BROOKINGS

Economic Activity

William C. Brainard and George L. Perry, Editors

2004

Ryan D. Nunn, Statistical Associate
Theodore Papageorgiou, Assistant to the Editors
Michael Treadway, Editorial Associate
Lindsey B. Wilson, Production Associate

BROOKINGS INSTITUTION

WASHINGTON, D.C.

BROOKINGS PAPERS ON

Economic Activity

2

William C. Brainard and George L. Perry, Editors

2004

Purpose	*Brookings Papers on Economic Activity* contains the articles, reports, and highlights of the discussions from conferences of the Brookings Panel on Economic Activity. The panel was formed to promote professional research and analysis of key developments in U.S. economic activity. Prosperity and price stability are its basic subjects.
	The expertise of the panel is concentrated on the "live" issues of economic performance that confront the maker of public policy and the executive in the private sector. Particular attention is devoted to recent and current economic developments that are directly relevant to the contemporary scene or especially challenging because they stretch our understanding of economic theory or previous empirical findings. Such issues are typically quantitative, and the research findings are often statistical. Nevertheless, in all the articles and reports, the reasoning and the conclusions are developed in a form intelligible to the interested, informed nonspecialist as well as useful to the expert in macroeconomics. In short, the papers aim at several objectives: meticulous and incisive professional analysis, timeliness and relevance to current issues, and lucid presentation.
	Articles appear in this publication after presentation and discussion at a conference at Brookings. From the spirited discussions at the conference, the authors obtain new insights and helpful comments; they also receive searching criticism about various aspects of the papers. Some of these comments are reflected in the published summaries of discussion, some in the final versions of the papers themselves. But in all cases the papers are finally the product of the authors' thinking and do not imply any agreement by those attending the conference. Nor do the papers or any of the other materials in this issue necessarily represent the views of the staff members, officers, or trustees of the Brookings Institution.
Correspondence	Correspondence regarding papers in this issue should be addressed to the authors. Manuscripts are not accepted for review because this journal is devoted exclusively to invited contributions.
Subscriptions	For information on subscriptions, please visit the Brookings web site at www.brookings.edu or contact the Brookings Institution Press, 1775 Massachusetts Avenue, N.W., Washington, D.C. 20036. Call 202/797-6258 or 800/275-1447. E-mail bibooks@brookings.edu.
	Brookings periodicals are available online through both Online Computer Library Center (contact OCLC subscriptions department at 800/848-5878, ext. 6251) and Project Muse (http://muse.jhu.edu).

Editors' Summary

THE BROOKINGS PANEL ON Economic Activity held its seventy-eighth conference in Washington, D.C., on September 9 and 10, 2004. This issue of *Brookings Papers on Economic Activity* includes the papers and discussions presented at the conference. The first paper evaluates unconventional measures available to monetary policymakers for stimulating the economy when interest rates are already near zero, a situation that may arise with price stability or negative inflation. The second paper presents empirical evidence on the effects of taxes, federal spending, and deficits on national saving, interest rates, and growth. The third paper explores the impacts on U.S. employment in recent years from conventional foreign trade in goods and from the rise in offshoring of service jobs. The fourth paper examines the effect of tax changes, such as those passed since 2000, on business capital formation.

CENTRAL BANKS USUALLY implement monetary policy by setting the short-term nominal interest rate that the bank controls, such as the federal funds rate in the United States. However, the success of many industrial countries over the years in reducing inflation and, consequently, average nominal interest rates has increased the likelihood that, during a recession, the policy rate will approach its lower bound of zero. When rates are at or near zero, a central bank can no longer stimulate aggregate demand by further rate reductions and must rely instead on "nonstandard" policy alternatives. An extensive literature examines these alternatives, but for the most part from a theoretical or historical perspective. Few studies have presented empirical evidence on their potential effectiveness in modern economies. Such evidence not only would help central banks plan for the contingency of the policy rate approaching zero, but also would bear directly on the choice of the appropriate inflation objective in normal times: the greater the confidence of central bankers that tools exist to help the economy escape the liquidity trap that occurs at the zero bound, the less need there is to maintain an inflation "buffer." Hence evidence of effective alternative policies would bolster the argument for a lower inflation objective. In the first article of this issue, Ben Bernanke, Vincent Reinhart, and Brian Sack apply the tools of modern empirical finance to the recent experiences of the United States and Japan to look for such evidence.[1]

Following earlier work by Bernanke and Reinhart, the authors group nonstandard policy alternatives into three classes: official communications designed to shape public expectations about the future course of interest rates; quantitative easing, which increases both assets (holdings of government securities) and liabilities (unborrowed reserves) on the central bank's balance sheet; and changes in the composition of that balance sheet through, for example, targeted purchases of long-term bonds aimed at reducing long-term interest rates.

The authors' investigation employs two approaches. First, they perform event-study analysis, measuring and analyzing the behavior of selected asset prices and yields over short periods surrounding central bank statements or other financial or economic news. Second, they estimate "no-arbitrage" models of the term structure of interest rates for both the United States and Japan. For any given set of macroeconomic conditions and stance of monetary policy, these models allow the authors to predict interest rates at all maturities. Using the predicted term structure as a benchmark, they are then able to assess whether factors not included in the model—such as the Bank of Japan's quantitative easing policy that began in 2001—have economically significant effects on interest rates.

Bernanke, Reinhart, and Sack begin with a discussion of nonstandard policies that might be effective in stimulating the economy when short-term rates are at the zero bound; the discussion draws on the historical experience with such policies in the United States and Japan as well as on existing theories of potential policy channels and previous empirical analysis. The first type of policy they consider is the use of central bank communications to influence the market's expectations about future policy and hence future short-term rates. According to some theories, shaping expectations about future short-term rates is essentially the only tool central bankers have. But the authors take a broader view, arguing that private sector bor-

1. The editors thank Bernanke, Reinhart, and Sack for providing an excellent nontechnical summary of their paper, on which this summary draws extensively.

rowing and investment decisions are more sensitive to longer-term yields than to short-term rates, and considering the possibility that long-term rates can be moved independently of expectations of short-term rates. This leads to a discussion of the potential importance of policy statements, credibility, and policy rules. Although the authors see "rule-like" central bank behavior, particularly state-contingent behavior, as an important means of shaping the public's policy expectations, they believe that a central bank would find it particularly difficult to establish in advance how it would react to highly unusual circumstances, such as when the short-term rate is near the zero bound. Hence in such cases statements about policy intentions and commitments are likely to be particularly important.

The second type of nonstandard policy, quantitative easing, involves purchasing government securities beyond what is required to drive the short-term rate to zero. The authors discuss three channels through which such a policy might operate to escape the liquidity trap. First, such purchases may lead to private sector rebalancing of portfolios, which in turn would raise the prices of other assets. However, the authors observe that there will be little incentive to rebalance if money is a good substitute for the short-term bills it replaces when the latter are paying close to zero interest. Second, a larger outstanding stock of money raises the prospect of higher seigniorage in the event of future inflation, substituting for direct taxes. The effectiveness of this "fiscal" channel requires that the public, in the midst of a deflation, expect future inflation and expect that the central bank will not withdraw the injected money when that inflation arrives. The authors believe that the fiscal channel could work if pursued aggressively enough and with a clear commitment not to reverse course. Third, the visible signal that quantitative easing provides makes it more believable that the central bank will hesitate to reverse such large purchases soon, perhaps because of the possible shock to money markets.

The third type of nonstandard policy involves altering the composition of the central bank's balance sheet by participating in all segments of the market in government debt, including inflation-indexed debt, so as to influence term, risk, and liquidity premiums. Using emergency provisions dormant since the 1930s, the Federal Reserve could even accept private financial and real assets as collateral for discount window loans. Although many economists are skeptical about the potential effectiveness of this channel, the authors note a number of historical examples of central banks effectively pegging long-term rates.

Bernanke, Reinhart, and Sack's own empirical investigation begins with an event study measuring the influence of Federal Reserve policy announcements by the response of three market-based indicators following selected decisions of the Federal Open Market Committee (the Federal Reserve's principal policymaking body) since 1991. The indicators are the current-month federal funds futures contract, the Eurodollar futures contract expiring in about a year, and the yield on Treasury securities of five years' maturity. The authors measure the responses of each indicator observed during the forty-five minutes following FOMC announcements; the very short time interval is chosen to minimize the extent to which other factors could be affecting rates. The change in the current-month federal funds futures contract simply measures the markets' reaction to news about the Federal Reserve's near-term funds target. The change in the year-ahead Eurodollar futures contract presumably incorporates both the effect of this funds rate surprise and the effect of any accompanying announcement on market expectations about policy actions and the economy over the coming year. The change in the five-year Treasury yield presumably includes both those effects plus those arising from revisions in expectations beyond a year. The authors decompose the second indicator into the part explained by the first factor, the funds "surprise," and the orthogonal residual, which they label a second factor. The change in the five-year rate not explained by the first two is designated a third factor. The authors find that only about 20 percent of the variance in the one-year-ahead rate during the forty-five-minute policy "window" is explained by the current policy surprise; unexplained movements in the year-ahead rate—the second factor—make up the remaining 80 percent. Again, this factor presumably captures any revisions in the private sector's expectations of future short-term rates due to information contained in the policy statement that accompanies the change in the funds rate.

Perhaps the most striking revelation of the authors' analysis is the high correlation between unexplained movements in the future one-year rate and the five-year Treasury yield: the second factor accounts for 68 percent of the variability of the five-year yield during the event window, and the policy surprise itself explains another 12 percent, leaving only 20 percent unexplained. Informal inspection of the historical behavior of the second factor reveals that it becomes increasingly important in the latter part of the sample, when policy statements came into regular use. In contrast, larger realizations of the first and third factors do not seem to line up with dates of policy statements. This leads the authors to a more formal investigation of the link between FOMC statements and the three factors. First, they regress the squared values of each of the factors on dummy variables indicating dates when statements were issued and the characteristics of those statements: The dummy variable STATEMENT takes a value of 1 on any date on which a statement was released. STATEMENT SURPRISE takes a value of 1 when, in the authors' judgment, the statement included information about the economy or the path of policy that most market participants would not have expected. Finally, PATH SURPRISE is set equal to 1 when, in the authors' judgment, the statement revealed new information about the likely future path of monetary policy. The authors attempt to assign "surprises" as objectively as possible, using commentaries written before and after each statement was released (including those of a leading financial firm that specializes in monitoring FOMC actions), internal Federal Reserve staff analyses of market reactions, pre-FOMC meeting surveys about expectations for the balance-of-risks part of the statement, and the results of a survey of expectations about the statement conducted by the New York Federal Reserve Bank. Of the 116 policy decisions in their sample, statements accompanied 56, and the authors identify 31 of them as having a significant element of surprise, and 9 of these, in turn, as path surprises.

In the regression explaining the first factor, the coefficient on STATE-MENT is positive and significant, and the authors attribute this result to the fact that, for much of the sample, statements were made only on days when the federal funds target was changed. These are days on which the policy rate surprise tends to be relatively large. The coefficient on STATE-MENT SURPRISE in this regression is negative and significant, suggesting that the FOMC viewed policy rate surprises and statements as substitutes, possibly because the FOMC was reluctant to issue surprising statements at the same time that it was also surprising the markets with the policy action. The PATH SURPRISE variable is insignificant.

The regressions explaining the second and third factors are of more interest, since they provide information about how FOMC statements affect market expectations. The mere issuance of a statement has essentially no effect on the variance of the second factor; in contrast, in periods when there is a statement surprise, the variance is nearly 200 basis points, and when there is also a path surprise, the variance is roughly 230 basis points. When the first two factors are controlled for, the five-year yield is not noticeably affected by policy statements, surprising or otherwise; thus statements do not appear to provide information about long-term yields independent of their influence on expectations about rates one year in the future.

FOMC statements often contain language that suggests the direction of future policy actions. Bernanke, Reinhart, and Sack investigate whether the direction of the response of the factors is consistent with whether a "surprise" statement appears hawkish, dovish, or neutral with regard to interest rates. They define two dummy variables, for statement and path surprises, each of which takes a value of +1 for surprises that are judged to be hawkish, −1 for those judged to be dovish, and zero otherwise. They find no significant response of either the first or the third factor to either of these dummies. However, they find that hawkish statement surprises increase, and dovish surprises decrease, the year-ahead rate by 12 basis points. The response to path surprises is an even greater 16 basis points. Both responses are highly significant. The authors note that, in addition to the official FOMC statements they study, the speeches and congressional testimony of FOMC members may be important in shaping expectations.

Beyond their direct effects, statements that are conditional—that is, that make the central bank's commitments contingent on specific economic developments—are likely to affect the market response to news about those events. For example, the statement that "[monetary] policy accommodation can be maintained for a considerable period," first introduced in Federal Reserve Chairman Alan Greenspan's semiannual report to Congress in July 2003, was, in subsequent FOMC statements, typically tied to labor market conditions and "slack" in the economy. A regression relating changes in the ten-year Treasury yield to surprises in the monthly payroll report shows greater sensitivity after August 2003 than in the preceding twelve years; this is consistent with the claim that this FOMC language heightened the market's attention to employment growth.

Although the event studies succeed in isolating the effects of FOMC policy announcements, they measure only very short term effects and do not take advantage of the restrictions linking yields of various maturities normally incorporated in term structure equations. Particularly when one is evaluating unusual policies, such as buybacks of longer-term Treasuries, it is useful to measure changes in yields against a "benchmark" term structure that incorporates these linkages and takes into account the observable macroeconomic factors that can affect the level and shape of the yield curve. For this purpose the authors use a "no-arbitrage" term structure model in which long-term yields are determined by two components: the expected future path of one-period interest rates, and a term premium in yields at various maturities that investors require as compensation for the risk in holding longer-term investments. The authors estimate a quarterly vector autoregression (VAR) for five observable factors that, taken together, provide a reasonable summary of economic conditions relevant to the term structure: the employment gap, the previous year's core inflation, expected inflation for the coming year (taken from the Blue Chip survey), the federal funds rate, and the year-ahead Eurodollar futures rate. The first component—the expected future path of one-period interest rates—can be computed by simply iterating the estimated VAR forward. The risks that are priced in the second component—the term premium—are the innovations in the VAR process, with prices that are assumed to depend only on the contemporaneous values of the variables in the VAR. The authors estimate these prices by fitting the model to zero-coupon Treasury yields at maturities of six months and one, two, three, four, five, seven, and ten years. The estimated effects of risks on the term structure are of interest in themselves. The authors find that the term premium for longer maturities has declined over time, presumably reflecting greater stability in the economy and in policy. The estimated model predicts the Treasury yield curve reasonably well at all maturities: the standard deviation of prediction error is 33 basis points at six months and increases to around 80 basis points for longer maturities. The authors' results show that the year-ahead futures rate makes an important contribution to the accuracy of the model's predictions, reducing the standard deviation of prediction error for the one-year yield by about 30 basis points, or 35 percent; smaller contributions are found for longer maturities, decreasing from about 20 basis points for the two- and three-year yields to a mere 7 basis points for the ten-year yield.

How large are the innovations in the year-ahead futures contracts according to the VAR, how does their magnitude compare with the earlier event-study estimates of the impact of policy surprises, and by how much do these innovations shift Treasury yields at various maturities? The authors show that the event-study estimates of the effect of policy on the futures rate are only a small fraction of the VAR innovations before July 2003, but that since then the standard deviation of VAR innovations has fallen and that of event-study shocks has risen, amounting to roughly 45 percent of the VAR innovations. Some of this difference may reflect communications effects not captured in the statements, and some must reflect responses of expectations to developments in the economy unrelated to FOMC communications. The authors examine in some detail the comparison of VAR innovations and event-study shocks during the period from August to December 2003, during which the FOMC used the "considerable period" language. During that period the results from the event study suggested that FOMC communications pushed down the Eurodollar futures rate by a cumulative 19 basis points, whereas the VAR innovation lowered that rate by 63 basis points. The model predicts that a 63-basis-point decline in the futures rate would shift the yield curve down 25 basis points at a two-year horizon and 7 basis points at a ten-year horizon. The authors guess that the true communications effect is somewhere between these two extremes.

The effectiveness of the third type of nonconventional policy, changes in the composition of the central bank's balance sheet, depends on whether substitution among assets is sufficiently imperfect that large purchases of a specific class of asset might affect its yield relative to the short-term interest rate. If composition matters, the FOMC has the ability to stimulate the economy even when the federal funds rate is constrained by the zero floor. Because the Federal Reserve has not undertaken large purchases of longer-term assets in recent years, the authors instead examine three recent episodes in which it seems plausible that many market participants came to anticipate significant changes in the relative supplies of Treasury securities. The first of these was the Treasury's announcement in 1999 of a plan to buy back government debt in the face of prospective budget surpluses; the second was the investment in Treasury securities by Asian official institutions intervening in exchange markets after the currency crises of 1998; the third was in the summer of 2003, when some financial market participants came to believe the Federal Reserve might purchase long-term Treasury securities in order to combat incipient deflation. For each episode the authors examine the movement of a number of yields in narrow windows surrounding important announcements and the movements of the residuals from the benchmark term structure model.

The dating of each episode is necessarily imprecise. The gradual elimination of government interest-bearing debt began with the surpluses that emerged in the early 1990s, and by the end of the decade many observers were forecasting that Treasury debt would disappear by 2010. Bernanke,

Reinhart, and Sack focus on two events that they believe were particularly salient in investors' minds: the mid-quarter refunding announcements of February 2000, when the under secretary of the Treasury suggested that the ten-year note would replace the thirty-year bond as the benchmark long-term security; and the November 2001 refunding announcement, when the Treasury confirmed it would stop selling the long bond. The authors report that in both cases the Treasury yield curve rotated down dramatically. Examination of their estimated term structure model that controls for variations in the economy and policy shows that the yield on twenty-year bonds dropped roughly 80 basis points below what was expected for this period. The authors view these results as only suggestive of the efficacy of decreasing the relative supply of long-term government debt, recognizing that the term structure model is unlikely to capture all the other factors that changed expectations about the supplies of bonds, and that it is hard to know the probability that investors assigned to a sizable paydown. They also note that the reaction of yields on long-term Treasuries did not translate into a reduction in interest rates on privately issued debt—long-term swap spreads widened noticeably during the period.

The beginning of the accumulation of Treasury securities by foreign official institutions is likewise difficult to date with any precision. Since 1998 the value of securities held in custody for foreign governments at the New York Federal Reserve Bank has almost doubled, reaching $1¼ trillion. Japanese authorities in particular intervened heavily in foreign exchange markets in 2003, when their purchases totaled $177 billion, and the first quarter of 2004, when they purchased $138 billion. Regressions of changes in two-, five-, and ten-year Treasury yields on the volume of dollar interventions, which the authors assume were immediately recognized by market participants, show small (less than 1 basis point per $1 billion of intervention) but statistically significant changes in the three-day period beginning with the intervention. Interestingly, swap spreads did not increase during this period, suggesting that the effects on the Treasury yields were transmitted to yields on private debt. Yields on five- and ten-year Treasuries remained 50 to 100 basis points below the predictions of the benchmark term structure model during this period. Although these findings are suggestive, the authors note that yields had begun to move down before the sizable Japanese interventions, perhaps because of fears of deflation.

The authors refer to the period between the fall of 2002 and the summer of 2003 as the "2003 deflation scare," a period when various Federal

Reserve officials spoke explicitly about the risks of deflation and the possible response of monetary policy should the funds rate approach its lower bound of zero. Although officials consistently described this possibility as remote, the authors observe that some market participants believed the Federal Reserve took the danger seriously enough to consider purchasing large amounts of longer-term Treasuries. The perceived likelihood seemed to peak with the May 2003 FOMC meeting statement. Such action was seen to be "taken off the table" when the June FOMC statement did not mention deflation and when Chairman Greenspan, in his July testimony, said, "situations requiring special policy actions are most unlikely to arise." The ten-year Treasury yield moved sharply with these events, falling 20 basis points with the May FOMC statement and rising abruptly with the June statement (10 basis points) and the chairman's July testimony (20 basis points). Residuals from the benchmark term structure were consistent with these responses. The authors caution against making too much of these results, particularly since the period of the "scare" overlapped that of large-scale purchases of Treasuries by foreign official institutions. But they express confidence that, if the Federal Reserve were willing to purchase an unlimited amount of a particular asset, they could establish the asset's price.

The authors' analysis of the recent experience in Japan focuses on two nonstandard policies recently employed by the country's central bank, the Bank of Japan. The first is the zero-interest-rate policy, under which the central bank, beginning in 1999, committed to keep its policy rate, the call rate, at zero until deflation had been eliminated; the second is the quantitative easing policy, announced in 2001, which consists of providing bank reserves at levels much greater than needed to maintain a policy rate of zero. The evidence for the effectiveness of these policies is more mixed than in the case of the United States. The authors' event-study analyses, which may be less informative in Japan because of small sample sizes, do not show any reliable relationship over the past few years between policy statements by the Bank of Japan and markets' one-year-ahead policy expectations. (The latter are measured in Japan's case as the portion of movements in the nearest Euroyen futures contract not explained by unexpected changes in the current policy setting.) But the residuals from an estimated term structure model for Japan similar to that used for the United States make a stronger case for nonconventional policies. The Bank of Japan's use of quantitative easing, with which the United States has no recent experience, appears to have lowered longer-term yields, as did the zero-interest-rate policy. Simulations of the model also indicate that interest rates at all maturities were noticeably lower under both nonstandard policies than they would have been otherwise.

Bernanke, Reinhart, and Sack believe that their results provide some grounds for optimism about the likely efficacy of two of their nonstandard policies. In particular, they confirm a potentially important role for central bank communications in shaping public expectations of future policy actions. In the United States, market expectations about the trajectory of the federal funds rate over the next year appear strongly linked to Federal Reserve policy statements. If such central bank "talk" does affect policy expectations, then policymakers retain some leverage over long-term yields, even if the current policy rate is at or near zero. Based on the recent episodes they examine, the authors further suggest that large changes in the relative supplies of securities may have economically significant effects on their yields.

Yet despite their relatively encouraging findings concerning the potential efficacy of nonstandard policies at the zero bound, the authors are cautious in making policy prescriptions because of the considerable uncertainty about the size and reliability of these effects. They therefore counsel a conservative approach—maintaining a sufficient inflation buffer and applying preemptive easing as necessary to minimize the risk of hitting the zero bound. But, recognizing that such policies cannot ensure that the zero bound will never be hit, they argue that refining our understanding of the potential usefulness of nonstandard policies for escaping the zero bound should remain a high priority.

IF, IN PRACTICE, FISCAL policy were conducted so as to keep federal budget balances within a moderate range, the implications of sustained large deficits would be of only academic interest. And in fact the budget balance averaged a modest deficit during the first three postwar decades, with mostly countercyclical fluctuations around that average. Fiscal discipline has eroded sharply twice since then, first in the early 1980s and then, after recovering, again in the early 2000s. The standardized budget balance, which adjusts for the effects of the business cycle, reached 5 percent of GDP in the mid-1980s and recovered to about half that size by the early 1990s, after the second Reagan tax reform. The deficit was steadily reduced between 1992 and 2000, turning into a surplus by the end of the period. At that point analysts found themselves wrestling with the problems that a vanishing national debt might bring. Today, through a combination of large tax cuts, weaker growth, higher defense spending, and the end of windfall revenue from the booming stock market, the budget is over $400 billion in deficit, and most private analysts project that deficits will remain a large fraction of GDP for the indefinite future under likely policy scenarios—a situation without precedent in U.S. economic history. In the second article of this issue, William Gale and Peter Orszag analyze the likely effects of tax cuts and deficits and apply their findings to the fiscal situation under present and projected policies.

The authors examine the consequences of deficits for the economy by conducting a careful empirical analysis of two channels through which those consequences should operate. The first is through saving, where the issue is the extent to which government saving or dissaving (the government budget balance) affects national saving, which is the sum of government and private saving. In what Gale and Orszag call the conventional case, private saving offsets little or none of a reduction in government saving, and so future national income and GNP are reduced by the returns forgone due to the reduction in national saving and investment. In the polar alternative, which, following the literature, the authors refer to as the Ricardian equivalence case, an increase in the deficit resulting from a tax cut induces an equal increase in private saving, so that national saving and investment are unchanged, and future GNP is unaffected. The second channel works through interest rates. If, as in the conventional case, the deficit reduces national saving, and that in turn raises rates, domestic investment will be reduced, lowering future GNP. In the absence of increased foreign investment into the United States, this will result in a corresponding reduction in GDP. To the extent foreign investment makes up for the reduced national saving, domestic investment, the domestic capital stock, and GDP will be unaffected, but national income and GNP will fall relative to GDP by the amount of the higher earnings paid to foreigners on their investment. In the Ricardian equivalence case, since there is no effect of tax cut-induced deficits on national income, deficits are not predicted to affect interest rates.

Gale and Orszag survey the extensive empirical literature that uses time-series data to estimate the effect of deficits on private saving; they also reexamine and extend some of the earlier work and perform their own, new tests. They first reestimate the consumption function used in a 1990 paper by Roger Kormendi and Philip Meguire, which relates aggregate consumption to the various flows that make up disposable income—NNP (net national product, equal to GNP minus capital depreciation) plus transfers and government interest payments, minus taxes and retained earnings of corporations—and to private net worth, the federal budget surplus, the stock of government debt, and government spending on goods and services. These authors and others interpret zero coefficients on taxes and transfers in this equation as support for the Ricardian case. Gale and Orszag note that this interpretation rests on the questionable assumption that neither changes in taxes nor changes in transfers are related to changes in future government purchases, so that higher taxes or lower transfers today imply lower taxes or higher transfers in the future. Nonetheless, they agree that the coefficients on taxes and transfers are relevant to the policy issue of how deficits affect future economic performance. By extending the data period to include the 1990s and the start of the 2000s, the authors can examine how the specification fits outside the original data period. These additional years may be particularly informative because deficits have fluctuated widely.

Using annual data, the authors estimate the consumption function for two measures of the dependent variable: the first (that used by Kormendi and Meguire) includes services of durables in consumption in addition to spending on nondurables and services; the second is the simple sum of nondurables and services, scaled up to preserve the mean level of total consumption. They try three transformations of the dependent and independent variables: first differences, first differences scaled by last year's NNP, and first differences of ratios to NNP. And they try some specifications of the independent variables that differ from those in previous work: separating federal from state and local spending, and adding marginal tax rates constructed so as to largely reflect legislative changes. The separation of federal from state and local taxes is motivated by the fact that state and local revenue come largely from sales taxes, which vary positively with consumption, and this change proves to be the most important. When the authors use Kormendi and Meguire's specification of the variables in ordinary least squares (OLS) regressions and end the sample period in 1992, they replicate the earlier authors' finding of no significant effect of taxes on consumption. However, that finding is reversed when the data period is extended, with the estimated effect of federal taxes largest when the estimation extends through 2002. For this period, and with the refined variables just described, estimates of the consumption response to federal tax changes in the year they occur range from

−0.34 to −0.46, with additional lagged consumption responses in subsequent years. The effects of transfers on consumption are generally even larger. These results with the Kormendi-Meguire equation thus overturn those its originators found.

Gale and Orszag turn next to an Euler equation formulation for estimating consumer behavior. In this formulation, as first developed by Robert Hall, farsighted and rational consumers who are not subject to borrowing constraints smooth their marginal utility over time; the path of their consumption is a random walk with drift. Building on modifications suggested by other researchers and their own work, the authors introduce a number of other possible influences on consumption. They allow for a fraction of consumers to be constrained by liquidity, so that their consumption is limited to current-period disposable income. They allow for wealth effects and for the possibility that consumers distinguish between private net worth and government bonds and that they adjust their consumption for expected changes in government purchases. They also allow for the possible incentive effects of marginal tax rates on personal and corporate income. The authors first examine this main case and then explore the effects of adding other explanatory variables that might be expected to influence consumption.

In the main Euler equation specification, when variables are expressed as the first difference in ratios to NNP, OLS estimates of tax effects are larger than those found using the Kormendi-Meguire specification. The coefficients range between −0.5 and −0.7, depending on whether marginal tax rates are included in the estimation equation. They are similar to the Kormendi-Meguire results for the other two expressions of the variables.

To address the possible bias from the endogeneity of the right-hand-side variables in OLS estimation, Gale and Orszag also use values of most of the right-hand-side variables with two or three lags as instruments for their current values, and similarly lagged values of consumption as an instrument for current income. They also present estimates in which all the explanatory variables are instrumented, and estimates in which private wealth and government bonds, measured at the end of the previous period, are not instrumented. The authors find the effect of federal taxes on consumption to be large and significant in all the regressions. With all variables included and instrumented, the coefficients are −1.0 and −0.9 for the two measures of consumption in the first-differences regressions, −0.6 and −0.5 in the first-differences-of-ratios regressions, and −0.7 in regressions with either consumption variable in ratios. The authors see these results as conclusive evidence of a substantial effect of changes in current taxes on current consumption. Before-tax income is the only other variable that significantly affects consumption across all the instrumental variables regressions. With two of the three transformations of the variables, its coefficient has a similar size (and opposite sign) as federal taxes; with the third, the transformation using first differences of ratios to NNP, before-tax income has a coefficient of about 0.9.

Turning to the second channel of fiscal policy—the impact of government deficits on interest rates—Gale and Orszag take pains to avoid contaminating their estimates with the well-established cyclical interrelationships among output, interest rates, and deficits, and to focus on fiscal developments to which forward-looking financial markets would be expected to respond. Their review of recent research confirms the downward bias that results from estimations that ignore these problems. For their main regressions the authors focus on the real interest rate on ten-year Treasury bonds for the period five years ahead, and they use five-year-ahead projections of several federal fiscal variables, all as percentages of GDP, as the principal explanatory variable. The fiscal variables are publicly held debt, the unified budget deficit, the primary deficit (which excludes interest payments), and revenue and primary outlays. Real interest rates are calculated using the zero-coupon yield curve for the period five to fourteen years ahead, adjusted for expected inflation. The fiscal variables are taken from projections of the Congressional Budget Office. All regressions also include expected GDP growth over the relevant period and a constant term.

The OLS estimates in the simplest model, using annual data for 1976-2004, show substantial and statistically significant effects on future interest rates using either the debt variable or any of the deficit variables: each of the deficit variables explains roughly twice as much of the variation in rates as does debt. A sustained increase in the unified deficit equal to 1 percent of GDP raises the forward long-term interest rate by 29 basis points. The same increase in the primary deficit raises the interest rate by 40 basis points. Consistent with this result, the same changes due solely to reduced revenue or solely to higher primary outlays raise rates by 42 and 37 basis points, respectively. The authors also add to the equation terms interacting their fiscal variables with dummy variables indicating recessions. When these are included, the estimated effects of the fiscal variables on interest rates rise modestly, suggesting that some business cycle effects remain in the initial estimates. Adding an assortment of other variables, some suggested by earlier research, reduces the coefficients on the fiscal variables somewhat, but their interpretation is not clear. The variable with the most significant effects, which the authors label the equity premium, is calculated from real long-term rates and GDP growth, which are already on the left- and right-hand sides of the estimating equation.

Gale and Orszag go on to estimate a number of additional specifications as a way of checking the robustness of their main results. They use the debt and unified deficit variables together in equations explaining forward real long-term rates, taking the projected debt at the end of four years and the projected deficit in the fifth year to avoid double counting. In both OLS and autoregressive moving average regressions for this specification, deficits always dominate debt: the coefficient on the latter has the wrong sign and is insignificant, and the deficit coefficient is larger than in the regressions using deficits alone. In regressions explaining current, rather than forward, real long-term interest rates, the estimated effects of the fiscal variables are, not surprisingly, somewhat smaller than in the main equation. In regressions explaining nominal forward long-term rates and including expected inflation as an additional explanatory variable, the latter consistently has a coefficient near 1.0, and the deficit effects are close to those in the main regressions. The least successful specification attempts to explain current nominal long-term rates. In these regressions the coefficient on expected inflation, the most significant explanatory variable, ranges nearer 2.0 than 1.0; the coefficients on the fiscal variables are smaller and often insignificant. The authors also vary the data period and demonstrate that their main results are not sensitive to the exclusion of either 1976-81 or 2000-2004, two periods that some analysts view as atypical.

Gale and Orszag conclude by addressing the current U.S. fiscal situation. They reason that realistic budget projections should assume that the 2001 and 2003 tax cuts are made permanent and that the alternative minimum tax is amended so as to leave only 5 million households affected by it. (They do not include the president's plan to partially privatize the Social Security system, which would significantly further enlarge deficits for decades.) Amending the official Congressional Budget Office projections accordingly, they calculate that the projected unified budget deficit will average 3.5 percent of GDP over the coming decade. Their empirical results imply that, compared with a decade of balanced budgets, sustained deficits of this size will reduce national saving by 2 to 3 percent of GDP and will raise long-term interest rates by 80 to 120 basis points. At the end of ten years, the lower saving rate will have reduced the assets owned by Americans by 20 to 30 percent of GDP from what they would have been. And, at a 6 percent rate of return on capital, this smaller capital stock would reduce national income by 1 to 2 percent by 2015 and in each year thereafter.

NONFARM PAYROLL EMPLOYMENT continued to decline for nearly two years after the recession trough in November 2001, and by mid-2004 it was barely back to its trough level. Employment in manufacturing, the sector most affected by international trade, has been much weaker. As of November 2004 it was 3.2 million below its March 1998 peak and still 1.4 million below its level at the recession trough. The fact that this weak employment recovery was accompanied by a large expansion in the trade deficit has led many to identify trade as the cause. What is more, the substantial public attention given to the offshoring of jobs to India in recent years has raised the specter that jobs in the services sector, traditionally less vulnerable than manufacturing jobs to foreign competition, might now be increasingly exposed. Although economists typically focus on the long-run gains from trade for the nation as a whole, the loss of important markets to foreign competition is costly to the affected workers and firms and adds to political pressure for trade protection. In the third article of this issue, Martin Baily and Robert Lawrence examine employment in the current recovery and analyze the role of foreign trade and of services offshoring in its performance.

The authors first review developments in manufacturing during the three years ending in 2003, the last for which detailed annual industry data are available. Over this period, manufacturing employment declined 16 percent, far more than the 1.4 percent decline in employment of the nonfarm business sector. The authors focus on two measures of the importance of trade to manufacturing's performance in this period. Measured as a share of manufacturing value added (the portion of GDP originating in the sector), the manufacturing trade deficit rose from 21.3 percent to 28.3 percent; as a share of gross output—sales by manufacturing to other sectors—the deficit rose from 11.9 percent to 15.6 percent. The explanation for this development lies more in export weakness than in import strength: manufactured exports fell 8.8 percent, while manufactured imports rose only 2.3 percent. Only one of nineteen broad categories of manufacturing industry, primary metals, saw its trade balance improve, and all nineteen suffered employment declines, the largest occurring in computer and electronic products, machinery, and fabricated metal products.

To examine these developments more closely at the industry level, Baily and Lawrence make use of the U.S. input-output tables for 1997, the most recent ones available from the Bureau of Economic Analysis at the requisite level of detail. Typically a sector's output goes both for final use and as an input to production in other sectors. For a dollar of final use of any product—consumption, exports, investment, or government expenditure—the coefficients in the input-output tables permit calculation of the required imports and output from each domestic sector, including the imports and domestic output used as inputs to other sectors. Both industry and final-use categories are specified at a highly detailed level and are taken from (three-digit) North American Industry Classification System trade data, plus domestic use. The authors aggregate the detailed industry categories in the input-output tables into the nineteen two-digit manufacturing industries, transform the gross output coefficients to value-added coefficients using the 1997 ratios, and calculate employment growth for each industry as the difference between growth in its value added and growth in its productivity. This allows them to trace the effect of any change in final use—exports less imports plus domestic spending—on employment in manufacturing and in each industry.

The use of input-output tables for calculating value added by industry reveals a picture of trade that may surprise observers accustomed to looking only at the direct exports of each industry. Because the input-output analysis traces through all intermediate as well as final uses of each industry's output, it accounts for the indirect exports of an industry (goods sold to other domestic firms for use as inputs in export production) as well as its direct exports. It also accounts for the direct and indirect import content of the industry's production, including its production for export. For 2003, this accounting reveals that primary metals is the most export-intensive U.S. manufacturing industry, with 54 percent of its jobs coming from exports. Shares for other heavily export-dependent industries are 37 percent in computers, 30 percent in textiles, 28 percent in chemicals and in machinery, 26 percent in "other transportation" (mainly aircraft), and 25 percent in petroleum and coal products.

Turning to manufacturing as a whole, where employment declined by 2.74 million between 2000 and 2003, Baily and Lawrence calculate the employment changes attributable to exports and imports. They take into account both the changes in exports and imports and the employment implications of productivity increases in the exporting and import-competing sectors. For a given level of exports, rising productivity reduces over time the number of "export-created" jobs. Similarly, raising productivity reduces the number of domestic jobs displaced by a given level of imports. Using this accounting, Baily and Lawrence attribute a drop of 742,000 jobs, or 28 percent of the total decline, to weak export growth (exports grew more slowly than productivity in those sectors producing exports) and a rise of 429,000 jobs to imports (imports grew more slowly than productivity in import-displaced sectors). Combining the export and import figures results in only 12 percent of the total decline of manufacturing employment being attributed to trade. The remaining 88 percent is associated with weaker domestic demand, the residual category in the allocation.

The authors recognize the conceptual issues that complicate any such allocation and that alternative assumptions would lead to somewhat different interpretations of the employment decline. For example, a different decomposition could attribute all of the employment decline to productivity, because productivity rose about as much as output in this period. Or, since imports respond predictably to changes in domestic demand, one could attribute to domestic demand the change in imports that the change in domestic demand would predict, and identify only the unpredicted part as the "shock" from imports. A decomposition closer to public perceptions would relate to the number of jobs lost because of lower exports or higher imports without taking into account the implications of domestic productivity growth. The authors briefly discuss such alternatives but regard their own calculations as the most useful for examining the role of trade in the employment decline.

The predominance of weak domestic demand is again evident when the authors examine the nineteen individual manufacturing industries. In this analysis only chemical products experience an employment increase due to increased domestic use. The importance of weak exports rather than strong imports is also evident in the individual industry results. Several industries experienced substantial employment declines due to weak exports. None experienced large employment declines due to imports, and eleven of the nineteen experienced increased employment because imports rose by less than productivity.

Baily and Lawrence next examine several potential explanations for the weakness in exports. Although world output growth slowed in the period they examine, accounting for some of the slowdown in U.S. export growth, they show that the decline in the United States' share of world trade also contributed importantly. Measured in dollars, the U.S. share of world exports rose in the 1990s, particularly after 1995, but has fallen sharply since 2000. When U.S. exports are valued by an index of other major currencies, this pattern is still evident, although not as strongly. The authors go on to break down the changes in U.S. exports into four components. The first reflects the change in exports that would have been required to maintain a constant U.S. share of world trade, and the second and third show the effects of changes in the composition of U.S. exports by commodity and destination, respectively. The fourth, residual component includes the effects of changes in competitiveness, along with any measurement errors and other factors not captured by the first three.

By the authors' calculations, keeping the U.S. share of world trade constant at its 2000 level would have required a $152 billion increase in exports rather than the $46 billion decline that occurred. Changes in the commodity composition of exports had little effect, but changes in destination country composition predicted (coincidentally) about a $46 billion decline. The residual is a decline of $156 billion, which is presumed to mainly reflect deteriorating competitiveness. Using established rules of thumb to trace the effects of exchange rate variations through time, the authors conclude that the strength of the dollar through much of this period can account for most, if not all, of this residual weakness in exports and the negative impact of trade on employment.

Foreign competition in manufactured goods has been a fact of economic life since countries first began to industrialize in the eighteenth century. The shifting of U.S. service jobs "offshore" is a recent development, however, made possible by the technological revolution in communications. To gain perspective on the importance of offshoring to the U.S. job market, Baily and Lawrence focus on jobs offshored to India, the country benefiting most from this new development. They start by confronting a serious data problem. Whereas economic analysis of goods trade can draw on a wealth of detailed data going back several decades, data on offshoring of service jobs are relatively scarce, and the two main sources tell seemingly very different stories. One source is NASSCOM, a trade association for emerging business services industries in India; the other is the Bureau of Economic Analysis (BEA), whose conventional trade data include data on services imports and exports between the United States and India. The BEA data, which do not detail the types of services traded, show that services imports from India more than doubled between 1995 and 2000, to $1.9 billion, and then fell to $1.7 billion in 2002. But the NASSCOM data indicate that exports to the United States in just two categories—software services (such as computer programming) and business process services (such as call centers and back office processing)—totaled $6 billion that year, or more than three times the BEA total. Possible sources of error in the BEA data include the difficulty of distinguishing hardware from the software bundled with it; the recording of packaged software as a good rather than a service; and the BEA's reliance on infrequently revised company surveys, which may cause it to miss services imports by sectors not traditionally associated with foreign trade.

The authors also observe that the decline in services imports recorded by the BEA in recent years is not consistent with the growing visibility of such imports. Some might consider it an error in the NASSCOM export data that some fraction of the services reported as Indian exports are actually performed in the United States—for example, by workers on assignment to U.S. client firms. However, they find no support in U.S. immigration data for an influx of Indian temporary workers large enough to explain the rise in employment reported by NASSCOM. And they note that such workers would not be counted in the U.S. payroll employment data they are trying to explain, and hence should be counted as displacing U.S. jobs regardless of where their work is located. The authors therefore choose to base their analysis on the NASSCOM data, which, if anything, set an upper bound on jobs lost to offshoring.

According to NASSCOM, employment in Indian services for export to the United States rose by 91,500 a year between (roughly) 2000 and 2003, divided about evenly between software and business processing services. Although this is only a small fraction of average annual growth in total U.S. services employment (2.1 million) during the 1990s, it is more than a quarter of the slow growth in U.S. services employment in 2000–03. Comparison with U.S. employment trends in services occupations that are closely related to those being offshored is complicated by the surge of jobs associated with Y2K. But, for the period from 1999 to 2003, employment rose by an average of 58,000 a year in high-wage IT occupations and fell by an average of 107,000 a year in low-wage IT-enabled occupations—categories comparable to software and business processing services, respectively, in the Indian data. Although each Indian job gained corresponds to one U.S. job lost only if productivity in both jobs is the same, offshoring has clearly been an important cause of the weak job markets in these sectors, particularly in the low-wage occupations.

To examine the kinds of changes in trade and in the composition of domestic output that can be expected from offshoring in the longer run, the authors use a macroeconomic model developed by the consulting firm Macroeconomics Advisers, together with projections by Forrester Research that indicate an additional 3.1 million service jobs will be lost to offshoring by 2015. The baseline macroeconomic model assumes that lower fiscal deficits and dollar devaluation will reduce the U.S. current account deficit to 0.5 percent of GDP in that year, with monetary policy adjusting so as to maintain full employment. The authors adjust the baseline for the assumed loss of 3.1 million additional service jobs to offshoring and examine what difference it makes. The authors' preferred way of modeling this rise in offshoring is through a shift in foreign supply resulting from improved productivity abroad that lowers the price the United States pays for services imports. In this case productivity growth quickens, and, by 2015, GDP is 2.6 percent higher and manufacturing employment 62,000 higher, all relative to baseline. Real compensation rises and real profits rise even more. Although the authors see these projected changes as no more than illustrative, they note that they are qualitatively consistent with the changes one would expect from a more conventional opening of trade such as might arise from reducing trade barriers.

In concluding, Baily and Lawrence broaden their field of view to consider the possible role of factors other than trade in the disappointing recent growth of U.S. employment. Productivity growth has been rapid in this same period, leading some to regard it as part of the explanation. But the authors note that, although higher labor productivity at a given level of output translates into lower employment, it may instead raise output by improving competitiveness, leaving the effect on employment ambiguous. They observe that the slowdown in productivity in the 1970s was accompanied by slower employment growth, whereas the acceleration of productivity in the second half of the 1990s was accompanied by faster employment growth and a reduction of unemployment to the lowest level in decades. As they see it, rapid productivity growth after 2000 meant that aggregate demand also would have had to grow rapidly to maintain employment growth. Although the 2001 recession was mild, the expansion of aggregate demand that followed was not rapid enough. As principal factors contributing to this inadequate growth in demand, the authors cite the uncertainties following 9/11, the war in Iraq, higher oil prices, and the rise in the dollar's exchange value, all of which also help explain the weakness in exports and the worsening trade balance.

THE STOCK MARKET BOOM of the late 1990s and the record rates of business investment that accompanied it were followed by an unusually large decline in investment during the recession of 2001. Although, historically, investment has declined during recessions, this time the decline was extraordinary—larger than that of GDP itself. Just as extraordinary has been the slow recovery of investment: two years after the recession trough, investment was still only slightly below its peak value of the second quarter of 2000. Many observers, positing a link between the stock market and investment booms, have blamed the depth of the investment decline and its slow recovery on an "overhang" of capital from the earlier period. The sluggish performance of investment has been used to justify sharp cuts in corporate taxes, in the form of accelerated depreciation for most types of investment and lower tax rates on dividends, to stimulate investment by lowering the cost of capital. In the fourth article of this issue, Mihir Desai and Austan Goolsbee look for evidence in support of the overhang story at the firm, asset, and industry levels and evaluate the effectiveness of the tax stimulants that were introduced in recent years.

Although the overhang story fits the aggregate behavior of the stock market and investment in the 1990s and early 2000s, the authors do not consider this evidence conclusive. It could be that the decline in investment during the recession took place in a different set of firms and industries than those that experienced the earlier run-up, in which case any overhang from a previous binge cannot explain the current situation. To examine this possibility, they investigate investment behavior at the industry and firm levels. They begin by performing a simple regression relating the change in the rate of investment from 2000 to 2002 to that between 1994 and 1999 for a sample of eighty-one nonoverlapping industries. Although the resulting point estimate of the effect of investment growth in the earlier period is negative—industries in which investment grew rapidly in the first five-year period did tend to have slower investment growth in the second—the effect is small and statistically insignificant. For manufacturing, the estimated negative relation is stronger: a 1-percentage-point faster rate of growth in investment during the earlier period is associated with approximately a half-percentage-point slower growth in the later period. (These results are for investment in both equipment and structures; the results are similar for investment in equipment alone and are highly significant.) The authors note, however, that manufacturing represents only about 20 percent of total investment, and so these results are consistent with a lack of significant mean reversion in the growth of total investment.

Desai and Goolsbee report similar results on mean reversion of the growth of investment by asset type across all industries. Examining twenty-five different categories of equipment and nine categories of structures, they again find that above-average increases in the rate of investment between 1994 and 1999 are followed by only slightly above average declines between 2000 and 2002, and the relationship is insignificant.

The authors examine in greater detail a set of data for all firms reported by Compustat; aggregate capital expenditure of the firms in this data set constitutes 85 to 90 percent of private nonresidential investment in the United States. Average growth rates of capital aggregated from the firm level into three broad sectors—manufacturing, computer and information businesses, and nonmanufacturing—display the same pattern as do the aggregate data for the overall economy, with large increases in investment rates during the 1990s followed by declines in 2000–02. The behavior of the computer and information sector was most dramatic, with investment more than doubling in the 1990s before falling back to less than 75 percent of its initial level by the end of 2002. However, regressions for the entire sample of firms show that changes in the growth rate of capital between 1994 and 1999 have only slightly negative effects on growth rates in the same firms in 2000–02. Without information from other periods, it is hard to know whether there was more or less mean reversion in the growth of investment, by firm or industry or asset type, in the early 2000s than is typical during a slowdown. But the authors find the lack of evidence of strong reversion suggestive, indicating that overhang may not be the dominant factor influencing investment in recent years.

Desai and Goolsbee do not explore the extent to which firms currently find themselves with excess capacity, or, for those that do, the extent to which it reflects excessive growth in capital in the 1990s rather than a reduction in demand for their product. In either case, excess capacity would be expected to result in lower investment and a lower market valuation relative to replacement cost—that is, a lower Tobin's q. Instead the authors are interested in knowing whether the extraordinary increases in firms' valuations or investment in the 1990s have reduced the responsiveness of investment to changes in q in the current recovery. Such a reduction would help explain the apparent ineffectiveness of the recent cuts in taxes on corporations and dividends in stimulating investment. Using Q (Tobin's q adjusted for the effect of the corporate profits tax and the tax treatment of depreciation) they first estimate an investment equation for the panel of Compustat firms covering 1962–2003. On the right-hand side, in addition to the firm's Q and its ratio of cash flow to capital, they include fixed year effects and, typically, fixed firm effects and, for the period 2000–03, a term that interacts Q with the change in q during the four-year period ending three years earlier. This interaction is expected to capture whether firms that experienced large increases in q during the stock market boom have a reduced sensitivity in subsequent years to Q and the tax effects it embodies. The estimated coefficients on Q are small but highly significant, whereas the interaction terms are unimportant. The same qualitative results are found for two subsets of firms, information and manufacturing. Although these results leave open the question of whether a capital overhang from the 1990s depressed Q, and therefore investment, after 2000, they do not suggest that investment became less responsive to Q.

The results are different, however, when the authors replace the past change in q in the interaction term with the past percentage increase in the firm's net capital stock. This time the interaction terms are significant, indicating that firms that had larger accumulations of capital in the 1990s were indeed less sensitive to Q in the 2000s. For the firm with the largest past increase in capital, the coefficient on Q falls by 0.004, which corresponds to roughly a 30 percent reduction in the sensitivity of investment to Q. For the median firm the reduction in sensitivity resulting from the investment boom is about 9 percent.

Before turning to an examination of the impact of the recent tax cuts on investment, the authors briefly review tax-adjusted q theory, pioneered by Lawrence Summers in the 1980s. According to the original q theory, investment in the absence of taxes is proportional to the difference between the marginal value of capital and its replacement cost, and the proportionality depends, inversely, on costs of adjustment. Summers recognizes four important features of the tax law: the corporate profits tax, investment tax credits and noneconomic depreciation, dividend taxes, and taxes on capital gains, each of which modifies one or the other of the terms in the nontax investment equation. The corporate profit tax scales both q and the cost of capital goods by $1/(1 - t)$, where t is the corporate profit tax rate, leaving the form of the equation unchanged. Introduction of an investment tax credit or accelerated depreciation simply modifies the cost-of-capital term and is equivalent to any other change in the price of capital goods.

Dividend and capital gains taxes are more complicated. Assuming that investors require a given after-tax rate of return, both dividend and capital gains taxes raise the required before-tax rate of return and hence lower market value, but their effect on investment is ambiguous because it depends on how firms finance their investment. If firms finance investment by issuing new equity, the dividend tax is relevant. In the short run a reduction in the dividend tax increases q and encourages investment; in long-run equilibrium the capital stock is larger than it would have been without the tax cut, earning a lower before-tax return but the same after-dividend-tax return, and q returns to its initial value of 1.0 (in the absence of an investment tax credit or noneconomic tax depreciation). In this case the dividend tax does not appear in the q investment equation, its effects being completely reflected in the firm's market value, which in turn affects investment. The authors label this case the "traditional" view and contrast it with what they call the "new" view of dividend taxes, according to which dividends affect firm market value but do not affect investment. This situation arises if a firm's earnings are more than sufficient to finance the desired level of investment, so that retained earnings are the marginal source of funds. It would make no sense for such a firm to sell new shares to finance investment while at the same time paying out earnings as dividends to shareholders, who would have to pay tax on those dividends.

Retaining and investing earnings increases the value of the firm's stock and delivers part of the return to investors through capital gains. Because investors typically hold stocks a considerable time before selling, the effective tax rate on capital gains is below the statutory gains rate, and well below the rate on dividends. A firm maximizing its value to shareholders invests retained earnings up to the point where the after-tax value of a marginal dollar of earnings invested equals that of a dollar paid as a dividend. A dollar of retained earnings that is used to purchase capital adds q to the value of the firm. Assuming they are acting only on behalf of the shareholders, a firm will invest until the value of q is significantly below 1.0. If it stopped adding to capital when q was 1.0, the after-tax value of the next dollar invested would be greater than the after-tax value of that dollar paid out as a dividend.

On this new view, a reduction in the dividend tax rate does not affect the level of either investment or dividends. It increases q by the same proportion as the increase in the after-tax value of dividends, so that a firm that previously was optimally balancing retained earnings and dividends will not want to change either. In contrast, a reduction in the capital gains rate, which also increases q in the short run, will lead the optimizing firm to increase investment and reduce dividends. In the long run the market value of the firm will be higher still, but q will be driven below its initial value.

Which of these two views, the "new" or the "traditional," is a more accurate description of reality? Given the importance to tax policy of knowing the answer, Desai and Goolsbee find it surprising that, with the exception of studies of aggregate investment in the United Kingdom by James Poterba and Summers, no one has attempted to directly estimate the effect of dividend taxes on aggregate investment or to use firm data to control for aggregate factors. In the case of the United States, part of the reason may be that, until the 2003 tax cut, dividend taxes were never cut in isolation from other tax changes.

Before turning to a direct performance comparison of new and traditional investment equations, the authors examine the performance of several other variants of the q equation in explaining investment of firms in their Compustat sample for 1962–2003. All of the equations include year and firm fixed effects. The authors try two different measures of q: one with and the other without adjustment for the corporate profits tax. Like most investment studies that, following theory, relate investment to q minus the cost of capital, they find that the coefficient is generally highly significant but quite small, implying unrealistically high adjustment costs. The authors believe that this small coefficient is likely to reflect measurement error in q that biases the coefficient toward zero. This leads them to estimate an investment equation that allows separate estimates of the response to q and the cost-of-capital terms for equipment and structures. They find that the coefficient on the cost of equipment (which represents roughly 80 percent of total investment) implies much more reasonable costs of adjustment. The coefficient on the cost of structures is insignificant, which the authors do not find surprising given the traditional difficulty in understanding the incentives for investment in structures. Using the earnings estimates of equity analysts as an instrument for q is another way to deal with the possibility of measurement error, and it likewise results in more reasonable estimates of the cost of adjustment.

Tax-adjusted q and unadjusted q perform comparably when entered singly, but when they are entered together, the coefficient on tax-adjusted q is much larger and of the correct sign, whereas unadjusted q takes on the wrong sign. Both estimates are highly significant. This is consistent with the presence of measurement error in q. The resulting errors in the tax-adjusted term can be offset by a negative coefficient on the q variable entered separately, allowing the variations in the tax rates to dominate the estimation of the coefficient on tax-adjusted q.

The authors regard these estimated investment equations as quite successful. The coefficient on the cost of equipment, which incorporates an adjustment for the tax treatment of depreciation, can be used to predict the effect of the substantial increases in depreciation allowances enacted in 2002 and expanded in 2003 on virtually every type of equipment. But since these equations do not account for the possible effects of capital gains and dividend taxes, they cannot be used to evaluate the effects on investment of the reduction in the capital gains tax rate from 20 percent to 15 percent in 2003, or of the even more dramatic reduction in dividend taxes that same year, from a maximum of 38.6 percent (the maximum tax rate on ordinary income) to the new capital gains rate. As discussed above, the effect of these changes should depend, crucially, on the financing margin facing firms. Desai and Goolsbee rerun the regressions on the panel of firms, this time including two q terms. The first one is appropriate for firms using equity financing of investment and reflects the traditional view, according to which the dividend tax rate should affect investment. The second is appropriate for a firm using retained earnings, reflecting the new view according to which the dividend tax rate should not affect investment. The new view q performs much better at predicting investment. For the entire sample its coefficient is positive and highly significant, whereas the coefficient on traditional-view q is insignificant and of the wrong sign. The same result holds for the subperiods 1962–96 and 1997–2003. The authors view the results for the latter period as especially relevant for assessing current tax policy, both because the current financial structure of firms is what currently matters and because this is the period when the tax rates on capital gains and dividends changed the most. Indeed, for this period the superiority of the new-view q is even greater: its coefficient is roughly twice that estimated using the entire sample. One awkwardness that arises with estimates for this period, however, is that the cost-of-capital terms, which were significant using the entire sample, are now insignificant.

The enactment of immediate expensing of 30 percent of investment in 2002 and 50 percent of investment in 2003 looks like a dramatic reduction that could have a major effect on investment incentives. But, given that investment in most forms of equipment could already be substantially written off in the first few years, the effects of immediate expensing are actually quite modest. The authors calculate the effect of the partial expensing on the cost of equipment, and on the cost of equipment plus structures, for industries at the three-digit classification level. Not surprisingly, the effects differ substantially across industries. Firms that invest mostly in long-lived assets, such as airlines, receive the largest benefit: expensing reduces the cost of their capital by over 3 percent. In industries such as real estate and hotels, in contrast, the reductions amount to only a fraction of a percent. Overall these reductions average about 3 percent for equipment and 2 percent for total investment. In comparison with earlier changes, such as the investment tax credit of 1962 or the Reagan depreciation allowance increases of 1981, all of which reduced capital costs by about 10 percent, the effects of these changes are quite small. The authors offer two reasons why: the corporate tax rate is lower today, so that the benefit of further reductions is smaller; and investment has shifted toward shorter-lived equipment such as computers. Even before the recent tax cuts, the present value of depreciation allowances for equipment was already only 10 percent less than that of full expensing.

Given their belief that dividend tax cuts do not significantly affect the required rate of return on capital, and given the modest effect that the 2002 and 2003 tax changes had on the tax-adjusted cost of equipment and structures, Desai and Goolsbee are not surprised that the Bush tax cuts have had little apparent effect on investment. Assuming a Cobb-Douglas production function, a 3 percent reduction in the cost of capital would increase the desired capital stock by 3.0 percent in the long run if, as the authors assume, output is held constant. If instead employment of labor is assumed to be unchanged or to respond to the higher labor productivity from capital deepening, the increase of the capital stock would be substantially greater. The authors estimate that costs of adjustment typically lead firms to move only about a third of the way toward the long-run goal each year. Using their assumption of constant output, the authors calculate the increase in capital, for a representative firm in each of the three-digit industries, using the capital share and reduction in the cost of capital that they estimate for each industry. They find that, on average, the increase in the capital stock between 2001 and 2003 attributable to the tax cuts is only 1 to 2 percent, and the average total increase is still less than 2 percent by the end of 2004.

Desai and Goolsbee draw three broad conclusions from their study. First, they see little evidence that a capital overhang from the 1990s plays a dominant role in explaining the differences in investment across industries, asset types, or firms in the 2000s. Second, the tax cuts of the early 2000s, despite their high revenue cost, had minimal, if any, impact on marginal investment incentives. The new view of investment, according to which dividend tax cuts are capitalized in share prices but do not affect investment, is a better description of firm behavior than the traditional view. Third, the partial expensing provisions passed in 2002 and 2003 were not large enough to provide much counterweight to the large declines in aggregate investment.

BEN S. BERNANKE
Board of Governors of the Federal Reserve System

VINCENT R. REINHART
Board of Governors of the Federal Reserve System

BRIAN P. SACK
Macroeconomic Advisers, LLC

Monetary Policy Alternatives at the Zero Bound: An Empirical Assessment

THE CONVENTIONAL INSTRUMENT of monetary policy in most major industrial economies is the very short term nominal interest rate, such as the overnight federal funds rate in the case of the United States. The use of this instrument, however, implies a potential problem: Because currency (which pays a nominal interest rate of zero) can be used as a store of value, the short-term nominal interest rate cannot be pushed below zero. Should the nominal rate hit zero, the real short-term interest rate—at that point equal to the negative of prevailing inflation expectations—may be higher than the rate needed to ensure stable prices and the full utilization of resources. Indeed, an unstable dynamic may result if the excessively high real rate leads to downward pressure on costs and prices that, in turn, raises the real short-term interest rate, which depresses activity and prices further, and so on.

Japan has suffered from the problems created by the zero lower bound (ZLB) on the nominal interest rate in recent years, and short-term rates in countries such as the United States and Switzerland have also come uncomfortably close to zero. As a consequence, the problems of conducting monetary policy when interest rates approach zero have elicited considerable attention from the economics profession. Some contributions have framed the

The views expressed are our own and are not necessarily shared by anyone else in the Federal Reserve System. We have benefited from conversations with many colleagues. We also thank Thomas Gallagher of the ISI Group and Jeffrey Young of Nikko/Citigroup for providing data on their real-time interpretations of, respectively, U.S. and Japanese monetary policies.

1

problem in a formal general equilibrium setting; another strand of the literature identifies and discusses the policy options available to central banks when the zero bound is binding.[1]

Although there have been quite a few theoretical analyses of alternative monetary policy strategies at the ZLB, systematic empirical evidence on the potential efficacy of alternative policies is scant. Knowing whether the proposed alternative strategies would work in practice is important to central bankers, not only because such knowledge would help guide policymaking in extremis, but also because the central bank's choice of its long-run inflation objective depends importantly on the perceived risks created by the ZLB. The greater the confidence of central bankers that tools exist to help the economy escape the ZLB, the less need there is to maintain an inflation "buffer," and hence the lower the inflation objective can be.[2]

This paper uses the methods of modern empirical finance to assess the potential effectiveness of so-called nonstandard monetary policies at the zero bound. We are interested particularly in whether such policies would work in modern industrial economies (as opposed to, for example, the same economies during the Depression era), and so our focus is on the recent experience of the United States and Japan.

The paper begins by noting that, although the recent improvement in the global economy and the receding of near-term deflation risks may have reduced the salience of the ZLB today, this constraint is likely to continue to trouble central bankers for the foreseeable future. Central banks in the industrial world have exhibited a strong commitment to keeping inflation low, but inflation can be difficult to predict. Although low inflation has many benefits, it also raises the risk that adverse shocks will drive interest rates to the ZLB.

Whether hitting the ZLB presents a minor annoyance or a major risk for monetary policy depends on the effectiveness of the policy alterna-

---

1. Examples of the first approach include Woodford (2003), Eggertsson and Woodford (2003a, 2003b), Benhabib, Schmitt-Grohé, and Uribe (2002), and Auerbach and Obstfeld (2004); examples of the second include Blinder (2000), Bernanke (2002), Clouse and others (2003), and Bernanke and Reinhart (2004).

2. Phelps (1972), Summers (1991), and Fischer (1996) have noted the relevance of the ZLB to the determination of the optimal inflation rate. Coenen, Orphanides, and Wieland (2004) and Adam and Billi (2004) provide simulation evidence on the link between the ZLB and the optimal inflation rate.

tives available when prices are declining. Following a recent paper by two of the present authors,[3] we group these policy alternatives into three classes: using communications policies to shape public expectations about the future course of interest rates; increasing the size of the central bank's balance sheet; and changing the composition of the central bank's balance sheet. We discuss how these policies might work, and we cite existing evidence on their utility from historical episodes and recent empirical research.

The paper's main contribution is to provide new empirical evidence on the possible effectiveness of these alternative policies. We employ two basic approaches. First, we use event-study methods to examine financial market responses to central bank statements and announcements. By using sufficiently narrow event windows, we can get precise estimates of the market's responses to central bank communications and to other types of financial or economic news. Second, we estimate no-arbitrage vector autoregression (VAR) models of the term structure of interest rates for both the United States and Japan.[4] For any given set of macroeconomic conditions and stance of monetary policy, these models permit us to project the expected level and shape of the term structure. Using the predicted term structure as a benchmark, we are then able to assess whether factors not included in the model—such as quantitative easing in Japan, or changes in the relative supplies of Treasury securities during the recent debt buyback episode in the United States—have economically significant effects on interest rates.

Our results provide some grounds for optimism about the likely efficacy of nonstandard policies. In particular, we confirm a potentially important role for central bank communications to shape public expectations of future policy actions. Our event studies for the United States confirm the result of Refet Gürkaynak, Brian Sack, and Eric Swanson that surprises in the setting of the current policy rate are not sufficient to explain the effect of monetary policy decisions on policy expectations and asset prices.[5] These effects, however, can be explained by the addition of a second factor that reflects revisions to private sector expectations about the course of the policy rate over the subsequent year. Changes in the second factor appear strongly linked to Federal Reserve policy statements, providing support to the view that central bank announcements can help to shape market expectations.

The U.S. record also provides encouraging evidence that changes in the relative supplies of securities significantly affect their relative returns. As we know from the classic paper by William Brainard and James Tobin,[6] if assets are imperfect substitutes for each other, then changes in the composition of the central bank's balance sheet might be an effective nonstandard policy. To assess this possibility, we apply the event-study methodology to three important episodes in which U.S. financial market participants received information that led them to expect large changes in the relative supplies of Treasury securities: the announcement of debt buybacks following the emergence of budget surpluses in the late 1990s, the massive foreign official purchases of U.S. Treasury securities over the past two years, and the "deflation scare" of 2003, during which market participants apparently believed that the Federal Reserve was seriously considering a program of targeted bond purchases. We supplement the event-study evidence with results from our estimated term structure model, which provides a benchmark against which to compare the actual behavior of Treasury yields during the above three episodes. Our evidence generally supports the view that financial assets are not perfect substitutes, implying that relative supplies do matter for asset pricing.

Our analysis of the recent Japanese experience focuses on two nonstandard policies recently employed by the Bank of Japan (BOJ). The first is the BOJ's zero-interest-rate policy (ZIRP), under which the Japanese central bank has committed to keeping its policy rate, the call rate, at zero until deflation has been eliminated; the second is the BOJ's quantitative easing policy, which consists of providing bank reserves at levels much greater than needed to maintain a policy rate of zero. Our evidence for the effectiveness of these policies is more mixed than in the case of the United States. In event-study analyses, which may be less informative in Japan because of small sample sizes and our use of daily rather than intraday data, we find no reliable relationship over the past few years between one-year-ahead policy expectations and policy statements by the BOJ. This result, taken on its own, suggests that the BOJ was either unwilling or unable to influence one-year-ahead expectations during the period considered (but see below).

---

6. Brainard and Tobin (1968).

On a more positive note, Japan provides the only evidence of recent vintage bearing on the second type of nonstandard policy, namely, changing the size of the central bank's balance sheet (or quantitative easing). Although the BOJ has used this strategy recently, many consider the manner in which it has done so to have been relatively restrained and limited. Moreover, other forces have no doubt been at work at the same time, making it difficult to parse out the effects of quantitative easing on the economy. Nevertheless, our estimated term structure model for Japan does suggest that yields in Japan were noticeably lower during the quantitative easing period than the model would have predicted—a bit of evidence for the effectiveness of this policy. A similar result emerges for the period when the ZIRP was in effect, suggesting that the event-study analysis may not have captured the full effect of the BOJ's policy commitments on longer-term yields.

Despite our relatively encouraging findings concerning the potential efficacy of nonstandard policies at the ZLB, we remain cautious about making policy prescriptions. Although it appears that nonstandard policy measures may affect asset yields and thus potentially the economy, considerable uncertainty remains about the size and reliability of these effects under the circumstances prevailing near the ZLB. Thus we still believe that the best policy approach is one of avoidance, achieved by maintaining a sufficient inflation buffer and easing preemptively as necessary to minimize the risk of hitting the ZLB. However, should that outcome prove unavoidable, we hope that our research will provide some guidance on the potential of nonstandard policies to lift the economy away from the zero bound.

Monetary Policy Options at the Zero Bound

It is not without some irony that the resurgence in work on the ZLB, which for a few generations of economists seemed to be a relic of the Depression era, traces to a remarkable achievement by central banks in the major industrial economies. Among those countries, annual consumer price inflation has fallen to around 2 percent, about one-third the pace of twenty years ago.[7] For instance, as shown in figure 1, the median inflation

7. October of 2004 marked an important turning point in those efforts: Twenty-five years ago, then–Federal Reserve Chairman Paul Volcker and the other members of the Federal Open Market Committee fired the initial salvo in the battle to conquer inflation in the United States.

Figure 1. Consumer Price Inflation in Advanced Economies, 1980–2005[a]

Percent

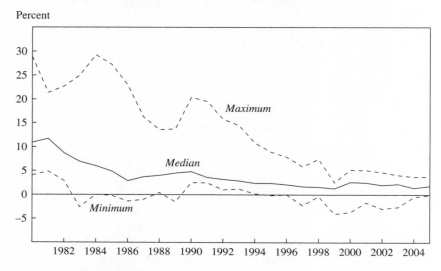

Source: International Monetary Fund, *World Economic Outlook* (April 2004).
a. International Monetary Fund definition of twenty-eight advanced economies, excluding Iceland and Israel.

rate among twenty-six countries labeled "advanced" in the International Monetary Fund's World Economic Outlook database has moved down steadily since 1980.[8] This disciplined pursuit of low inflation has no doubt generated macroeconomic benefits and should be considered a singular accomplishment, but it also has been associated with episodes of very low inflation and sometimes outright deflation.[9] The minimum inflation rate observed among these twenty-six economies has often been negative— and consistently so over the past ten years. In the case of Japan, deflation over the past five years implies that the current level of consumer prices is now slightly lower than in 1995.

With inflation low and likely to remain so, industrial countries are at risk of encountering the ZLB on nominal interest rates periodically in the future. This raises the stakes for answering the question: What options

8. Data from Iceland and Israel, which both experienced bouts of very high inflation, are excluded from the sample because they distort the maximums shown in the figure.

9. Key references on the potential benefits and costs of low inflation include Friedman (1969), Feldstein (1997), and Akerlof, Dickens, and Perry (1996).

exist for monetary policy when lowering the nominal short-term interest rate, the usual response to a weak economy, is no longer possible? Many previous studies have discussed possible answers to this question, and we will not review this extensive literature in detail. Instead, as background for the empirical results to be presented later, we provide an overview that focuses on some key debates about the effectiveness of alternative nonstandard policies and describes existing empirical evidence bearing on these debates.

Bernanke and Reinhart discuss three alternative, although potentially complementary, strategies when monetary policymakers are confronted with a short-term nominal interest rate that is close to zero.[10] As discussed in the introduction, these alternatives involve either shaping the expectations of the public about future settings of the policy rate; increasing the size of the central bank's balance sheet beyond the level needed to set the short-term policy rate at zero (quantitative easing); or shifting the composition of the central bank's balance sheet in order to affect the relative supplies of securities held by the public. We use this taxonomy here as well to organize our discussion of nonstandard policy options at or near the ZLB.

Shaping Policy Expectations

Commentators often describe the stance of a central bank's policy in terms of the level of the short-term nominal interest rate. For example, the very low short-term rates seen in Japan in recent years have led many to refer to the BOJ's monetary policy as "ultra-easy."[11] However, associating the stance of policy entirely with the level of the short-term nominal interest rate can be seriously misleading. At a minimum, a distinction needs to be drawn between the nominal short-term rate and the real short-term rate; in a deflationary environment, a nominal interest rate near zero does not preclude the possibility that real interest rates are too high for the health of the economy.

A more subtle reason that the level of the policy rate does not fully describe the stance of monetary policy is that a given policy rate may coexist with widely varying configurations of asset prices and yields, and hence with varying degrees of policy stimulus broadly considered. In the

10. Bernanke and Reinhart (2004).
11. "BOJ Leaves Policy Unchanged, Keeps Ultra-Easy Stance," *Japan Policy and Politics,* November 5, 2001.

United States, at least, the short-term policy rate has little direct effect on private sector borrowing and investment decisions. Rather, those decisions respond most sensitively to longer-term yields (such as the yields on mortgages and corporate bonds) and to the prices of long-lived assets (such as housing and equities). A given short-term rate may thus be associated with relatively restrictive financial conditions (for example, if the term structure is sharply upward sloping and equity prices are depressed) or, alternatively, with relatively easy conditions (if the term structure is flat or downward sloping and equity prices are high). Indeed, copious research by financial economists has demonstrated that two and possibly three factors (sometimes referred to as level, slope, and curvature) are needed to describe the term structure of interest rates, implying that the short-term policy rate alone can never be sufficient to fully describe even the term structure, let alone the broad range of financial conditions.

Financial theory also tells us that the prices and yields of long-term assets, which play such an important role in the transmission of monetary policy, depend to a significant extent on financial market participants' expectations about the future path of short-term rates. In particular, with the relevant term, risk, and liquidity premiums held constant, expectations that short-term rates will be kept low will induce financial market participants to bid down long-term bond yields and (for given expectations about future corporate earnings) bid up the prices of equities. Because financial conditions depend on the expected future path of the policy rate as well as (or even more than) its current value, central bankers must be continuously aware of how their actions shape the public's policy expectations. The crucial role of expectations in the making of monetary policy, in normal times as well as when the policy rate is near the ZLB, has recently been stressed in two important papers by Gauti Eggertsson and Michael Woodford (EW).[12] Indeed, in the context of their theoretical model, EW obtain the strong result that shaping the interest rate expectations of the public is essentially the only tool that central bankers have—not only when the ZLB binds, but under normal conditions as well. We will have several occasions to refer to the EW result below and to suggest that the levers of policy are greater in number than they contend.

---

12. Eggertsson and Woodford (2003a, 2003b).

How, then, can a central bank influence private sector expectations? EW, like most of the literature, emphasize the importance of the central bank's committing in advance to a policy rule. Under the assumption that such a commitment is feasible, they focus on the problem of designing policy rules that perform reasonably well both close to and away from the ZLB. EW are surely correct that predictable, rule-like behavior on the part of central banks is an important means of shaping the public's policy expectations. Central banks have generally become more predictable in recent years, reflecting factors such as increased transparency and, in some cases, the adoption of explicit policy frameworks such as inflation targeting. However, there are limits in practice to the ability of central banks to commit "once and for all" to a fully specified policy rule, as envisioned by theoretical analyses of monetary policy under commitment. Although a theoretician might be able to specify the appropriate state-contingent policy plan for a given model, in practice a central bank would likely find it particularly difficult to describe the details of its reactions to highly unusual circumstances, such as those associated with the policy rate being constrained by the ZLB.

Given that their ability to commit to precisely specified rules is limited, central bankers have found it useful in practice to supplement their actions with talk, communicating regularly with the public about the outlook for the economy and for policy. That is not to say that talk is an independent instrument of policy, because statements by a central bank will be believed by the public only if the central bank has a proven track record of delivering on its stated commitments. However, if central banks perceive a sufficient reputational cost to being seen to renege on earlier statements, communication in advance may enhance the central bank's ability to commit to certain policies or courses of action. Moreover, at all times such communication can be helpful in achieving a closer alignment between the policy expectations of the public and the plans of the central bank.

Although communication is always important, its importance may be elevated when the policy rate is constrained by the ZLB. In particular, even with the overnight rate at zero, the central bank may be able to impart additional stimulus to the economy by persuading the public that the policy rate will remain low for a longer period than was previously expected. One means of doing so would be to shade interest rate expectations downward by making a commitment to the public to follow a policy of extended monetary ease. This commitment, if credible and not previously expected, should lower longer-term rates, support other asset prices, and boost aggregate demand.

In effect, public statements by the central bank may foster the expectation that it intends to follow what EW refer to as optimal monetary policy under commitment rather than prematurely remove policy accommodation in the future (as happens in EW's no-commitment case).[13] The expectation that the nominal short-term rate will be kept sufficiently low for long enough to ward off deflation should also prevent inflation expectations from falling, which would otherwise raise real interest rates and impose a drag on spending. Because interest rate commitments have implications for inflation expectations in equilibrium, our description of policy in terms of expected interest rate paths is closely related to the types of policies analyzed by Paul Krugman and Lars Svensson.[14] These authors stress the importance of the central bank committing to generate sufficient future inflation to reduce the expected real interest rate to levels supportive of aggregate spending. Our emphasis, as in EW, is on policies under which the central bank commits to keeping the short-term nominal rate low for long enough to achieve the same results.

Bernanke and Reinhart note that, in principle, such commitments could be unconditional (that is, linked only to the calendar) or conditional (linked to developments in the economy).[15] Unconditional commitments are rare. The Federal Reserve's commitment to peg short-term and long-term rates during the decade after 1942, discussed below, might be considered an example of an unconditional commitment, in that the pegging operation was open-ended and did not specify an exit strategy. More usually, central bank commitments about future policies are explicitly conditional.

An important recent example of a conditional commitment is the zero-interest-rate policy of the Bank of Japan. The BOJ reduced the call rate to a level "as low as possible"—to zero, for all practical purposes—in February 1999. In April 1999 then-Governor of the BOJ Masaru Hayami announced that the BOJ would keep the policy rate at zero "until defla-

---

13. Also see Reifschneider and Williams (2000) on the importance of committing to keeping rates low.

14. Krugman (1998); Svensson (2001, 2003).

15. Bernanke and Reinhart (2004).

tionary concerns are dispelled," clearly indicating that the policy commitment was conditional.[16] However, in a case of what might be called commitment *interruptus*, the BOJ then raised the call rate to 25 basis points in August 2000. In February 2001, following a subsequent weakening in economic conditions, the rate increase was partly retracted. The ZIRP was then effectively reinstated in March 2001, when the BOJ announced that it would henceforth target bank reserves at a level well above that needed to bring the call rate to zero (a policy of quantitative easing; see below). Since that time the BOJ has attempted to assure the markets that the reconstituted ZIRP, together with its other extraordinary policy measures, will be maintained as long as deflation persists. Indeed, under Hayami's successor as BOJ governor, Toshihiko Fukui, the BOJ has become more explicit about the conditions required to move the call rate from its zero floor, asserting that the ZIRP will not end until year-over-year core inflation has been positive for several months *and* is expected to remain positive.

A relevant, although less explicit, example of policy commitment is also available for the United States. From the latter part of 2002 through much of 2003, Federal Reserve officials expressed concerns about what they described as a "remote" possibility of deflation. Subsequently, in late 2003 and early 2004, although the deflation risk had receded, the slow pace of job creation heightened concerns about the sustainability of the economic recovery from the 2001 recession. Although the Federal Reserve's policy rate remained at least 100 basis points above zero throughout this period, policymakers became more specific in communicating their outlook for policy in the attempt to shape expectations. For example, the August 2003 statement of the Federal Open Market Committee (FOMC, the body responsible for the conduct of monetary policy in the United States) that "policy accommodation can be maintained for a considerable period" may be interpreted as an example of conditional commitment.[17] The conditional nature of the commitment was made clear in the committee's December 2003 policy statement, which explicitly linked continuing policy accommodation to the low level of inflation and slack in resource use. Likewise, the FOMC's stated plan in 2004 to "remove

---

16. Fujiki and Shiratsuka (2002).

17. The full texts of the FOMC's statements can be found at www.federalreserve. gov/fomc.

policy accommodation at a pace that is likely to be measured" gave the market information about the likely direction of the policy rate but also emphasized that future actions would be linked explicitly to the condition that inflation remain under control.

Empirical evidence on the ability of central banks to influence policy expectations through statements, speeches, and other forms of talk is relatively limited. For the United States, Donald Kohn and Sack present evidence that the issuance of FOMC statements increases the variability of market interest rates on the day of the statement, suggesting that these statements convey information to financial markets over and above the information in any accompanying policy action.[18] However, they do not specifically address the ability of the FOMC to influence expectations of future policy in the desired direction or at longer horizons. In the next section we extend the work of Kohn and Sack to provide additional evidence on the effects of FOMC statements on policy expectations and asset prices.

More work has been done on the effects of the BOJ's ZIRP, primarily by researchers at the Bank of Japan and affiliated research institutions. The majority of this research suggests that the ZIRP has been successful at affecting policy expectations, and thus at affecting yields, although the greatest impact is observed at the short end of the maturity spectrum.[19] Also, studies that include both the early ZIRP period, before August 2000, and the later application of the policy, which commenced in March 2001 with the introduction of the quantitative easing policy, tend to find modestly stronger effects in the latter period.[20] In an interesting paper, Kohei Marumo and others use an estimated model of the Japanese term structure to back out the evolution of market participants' beliefs about how long the ZIRP would hold.[21] They find that, over the period from February 1999 to August 2000, the mode of the probability distribution over the expected remaining time of the policy ranged from less than one year to about three years. For the second incarnation of the ZIRP, after March 2001, they find that modal expectations of the time to the end of

---

18. Kohn and Sack (2003).
19. Fujiki and Shiratsuka (2002); Takeda and Yajima (2002); Okina and Shiratsuka (2004).
20. Nagayasu (2004).
21. Marumo and others (2003).

the policy varied from approximately two to three years. Kunio Okina and Shigenori Shiratsuka obtained similar results, ultimately concluding that "[t]he policy duration effect was highly effective in stabilizing market expectations regarding the future path of short-term interest rates, thereby bringing longer-term interest rates down to flatten the yield curve."[22]

A shortcoming shared by most of these studies, however, is the absence of an adequate benchmark for the term structure. That is, most existing studies do not effectively answer the question of what yields would have been in the absence of the ZIRP. Hence we really do not know (for example) whether the exceedingly low level of longer-term government bond yields in Japan during recent years primarily reflects expectations of low future policy rates or the belief that Japan faces a protracted period of deflation. In an interesting recent paper, Naohiko Baba and others address the benchmark issue by estimating a "macro-finance," no-arbitrage model of the term structure (discussed in more detail in the next section).[23] They use this model to estimate what yields in Japan would have been at each date, given the state of the economy, under the counterfactual assumption that no ZIRP was in place. A comparison of the actual term structure with the estimated benchmark permits inferences about the effects of the ZIRP. Notably, these authors find somewhat stronger net effects of the ZIRP on long-term yields than does much of the earlier work. We apply a similar strategy in our empirical analysis below.

Our discussion, like much of the literature, has focused on regimes in which the short-term nominal interest rate is the instrument of monetary policy. However, other variables can and have served as a nominal anchor for the system and thus as a target or instrument for the central bank. Svensson has called attention to the nominal exchange rate as an alternative policy instrument when the ZLB binds, noting that monetary policies that can be defined in terms of current and future values of the short-term nominal interest rate can equally well be expressed in terms of paths for the nominal exchange rate.[24] Switching the policy instrument from the short-term interest rate to the exchange rate does not eliminate

---

22. Okina and Shiratsuka (2004, p. 75). However, these authors also argue that the ZIRP did not help the economy much, "since [the] transmission channel linking the financial and non-financial sectors has remained blocked."
23. Baba and others (2004).
24. Svensson (2001, 2003).

the constraints imposed by the zero bound: some paths for the nominal exchange rate cannot be engineered by the central bank, because the values of the short-term nominal interest rate implied by interest rate parity would violate the ZLB. Nevertheless, we agree with Svensson that commitments by the central bank to future policies may be more credible when expressed in terms of a planned path for the exchange rate rather than in terms of future values of the short-term nominal interest rate. One obvious benefit of expressing policy commitments in terms of the exchange rate is that such a commitment is verifiable, in that the central bank's announcement can be accompanied by an immediate and visible change in the exchange rate; promises about future values of the short-term interest rate cannot be accompanied by immediate action, if the current policy rate is at the ZLB.[25]

These considerations suggest that exchange rate–based policies may be the best way for smaller open economies to break the hold of the ZLB. For example, the Swiss National Bank increased its use of the exchange rate as a policy indicator during its recent struggle with the ZLB. Whether large economies like the United States or Japan can have success with exchange rate–based policies is more controversial. Skeptics have argued that the strongest short-term effects of the devaluation suggested by Svensson would be felt on the patterns of trade, raising the possibility that the large country's trading partners would accuse it of following a beggar-thy-neighbor policy. Svensson has replied that growth in domestic demand would ultimately raise imports, offsetting the terms-of-trade effects created by the devaluation. Whether these second-round effects would develop quickly enough to help defuse the political problem, however, is difficult to judge, and we have nothing to add to this controversy. Because large industrial countries have traditionally emphasized interest rates and money growth as policy instruments, the remainder of the paper focuses on these variables. That said, we believe that empirical study of the use of the exchange rate as a policy indicator when the ZLB is binding would be highly worthwhile.

---

25. In principle, a policy that relies on nominal interest rates could be made similarly verifiable by announcing a desired range for an intermediate- or longer-term yield, perhaps in conjunction with central bank purchases in the corresponding segment of the market, a question we discuss below. Up to now the literature has tended to focus on the exchange rate, not a note or bond price, as the intermediate policy target.

Increasing the Size of the Central Bank's Balance Sheet (Quantitative Easing)

Central banks normally lower their policy rate through open-market purchases of bonds or other securities, which have the effect of increasing the supply of bank reserves and putting downward pressure on the rate that clears the reserves market. A sufficient injection of reserves will bring the policy rate arbitrarily close to zero, so that the ZLB rules out further interest rate reduction. However, nothing prevents the central bank from adding liquidity to the system beyond what is needed to achieve a policy rate of zero, in a policy known as quantitative easing. As already noted, Japan has actively pursued this policy approach in recent years. Announced in March 2001, the BOJ's quantitative easing policy might initially have been interpreted as a recommitment to the policy of keeping the short-term rate at zero—that is, of maintaining the ZIRP. However, the BOJ raised its target for current account balances at commercial banks (essentially, bank reserves) a number of times, to the point that reserves substantially exceeded the level needed to pin the call rate at zero. (The BOJ's target for current account balances reached 30-35 trillion yen in January 2004, compared with required reserves of approximately 6 trillion yen, and the monetary base grew by two-thirds in the three years following the initiation of the quantitative easing policy.)[26] However, as has been frequently noted, growth in bank reserves and base money in Japan has not resulted in comparable growth in broader monetary aggregates. In large part this limited effect stems from the poor condition of banks' and borrowers' balance sheets, which makes profitable lending difficult and induces banks to hold large quantities of idle balances.

Whether quantitative easing can be effective in relieving deflationary pressures and, if so, by what mechanism, remains controversial. As already noted, EW have provided theoretical reasons to doubt the efficacy of quantitative easing as an independent tool of policy. They show that, in a world in which financial frictions are sufficiently minimal to permit full insurance against idiosyncratic consumption risks, and in which effects of monetary policy on the government's budget constraint are ruled out, quantitative easing will have *no* effect, except perhaps to the extent that the extra money creation can be used to signal the central bank's intentions regarding future

---

26. As reported in Baba and others (2004).

values of the short-term interest rate. The assumptions that financial markets are essentially frictionless and that fiscal budget constraints are independent of monetary policy are rather strong. If these assumptions do not hold, we may have some basis for believing that quantitative easing will be effective.

Why might injections of liquidity that go beyond the point necessary to drive the short-term policy rate to zero help the economy? One argument for quantitative easing is what might be called the *reduced-form argument*. Broadly, those making this argument are agnostic about the precise mechanisms by which quantitative easing may have its effects. Instead, in support of quantitative easing as an anti-deflationary tool, they point to the undeniable fact that, historically, money growth and inflation have tended to be strongly associated. It follows, according to this argument, that money creation will raise prices independent of its effects on the term structure.

Basing policy recommendations on reduced-form evidence of this sort is problematic, however. As the Lucas critique warns us, historical relationships are prone to break down in novel circumstances. In particular, there is no reason to expect the velocity of money to be stable or predictable when the short-term interest rate (the opportunity cost of holding money) is close to zero, and thus no reason to expect a stable relationship between money growth and nominal income under those conditions. To make the case for quantitative easing, we need more explicit descriptions of how additional money growth might stimulate the economy even when the short-term interest rate has reached zero.

At least three channels through which quantitative easing may be effective have been advanced. The first builds from the premise that money and other financial assets are imperfect substitutes.[27] According to this view, open-market purchases of securities will raise the amount of money relative to nonmoney assets in the public's portfolio. The private sector's collective attempt to rebalance portfolios will tend to raise the prices and lower the yields of nonmoney assets if money and nonmoney assets are imperfect substitutes. Higher asset values and lower yields, in turn, stimulate the economy, according to this view. Recently, Javier Andres, David Lopez-Salido, and Edward Nelson have shown how these

27. This view is associated both with monetarist expositions, such as Meltzer (2001), and with Keynesian classics, such as Brainard and Tobin (1968) and Tobin (1969).

effects might work in a general equilibrium model that includes sufficient financial market frictions.[28]

So long as technology has not made it possible to pay a grocery bill with a stock certificate or the deed to a home, it is difficult to dispute the premise that, as a general matter, money and nonmoney assets are imperfect substitutes. However, in the special situation of a binding ZLB, large additional injections of liquidity may satiate the public's demand for money, implying that, at the margin, extra cash provides no transactions services to households or firms. If money demand is satiated, money becomes (at the margin) just another financial asset, one that happens to pay a zero nominal rate, to be riskless in nominal terms, and to have an indefinite maturity. In this situation it is no longer obvious that money is a particularly poor substitute for nonmonetary assets. For example, with the important exception of its maturity, money's characteristics are very close to those of short-term Treasury bills paying close to zero interest. Of course, even in this situation there will be assets—real estate, for example—that are not very substitutable with money, implying that the central bank's choice of assets to buy may matter a great deal.

A second possible mechanism for quantitative easing to influence the economy is the fiscal channel. This channel relies on the observation that sufficiently large monetary injections will materially relieve the government's budget constraint, permitting tax reductions or increases in government spending without increasing public holdings of government debt.[29] Effectively, the fiscal channel is based on the government's substitution of seigniorage (a tax with little or no deadweight loss in a deflationary environment) for direct taxes such as income taxes. Alan Auerbach and Maurice Obstfeld provide a detailed analysis of both the macroeconomic and the welfare effects of the fiscal channel and find that they are potentially quite substantial.[30] These authors also note, however, that the fiscal effect of quantitative easing will be attenuated or absent if the public expects today's monetary injections to be withdrawn in the future.[31] Broadly, if the public expects quantitative easing to be reversed at the first sign that

---

28. Andres, Lopez-Salido, and Nelson (2003).

29. Bernanke (2003); Auerbach and Obstfeld (2004).

30. Auerbach and Obstfeld (2004).

31. Their point is closely related to Krugman's (1998) important analysis, which emphasized the crucial role of central bank credibility in most nonconventional monetary policies.

deflation has ended, they will likewise expect that their money-financed tax cuts will be replaced by future tax increases as money is withdrawn, and this expectation will blunt the initial impact of the policy. Thus it is crucial that the central bank's promises to maintain some part of its quantitative easing as the economy recovers be perceived by the public as credible. Auerbach and Obstfeld show that, if the central bank is known to be willing to tolerate even a very small amount of inflation, the promise to maintain quantitative easing will be credible. A similar result would likely obtain if the central bank associates even a relatively small cost with publicly reneging on its promises. Thus it seems reasonable to expect that the fiscal channel of quantitative easing would work if pursued sufficiently aggressively.

A third potential mechanism of quantitative easing, admittedly harder to pin down than others, might be called the signaling channel. Simply put, quantitative easing may complement the expectations management approach by providing a visible signal to the public about the central bank's intended future policies. For example, if the public believes that the central bank will be hesitant to reverse large amounts of quantitative easing very quickly, perhaps because of the possible shock to money markets, this policy provides a way of underscoring the central bank's commitment to keeping the policy rate at zero for an extended period.

More speculatively, quantitative easing may work through a signaling channel if its implementation marks a general willingness of the central bank to break from the cautious and conventional policies of the past. A historical episode that may illustrate this channel at work (although the policymaker in question was the executive rather than the central bank) was the period following Franklin D. Roosevelt's inauguration as U.S. president in 1933. During 1933 and 1934 the extreme deflation seen earlier in the decade suddenly reversed, stock prices jumped, and the economy grew rapidly. Christina Romer has argued persuasively that this surprisingly sharp recovery was closely associated with the rapid growth in the money supply that arose from Roosevelt's devaluation of the dollar, capital inflows from an increasingly unstable Europe, and other factors.[32] Because short-term interest rates remained near zero throughout the period, the episode is reasonably characterized as a successful application of quantitative easing. Romer does not explain the mechanism by which quantita-

32. Romer (1992).

tive easing worked in this episode, other than to observe that real interest rates declined as deflation changed to inflation.[33] Peter Temin and Barrie Wigmore addressed that question, arguing that the key to the sudden reversal was the public's acceptance of the idea that Roosevelt's policies constituted a "regime change."[34] The policymakers who preceded him had shown little inclination to resist deflation and, indeed, seemed to prefer deflation to even a small probability of future inflation. In contrast, Roosevelt demonstrated clearly through his actions that he was committed to ending deflation and reflating the economy. Although the president could have simply announced his desire to raise prices, his adoption of policies that his predecessors would have considered reckless provided a powerful signal to the public that the economic situation had fundamentally changed. If one accepts the Temin-Wigmore hypothesis, it appears that the signal afforded by Roosevelt's exchange rate and monetary policies was central to the conquest of deflation in 1933–34.[35]

Outside of the suggestive evidence from the interwar period just discussed, there has been little empirical analysis of the quantitative easing channel. The only recent experience to draw upon, of course, is that of Japan since March 2001. Masaaki Shirakawa reviewed the quantitative easing policy after one year and argued that, although the policy may be credited with reducing liquidity premiums in some markets, it did not have discernible effects on the prices of most assets, including government bonds, equities, or foreign currency, nor did it increase bank lending.[36] Takeshi Kimura and others studied the effects of quantitative easing by vector autoregression methods and by estimating a money demand equation. They concluded that any effects of quantitative easing have been very small and highly uncertain.[37]

---

33. Dollar devaluation, of course, improved the competitiveness of U.S. exports and raised the prices of imports. But, in an economy that was by this time largely closed, the direct effects of devaluation seem unlikely to have been large enough to account for the sharp turnaround. Eichengreen (1992) argues persuasively that the devaluation stimulated the economy by freeing up the money supply rather than by changing relative prices.

34. Temin and Wigmore (1990).

35. Meltzer (1999) has also drawn on the experience of the first half of the twentieth century, including episodes in 1920–21, 1937–38, and 1947–48, to argue for the potential benefits of quantitative easing.

36. Shirakawa (2002).

37. Kimura and others (2002).

20   *Brookings Papers on Economic Activity, 2:2004*

The recent moderating of deflation in Japan and the signs of recovery there are, of course, a bit of evidence in favor of the effectiveness of the BOJ's quantitative easing policy. Unfortunately, however, they are far from decisive. Other factors have certainly played a role in the recent improvement in the Japanese economy, including structural and banking reforms, a strengthening world economy, and the ZIRP. The quantitative easing policy, although an important departure from the standard policy framework, has in fact been somewhat conservative in its execution. Despite some interesting initiatives intended to promote the development of various financial markets, the BOJ has largely restricted its open-market purchases to the usual suspects—government securities—thereby inhibiting any effect that might work through imperfect substitutability. Even more important, there has been a notable absence of cooperation between the monetary and the fiscal authorities (indeed, the BOJ has expressed repeated concerns that monetary ease might facilitate fiscal indiscipline), and the communication and signaling aspects of policy have been subdued. We will present some evidence that is consistent with quantitative easing having been effective in Japan, but our findings do not clearly isolate the effects of quantitative easing from other influences. The reality may well be that the Japanese experience does not support strong conclusions about the potential efficacy of this particular nonstandard policy.

Altering the Composition of the Central Bank's Balance Sheet

The composition of the assets on the central bank's balance sheet offers another potential lever for monetary policy. For example, the Federal Reserve participates in all segments of the Treasury market, including inflation-indexed Treasury debt: its asset holdings of about $700 billion are distributed among Treasury securities with original maturities ranging from four weeks to thirty years. Over the past fifty years, the average maturity of the Federal Reserve System's holdings of Treasury debt has varied considerably within a range from one to four years. By buying and selling securities of various maturities or other characteristics in the open market, the Federal Reserve could materially influence the relative supplies of these securities. In a frictionless financial market, as EW point out, these changes in supply would have essentially no effect, because the pricing of any financial asset would depend exclusively on its state- and date-contingent payoffs. However, in a world with transactions costs and in which financial markets are incomplete in important ways, the Federal Reserve's action might be able to influence term, risk, and liquidity premiums—and thus overall yields.[38] The feasibility of this approach is, of course, closely related to the issue of whether different types of assets are imperfect substitutes for each other, as discussed earlier.

The same logic would apply, of course, to other financial and real assets that the central bank might buy or sell. Except under certain emergency provisions dormant since the 1930s, however, the Federal Reserve is restricted to purchasing a limited range of assets outside of Treasury securities, including some foreign government bonds, the debt of government-sponsored enterprises, and some municipal securities.[39] Various methods might effectively make these restrictions less binding. For example, the Federal Reserve has the authority to accept a wide range of assets as collateral for loans from its discount window. Some other central banks face fewer restrictions on the assets they can hold; for example, the BOJ's expansionary efforts have involved purchases not only of treasury bills and Japanese government bonds, but also of commercial paper, various asset-backed securities, and equities (from commercial banks).

Perhaps the most extreme example of a policy keyed to the composition of the central bank's balance sheet is the announcement of a ceiling on some longer-term yield that is below the rate then prevailing in the market. Such a policy would entail an essentially unlimited commitment to purchase the targeted security at the announced price. If these purchases were allowed to affect the size of the central bank's balance sheet as well as its composition, ultimately the policy might also involve quantitative easing. A "pure" pegging policy would require the central bank to sell other securities equal in amount to its purchases of the targeted security. A commitment to peg a longer-term yield may also help to convince the public that the central bank intends to keep the short-term rate low for a considerable period; such a policy would thus include an element of expectations shaping as well.

---

38. In carrying out such a policy, the Federal Reserve would need to coordinate with the Treasury, to ensure that the latter's debt issuance policies did not offset the former's actions. In principle, the Treasury could alter its debt management patterns to achieve the same effect, much along the lines discussed by Tobin (1963).

39. Clouse and others (2003) review the Federal Reserve's legal authority.

As with quantitative easing, whether policies based on manipulating the composition of the central bank's balance sheet can have significant effects is a contentious issue. A fair characterization of the prevailing view among financial economists is that changes in the relative supplies of assets within the range of U.S. experience are unlikely to have a major impact on these premiums and thus on overall yields.[40] We will present new evidence on this issue later in the paper. If the view is correct that financial pricing approximates the frictionless ideal, then attempts to enforce a ceiling on the yields of long-term Treasury securities would be successful only if the targeted yields were broadly consistent with investor expectations about future values of the policy rate. If investors doubted that rates would be kept low, this view would predict that the central bank would end up owning all or most of the targeted security. Moreover, even if large purchases of, say, a long-dated Treasury security were able to affect the yield on that security, the yield on that security might become "disconnected" from the rest of the Treasury term structure and from rates on private sector securities, thus reducing the economic impact of the policy.

Such caveats notwithstanding, history offers a number of examples of rate pegs by central banks. During the twentieth century, central banks in a number of countries successfully pegged (or imposed a ceiling on) long-term government bond rates in order to facilitate the financing of war or postwar reconstruction. In the United States, the Federal Reserve maintained ceilings on Treasury yields at seven different maturities between 1942 and the 1951 Accord; among these were caps of ⅜ percent on ninety-day Treasury bill rates (raised to ¾ percent in July 1947) and of 2½ percent on very long term bonds. The peg on bills appeared to be binding, in that for most of the period the rate on bills remained precisely at the announced level, and Federal Reserve holdings of bills grew steadily, exceeding 90 percent of the outstanding stock by 1947.[41] In contrast, the 2½ percent cap on very long term bond yields was maintained

---

40. Reinhart and Sack (2000) show that a simple mean-variance model of portfolio choice predicts that even sizable changes in the composition of the public's asset holdings would have only small effects on yields. However, a number of studies, including Roley (1982) and Friedman and Kuttner (1998), have provided evidence of imperfect substitution among broad asset classes.

41. Toma (1992).

without active intervention throughout much of the period, suggesting that the cap was not a binding constraint. There were exceptions to this generalization, however: Notably, from the beginning of the regime in April 1942 through December 1944, long-term bond yields fluctuated in a narrow range between 2.43 percent and 2.50 percent, suggesting that the cap had some influence.[42] Also, between October 1947 and December 1948, the Federal Reserve appears to have intervened actively to keep bond yields just below the peg, in the process raising the central bank's holdings of bonds from near zero to about 13 percent of the outstanding stock.[43]

The relative ease with which the Federal Reserve maintained the ceiling on long-term government bond yields for an entire decade raises intriguing questions. During the early part of the pegging period, memories of the low interest rates of the 1930s and ongoing low inflation (enforced in part by wartime price controls) plausibly implied equilibrium long-term yields either below or not far above the ceiling. After the war and the elimination of wartime controls, however, inflation rose quite sharply. Yet the long-term peg remained intact. Barry Eichengreen and Peter Garber argue that the public was confident that the Federal Reserve would reverse the postwar inflation and hence remained content to hold low-yielding bonds.[44] Likewise, Mark Toma notes that there is no logical inconsistency in promising a monetary policy that is easy in the short run but anti-inflationary in the long run, as the pegging policy seemed to do.[45] In this paper we focus our empirical analysis on more recent episodes, and so we confine ourselves here to raising a few questions about the pre-Accord period that we believe merit further analysis. First, if we accept the Eichengreen-Garber argument that long-term inflation expectations were well behaved during this period, we might still ask how, if at all, the Federal Reserve's pegging policy influenced those expectations. For example, did the pegging policy communicate a commitment to low inflation, perhaps because the public understood that the Federal Reserve would do all it could to avert the capital losses to banks and on its own account that would be suffered if inflation and long-term rates rose

42. Hutchinson and Toma (1991).
43. Toma (1992).
44. Eichengreen and Garber (1991).
45. Toma (1992).

sharply? Second, did the pegging policy affect term premiums, for example by reducing the perceived risk in holding long-term bonds? Finally, did the Federal Reserve in fact succeed in pegging long-term yields below their equilibrium levels in 1942–44 and 1947–48, and, if so, what were the consequences?

A second well-known historical episode involving the attempted manipulation of the term structure was the so-called Operation Twist. Launched in early 1961 by the incoming Kennedy administration, Operation Twist was intended to raise short-term rates (thereby promoting capital inflows and supporting the dollar) while lowering, or at least not raising, long-term rates.[46] The two main actions underlying Operation Twist were, first, the use of Federal Reserve open-market operations and Treasury debt management operations to shorten the average maturity of government debt held by the public, and second, some easing of the interest rate restrictions on deposits imposed by Regulation Q. The current view, shaped largely by the classic work by Franco Modigliani and Richard Sutch,[47] is that Operation Twist was a failure.[48] Their empirical estimates of the "habitat model" of interest rate determination led them to conclude that Operation Twist narrowed the spread between long-term and short-term yields by amounts that "are most unlikely to exceed some ten to twenty base points—a reduction that can be considered moderate at best."[49] However, Modigliani and Sutch also noted that Operation Twist was a relatively small operation and, indeed, that over a slightly longer period the maturity of outstanding government debt rose significantly, rather than fell.[50] Thus Operation Twist does not seem to provide strong evidence in either direction as to the possible effects of changes in the composition of the central bank's balance sheet. In the next section we consider the effects of more significant changes in relative supplies of government bonds of different maturities than were observed during Operation Twist.

---

46. Modigliani and Sutch (1966).
47. Modigliani and Sutch (1966, 1967).
48. The Modigliani-Sutch conclusion was not uncontroversial; see, for example, Holland (1969).
49. Modigliani and Sutch (1966, p. 196)
50. This was also noted by Tobin (1974).

The Potential Effectiveness of Nonstandard Policies:
Evidence from the United States

Although the federal funds rate declined to 1 percent in 2003, short-term nominal interest rates in the United States have not been effectively constrained by the ZLB since the 1930s. Nevertheless, the recent experience of the United States provides some opportunities to test the potential effectiveness of nonstandard monetary policies in a modern, financially sophisticated economy.

The previous section classified nonstandard monetary policies under three headings: using communications to shape policy expectations; increasing the size of the central bank's balance sheet beyond what is needed to bring short-term rates to zero (quantitative easing); and changing the composition of the central bank's balance sheet in order to affect the relative supplies, and thus possibly the relative prices, of targeted securities. As far as we can see, the recent experience of the United States does not contain any episodes useful for studying the potential of the second type of nonstandard policy. However, as we discuss in this section, recent U.S. experience does provide valuable evidence, both direct and indirect, on the effectiveness of the first and third types.

We first address the question of whether the recent communication policies of the Federal Open Market Committee have influenced market expectations of future short-term interest rates, as would be required to affect longer-term rates by shaping market expectations (the first class of nonstandard policies). Our principal methodology is event-study analysis; that is, we draw inferences about the impact of FOMC statements from the behavior of market-based indicators of policy expectations in a narrow window surrounding FOMC announcements. We also use the event-study approach to determine whether FOMC statements affect the responsiveness of policy expectations to other types of news, such as employment reports. The event-study analysis shows that FOMC policy statements do in fact have a substantial impact on market expectations of future policy, both directly and indirectly, suggesting that the committee does have some scope to use communication policies to influence the yields and prices of longer-term assets. To assess further the magnitude of these effects, we next estimate a macrofinance model of the term structure of Treasury yields, which links the term structure to macroeconomic conditions and to indicators of monetary policy. Comparison of this benchmark model of the term structure with the actual evolution of yields provides additional information on the magnitude and duration of the effects of FOMC "talk" on the term structure.

In the second part of this section, we present evidence that bears on the possibility that changes in the composition of the Federal Reserve's balance sheet might influence asset prices—the third type of nonstandard policy. The key issue here is whether changes in the relative supplies of assets, such as government bonds of different maturities, have significant effects on prices and yields, holding macroeconomic conditions and policy interest rates constant. We address this issue indirectly by considering the market effects of three recent episodes: first, the period of Treasury debt buybacks of the late 1990s, during which the Treasury announced its intention to shorten significantly the maturity structure of U.S. debt; second, the large purchases of U.S. Treasuries by Japan's Ministry of Finance during the period of Japan's exchange rate interventions after 1998; and third, the "deflation scare" episode of 2003, during which bond market participants purportedly saw a significant probability that the Federal Reserve might use securities purchases to try to affect longer-term yields. Using the same two methodologies as applied in the study of FOMC statements—that is, an event-study approach and the use of an estimated model of the term structure as a benchmark for comparison—we find evidence that "supply effects" have at times significantly influenced bond yields, suggesting that targeted purchases of bonds at the ZLB could be effective at lowering the yields on longer-dated securities. However, the duration and magnitude of these effects remain somewhat unclear from our analysis.

Do FOMC Statements Influence Policy Expectations?

Has the FOMC historically exerted any influence on investors' expectations about the future course of policy? Although members of the FOMC communicate to the public through a variety of channels, including speeches and congressional testimony, official communications from the FOMC as an official body (ex cathedra, one might say) are confined principally to the statements that the FOMC releases with its policy decisions.[51] In this section we investigate whether FOMC statements have

51. Some testimony, notably the Federal Reserve chairman's semiannual report to Congress, might also be interpreted as reflecting the collective views of the FOMC. Speeches by the chairman are not technically official communications, but, because of the chairman's influence on policy decisions, they are watched carefully by market participants.

observable effects on financial markets over and above the effects of policy changes themselves. We undertake a similar exercise for the Bank of Japan later in the paper.

The FOMC has moved significantly in the direction of greater transparency over the past decade. Before 1994, no policy statements or descriptions of the target for the federal funds rate were released after FOMC meetings. Instead, except when changes in the federal funds rate coincided with changes in the discount rate (which were announced by a press release of the Federal Reserve Board), the FOMC signaled its policy decisions to the financial markets only indirectly, through open-market operations, typically on the day following the policy decision. In February 1994 the FOMC began to release statements noting changes in its target for the federal funds rate, but it continued to remain silent following meetings where no policy changes occurred. Since May 1999, however, the committee has released a statement after every policy meeting.

The FOMC statements have evolved considerably. In their most recent form they briefly describe the current state of the economy and, in some cases, provide some hints about the near-term outlook for policy. They also contain a formulaic description of the so-called balance of risks with respect to the outlook for output growth and inflation. A consecutive reading of the statements reveals continual tinkering by the committee to improve its communications. For example, the balance-of-risks portion of the statement replaced an earlier formulation, the "policy tilt," which characterized the likely future direction of the federal funds rate. Much like the policy tilt statement, the balance-of-risks statement hints about the likely evolution of policy, but it does so more indirectly by focusing on the committee's assessment of the potential risks to its dual objectives rather than on the policy rate. The relative weights of forward-looking and backward-looking characterizations of the data and of policy have also changed over time, with the FOMC taking a relatively more forward-looking stance in 2003 and 2004.

Of course, investors read the statements carefully to try to divine the FOMC's views on the economy and its policy inclinations.[52] This careful

---

52. It has been said that a mark of great literature is that readers can find meanings in the text that the author did not consciously intend. On this criterion FOMC statements certainly qualify as great literature.

attention is prima facie evidence that what the committee says, as well as what it does, matters for asset pricing. Here we support this observation with more formal evidence and try to judge the magnitude of the effect.

To measure the influence of these FOMC announcements, we first take an event-study approach. We look at the movements in three market-based indicators of the private sector's monetary policy expectations during the periods surrounding FOMC decisions—including both decisions made at scheduled FOMC meetings and decisions made between regular meetings—since July 1991.[53] The first of the three indicators is a now-standard measure of the surprise component of current policy decisions. This measure, derived from the current-month federal funds futures contract in the manner described by Kenneth Kuttner,[54] provides a market-based estimate of the difference between the federal funds rate target set by the FOMC and the value of the funds rate target that market participants expected just before the FOMC's announcement. (Essentially, the change in the near-term federal funds contract in response to the decision, when scaled by the number of days remaining in that month-long contract, provides a measure of the change in expectations.) The second indicator is the rate on the Eurodollar futures contract expiring about a year ahead. Roughly speaking, the change in this rate during the period that spans the announcement of the FOMC's decision is a measure of the change in year-ahead policy expectations (and movements in the term premium associated with those changes) induced by the committee's decisions. Finally, we also consider changes in the yield on Treasury securities of five years' maturity, which provide an indication of changes in market expectations of policy (as well as associated changes in term premiums) at a five-year horizon. To isolate the effects of policy events on these indicators as cleanly as possible, we focus on movements in the three market-based indicators over the one-hour window (from fifteen minutes before to forty-five minutes after) surrounding the policy announcements.

We would like to test whether the private sector's policy expectations over the hour surrounding an FOMC announcement are affected solely by

53. Determining precisely when each decision was conveyed or signaled to the markets is a tedious process. See the text and especially the appendix of Gürkaynak, Sack, and Swanson (2004) for a discussion and a detailed listing of the timing of decisions.
54. Kuttner (2001).

the unexpected component of the policy action itself, or whether there is room for additional influences on expectations arising from the committee's statement. The earlier literature has mostly considered the effects on asset prices and yields of the current policy surprise only.[55] If the "one-factor" view of the effects of FOMC decisions implicit in these studies is correct, there can be no independent effect of the committee's statements on policy expectations or asset prices. To investigate this issue, we follow an approach similar to that of Gürkaynak, Sack, and Swanson to determine whether significant factors independent of the current policy surprise are needed to account for the response of policy expectations at the one-year and five-year horizons.[56] Specifically, we construct a candidate set of factors through a Cholesky decomposition of our three indicators of changes in policy expectations. We assume that the first factor equals the current policy surprise, as inferred from the federal funds futures market, which also affects the year-ahead futures rate and the five-year yield. The second candidate factor equals the portion of the change in year-ahead policy expectations (as measured by the change in the Eurodollar futures contract) not explained by (that is, orthogonal to) the first factor, which is also allowed to influence the five-year yield. As a residual, the third candidate factor is the change in the five-year Treasury yield not explained by (orthogonal to) the first two factors. If the one-factor view of the effects of policy decisions is correct, then the second and third candidate factors should account for only a small portion of the changes in longer-horizon interest rates in the period surrounding FOMC decisions, and they should be unrelated to aspects of the FOMC decision (such as the statement) other than the change in the policy rate.

The loadings of the three market indicators of policy expectations on the three factors, as determined by the Cholesky decomposition, are shown in the top panel of table 1. By construction, each of the diagonal elements of the table is equal to unity. As already mentioned, the first factor has

55. Kuttner (2001); Bernanke and Kuttner (forthcoming).
56. Our analysis extends the work of Gürkaynak, Sack, and Swanson (2004) in two ways. First, we analyze the relationship of the policy factors to FOMC statements in greater detail. Second, as discussed later in the paper, we extend the analysis to the case of Japan. Methodologically, our approach also differs from theirs in some respects. In particular, Gürkaynak, Sack, and Swanson use four futures contracts covering policy expectations out to a year; we use only one contract to measure year-ahead expectations but use a longer-term yield as well. In addition, we use different methods than Gürkaynak, Sack, and Swanson to identify the underlying factors.

Table 1. Factor Decomposition of Monetary Policy Indicators, United States[a]

Effect or standard deviation	Factor 1	Factor 2	Factor 3
Loading of factor on[b]			
Current policy setting	1.00	0.00	0.00
Year-ahead futures rate	0.51	1.00	0.00
Five-year yield	0.27	0.64	1.00
Standard deviation of effect of factor on[c]			
Current policy setting	10.0	0	0
Year-ahead futures rate	5.1	10.1	0
Five-year yield	2.7	6.5	3.5

Source: Authors' calculations based on data from the Chicago Board of Trade, the Chicago Mercantile Exchange, and GovPX.

a. Factors are constructed by means of a Cholesky decomposition, in which the first factor is the policy surprise contained in a policy statement, as inferred from the federal funds futures market; the second is the portion of the change in year-ahead policy expectations (as measured by the change in the Eurodollar futures contract) not explained by (that is, orthogonal to) the first factor; the third is the change in the five-year Treasury yield not explained by (orthogonal to) the first two factors.

b. Sample period is July 1991 to the present.

c. In basis points. Sample period is April 1998 to the present.

been set equal to the surprise component in the current policy decision, as measured by the method of Kuttner.[57] Note that the second and third elements of the first column show the effect of a one-unit increase in the current policy surprise on policy expectations one year and five years ahead, respectively. As found by Kuttner, the effects of a current policy surprise on yields diminish as the horizon lengthens. The second factor has (again, by design) a unitary effect on year-ahead policy expectations and a diminishing effect on the five-year yield, whereas the third factor (by design) affects only the five-year yield.

An important finding is that the second factor (defined, again, as the part of the change in the year-ahead rate that is orthogonal to the surprise in the federal funds rate) plays a substantial role in determining policy expectations. This point can be seen in the bottom panel of table 1, which reports the standard deviation of the effect of each factor on the three market indicators of expectations in the period since 1998.[58] The standard deviation of the component of the year-ahead futures rate accounted for by the second factor (10.1) is twice that of the component accounted for by the first factor (5.1). Putting the results in terms of variances, we can infer from the bottom panel of table 1 that only about one-fifth of the

57. Kuttner (2001).

58. The post-April 1998 subsample in the bottom panel of table 1 is chosen for comparability to the results presented below for the Bank of Japan. The results reported in the table are similar if the full sample is used.

variance in the year-ahead futures rate in the hour around policy decisions is explained by current policy surprises (the first factor), and that
the other four-fifths of the variance is captured by the second factor. This
result confirms a primary conclusion of Gürkaynak, Sack, and Swanson,[59] who argue that two factors are needed to explain the influence of
FOMC announcements on monetary policy expectations out to a horizon
of a year.

Also significant is the finding that the second factor makes the largest
contribution to the variability in the five-year Treasury yield during the
hour around FOMC decisions. In terms of standard deviations, the contribution of the second factor to the variation in the five-year yield is about
twice that of either the first or the third factor. In terms of variances, the
second factor accounts for 68 percent of the variability of the five-year
yield during the event window, whereas the first factor explains 12 percent and the third factor 20 percent of the variance.

Having determined that policy expectations are determined to an
important degree by a second factor that represents influences on market
expectations of policy not captured in the policy decision itself, we next
ask whether the second factor is related to the FOMC's communications.[60] Informal inspection of the historical realizations of the various
factors reveals that the second factor has become increasingly important
in the latter part of the sample—the period when policy statements came
into regular use. Even during the years from 1994 to 1999, when policy
statements were used more sporadically, many of the large realizations of
the second factor coincided with policy statements. In contrast, larger
realizations of the first and third factors do not seem to line up with dates
of policy statements.

To investigate more formally the link between FOMC statements and
the three factors, we follow an approach similar to that employed by Kohn
and Sack.[61] As described in the previous section, Kohn and Sack showed
that, for given values of the policy surprise, the issuance of statements by
the FOMC increases the variability of market interest rates, suggesting
that statements contain information relevant to financial markets. Here we
extend their approach in several ways, in part by examining the effects on

59. Gürkaynak, Sack, and Swanson (2004).
60. Gürkaynak, Sack, and Swanson (2004) also address this issue and conclude that the
second factor is indeed related to FOMC statements.
61. Kohn and Sack (2003).

expectations of different types of statements (including "anticipated" and "unanticipated" statements), by linking statements to policy expectations at differing horizons (as summarized by the three factors), and by checking whether the directional effects of policy statements on policy expectations seem reasonable.[62]

As a first step, and in a manner analogous to Kohn and Sack's approach, we regress the squared values of each of the factors on several dummy variables related to policy statements, to determine whether statements "matter" for policy expectations at different horizons, as summarized by the three factors, without having to quantify the statements. We define the first dummy, which we call STATEMENT, to equal 1 on any date on which the FOMC released a policy statement following its meeting, and zero otherwise. A positive estimated coefficient on STATEMENT implies that this particular factor tends to be larger in magnitude on dates on which a statement is released. Of the 116 policy decisions in our sample, 56 were accompanied by statements.

Of course, a statement that market participants fully anticipated would not be expected to generate a market reaction. With this in mind, we define a second dummy variable (called STATEMENT SURPRISE) that equals 1 on dates when the issued statement included important information about the state of the economy or the path of monetary policy that a substantial portion of market participants did not expect.

Obviously, assigning values to STATEMENT SURPRISE involves some subjectivity, because investors' expectations about statements cannot be quantified as easily as their expectations for settings of the policy rate. To construct this dummy variable, we read a set of commentaries written before and after each statement was released, to determine whether the statement was substantially as expected by market participants or instead surprised the markets. After-the-fact commentaries that we examined included internal staff analyses from both the Federal Reserve Bank of New York and the Board of Governors of market reactions to the policy decision and the statement, as well as next-day articles about the FOMC's decision from the *Wall Street Journal*. A drawback of relying on after-the-fact analyses to determine which statements were surprises, of course, is that the authors' interpretations may have been influ-

---

62. Also, unlike Kohn and Sack (2003), who use daily data, we continue to use intraday data.

enced, consciously or unconsciously, by the observed market responses.[63] To guard against this source of bias, we also used several before-the-fact sources, including a pre-FOMC-meeting survey of expectations for the balance-of-risks (or policy bias) part of the statement, conducted by Money Market Services and its successor Action Economics; commentaries put out just before each meeting by the ISI Group, a leading financial firm that specializes in monitoring FOMC action; and the results of a survey conducted by the Federal Reserve Bank of New York that asks primary dealers about their expectations for the statement. We took all occasions when the policy bias or the balance of risks differed from the median survey response as surprises. Using these materials, we identified thirty-one of the fifty-six statements in our sample period as involving some nonnegligible surprise.[64]

Table 2 presents the regression results; we focus first on the odd-numbered columns. Column 2-1 shows the results from regressing the square of the first factor (the current policy surprise) against a constant term and the two dummy variables. The first dummy, which indicates the presence of any statement accompanying an FOMC policy decision, enters the regression with a positive and significant coefficient. The most likely explanation for this result is that, for much of the sample period, statements were released only on days on which the federal funds rate was changed; not surprisingly, policy rate surprises tend to be larger on days when the federal funds rate target was changed than on days when no change in the target was made. The coefficient on the second dummy variable, STATEMENT SURPRISE, is negative and significant, which suggests that the FOMC views surprises in the policy rate and in the statement as substitutes, or possibly that the FOMC was simply reluctant to issue surprising statements at the same time that it was also surprising the markets with its policy action.

The regression reported in column 2-3 shows that the squared second factor, by contrast, appears to be driven entirely by statement surprises. The coefficient on STATEMENT SURPRISE is both highly statistically significant and economically important; the regression results imply that,

---

63. Although written after the fact, the Federal Reserve staff analyses not infrequently reported that the market's reaction was different from their ex ante assessment of the likely response, suggesting that the retrospective bias may not have been severe.

64. The breakdown of statements into surprises and nonsurprises, together with a brief commentary, is available from the authors on request.

Table 2. Regressions of Squared Factors on Dummy Variables for Federal Reserve Policy Statements[a]

	Dependent variable					
	Factor 1		Factor 2		Factor 3	
Independent variable	2-1	2-2	2-3	2-4	2-5	2-6
Constant	64.7	64.7	24.1	24.1	3.2	3.2
	(1.85)	(1.82)	(1.48)	(1.51)	(1.10)	(1.10)
STATEMENT[b]	131.6**	131.6**	18.3	18.3	6.3	6.3
	(2.04)	(2.03)	(0.61)	(0.63)	(1.18)	(1.17)
STATEMENT	−149.4**	−139.5	153.3**	120.7**	8.1	7.9
SURPRISE[c]	(−2.05)	(−1.75)	(4.54)	(3.35)	(1.33)	(1.19)
PATH SURPRISE[d]		−34.2		112.5**		0.6
		(−0.32)		(2.31)		(0.07)
Adjusted R^2	.04	.04	.26	.30	.07	.07

Source: Authors' regressions.

a. Numbers in parentheses are t statistics. ** indicates statistical significance at the 95 percent level. Factors are as defined in table 1.

b. Dummy variable set equal to 1 on dates when the FOMC released a policy statement following its meeting, and zero otherwise.

c. Dummy variable set equal to 1 on dates when the FOMC issued a statement that included important information about the state of the economy or the path of monetary policy that a substantial portion of market participants did not expect, and zero otherwise.

d. Dummy variable set equal to 1 on dates when the FOMC issued a statement that included important information about the path of monetary policy that a substantial portion of market participants did not expect, and zero otherwise.

on average, the variance of the second factor during the one-hour window surrounding the release of the statement is about 196 basis points (the sum of the constant term and both regression coefficients) when the statement is surprising, but only about 42 basis points (the constant term plus the first coefficient) when the statement is as expected. Moreover, the variance of the second factor is not significantly different from zero on days when no statement is released or when the statement is as anticipated. This result suggests that surprise statements have a major impact on policy expectations a year ahead.

The magnitude of the third factor seems unrelated to policy statements, because neither dummy variable enters significantly into the regression for the square of that factor (column 2-5). In other words, we find no evidence that FOMC statements affect the five-year Treasury yield independent of their effect on year-ahead expectations. (However, recall from table 1 that independent variation in year-ahead policy expectations—the second factor—accounts for the bulk of the variance of the five-year Treasury yield during the periods surrounding FOMC decisions. Thus, holding the current policy decision constant, a surprising statement has an important effect on yields at the five-year horizon, albeit indirectly through its effects on one-year-ahead policy expectations.) As we saw above, the third factor is quite small and may simply reflect residual noise in the five-year yield.

Investors are most interested in statements that provide hints about the FOMC's inclinations regarding future policy actions (as opposed to, for example, statements that describe past economic developments). From the committee's point of view, the effects on market expectations of statements bearing on the future course of policy should also be of particular interest, since this is the type of statement that theory suggests should be most useful when the policy rate is near the zero bound. To examine whether statements that provide new information about the likely future path of monetary policy are particularly influential, we used the sources noted above to identify nine statements among the thirty-one surprise statements that seemed most explicitly focused on the likely future path of policy. The dummy variable PATH SURPRISE takes a value of 1 on the dates of these statements.

A number of these statements occurred recently, in a period when the FOMC was attempting to provide additional stimulus to the economy despite the fact that the federal funds rate had already been reduced to as little as 100 basis points. For example, in August 2003 the FOMC stated that "policy accommodation can be maintained for a considerable period," marking the first time that the FOMC statement discussed an extended outlook for its policy path.[65] This phrase was repeated in FOMC statements following the September, October, and December meetings. At its January 2004 meeting the FOMC replaced the "considerable period" phrase with the assertion that "the Committee believes that it can be patient in removing its policy accommodation." This substitution caused long-dated Treasury yields to jump 15 to 25 basis points, a clear indication that the committee's language was important in shaping longer-term policy expectations. Policymaking by thesaurus continued through 2004. After repeating the "patient" language after its March meeting, the FOMC in its May statement replaced this phrase with the statement that it "believes that policy accommodation can be removed at

---

65. The "policy bias" that was part of the statement for the brief period from May 1999 to December 1999 was usually interpreted as pertaining to a much shorter time frame, such as the period between FOMC meetings.

a pace that is likely to be measured," and it maintained that assessment through the end of our sample. These statements, because they are so explicitly focused on the policy path, may provide the best natural experiments for assessing what could be accomplished at the zero bound.

As can be seen in the even-numbered columns in table 2, the PATH SURPRISE dummy enters significantly only in the regression explaining the square of the second factor, further confirming the association of this factor with policy statements. Relative to a situation in which an unsurprising statement is issued, a surprise statement about the likely future course of policy increases the variance of the second factor during the event window by 233 basis points (the sum of the coefficients on surprise statements and policy path surprise statements), indicating that statements providing new information about the prospective path of policy have a powerful effect on year-ahead policy expectations and, hence, indirectly on the five-year Treasury yield as well.

So far we have shown that year-ahead policy expectations react strongly to unexpected changes in the FOMC's statement, in the sense that the absolute change in year-ahead expectations tends to be much larger when the content of the statement is unexpected. We have not yet shown that the change in expectations is in the predicted direction, for example that unexpectedly "hawkish" statements cause expectations to shift toward a greater degree of policy tightening. To take this additional step, while recognizing once again that the quantification of purely qualitative statements is necessarily hazardous, we used the source materials described earlier to "sign" the thirty-one surprise statements in terms of their apparent implications for subsequent monetary policy actions. We summarized this information in a dummy variable, SIGNED STATE-MENT, which is assigned the value of +1 for surprise "hawkish" statements (those that implied a higher future path of the federal funds rate than previously expected), −1 for surprise "dovish" statements, and zero for all other observations, including those with nonsurprising statements or no statements at all. We then regressed the *levels* (not the squares) of each of the three factors on the signed dummy variable. We also tried regressing the levels of the factors on the signed values of statements corresponding to policy path surprises (SIGNED PATH, defined as the product of the SIGNED STATEMENT and PATH SURPRISE dummies.)

The results, shown in table 3, further strengthen our findings. Columns 3-1, 3-2, 3-5, and 3-6 show that no significant relationship exists between

Table 3. Regressions of Factors on Signed Dummy Variables for Federal Reserve Policy Statements[a]

| | Dependent variable | | | | | |
| | Factor 1 | | Factor 2 | | Factor 3 | |
Independent variable	3-1	3-2	3-3	3-4	3-5	3-6
SIGNED STATEMENT SURPRISE[b]	1.4 (0.83)		11.5** (10.21)		−0.4 (−0.68)	
SIGNED PATH SURPRISE[c]		−1.5 (−0.49)		15.8** (6.38)		1.3 (1.37)
Adjusted R^2	−.03	−.03	.47	.26	−.02	−.01

Source: Authors' regressions.

a. Numbers in parentheses are *t* statistics. ** indicates statistical significance at the 95 percent level. Factors are as defined in table 1.

b. Dummy variable assigned the value of +1 on dates when the FOMC issued a surprise "hawkish" statement (implying an increase in the federal funds rate), −1 on dates of surprise "dovish" statements (implying a decrease), and zero otherwise.

c. Product of PATH SURPRISE (see table 2 for definition) and SIGNED STATEMENT SURPRISE variables.

the signed statement surprises and either the first or the third factor. In contrast, signed surprises have a large and highly statistically significant effect on the second factor, with hawkish statements raising and dovish statements lowering year-ahead policy expectations by 12 basis points on average (column 3-3). The effects are even larger (16 basis points) when we restrict our attention to the nine policy path surprises (column 3-4). Recalling from table 1 that the loading of the five-year yield on the second factor is 0.64, we can also estimate that, with the current policy surprise held constant, a surprisingly hawkish statement raises the five-year yield by about 8 basis points and a hawkish statement about the policy path raises the yield by about 10 basis points.

Conditioning Effects of Policy Statements

The immediate effects of official FOMC statements on policy expectations likely underestimate the overall impact of FOMC communications on expectations; for example, our focus on statements alone ignores the potential effects of speeches and testimony by FOMC members. Also, beyond their immediate effects, FOMC statements may affect the formation of policy expectations by influencing how those expectations respond to various sorts of incoming data. In particular, to the extent that FOMC policy commitments are conditional, that is, tied to specific economic developments, policy expectations should react more strongly to macroeconomic news that bears on those developments.

A leading example is the market's responsiveness to monthly reports on payroll employment.[66] Throughout the recent period, the FOMC was concerned about the "jobless" nature of the economic recovery and repeatedly pointed to weakness in the labor market as a key factor shaping the outlook for policy. When Federal Reserve Chairman Alan Greenspan introduced the phrase "considerable period" in his semiannual report to Congress in July 2003, he indicated the Federal Reserve's concerns about resource utilization and "unwelcome disinflation." (On several occasions in congressional testimony, Greenspan has also indicated his preference for the payroll employment series over the household employment series as a measure of current conditions in the labor market.) Each FOMC statement that used the "considerable period" language also discussed labor market conditions, and the December 2003 statement tied the "considerable period" outlook for policy closely to slack in resource use. Statements since December 2003 have continued both to place substantial weight on labor market conditions (as well as inflation) and to provide information about the FOMC's policy expectations.

With this background, if FOMC communication is effective, one might expect to find that financial markets have become more sensitive to news about payroll employment. Figure 2 confirms this hypothesis: it shows the responsiveness, over a thirty-minute window, of the ten-year Treasury yield to surprises in monthly payrolls, where the surprise is defined as the reported payroll number less the median survey expectation as reported by Money Market Services. The sample is divided into the period through August 2003, just before the meeting when the "considerable period" language was introduced, and the period from September 2003 to the present. In the earlier period, as indicated by the thin regression line in figure 2, a positive surprise of 100,000 payroll jobs translated into a 4-basis-point increase in ten-year Treasury yields during the thirty-minute window. Since September 2003 this responsiveness has strengthened, as is visible from the larger data points. The regression line for the recent subsample shows that ten-year Treasury yields increased by 11 basis points for every surprise of 100,000 jobs above the consensus expectation. The difference in coefficients is statistically significant.

---

66. A second important example, not pursued here, is the responsiveness of the market to data on core inflation.

Figure 2. Response of Ten-Year Treasury Yields to Surprises in Monthly Employment Reports, 1991–2004

Change in yield (basis points)[a]

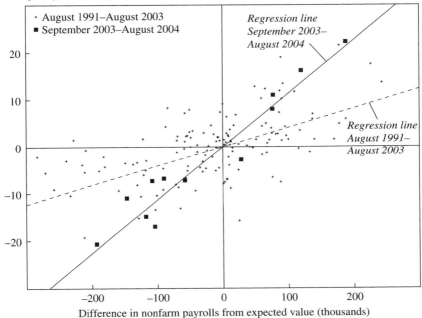

Difference in nonfarm payrolls from expected value (thousands)

Sources: GovPX, Bloomberg, and Money Market Services.
a. Change in market yield from 8:25 a.m. to 8:55 a.m. on the days of employment reports (released at 8:30 a.m.). A few large observations are excluded from the graph but included in the regression estimation.

If FOMC communications are responsible for the increased responsiveness of yields (and the associated policy expectations) to unexpected changes in payroll employment, it should also be the case that markets have responded less to macroeconomic developments not flagged by the committee as likely to have a strong bearing on policy decisions. This should especially be the case over the period when, conditioned on the ongoing sluggishness of hiring, the FOMC indicated that policy would remain highly accommodative. That this latter conjecture is likely to be true is shown by figure 3, which reports implied volatility measures derived from options on Eurodollar futures. These measures are market-based estimates of the expected volatility of short-term interest rates over two horizons: four months and one year. As the figure shows, the short-horizon volatility

Figure 3. Implied Volatility of the Federal Funds Rate, 1990–2004[a]

Percentage points

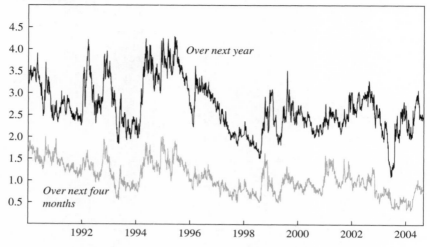

Source: Authors' calculations based on data from the Chicago Mercantile Exchange.
a. Data are widths of a 90 percent confidence interval for the federal funds rate over the indicated horizon, derived from the volatility of the three-month Eurodollar rate implied by options on Eurodollar futures.

measure fell to historic lows during the second half of 2003, but the same result does not hold at the longer horizon. These data provide a bit of evidence that the FOMC's communications in the second half of 2003 reduced the volatility of (or "anchored") near-term policy expectations. Since we have seen that policy expectations simultaneously became more sensitive to certain types of macroeconomic news, such as the payroll report, the decline in overall volatility suggests that the responsiveness of markets to other types of news declined.

Shaping Policy Expectations: Evidence from a Macrofinance Model of the Term Structure

Our event studies confirm that FOMC statements have important influences, both direct and indirect, on private sector policy expectations. Event studies have the drawback, however, of showing only very short term effects. They may overstate the more important longer-term effects, if, for example, yields tend to overreact in the period just around announcements; or they may understate the longer-term effects, for example by not accounting for types of communication other than statements. In this section we address this issue by developing a benchmark macrofinance model of the term structure. Here and in additional exercises in the remainder of the paper, our model provides estimates of what the term structure would have been on a given date, given the state of the economy and the stance of monetary policy but excluding other factors. By comparing this benchmark estimate of the term structure with the actual term structure at crucial junctures, we may be able to get a sense of the quantitative impacts of these other factors on the maturity structure of interest rates.

To develop a baseline model of the Treasury yield curve, we estimate an affine term structure model (that is, a model that is linear in the factors).[67] The affine term structure model imposes a no-arbitrage condition that links yields at every maturity of the term structure, thereby increasing the efficiency of estimation and allowing us to forecast the entire yield curve as a function of the variables designated as underlying factors. We differ from most of the previous literature in identifying the underlying factors that determine the term structure by means of observable indicators of macroeconomic conditions and the stance of monetary policy, and not relying on unobserved factors or longer-term yields as the assumed drivers of term structure dynamics.

As to the dynamics of the underlying factors, we employ a vector autoregression (VAR) in five observable variables: a measure of the employment gap (payroll employment, detrended by a Hodrick-Prescott filter); inflation over the past year, as measured by the deflator for personal consumption expenditures, excluding food and energy; expected inflation over the subsequent year, taken from the Blue Chip survey and with inflation defined in terms of the GDP deflator (the Blue Chip survey does not forecast core inflation); the federal funds rate; and the year-ahead Eurodollar futures rate. Together these variables should provide a reasonable summary of economic conditions, including the current setting of monetary policy (as reflected in the federal funds rate) and the expected path of policy over the near term (as captured by the Eurodollar futures rate). The data are monthly from June 1982 (when the Eurodollar data

---

67. Affine term structure models were popularized by Duffie and Kan (1996), whose formalization encompasses earlier models due to Vasicek (1977), Cox, Ingersoll, and Ross (1985), and Longstaff and Schwartz (1992), among others. Bolder (2001) provides a useful introduction to these models.

first became available) to the present, and four lags of each variable are included in the VAR.

As already noted, to measure the influence of these observed indicators on the Treasury yield curve, we construct a no-arbitrage term structure model in which the five economic and monetary indicators are treated as factors. In general, Treasury yields are determined by two components: the expected future path of one-period interest rates, and the excess returns that investors demand as compensation for the risk of holding longer-term instruments. The estimated VAR can be iterated to provide forecasts for the one-period interest rate at each horizon (where we treat the monthly average federal funds rate as the "one-period interest rate"). In addition, we make a standard assumption of affine models of the term structure, namely, that equilibrium prices of risk are linear functions of the factors (the variables in the VAR). With that assumption, the entire Treasury yield curve can be priced from the VAR estimates.

To be more specific, suppose we write the estimated VAR in the following form:

$$(1) \qquad \mathbf{X}_t = \mu + \Phi \mathbf{X}_{t-1} + \Sigma \varepsilon_t,$$

where $\mathbf{X}_t$ is the vector of state variables. To develop the no-arbitrage part of the model below, it will be convenient for the state variables to follow a first-order autoregressive process. Thus in equation 1 we have stacked the VAR variables so that the state vector $\mathbf{X}_t$ includes the contemporaneous values of the five variables and three lags of the variables (hence $\mathbf{X}_t$ is a 20 × 1 column vector).[68]

We assume that there is no arbitrage in the bond market, implying that a single pricing kernel determines the values of all fixed-income securities. The pricing kernel is determined by investors' preferences for state-dependent payouts. Specifically, the value of an asset at time t equals $E_t[m_{t+1}Y_{t+1}]$, where Y_{t+1} is the asset's gross return in period $t+1$, and m_{t+1} is the one-period pricing kernel. Because we will be considering zero-coupon bonds, the payout from the bonds is simply their value in the following period, so that the following recursive relationship holds:

$$(2) \qquad P_t^n = E_t[m_{t+1}P_{t+1}^{n-1}],$$

---

68. Thus the first five rows of the matrix Φ include the VAR estimates, and the rest of the matrix contains zeros and ones at the appropriate locations.

where n is the remaining life of the bond, and the terminal value of the bond, P_{t+n}^0, is normalized to equal 1.

Following the approach of Andrew Ang, Monika Piazzesi, and Min Wei,[69] we assume that the pricing kernel is conditionally log-normal, as follows:

$$(3) \qquad m_{t+1} = \exp(-y_t^{(1)} - \tfrac{1}{2}\lambda_t'\lambda_t - \lambda_t'\varepsilon_{t+1}),$$

where the λ_t are the market prices of risk associated with the VAR innovations (the source of uncertainty in the model), and $y_t^{(1)}$ is the one-period interest rate expressed on a continuously compounded basis. As already noted, we assume that the prices of risk are linear in the state variables:

$$(4) \qquad \lambda_t = \lambda_0 + \lambda_1 \mathbf{X}_t.$$

We restrict the prices of risk to be zero for all but the first five elements of λ_t, and we assume that those prices of risk depend only on the contemporaneous values of the VAR. (Recall that the final fifteen elements of the stacked column vector $\mathbf{X}_t$ are lags of the five factors.) These assumptions imply that only thirty parameters must be estimated in this block of the model, a manageable number while still allowing the model the flexibility needed to provide a good empirical fit of the term structure data.

Manipulation of equations 1 through 3 shows that the zero-coupon yields can be written as linear functions of the state variables, as follows:

$$(5) \qquad y_t^{(n)} = a_n + b_n'\mathbf{X}_t,$$

where $a_n = -\mathbf{A}_n/n$ and $b_n = -\mathbf{B}_n/n$, and the vectors $\mathbf{A}_n$ and $\mathbf{B}_n$ are determined by the following recursive formulas:

$$(6) \qquad \mathbf{A}_{n+1} = \mathbf{A}_n + \mathbf{B}_n'(\mu - \Sigma\lambda_0) + \tfrac{1}{2}\mathbf{B}_n'\Sigma\Sigma'\mathbf{B}_n - \delta_0$$

$$(7) \qquad \mathbf{B}_{n+1} = (\Phi - \Sigma\lambda_1)'\mathbf{B}_n - \delta_1.$$

The starting values for these equations are $\mathbf{A}_1 = -\delta_0$ and $\mathbf{B}_1 = -\delta_1$, and the parameters δ_0 and δ_1 describe the relationship of the one-period yield to

---

69. Ang and Piazzesi (2003); Ang, Piazzesi, and Wei (2003).

the state vector, that is, $y_t^{(1)} = \delta_0 + \delta_1' \mathbf{X}_t$. In our application, because the one-period yield (the federal funds rate) is included in the state variable, this relationship is trivial: All elements of δ_0 and δ_1 are zero except for the element of δ_1 that picks out the current value of the federal funds rate, which is set to unity.

Given a set of prices of risk, the entire Treasury yield curve can be derived using equation 5. We estimate the prices of risk by minimizing the sum of squared prediction errors for zero-coupon Treasury yields at maturities of six months and one, two, three, four, five, seven, and ten years. Our data are zero-coupon Treasury yields, based on the Fisher-Nychka-Zervos yield curve for the period 1982 to 1987 and on the zero-coupon yield curve constructed at the Board of Governors for the period since 1987.[70] Note that to some extent we are explaining one set of interest rates by another, since the federal funds rate and the year-ahead Eurodollar rate are included in the VAR and thus serve as factors. As already mentioned, however, including the latter indicators in the VAR serves the important function of capturing the effects of current and expected monetary policy actions on the Treasury term structure; this will be important later when we use the model to isolate relative supply effects on Treasury yields. Moreover, our procedure implies no internal inconsistency, because both indicators of monetary policy differ in substantive respects (for example, in credit risk, liquidity, and maturity) from the Treasury rates that they are being used to model.

Our model contributes to the growing literature that includes macroeconomic variables in no-arbitrage term structure models. An appealing feature of our framework is the substantial simplification in estimation and analysis achieved by our assumption that all the factors driving the term structure are observable economic and monetary variables. As noted earlier, related models typically include unobserved factors as determinants of the term structure and even of the observed economic variables in the system.[71] The use of unobserved factors has advantages in some applications, but it greatly complicates estimation and may make the economic

---

70. Fisher, Nychka, and Zervos (1995).
71. Related models include those of Ang and Piazzesi (2003) and Rudebusch and Wu (2003).

interpretation of the results more difficult.[72] Our approach instead directly links the term structure to observable economic conditions, thereby providing us with an easily interpretable benchmark for gauging the potential effects of unusual monetary policy strategies.

The estimated model does a quite creditable job of explaining the behavior of the term structure over time. Figure 4 compares the fitted and actual time series for the two-year and ten-year Treasury yields. The model predicts Treasury yields reasonably well at all maturities: as reported in the first column of table 4, the standard deviation of the model's prediction error is 33 basis points at the six-month maturity and increases to around 80 basis points for longer maturities. Also shown in figure 4 are the two-year and ten-year "risk-neutral" yields. These are derived by setting the prices of risk equal to zero—that is, they are the rates that investors would demand if they were risk neutral. The differences between these lines and the predicted yields, then, are estimated term premiums. Figure 4 shows that estimated term premiums for longer-dated securities have declined over time, presumably reflecting greater stability in the economy and in policy, but they remain fairly large. Of particular note is that variations in the term premium are estimated to account for a significant portion of the variation in long-term yields; part of the reason is likely to be that the forecasting model does a better job capturing low-frequency movements in the data than high-frequency ones. Those residuals in predicting high-frequency movements, then, are imputed to the term premium.

In the event-study analysis described earlier, we found that an important part of the effect of a monetary policy decision is transmitted through its impact on year-ahead policy expectations, but that expectations also depend importantly on FOMC statements. The importance of year-ahead policy expectations for longer-dated yields is generally confirmed by our term structure fitting exercise. We can assess the importance of innovations of the futures rate by ordering it last in a Cholesky decomposition. In doing so, we are attributing as much as possible of the movements in futures rates to the other variables. Even so, innovations to the futures rate

72. Ang, Piazzesi, and Wei (2003) employ a model in which, as in our analysis, the pricing kernel is assumed to be a function of observable variables. However, the only macroeconomic variable in their model is GDP growth, and they do not focus on the properties of the term structure model itself but rather on the implications of their framework for predicting GDP growth.

Figure 4. Actual and Predicted Zero-Coupon Treasury Yields, 1982–2004[a]

Two-year

Percent a year

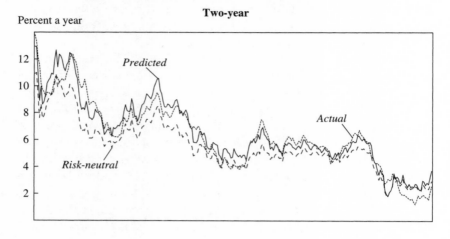

Ten-year

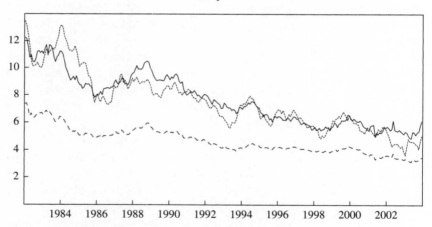

Source: Authors' calculations based on data from the Bureau of Labor Statistics, the Bureau of Economic Analysis, Blue Chip Financial Forecasts, the Chicago Mercantile Exchange, and the Federal Reserve.
a. The predicted Treasury yields are generated by the term structure model, as described in the text. The risk-neutral Treasury yields are generated by the same model, but with the prices of risk set equal to zero.

Table 4. Prediction Errors for Treasury Yields in the Term Structure Model
Basis points

	Standard deviation of predicted yield	
Maturity	*VAR with Eurodollar shocks*	*VAR without Eurodollar shocks*
6 months	33.0	62.1
1 year	50.3	78.9
2 years	73.3	97.4
3 years	81.2	100.7
4 years	82.5	98.3
5 years	81.5	95.0
7 years	83.3	93.3
10 years	80.8	87.8

Source: Authors' calculations based on data from the Bureau of Labor Statistics, the Bureau of Economic Analysis, Blue Chip Financial Forecasts, the Chicago Mercantile Exchange, and the Federal Reserve.

are important for explaining movements in the yield curve. As can be seen in the second column of table 4, excluding the year-ahead futures rate innovations from the VAR causes a significant deterioration in the fit of the estimated model, particularly at shorter horizons. For example, doing so raises the standard deviation of the prediction error for the two-year Treasury yield from 73 basis points to 97 basis points. The inclusion of a variable such as the year-ahead futures rate, and to a lesser extent the survey measure of inflation looking one year ahead, has the advantage of improving the fit of the model. But it also implies that some of the influence of policy in shaping expectations will be captured by those variables in the forecasting model. If so, our later attempt to interpret deviations of actual yields from those predicted by the model will tend to be conservative, in that the macrofinance model may well capture some expectations effects.

It is tempting to combine the result of the event study (that FOMC statements have a substantial influence on year-ahead policy expectations) with the result from the term structure fitting exercise (that year-ahead policy expectations are important determinants of Treasury yields) to conclude that FOMC statements have an important influence on the term structure. That conclusion may be a bit premature. Notably, the innovations to the Eurodollar futures rate obtained from the VAR need not correspond closely to the innovations to the same variable obtained from the high-frequency event study. To illustrate this point, table 5 compares, for various

Table 5. Year-Ahead Futures Shocks in Vector Autoregression and in Event Study
Basis points

	Standard deviation of innovations to the year-ahead Eurodollar futures rate	
Sample period[a]	*VAR shock*	*Event-study shock*[b]
July 1991 to January 1994	35.9	4.2
February 1994 to April 1999	35.2	6.8
May 1999 to July 2003	40.1	8.2
August 2003 to May 2004	25.2	11.7

Source: Authors' calculations based on data from sources listed in tables 1 and 4
a. Overall period begins in July 1991, the earliest date covered by the event study. Break dates include the date at which the FOMC began announcing interest rate decisions (February 1994), the date at which the FOMC began issuing statements after every meeting (May 1999), and the date at which the FOMC adopted the "considerable period" language (August 2003).
b. Aggregated to a monthly variable for comparability with the VAR shock.

subsamples, the monthly standard deviation of innovations to the year-ahead Eurodollar futures rate, as calculated from the VAR (first column) and by summing the changes in the Eurodollar rate around FOMC decisions (second column). In general, the variance of the VAR innovations to the Eurodollar rate is significantly greater than the variance of innovations to the Eurodollar rate directly associated with FOMC decisions. Several plausible explanations for this difference come to mind: First, the movements of the Eurodollar rate in the hour around FOMC decisions certainly do not capture all of the effects of FOMC communications, including the effects of speeches and testimonies and the point, demonstrated earlier, that FOMC statements can affect the responsiveness of policy expectations to various kinds of macroeconomic news. Indeed, as table 5 illustrates, as the FOMC has made greater use of communications strategies, particularly since mid-2003, the variation of the Eurodollar rate around FOMC decisions has risen, while the variation in the corresponding VAR innovation has actually fallen, possibly reflecting better anchoring of short-term policy expectations. That said, it seems clear that not all of the VAR innovation represents unmeasured communication effects; certainly, some part of the VAR innovations to the Eurodollar futures rate reflects responses of policy expectations to developments in the economy unrelated to FOMC communications (and not captured by the economic variables included in the VAR).

As a simple case study, we considered in more detail the VAR innovations and the event-study innovations during the period in which the FOMC

Figure 5. Effects of Unexpected Futures Rate Outcomes on Treasury Zero-Coupon Yield Curve, August–December 2003[a]

Basis points

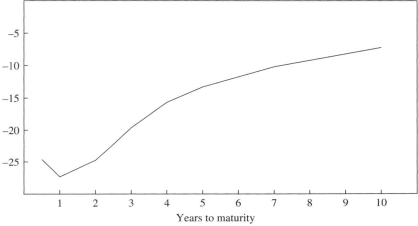

Years to maturity

Source: Authors' calculations based on data from the sources listed in figure 4.
a. Cumulative shift in Treasury yields of the indicated maturity predicted by the futures rate shocks from the VAR described in the text.

introduced the "considerable period" language (August to December 2003). During that period, according to the event study, FOMC communications pushed down the Eurodollar futures rate by a cumulative 19 basis points, whereas the VAR shocks lowered the future rate by 63 basis points.[73] As an upper bound on the effect of the "considerable period" language on the term structure, figure 5 uses our estimated model of the term structure to show the effect on the yield curve associated with a 63-basis-point decline in the Eurodollar futures rate. The model predicts an effect of the "considerable period" language ranging from about 25 basis points at the two-year horizon to about 7 basis points at the ten-year horizon.[74]

73. Because the VAR models month-average variables, we sum the realization through January 2004, because the "considerable period" language was not removed until the end of that month.

74. Note that an innovation to the Eurodollar futures rate has an effect on Treasury yields that is less than one for one at all maturities, suggesting that the futures rate measured here has excess variation relative to Treasury yields. This could reflect the (presumably small) credit risk premium embedded in the futures rate, premiums for the relative liquidity of the two instruments, or simply measurement noise.

Overall, the evidence suggests that FOMC statements have importantly shaped the policy expectations of investors, particularly over the past five years. Indeed, yield curve movements around FOMC decisions cannot be adequately described by the unexpected component of policy decisions, but are instead influenced to a greater extent by a second factor, which appears to be associated with surprises in the policy statements. These findings suggest that policymakers may have some scope for influencing investors' expectations if the federal funds rate were to fall to the zero bound.

The Effects of Changing the Supply of Assets

We turn now to evidence bearing on the third type of nonstandard policy, namely, changes in the composition of the central bank's balance sheet or targeted asset purchases. The question is whether substitution among assets is sufficiently imperfect so that large purchases of a specific class of asset might affect its yield, over and above any influence those purchases might have on investors' expectations about the future course of the short-term interest rate. Of course, the Federal Reserve has not undertaken any such actions in recent years. However, it still may be possible to learn about the effects of such actions by looking at the effects on yields of other actual or expected changes in the relative supplies of assets.

We identified three episodes in the past five years in which market participants in the United States came to anticipate significant changes in the relative supplies of different Treasury securities. These three natural experiments are, first, the Treasury's announcement in 1999 of a plan to buy back government debt in the face of prospective budget surpluses; second, the investment in Treasury securities by Asian official institutions of the proceeds of their foreign exchange market interventions since 2002; and third, the emerging belief on the part of some financial market participants in the spring of 2003 that the Federal Reserve might resort to targeted purchases of long-term Treasury securities in order to combat incipient deflation.

We look at each episode through two prisms. First, we consider the movement in a number of yields in narrow windows surrounding important announcements—in essence relying on an event-study methodology to isolate the market response to news. Then we apply our no-arbitrage model of the U.S. term structure to provide a benchmark estimate of the pattern of yields, attributing residual movements to relative supply effects.

THE PAYDOWN OF TREASURY BONDS. We begin with "the case of the disappearing Treasury bonds," that is, the debt buyback episode of 1999–2000. In the mid-1990s a confluence of economic forces and policy changes turned federal budget deficits into surpluses. By the end of the decade, extrapolation of those trends led to forecasts that Treasury debt would disappear by 2010.[75] The Treasury dealt with that windfall in three stages. Initially, it cut the issuance of Treasury bills as the deficit shrank, which reportedly led to some deterioration of liquidity in that segment of the market and a shift toward three-month Eurodollar instruments as the hedging vehicles of choice. Next, the Treasury trimmed the issuance of longer-term securities by eliminating a few maturities and scaling back the volume of the remainder. Third, the Treasury announced in August 1999 that it was considering buying back some older, off-the-run issues, so that its remaining auctions would remain sizable enough to retain investors' interest.

Developments in the market for Treasury bonds are most interesting for our purposes because the expected supply of those securities changed abruptly. Two events stand out as marking a significant shift in investors' view of the prospects for Treasury bond issuance, namely, the midquarter refunding announcements of February 2000 and November 2001. At the 2000 refunding, the under secretary of the Treasury for domestic finance, Gary Gensler, made a comment suggesting that the ten-year note would replace the thirty-year bond as the benchmark long-term security, triggering speculation that the issuance of thirty-year bonds would be discontinued. At the November 2001 refunding announcement, the Treasury confirmed that it would stop selling the long-term bond.

The supply of bonds was also being reduced by Treasury debt buybacks. Actual market repurchases began in March 2000 and had cumulated to $67 billion when the repurchases ended in 2002. Only bonds were purchased, the bulk of which matured beyond 2015. These debt buybacks represented a significant relative supply shock, as they were

---

75. Reinhart and Sack (2000) review the economic consequences of such an outcome. Auerbach and Gale (2000) provided a real-time reminder of the fickleness of far-ahead fiscal forecasts.

Table 6. Changes in Treasury Yields around Quarterly Refunding Announcements[a]
Basis points

Maturity	Date of quarterly refunding	
	February 2000	November 2001
2 years	−5	1
5 years	−13	−9
10 years	−13	−20
30 years	−27	−43

Source: GovPX.
a. Changes in the yields of on-the-run issues from the day before the announcement to the day after.

concentrated in one maturity segment and amounted to about one-tenth of the outstanding stock of bonds (as of the beginning of 2000). Moreover, the buybacks were widely expected to be much larger than they were, with some dealers in early 2000 estimating that they would reach $100 billion a year soon thereafter. Thus, in terms of anticipated supply, the shock was much larger.

Views about the magnitude of debt buybacks seem to evolve over time and thus do not lend themselves easily to event-study analysis. However, we can look at the immediate market impact of the two quarterly refunding announcements, identified above, that provided information about the discontinuation of bond issuance. The news from these announcements bore primarily on the pattern of sales rather than on the outlook for net issuance of government debt. Even so, as shown in table 6, the Treasury yield curve rotated down dramatically in both cases when investors learned that the managers of the government debt would shy away from longer-maturity securities.

The market's reaction is seen more starkly in the movement in yields across the maturity spectrum in the month bracketing the February announcement, as plotted in figure 6.[76] No doubt, macroeconomic news relevant to interest rate expectations and risk attitudes and perceptions also came out during that month. But the fact that yields on bonds as opposed to notes declined sharply over a month in which important infor-

---

76. For the past three decades, the longest-maturity security the Treasury issued has been either the ten-year or the thirty-year bond. Points on the yield curve beyond the ten-year maturity, accordingly, come from thirty-year securities of varying issue dates. The four-year gap in the figure corresponds to a gap in Treasury issuance.

Figure 6. Treasury Yield Curve before and after Announcement of the Debt Buyback Program[a]

Percent a year

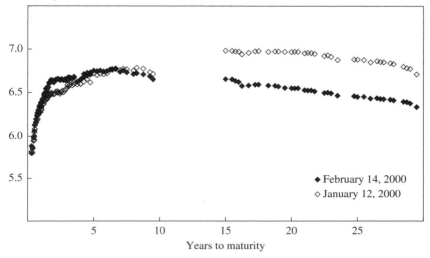

Years to maturity

◆ February 14, 2000
◇ January 12, 2000

Source: Federal Reserve data.
a. Yields are for all outstanding Treasury notes and bonds, excluding callable issues.

mation about the elimination of the issuance of long-term securities was released seems suggestive of the possibility that relative supplies matter.

We can also look at this episode using our estimated term structure model to control for variations in the economy and monetary policy over the period surrounding the buyback news. Figure 7 shows the prediction error of the model for the twenty-year Treasury yield in the period around the debt buyback.[77] We see that yields during this period dropped from about 20 basis points above to about 80 basis points below the prediction of the model (which, again, controls for the effects of current and expected monetary policy).

The decline in bond yields during the buyback period is significant in economic terms. To make a rough assessment of their statistical significance, we performed a simple bootstrapping exercise with the model by first forecasting the yield curve for January and February 2000 (about the

77. In order to include the twenty-year Treasury yield in the model, we reestimated the prices of risk. The predicted yields at other maturities did not change materially.

Figure 7. Prediction Errors of the Term Structure Model for Twenty-Year Zero-Coupon Treasury Yields, 1993–2002[a]

Basis points

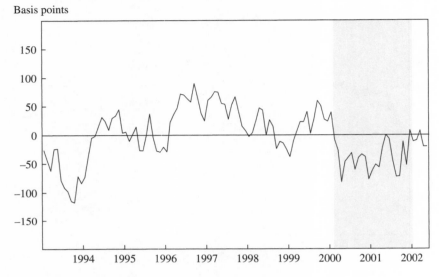

Source: Authors' calculations based on data from the sources listed in figure 4.
a. Figure shows difference between actual and predicted Treasury yields. Shading indicates bond paydown period.

middle of the episode), conditional on economic and yield curve data observed just before the start of the period. We then added shocks by randomly drawing observations from the set of historical errors of both the macroeconomic and yield curve variables over the entire period. By repeating this process 10,000 times, we were able to get some sense of whether the observed errors were outside standard confidence bands. In fact, conditional on our model, the fall in the twenty-year Treasury yield early in 2000 had an ex ante probability of occurring of less than 10 percent—that is, the observed decline in the twenty-year yield appears to be statistically significant. The ex post errors observed along the yield curve at shorter maturities, however, were much more likely to have occurred by chance. These results support the intuition derived from the marked shift in the yield curve already shown in figure 6: the buybacks significantly altered the shape of the long end of the Treasury yield curve and had no material effects on shorter maturities, supporting the view that relative supplies matter.

Figure 8. Interest Rate Swap Spreads, 1997–2004[a]

Basis points

Source: Bloomberg.
a. Shading indicates bond paydown period.

These results are only suggestive, of course, in that the term structure model is unlikely to capture all the determinants of yields or to control adequately for shifts in expectations. In addition, the precise magnitude of the effects is not clear: the size of the shock is hard to determine because we do not know the probability that investors were attaching to a sizable paydown. Moreover, we cannot be sure that the effects shown here are scalable in a predictable manner; hence these results give little quantitative information to policymakers contemplating targeted asset purchases. Finally, as discussed earlier, movements in Treasury yields arising from targeted purchases need not pass through to the interest rates on private transactions that presumably influence spending decisions. As a bit of evidence on this last point, swap spreads—a good indicator of risk premiums on private sector securities—widened noticeably at the thirty-year maturity (but not at the two-year maturity) during the period when long-dated Treasury yields declined (figure 8). The sharp increase in long-term swap spreads and its subsequent unwinding coincide closely with the dip in prediction errors in figure 7. Thus private sector interest rates apparently did not follow the long end of the Treasury curve down as investor concerns regarding the availability of certain maturity classes of Treasuries mounted.

FOREIGN OFFICIAL PURCHASES OF U.S. TREASURY SECURITIES. In the wake of the Asian currency crisis in 1998, policymakers in many Asian economies apparently decided that it was desirable to limit fluctuations of their currencies against the dollar. The result has been a steady accumulation of dollar reserves, often in the form of Treasury securities. For instance, securities held in custody at the Federal Reserve Bank of New York on behalf of foreign official institutions now total about $1¼ trillion, about double the amount at the end of 1998. Japanese authorities, in particular, intervened heavily in foreign exchange markets from 2003 to the first quarter of 2004 in an effort to counter or slow the yen's appreciation against the dollar. Japanese intervention purchases totaled $177 billion in 2003 and $138 billion in the first quarter of 2004. The Japanese Ministry of Finance holds the proceeds of its intervention activities as either bank deposits or Treasury securities, and its deposit holdings generally are reinvested in Treasuries over time. According to market reports, those purchases have tended to be concentrated in maturities of no more than ten years. The Japanese interventions in the five quarters ending in 2004:1 cumulated to about $300 billion, which bond market participants anticipated would be invested in Treasury securities. Since the Japanese interventions were presumably only weakly linked at best to expectations about future U.S. monetary policy, these purchases provide the basis for a second natural experiment for testing the relationship between relative asset supplies and yields.

The simplest exercise is to regress the change in various Treasury yields on the dollar volume of intervention.[78] Although the interventions were not publicly announced, an examination of newspaper articles indicates that operations were immediately recognized by market participants, who also generally appeared to have an accurate understanding of the scale as well. Thus, even though foreign exchange market transactions settle two days after the transaction ($t + 2$), the effects on Treasury yields should occur at date t, as market participants anticipate near-term purchases of Treasury securities. However, to allow for the possibility that in

---

78. We have benefited from discussions with Alain Chaboud and Jonathan Wright on this topic.

Table 7. Response of Treasury Yields to Japanese Foreign Exchange Intervention[a]
Basis points per $1 billion

Maturity	All days in sample period	Excluding days of major U.S. data releases[b]
3 months	−0.18	−0.18
	(−1.16)	(−0.80)
2 years	−0.78**	−0.55**
	(−3.00)	(−1.99)
5 years	−0.83**	−0.66**
	(−2.37)	(−1.98)
10 years	−0.73**	−0.66**
	(−2.29)	(02.14)
No. of observations	1,086	892
No. of interventions	140	112

Source: Authors' regressions.
a. Table reports coefficients from a regression of the change in the yield of off-the-run issues from the day before an intervention to the day of settlement (two days later) on the size of the intervention; the sample period is January 2000 to March 2004. Numbers in parentheses are *t* statistics, where standard errors are adjusted for autocorrelation and heteroskedasticity using the approach of Hodrick (1992).
b. Days excluded are those of the release of reports on employment, GDP, business activity (ISM), retail sales, or consumer confidence.

this case the market did not recognize the interventions until the date of settlement, we looked at changes in yields from day $t-1$ to day $t+2$. The sample includes all Japanese interventions from January 3, 2000, to March 3, 2004. As can be seen in the first column of table 7, two-, five-, and ten-year Treasury yields all fell sharply on dates around Japanese interventions, and the estimated coefficients are highly statistically significant. Treasury bill yields did not react to the interventions, however, perhaps because they are pinned down by the current and near-term expected path of the federal funds rate.

Returning to figure 8, swap spreads did not move materially in the period of heavy Japanese intervention, suggesting that any effects on benchmark Treasury yields were transmitted to yields on private securities. This contrasts with the experience during the bond paydown episode and may be due to the fact that the Treasury buybacks were concentrated exclusively at the long end of the yield curve, whereas Japanese purchases probably spanned a wider band of the maturity spectrum, in which both the Treasury and private markets are deeper.

Although these results are suggestive of an important role for relative asset supplies in the determination of yields, they suffer from potential problems of joint endogeneity. For example, weak economic data could cause Treasury yields to fall and the dollar to weaken, with the latter prompting foreign exchange intervention by the Japanese finance ministry. To try to address this problem, we excluded from the sample all days with major U.S. data releases (see the notes to table 7). Their exclusion produced smaller and less statistically significant coefficients (shown in the second column of table 7), but the results remain broadly unchanged.

This episode provides us another opportunity to apply the no-arbitrage term structure model to control for a changing macroeconomic environment. The results, shown in figure 9, indicate that both five-year and ten-year Treasury yields remained below the model's predictions by an average of 50 to 100 basis points over the period January 2000 to March 2004. This suggests that some force not captured in the model was exerting downward pressure on yields over this period. But although the evidence is suggestive of effects from Ministry of Finance purchases, it is not conclusive. Indeed, yields moved down to those levels in advance of the sizable Japanese intervention (but of course did not move back). Moreover, as table 4 indicated, prediction errors of this magnitude are not uncommon.

To assess the statistical significance of these findings, we repeated the bootstrapping procedure described earlier, this time with the goal of putting confidence bands around yield predictions from May 2002 to April 2003. Those results suggest that the underprediction of yields of Treasury securities with maturities from one to ten years was quite unlikely given the structure of the model, as the observed errors differed significantly from zero at better than the 10 percent confidence level. We would hesitate, however, to ascribe this effect exclusively to foreign purchases of Treasury securities because, as we discuss next, other important events were leaving their imprint on yields at about the same time.

THE 2003 DEFLATION SCARE. From the fall of 2002 through the summer of 2003, with the economy remaining weak, inflation low and apparently falling, and the federal funds rate quite low, FOMC members began to talk about the risks of deflation in the United States and the possible responses of monetary policy if the federal funds rate were to hit its lower bound. Table 8 provides a brief chronology of relevant speeches and testimonies by Federal Reserve officials during this period.

Although Federal Reserve officials consistently referred to the risk of deflation as "remote" and the FOMC's planning for the contingency of

Figure 9. Prediction Errors of the Term Structure Model for Five- and Ten-Year Zero-Coupon Treasury Yields, 1995–2004[a]

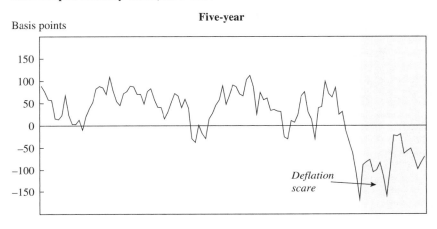

Basis points

Five-year

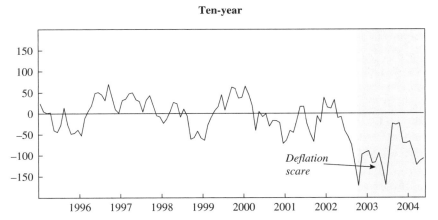

Ten-year

Source: Authors' calculations based on data from the sources listed in figure 4.
a. Shading indicates period of Japanese Ministry of Finance purchases.

hitting the ZLB as purely precautionary in nature, some market participants apparently interpreted these and other public comments as indicating that the Federal Reserve was seriously considering "unconventional" policy measures—in particular, purchasing large amounts of longer-term Treasuries. The perceived likelihood of such actions seemed to peak after the May FOMC meeting, when the committee pointed to the (remote) risk of a substantial decline in inflation. The possibility of direct purchases of longer-term Treasuries was seen to be taken off the table when the June FOMC statement did not mention it, and when Chairman Greenspan testified to Congress in July that "situations requiring special policy actions are most unlikely to arise."[79] Again, large movements in Treasury yields were observed on many of those days, with little alternative explanation.[80] Most notably, the ten-year Treasury yield fell sharply on the May FOMC statement (20 basis points) and after the chairman's speech in early June (10 basis points), and then rose abruptly following the June FOMC statement (26 basis points) and the chairman's testimony in July (20 basis points).

Of course, the FOMC never undertook targeted purchases of Treasury securities, but in an efficient market even the incorrect anticipation of such an event should affect yields. Figure 9 shows a sharp downward spike in the model errors in May and June 2003, which is reversed in July. These findings, taken at face value, suggest that the perceived possibility of Treasury purchases had an impact on the order of 50 basis points or more. The unexplained dip in yields in May and June is highly statistically significant, based on a bootstrapping exercise similar to that described above. Once again, however, one must be particularly wary of identification issues. The events that conveyed information about the possibility of Federal Reserve purchases of Treasuries most likely also conveyed information to the public about the risk of deflation. Changes in the perceived risk of deflation would affect long-term yields independent of supply effects. Moreover, some overlap exists between this episode and the period of Ministry of Finance purchases, discussed earlier.

If the Federal Reserve were willing to purchase an unlimited amount of a particular asset—say, a Treasury security—at a fixed price, there is little doubt that it could establish that asset's price. Presumably, this would be true even if the Federal Reserve's commitment to purchase the long-lived asset were promised for a future date.

---

79. Board of Governors of the Federal Reserve System, "Testimony of Chairman Alan Greenspan: Federal Reserve Board's Semiannual Monetary Policy Report to the Congress," July 15, 2003 (www.federalreserve.gov/boarddocs/hh/2003/july/testimony.htm).

80. The fact that rates did not uniformly change by large amounts on all the dates listed is not surprising, because other, unrelated news important to financial markets may have been released on some days and because the events themselves varied in the extent they provided new information.

Table 8. Notable Events and Changes in Treasury Yields during the 2003 Deflation Scare

Date	Event	Content	Change in yield[a]	
			2-year	10-year
November 21, 2002	Bernanke speech	Presents arguments for making sure "it" (deflation) doesn't happen in United States	7	6
December 19, 2002	Greenspan speech	Says United States is nowhere close to sliding into a "pernicious" deflation	−7	−10
March 30, 2003	Reinhart speech	Discusses policy options at the zero bound	−5	−9
May 6, 2003[b]	FOMC statement	Points to risk of an "unwelcome substantial fall in inflation"	−9	−20
May 22, 2003	Greenspan testimony	Argues deflation is a "serious" issue but the risks are "minor"	−1	−5
May 31, 2003	Reinhart speech	Emphasizes importance of shaping expectations	7	2
June 3, 2003	Greenspan speech	Mentions continued risk of declining inflation, need for a "firebreak"	−13	−10
June 25, 2003[b]	FOMC eases, issues statement	Smaller-than-expected easing; statement does not mention unconventional policy measures	29	26
July 15, 2003	Greenspan testimony	"Situations requiring special policy actions are most unlikely to arise"	9	20
July 23, 2003	Bernanke speech	FOMC should be willing to cut the federal funds rate to zero if necessary	−4	−4
August 12, 2003	FOMC statement	Drops "substantial" from statement on risk of "unwelcome fall in inflation"	5	20

Source: GovPX.

a. Except where noted otherwise, changes are daily changes in on-the-run Treasury yields. Dates of changes that were strongly associated with the event listed are in italics.

b. Changes in yields are two-day changes, since the market continued to respond on the day after the FOMC meeting.

Conceptually, it is useful to think of the Federal Reserve as providing investors in that security with a put option allowing them to sell back their holdings to the central bank at an established price. We can use our term structure model to price that option. As a purely illustrative example, suppose the Federal Reserve announced its willingness to purchase the current ten-year, zero-coupon Treasury security one year hence at a yield of 5½ percent. We will consider the value of this option, jumping off from the last observation used in estimating our model, that of May 2004. (We assume that the rate in May 2004 equals the value predicted by our model rather than the actual rate prevailing in that month.) Without this commitment, according to our model, the yield on that security would be expected to be 5.67 percent one year hence, implying that the put option has a 58 percent chance of ending up in the money. (The yield is given by $y_{t+12}^{(9)} = a_9 + b_9 X_{t+12}$.) The strike price of the option will be $K = \exp(-9 \times cap)$, where in our example $cap = 0.055$.

The price of the put option is

$$(8) \qquad \text{put} = E_t \left\{ m_{t+1} \, m_{t+2} \, m_{t+3} \ldots m_{t+12} [K - \exp(-a_9 - b_9' X_{t+12})]^+ \right\}.$$

We can compute this expectation by doing 10,000 simulations of the model. Note that the simulations determine the correlation between the payouts on the option and the value that risk-averse investors place on those payouts (which depends on the evolution of the state variables on the path to the payout). The results indicate that this option would lower today's ten-year rate by 34 basis points, or more than the 17 basis points by which the option is in the money because the convexity of the option gives it value.

Thinking of a pegging strategy in terms of options also highlights the potential that the pass-through to private securities of such a strategy might be limited. In this case, those investors holding a ten-year Treasury security receive the put option, but the holder of, say, a ten-year high-grade corporate bond does not. Thus the value of the put option would be reflected in the price of the corporate bond only to the extent that the marginal investor viewed Treasury and corporate securities as close substitutes. As shown in figure 8, and in contrast to the prediction of theory, swap spreads actually narrowed in the first half of 2003, when deflationary fears were building, and widened after those fears lifted later in the year. The range of variation, however, is quite narrow and so may relate to other macroeconomic and idiosyncratic developments.

Japan: A Modern Industrial Economy at the Zero Bound

So far we have made use of a variety of natural experiments from recent U.S. experience to try to gauge the potential effectiveness of policy tools at or near the ZLB. In particular, we have analyzed the effects on market expectations of FOMC statements (relevant for strategies that involve the shaping of policy expectations) and considered how the net supply of various Treasury securities influences the yield curve (relevant for strategies that involve the size or composition of the central bank's balance sheet). The possible effectiveness of such policies in the U.S. context is of great interest, but of course the inferences made are necessarily somewhat indirect, because the policy rate in the United States has remained at least 100 basis points above zero. In contrast, Japan is a modern industrial economy that has actually grappled with the ZLB for some seven years now; and although the Japanese economy differs from that of the United States in many ways (notably in its financial structure), its experience still should provide useful lessons for the United States and other industrial countries. In this section we apply some of the same methods used in the U.S. analysis toward understanding the experience of Japan.

An Event Study of Policies of the Bank of Japan

We begin our analysis of Japanese monetary policy by conducting an event study analogous to the one we conducted for the United States. As in the U.S. case, the objective is to analyze how monetary policy expectations at different horizons (as measured in financial markets) respond to central bank statements. Because the Bank of Japan in recent years has used its statements not only to try to shape expectations, but also to provide information regarding its programs of quantitative easing and targeted asset purchases, in principle the event study should cast light on the effectiveness of all three types of nonstandard policy options available to an economy at or near the ZLB. In practice, the relatively small number of BOJ policy statements in our sample leads to results that are less sharp than we would like. In the latter part of this section, therefore, we report results based on estimation of the term structure model for Japan.

Two preliminary issues must be addressed before proceeding to the details of the event study. First, the BOJ did not gain its independence until April 1998, which shortens the available sample considerably. (Before the BOJ became independent, monetary policy in Japan was largely controlled by the Ministry of Finance.) We include in our sample all policy meetings and dates of policy decisions by the BOJ since independence, which gives us 110 observations. Note that, during most of the sample period, the overnight interest rate was very close to zero. Second, intraday financial data are difficult to obtain for Japan, and so we are forced to rely on daily data. To complicate matters further, on some occasions BOJ statements have been released just before the close of Japanese financial markets, whereas at other times they were released just after the close. Because we could not easily ascertain the exact timing of all releases, to avoid contamination of the results we examine two-day changes in the financial market variables considered, from the day before each policy meeting to the day after. The use of a considerably longer event window than in the U.S. analysis increases the scope for factors other than policy actions or announcements to influence the financial variables. The extra noise will reduce the efficiency of our estimates but should not bias the results.

As in the event study for the United States, we employ three market-based measures of policy expectations at various horizons. The first is intended to capture the unexpected component of changes in the policy interest rate, the (overnight) call rate. Unfortunately, we cannot measure these surprises in exactly the same way as we do for the FOMC, because there is not an active futures market on the call rate in Japan. Instead we measure current policy surprises as the change during the event window in the first Euroyen futures contract to expire, which reflects unexpected changes in the policy rate over a slightly longer horizon.[81] Innovations to policy expectations at the one-year and the five-year horizons are measured as changes during the event window in the year-ahead Euroyen futures rate and in the five-year zero-coupon Japanese government bond (JGB) yield. These two indicators of policy expectations are essentially

---

81. These contracts are written on the three-month Euroyen deposit rate at the time of expiration; in practice, the ease with which investors can switch among money-market assets ensures that this rate will be closely tied to the average policy rate expected to prevail over that interval. The Euroyen futures contract expires 1½ months ahead on average, implying that the futures rate corresponds approximately to the expected call rate from 1½ to 4½ months ahead.

Table 9. Factor Decomposition of Monetary Policy Indicators, Japan[a]

Effect or standard deviation	Factor 1	Factor 2	Factor 3
Loading of factor on			
Current policy setting	1.00	0.00	0.00
Year-ahead futures rate	0.55	1.00	0.00
Five-year yield	0.32	0.64	1.00
Standard deviation of effect of factor on[b]			
Current policy setting	3.4	0	0
Year-ahead futures rate	1.9	3.0	0
Five-year yield	1.1	1.9	3.5

Source: Authors' calculations based on data from Bloomberg, the Chicago Mercantile Exchange, and the Bank of Japan.

a. Factors are constructed by means of a Cholesky decomposition, in which the first factor is the policy surprise contained in a policy statement, as inferred from the nearest Euroyen futures contract; the second is the portion of the change in year-ahead policy expectations (as measured by the change in the year-ahead futures contract) not explained by (that is, orthogonal to) the first factor; and the third is the change in the five-year zero-coupon JGB yield not explained by (orthogonal to) the first two factors. Sample period is April 1998 to the present.

b. In basis points.

identical in concept to the analogous rates in our event study for the United States.[82]

As in the U.S. event study, we apply a Cholesky decomposition to derive three candidate factors to explain the movements in the market-based policy indicators in the period around BOJ decisions. By construction, the first factor corresponds to unexpected changes in the current policy setting during the period around BOJ decisions, as measured by the change in the nearest Euroyen futures contract. The second factor, equal to the part of the change in the year-ahead futures contract that is orthogonal to the first factor, is intended to represent year-ahead policy expectations not explained by changes in the current policy setting. Finally, the third factor equals the change in the five-year zero-coupon JGB yield not explained by the first two factors.

The links between these factors and the policy indicators, shown in the top panel of table 9, are remarkably similar to those found for the FOMC (top panel of table 1). Notably, as in the U.S. event study, we find in the case of Japan that the first factor has an effect on longer-term interest rates that diminishes with maturity, and that the loading of the five-year yield on the second factor is significantly greater than that on the first factor.

82. The Euroyen futures contracts trade on the Chicago Mercantile Exchange. Data for the zero-coupon five-year JGB yield were taken from Bloomberg.

However, the magnitudes of the three factors, shown in the bottom panel of table 9, differ from the U.S. case. In particular, the first and second factors are much smaller (as measured by their standard deviations, the diagonal elements in the table) than in the U.S. event study (bottom panel of table 1). That is, changes in both current and year-ahead policy expectations in periods around BOJ decisions have been more subdued than in the U.S. case. However, the standard deviation of the third factor, which reflects longer-horizon policy expectations, is about the same, at 3.5 basis points, in the Japanese and the U.S. cases. The influence of the ZLB may explain the limited variation in the first two factors: both current and year-ahead futures rates were near zero over much of the sample, which restricted changes in policy expectations and rates in the downward direction at least. However, the ZLB is not the whole story; even in the period before 2001, when the year-ahead futures rate was generally above 50 basis points, the standard deviation of the second factor was only slightly higher (3.9 basis points) than in the sample as a whole (results not shown). Overall, it appears that the scope for the Bank of Japan to "use" the second factor, or its willingness to do so, was less than in the case of the Federal Reserve over the same period.[83]

As in the U.S. event study, we are interested in examining the relationship between the three factors describing changes in policy expectations and the statements issued by the central bank. We again define a dummy variable, STATEMENT, that equals 1 on dates when the BOJ released policy statements and zero otherwise. As in the U.S. analysis, we also define a dummy variable, STATEMENT SURPRISE, that indicates statements deemed to be surprising in significant aspects to market participants. To determine which statements were surprises, we again relied on several after-the-fact documents, including internal write-ups prepared by the staff of the Federal Reserve Bank of New York and articles in the *Wall Street Journal,* and one before-the-fact source, a series of commentaries prepared by Nikko/Citigroup just before each BOJ meeting.

Of the 110 observations in our sample, 19 involved the release of statements about the economy or monetary policy; we exclude 10 statements concerned only with various technical aspects of monetary policy opera-

---

83. An institutional explanation for the smaller second factor in Japan is the BOJ's practice of releasing policy statements only in conjunction with policy actions, rather than after every scheduled meeting.

tions without implications for the economic or policy outlook. Of these 19 statements, 10 were identified by our methods as surprises.[84]

As in the U.S. event study, we proceeded by regressing the squared factors on the dummy variables indicating statements and surprising statements. Again, following Kohn and Sack,[85] the use of the squared factors as dependent variables allows us to determine whether statements were associated with large changes in policy expectations (large realizations of the factors), without requiring us to specify the "direction" of the statements.

The regression results, shown in table 10, differ considerably from those found for the Federal Reserve (table 2). First, we find that the square of the first factor has a statistically significant relationship to STATEMENT SURPRISE but not to STATEMENT. One interpretation is that, unlike the FOMC, which appears reluctant to surprise the market in terms of both the policy setting and the statement at the same meeting, the BOJ often did so. Indeed, a review of the record shows that the BOJ on several occasions combined announcements of major policy innovations with unexpected changes in the setting of the interest rate. Notably, the announcement of the adoption of the zero-interest-rate policy on February 12, 1999, coincided with a 9-basis-point policy rate surprise by our measure, as the call rate was reduced from 25 basis points to a value "as low as possible," initially 15 basis points; and the introduction of quantitative easing on March 19, 2001, coincided with an 11-basis-point policy surprise, as the call rate was reduced from 12.5 basis points to essentially zero.

Second, and in striking contrast with the results for the FOMC, we find no evident relationship between the second factor and the BOJ's release of statements, whether surprising or not. This result, together with the small magnitude of the second factor already reported, suggests again that the BOJ was either unable or unwilling to influence year-ahead policy expectations with its statements. (In making this interpretation, however, we again note that the Japanese sample is much smaller and that a coarser two-day window was used rather than the one-hour time span in the U.S. case.)

---

84. A description of all statements over the period and our method of coding them is available from the authors on request.

85. Kohn and Sack (2003).

Table 10. Regressions of Squared Factors on Dummy Variables for Bank of Japan Policy Statements[a]

	Dependent variable		
Independent variable	*Factor 1*	*Factor 2*	*Factor 3*
Constant	7.4	8.2**	10.9**
	(1.79)	(2.78)	(4.18)
STATEMENT	−1.2	−1.2	−5.7
	(−0.09)	(−0.12)	(−0.66)
STATEMENT SURPRISE	50.5**	10.4	25.8**
	(2.79)	(0.81)	(2.25)
Adjusted R^2	.12	.01	.06

Source: Authors' regressions.

a. Numbers in parentheses are t statistics. ** indicates statistical significance at the 95 percent level. Factors are as defined in table 9. Independent variables are defined in a manner analogous to the definitions in table 2 for the United States.

Third, in Japan, unlike in the United States, the magnitude of the realization of the third factor is linked to the issuance of surprising statements by the central bank. However, this finding is largely the product of a single observation, the February 12, 1999, statement announcing the introduction of the ZIRP. Standard reasoning suggests that the announcement of the ZIRP should have influenced the third factor by leading to a drop in long-term bond yields; surprisingly, the third factor actually rose by 14 basis points that day. Our reading suggests that market participants were disappointed that the statement did not announce large-scale BOJ purchases of JGBs, as had been rumored. Perhaps, then, we should think of this important observation as consisting of two surprises working in opposite directions.

To examine the effects of BOJ statements further, we categorized the surprising statements into three types: statements providing new information about the likely path of policy (PATH SURPRISE, analogous to the variable of that name in the event study for the Federal Reserve); statements announcing an unexpected change in the BOJ's target for purchases of JGBs (JGB SURPRISE); and statements announcing unexpected changes in the BOJ's target for commercial banks' current account balances, in the period following the introduction of quantitative easing (CAB SURPRISE). In principle, this categorization should provide information on the relative effects of changes in policy expectations, targeted purchases of securities, and quantitative easing. Statements were allowed to fall into more than one category, if appropriate.

Again, the problems arising from a small sample are apparent, as the number of statements in each category is relatively small. We identified only two statements as potential path surprises: the introduction of the ZIRP in February 1999 and the introduction of quantitative easing in March 2001. These, of course, represented major shifts in policy strategy, and thus their effects may differ from those of the policy path surprises identified in the U.S. event study. Five BOJ statements announced changes in the target for JGB purchases (including the implementation of the quantitative easing program), three of which we identified as surprises to the market. Ten statements during the sample period announced changes in the target for banks' current account balances (including the statement that initiated the program), of which six were identified as surprises to the market.

Because the direction as well as the magnitude of statement effects is important, we report here results based on the "signed" dummy variable approach introduced in the earlier section.[86] Specifically, for each dummy variable corresponding to a surprising statement, we assigned a value of 1 for statements that would be expected to increase interest rates and a value of −1 for statements that would be expected to lower interest rates. Nonsurprising statements were coded as zeros. We then regressed the levels of each of the three factors on the signed dummy variables, allowing us to judge not only whether statements influenced expectations but also whether expectations were influenced in the expected direction.

We added one further innovation to the analysis at this point. Our focus thus far has been on the link at various horizons between central bank policy actions and statements, on the one hand, and interest rates, on the other. However, the logic of quantitative easing and targeted asset purchases implies that the most important effects of these policies may be felt on the prices of assets other than government bonds. To investigate this possibility, we included a fourth candidate factor in this event study, defined as the portion of the change in the Nikkei 500 stock index during the event window that is orthogonal to the other three factors. That is, the fourth factor reflects the impact of the BOJ's action and statement on prices of Japanese equities (an important alternative class of asset), holding

---

86. We also tried regressing the squared values of the factors on the various dummies; this exercise did not add much information to that already reported in table 11.

market expectations about current and future interest rates constant.[87] If BOJ policy decisions are influencing asset prices other than through expectational channels, this factor should pick that up.

The results, shown in table 11, amplify but also generally confirm the results discussed earlier in this section. We saw earlier that surprises in the policy setting (the first factor) and in the statement tend to be associated in Japan. Column 11-1 of table 11 shows that these surprises tend to be in the same direction (that is, both toward tightening or both toward ease), consistent with the earlier discussion. Further, as column 11-2 shows, unanticipated changes in the policy setting also seemed to be associated with statements that provide information on the future path of policy (that is, the PATH SURPRISE dummy accounts for the entire relationship between the first factor and statement surprises). This result is driven primarily by the announcements of the ZIRP and the quantitative easing program, which, as already mentioned, were associated with surprises in the policy setting as well.

We continue to find no significant relationship between the second factor (the innovation in year-ahead policy expectations) and BOJ statements, even with this finer categorization of statements (columns 11-3 and 11-4). This result is the strongest and most important contrast between the findings for the BOJ and for the Federal Reserve.

The level of the third factor (which, again, corresponds to the fluctuation in the yield on JGBs during the event window that is not explained by current or year-ahead policy expectations) appears to be linked with certain types of statements. As column 11-6 shows, a statement that surprises the market in suggesting that policy will be tighter in the future (that is, a positive path surprise) causes five-year yields to fall; the effect is statistically significant. This finding can be rationalized by the argument that a near-term tightening lowers inflation expectations and thus nominal interest rates at long horizons. Perhaps more interesting, the third factor also has a statistically significant link to JGB surprises; that is, BOJ statements announcing unexpectedly large targets for JGB purchases (an easing move, therefore coded as −1) are associated with declines in the yield on five-year JGBs, as should be the case if targeted bond purchases by the

---

87. It turns out that 99.2 percent of the variance of stock prices during the event window is orthogonal to the first three factors; that is, almost all of the change in stock prices is explained by the fourth factor, unrelated to interest rates.

Table 11. Regressions of Factors on Signed Dummy Variables for Bank of Japan Policy Statements[a]

	Dependent variable							
	Factor 1		Factor 2		Factor 3		Factor 4	
Independent variable	*11-1*	*11-2*	*11-3*	*11-4*	*11-5*	*11-6*	*11-7*	*11-8*
SIGNED STATEMENT SURPRISE	4.75** (4.80)		1.1 (1.14)		0.5 (1.11)		−1.12 (−1.90)	
SIGNED PATH SURPRISE		9.8** (4.13)		−2.2 (−1.01)		−6.3** (−2.54)		−1.94 (−1.45)
SIGNED JGB SURPRISE		0.9 (0.53)		−2.7 (−1.64)		5.1** (2.80)		−1.16 (−1.17)
SIGNED CAB SURPRISE[b]		0.4 (0.26)		0.4 (0.28)		−0.0 (−0.02)		−1.70** (−2.0)
Adjusted R^2	.17	.16	.01	.03	.06	.13	.02	.10

Source: Authors' regressions.
a. Factors are as defined in table 9. Independent variables are defined in a manner analogous to the definitions in tables 2 and 3 for the United States. Numbers in parentheses are *t* statistics; ** indicates statistical significance at the 95 percent level.
b. CAB, current account balances (at commercial banks).

central bank affect their yields. However, the estimated effect, although statistically significant, is not large (5 basis points) and is of necessity based on relatively few observations.

The results for the fourth factor, which is essentially the change in stock prices during the event window, are of interest. Columns 11-7 and 11-8 of table 11 show that the Japanese stock market index drops between 1 and 2 percent on average when the BOJ issues a surprisingly hawkish statement. The statistically strongest link is to BOJ announcements of new current account balance targets. Inspection of the data shows that, on three of the six occasions when the BOJ made surprise announcements of increases in its target for current account balances, the Nikkei 500 rose between 3 and 6 percent, including a 5.9 percent increase on the announcement of the quantitative easing policy. On one other such occasion the market rose nearly 2 percent. Thus, in the event study at least, quantitative easing appears to provide a positive impetus to the stock market, with both current and future interest rate expectations held constant.

Two general conclusions emerge from the BOJ event study. First, there is little evidence that the BOJ used its statements to influence near-term policy expectations during this period. This contradicts the finding of other research that the ZIRP was effective; we revisit this issue below. Second, our findings provide some tentative support for the view that asset prices respond to quantitative easing and targeted asset purchases; specifically, we find statistically significant links between JGB purchases and JGB yields on the one hand, and between quantitative easing and stock prices on the other. Whether these latter effects were large enough to have a significant influence on the Japanese economy will be addressed next.

A Benchmark Term Structure Model for Japan

As a final exercise, we estimate a benchmark term structure model for Japan and compare the results with actual term structure behavior. As in the U.S. case, the model is a no-arbitrage affine term structure model driven by observable factors. The underlying factors are assumed to be the unemployment rate, the inflation rate (the twelve-month change in the consumer price index), the overnight call rate, and the year-ahead Euro-yen futures rate. These variables are closely analogous to those used for the U.S. estimation, except that we do not have a monthly inflation expectations measure for Japan to include. The dynamics of the factors are determined by an estimated VAR with four lags, where the estimation uses monthly data over the sample period June 1982 to May 2004.[88]

With the estimated VAR in hand, we then fit the no-arbitrage term structure model using data from the JGB market. The data on JGB yields are month-average zero-coupon yields at maturities of six months and one, two, three, five, seven, and ten years, obtained from Bloomberg for the period since April 1989. The prices of risk are estimated using yield curve data from April 1989 to December 1997, based on the VAR dynamics estimated over the full sample. The fit of the model is quite good (figure 10). We show the fit of the model through 1997 only; as we will discuss next, for the period after 1997 we need to make an adjustment for the proximity of short-term yields to the ZLB.

When short-term interest rates fall to very low levels, the ZLB constraint begins to influence the shape of the yield curve. One effect is that

---

88. Data on the Euroyen futures rate are available only from June 1989; for earlier dates we regressed the futures rate on the five-year JGB yield and the call rate for the sample period June 1989 to May 1999 and used the fitted values from this regression as a proxy for the actual futures rate.

Figure 10. Actual and Predicted Japanese Government Zero-Coupon Yields, 1989–97[a]

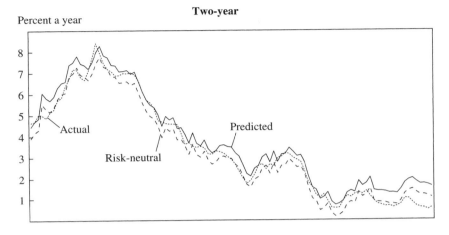

Two-year

Percent a year

Ten-year

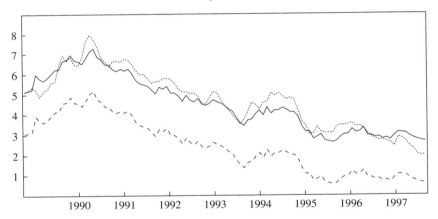

Source: Authors' calculations based on data from Datastream, the Chicago Mercantile Exchange, and Bloomberg.
a. The predicted yields are generated by the term structure model, as described in the text. The risk-neutral yields are generated by the same model, but with the prices of risk set equal to zero.

the ZLB reduces the possibility of declines in interest rates (and obviously eliminates them at short-term maturities), which limits the scope for capital gains on fixed-income securities. To compensate for this, investors will demand higher yields on fixed-income assets,[89] thereby steepening the yield curve.

We can account for this effect in our VAR model. The price of a two-year note, for example, should equal the expected product of the pricing kernel over the next twenty-four months:

$$(9) \qquad P_t^{24} = E_t[m_{t+1} \, m_{t+2} \, m_{t+3} \dots m_{t+24}].$$

We computed the bond price defined by equation 9 by performing 10,000 simulations of the model over the subsequent twenty-four months, determining the path of the pricing kernel in each iteration, and then taking the average of the product of the pricing kernel over all simulations. This exercise can be performed either ignoring the ZLB or imposing it.

If we perform the simulations without imposing the ZLB, the predicted bond prices will (asymptotically) be the same as those obtained directly from the VAR (such as those shown in figure 10), since the VAR dynamics do not recognize the presence of the ZLB constraint. To impose the ZLB, in each simulation we assume that, in any month that the policy rate would go negative, there is a shock to the policy rate sufficient to pull it back to zero.[90] We can rigorously price fixed-income assets according to equation 9 under these alternative simulations, which then allows us to estimate the effects of the ZLB on the term structure. In this exercise we account for the fact that investors, in valuing bonds, take into account the effect of the ZLB on the future path of short-term interest rates, as well as its effects on all of the state variables that affect the prices of risk.[91]

89. As described in Bomfim (2003); see also Ruge-Murcia (2002).
90. The year-ahead futures rate is assumed to respond endogenously to these policy shocks, based on a Cholesky decomposition in which the policy rate is ordered second to last and the futures rate is ordered last. Without this endogenous response, the futures rate would often go negative.
91. This exercise seems to get us a long way toward properly accounting for the effects of the ZLB on the term structure of interest rates, but it still has some shortcomings. Specifically, the dynamics of the VAR and the relationship between risk prices and economic variables may change in important ways near the zero bound, so that their dynamics are not well captured by the VAR with policy shocks. A similar criticism applies to other work on the effects of the ZLB, such as that of Bomfim (2003).

Figure 11. Yield Curve on Zero-Coupon Japanese Government Bonds before and after Bank of Japan Policy Announcements

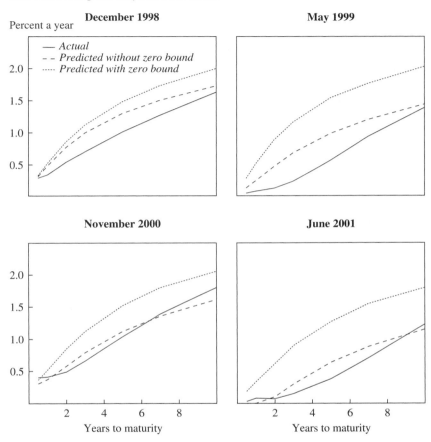

Source: Authors' calculations based on data from the sources listed in figure 10.

Figure 11 shows the results from this exercise for four representative months: December 1998 (several months before the introduction of the ZIRP), May 1999 (several months after its introduction), November 2000 (several months after the end of the ZIRP but before the introduction of the quantitative easing policy), and June 2001 (several months after the introduction of the quantitative easing policy). The influence of the ZLB (shown by the shift in the predicted yield curve) is to shift the yield curve upward in all cases, the magnitude of the shift depending on the proximity of rates to the ZLB. More important, the predicted yield curves (considering the ZLB) tend to lie above the corresponding actual yield curves. In other words, the VAR term structure model has difficulty explaining the low JGB yields during this period.

This result holds even though the VAR offers a very pessimistic view of the Japanese economy over this period. For most of the period since 1998, the VAR predicts that deflation will persist for some time and that short-term interest rates will remain very low. This forecast, however, probably should be regarded with some skepticism. The VAR is estimated over a sample period in which unemployment was rising and inflation falling; as a result, it finds that these variables are very persistent and extrapolates these trends. One could presumably improve upon that forecast by taking into consideration additional information or a more detailed model. Nevertheless, the interesting finding for our purposes is that, even given the VAR's downbeat projections of short-term interest rates, actual longer-term JGB yields seem to have been even lower than projected by the model.

An interesting question, then, is whether the low level of JGB yields was associated with the policies of the BOJ. Figure 11 suggests that the ZIRP and the quantitative easing policy may have played some role: the deviation between the predicted yields (taking account of the ZLB) and actual yields widened after the introduction of the ZIRP, narrowed once the policy was abandoned, and widened again after the introduction of the quantitative easing policy. Also of interest is that, in May 1999, after the introduction of the ZIRP, the spread between actual and predicted yields is greatest at the short end of the maturity structure—a result consistent with earlier research on the ZIRP, as discussed above.

As noted earlier, assessing the effects of the ZIRP and especially the quantitative easing policy is in general difficult because of the problems of controlling for other factors that influenced yields over the periods when these policies were in effect. It is intriguing that, when we control (at least roughly) for macroeconomic conditions and the current stance of monetary policy, as well as for the effects on longer-term rates of the option created by the presence of the ZLB, we still find that the Japanese term structure has recently been lower than predicted. Moreover, the deviation of the actual term structure and the predicted pattern of yields increased immediately following the introduction of the ZIRP and later of the quantitative easing policy. This evidence, more than the event-study analysis described above, gives some reason to believe that nonstandard policies in Japan have been effective at lowering longer-term interest rates. Whether the lower rates led to a material strengthening of the economy is beyond the scope of our discussion.

Conclusion

This paper has developed new empirical evidence on the likely effects of nonstandard monetary policies when nominal interest rates are near their zero lower bound. Although the evidence is to some degree indirect, it generally supports the view that nonstandard policies would be effective when the policy rate is at zero. Notably, the Federal Reserve has successfully used its communications to affect expectations of future policies and thus longer-term yields. We also find some evidence that relative supplies of securities matter for yields in the United States, a necessary condition for achieving the desired effects from targeted asset purchases. The event studies for Japan provide only limited evidence that the Bank of Japan has been successful in using nonstandard policies, but the analysis based on an estimated model of the term structure for that country does suggest that longer-term yields have been lower than might have been expected in recent years. The latter result holds open the possibility that the zero-interest-rate policy and quantitative easing policies have had expansionary effects.

Despite finding evidence that alternative policy measures may prove effective, we remain cautious about relying on such approaches. We believe that our findings go some way toward refuting the strong hypothesis that nonstandard policy actions, including quantitative easing and targeted asset purchases, cannot be successful in a modern industrial economy. However, the effects of such policies remain quantitatively quite uncertain. Thus we believe that policymakers should continue to maintain an inflation buffer and to act preemptively against emerging deflationary risks.[92] There are trade-offs, of course, in that erring toward the side of ease when rates are low tends to create an inflation bias, but the goal of zero inflation seems unwise in any case. Moreover, a systematic tendency to err toward an easier policy when adverse shocks bulk large

---

92. Reifschneider and Williams (2000).

and nominal interest rates are low can be offset by a willingness to unwind that accommodation quickly once the situation clears.

Shaping investor expectations through communication does appear to be a viable strategy, as suggested by Eggertsson and Woodford.[93] By persuading the public that the policy rate will remain low for a longer period than expected, central bankers can reduce long-term rates and provide some impetus to the economy, even if the short-term rate is close to zero. However, for credibility to be maintained, the central bank's commitments must be consistent with the public's understanding of the policymakers' objectives and outlook for the economy.

93. Eggertsson and Woodford (2003a, 2003b).

Comments and Discussion

Benjamin M. Friedman: This paper by Ben Bernanke, Vincent Reinhart, and Brian Sack is a welcome contribution to the new line of literature that examines, in a far more eclectic way than used to be done, how monetary policy works and what effects it has on the financial markets and the nonfinancial economy. The paper is valuable both because the question it asks is important—whether what the authors call nonstandard policy measures can be effective when ordinary monetary policy actions are constrained by the zero lower bound on short-term nominal interest rates—and because the analysis it brings to bear on this question is largely empirical. The paper also reaches what I regard as a sensible conclusion: that the potential efficacy of these nonstandard measures notwithstanding, it is wise for monetary policy both to aim at an inflation rate distinctly above zero, so as to allow for a buffer against disinflationary shocks, and to ease policy preemptively when necessary to avoid significant risk of hitting the zero lower bound on interest rates. Finally, the paper is important also because of who wrote it, but more on that below.

The authors consider three conceptually distinct classes of nonstandard monetary policy measures: central bank communications, changes in the *size* of the central bank's balance sheet, and changes in the *composition* of the central bank's balance sheet. (The last of these is what would normally be called debt management policy if it were executed by a country's fiscal authority rather than by its central bank.) It is important to point out, however—and this is the focus of my one major concern about the paper—that even when the authors are addressing the effects of changes in the size or composition of the central bank's balance sheet, what they are actually analyzing in their empirical work is still communications. Most of their empirical exercises focus not on policy actions but on official statements regarding intended future actions. Even when they examine such episodes as the U.S. Treasury's buyback of Treasury securities, during the happy but all-too-brief period in the late 1990s when the U.S. government ran surprisingly large budget surpluses instead of shamefully large deficits, their attention is more on what the Treasury said than on what it did.

In principle, of course, credible statements about future actions *should* matter for the pricing of medium- and long-term assets in speculative markets. The ground for concern is rather in how this approach to addressing questions of monetary policy reinforces the increasingly exclusive focus in recent literature on what many economists engaged in this line of research (for example, Gauti Eggertsson and Michael Woodford in a Brookings Paper last year)[1] call "expectations management."

Surely everyone today believes that expectations matter, and therefore that whatever influences the public's expectations, including communication from the central bank, matters as well. I am also sympathetic to the authors' presumption that, when an economy has reached the zero lower bound on short-term interest rates, central bank communications may be even more important than normally. But the net impression, delivered both by the authors' discussion and by the battery of empirical tests they perform, nonetheless resonates too strongly, at least for my taste, with the idea, which they attribute to Eggertsson and Woodford, that "shaping the interest rate expectations of the public is essentially the only tool that central bankers have—not only when the ZLB binds, but under normal conditions as well." (I will not repeat here my criticism of this view, but interested readers can refer to my remarks as a discussant of the Eggertsson-Woodford paper.)

This concern aside, I regard the authors' empirical analysis of the effect of Federal Reserve and Treasury statements on market interest rates as carefully crafted, and I find their conclusions easily credible. I especially admire their willingness to go beyond the standard event studies and use a multifactor term structure model to try to identify the role of "surprise" elements of Federal Reserve statements, as distinct from the policy actions that these statements accompanied. One might quibble with some of the details, and no doubt subsequent researchers will suggest alternative specifications, but that is not my purpose.

---

1. Eggertsson and Woodford (2003a).

My only real regret about this part of the paper is that the authors never say what they think of the specifics of the two recent Federal Open Market Committee statements they examine: the August 2003 statement that "policy accommodation can be maintained for a considerable period" and the May 2004 statement that the committee intends to remove policy accommodation "at a pace that is likely to be measured." How do they think these statements measure up to the now-conventional mantra that central bank communications with the market (and the general public) should be clear and transparent? What are we to read into their highly quotable remark about "policymaking by thesaurus"? FOMC practice may perhaps require a certain opacity, but publication in the Brookings Papers presumably does not.

The authors' extended analysis of what amounts to debt management policy (actually, *statements* about debt management policy) is a further strength of the paper, and it, too, merits comment. The basic principle at work here is that the vector of market-clearing expected returns on all traded assets emerges as a consequence of the equilibrium of respective asset supplies and asset demands. Given the conditions underlying the public's asset demands—importantly including the risk properties of specific assets, investors' risk tolerance, and investors' assessment of the magnitudes of various risks and of the relationships among them—changes in the relative supplies of any "outside" assets (that is, assets supplied by issuers, such as government, whose portfolio behavior lies outside the model of market equilibrium) normally result in changes in the entire vector of market-clearing relative returns. Whether the degree of imperfect substitutability among the relevant assets (especially longer-term obligations that are likely to be closer substitutes to equities and other claims on capital) is sufficient to render policy interventions of this kind potentially important is then an empirical question.

The authors rightly question the familiar presumption that the Federal Reserve's "Operation Twist" effort in the early 1960s provides evidence against the effectiveness of debt management policy. Not only did the Treasury's choice of maturity for its new issues offset the Federal Reserve's policy of buying in long bonds and selling bills, as James Tobin often rightly pointed out; indeed, the situation was worse than that. Treasury data show that the early 1960s was a quite exceptional time. In the three decades immediately following World War II, during which the mean maturity of the outstanding Treasury debt declined from ten years to just two-and-a-half years, this was the only time when the mean maturity *lengthened*. Why *should* the yield curve have flattened during these few years?

The authors' empirical efforts show a modest impact on the yield curve from the Treasury's statements about its late-1990s buyback program. I find these estimates credible. Indeed, they are close to what I myself found some years ago, using a structural supply-demand model for different debt instruments to estimate the impact of debt management policy. Specifically, I used my estimated model to simulate the effects of a switch out of long-term Treasury bonds and into short-term Treasury bills, in a quantity that was fairly large back in the pre-Reagan days when there was not much debt outstanding. My estimates indicated that, in response, the Treasury bill rate would rise by 18 basis points, the rate on three- to five-year securities would rise by 7 basis points, the rate on six- to eight-year maturities would fall by 21 basis points, and the rate on thirty-year maturities would fall by 25 basis points. These higher bill rates and lower bond rates, in turn, would induce private borrowers to shift their debt issuance from the short toward the long end of the available maturity range. As a result, although the rate on long-term government bonds went down by 25 basis points in my estimates, the rate on long-term corporate bonds—which is presumably what matters more for real economic activity—went down by only 12 basis points.

My only reservation about this part of the paper concerns the framing of the analysis in terms of the zero lower bound on nominal interest rates. What the authors are investigating is debt management policy (or, to repeat, statements about debt management policy). There is no reason to believe that the effects of debt management policy are any larger at or near the zero lower bound, nor is it necessarily the case that debt management policy is uninteresting *away* from the zero lower bound.

My reaction to the authors' treatment of changes in the *size* of the central bank's balance sheet likewise focuses not on what they did or what they found, but on how they describe this inquiry. Although they are careful to use language that does not make the point explicit, the question they are really asking here is whether changes in the quantity of money matter—even for prices! And their answer is mostly no, or at least that they do not matter under the economic conditions they have in mind.

It is a mark of how far the economics profession has come in the last two decades that it is possible to ask this question, and to give this answer, in the totally innocuous way the authors do. Twenty years ago most economists (although not everyone around the Brookings Panel table) automatically assumed that increasing the money stock would lead, at the least, to rising prices. Changes in money were what monetary policy was about. The idea that, once interest rates fell low enough, money and short-term securities became perfect substitutes, so that further increases in money no longer mattered and monetary policy became impotent—that policymakers could not "push on a string"—was anathema. Today the whole conversation about monetary policy is couched in terms of interest rates, and any notion that the central bank would seek to increase or decrease the quantity of money, or that such changes in money would have any effect, in the absence of changes in interest rates is labeled "nonstandard." Indeed, the whole discussion now takes place without requiring mention of the word "money." Who ever said there is no such thing as intellectual progress?

Two smaller matters also merit at least some comment: First, why does the definition of a "pure pegging policy" require that the central bank match purchases or sales of the pegged security with sales or purchases of some other security, rather than with changes in the monetary base? In a model with only one kind of bond, "pegging the interest rate" always means being willing to vary the monetary base for this purpose. Why preclude that usage in a world with two or more kinds of bonds? And second, although I understand the desire of policymakers to take credit for all sorts of benefits that follow from "greater stability in the economy and in policy," I suspect that a major contributor to the decline in long-horizon risk premiums over the last decade and more, to which the authors point, has been the improvement in the efficiency and availability of the market's hedging facilities.

Let me close by returning to my remark at the outset that one reason this paper is welcome is simply that the authors are who they are. I have always regretted a certain cultural difference between policymakers in different domains: It is de rigueur for former active participants in foreign policy, for example, to write after-the-fact accounts of how policies were made, typically including details of the push and pull of how their institution or organization went about reaching its decisions. The practice among monetary policymakers, by contrast, is far more close-mouthed (or empty-penned). One can cite Sherman Maisel's book of a generation ago, and more recently books by Alan Blinder and Laurence Meyer, as well as by John Crow in Canada. But the serious student of the subject longs for books that were never written—in the United States alone by William McChesney Martin, Allen Sproul, Alfred Hayes, or other key players of that day; by Paul Volcker, or Anthony Solomon, or Gerald Corrigan; or by Alan Greenspan (although his would still be premature). Such books might not have the same *public* appeal as the classics of diplomacy by George Kennan and Dean Acheson and Henry Kissinger, but for students of our discipline they would be invaluable. I hope Governor Bernanke continues to engage in written reflection and analysis of his and his colleagues' actions, and of the thinking and discussions behind those actions, and that the book he will write in time will add to a literature that still stands much in need of further contributions.

Lars E. O. Svensson:[1] This paper by Ben Bernanke, Vincent Reinhart, and Brian Sack is an important and interesting one, with a good theoretical discussion of and new empirical results on monetary policy alternatives at the zero lower bound (ZLB) on nominal interest rates. The paper is important and interesting also for the obvious reason that two of its authors are important and influential insiders at the Federal Reserve System. Notwithstanding the qualification that the views expressed are not necessarily shared by anyone else in the organization, the paper reveals some aspects of the Federal Reserve's thinking about and preparation for the possibility that the ZLB might bind at some future time.

I have no disagreements with the substance of the paper or the empirical results that the authors find. However, I believe that the paper's focus and emphasis are not quite right.

Consider a liquidity trap—a situation when the ZLB is strictly binding, in the sense that it prevents the central bank from setting the interest rate that is its instrument rate (the federal funds rate, in the case of the Federal Reserve) at its optimal level. What is the problem in a liquidity trap? The problem is that, even though the instrument rate is at zero, the real (short-term) interest rate is too high, and as a consequence the economy is in a recession or inflation is too low (perhaps even negative), or both. The central bank would prefer a lower real interest rate and a more expansionary monetary policy stance, if that were possible.

How can the problem be solved? The central bank can lower the real interest rate if it can induce the private sector to expect a higher price level in the future. If expected inflation increases, the real interest rate falls, even

1. I thank Kathleen Hurley for secretarial and editorial assistance.

if the nominal interest rate is unchanged at zero. But how can the central bank induce such expectations of a higher future price level? Indeed, this is the real problem in a liquidity trap. Consequently, in assessing policy alternatives in a liquidity trap, the focus should be on how effective each of those alternatives is in affecting expectations of the future *price level*. In this paper, however, the focus is mostly on affecting expectations of future *interest rates,* which is likely to be much less effective.[2]

Price-Level Expectations in a Liquidity Trap

Let me illustrate with a simple New Keynesian model. Let $x_t \equiv y_t - \bar{y}_t$ denote the output gap in the current period t, where y_t denotes (log) output and $\bar{y}_t$ (log) potential output. Potential output is assumed to be an exogenous stochastic process. Let r_t denote the (short-term) real interest rate:

$$r_t \equiv i_t - \pi_{t+1|t} \equiv i_t - \left(p_{t+1|t} - p_t \right),$$

where i_t denotes the nominal interest rate (the instrument rate), $\pi_{t+1|t}$ denotes private sector expectations of one-period-ahead inflation, p_t denotes the (log) price level, and $p_{t+1|t}$ denotes the expected one-period-ahead (log) price level. Let $\bar{r}_t$ denote the neutral (real) interest rate—that is, the Wicksellian natural interest rate, the real interest rate that would arise in a hypothetical flexible-price economy with output equal to potential output. In the simplest case, the neutral interest rate is given by

$$\bar{r}_t \equiv \rho_t + \left(1/\sigma \right)\left(\bar{y}_{t+1|t} - \bar{y}_t \right),$$

where ρ_t is the rate of time preference (an exogenous stochastic process) and the positive constant σ is the intertemporal elasticity of substitution for consumption. Hence the neutral interest rate is determined by the rate of time preference and expected growth of potential output. The output gap depends positively on the expected future output gap, $x_{t+1|t}$,

---

2. Although, in some cases, a particular path of future interest rates may induce desirable price-level expectations in equilibrium, this way of affecting price-level expectations is certainly very indirect and in practice fraught with many difficulties. Furthermore, an interest rate commitment alone may not be sufficient to uniquely determine the price level, as emphasized long ago by Sargent and Wallace (1975) and more recently—in the context of a liquidity trap—by Benhabib, Schmitt-Grohé, and Uribe (2002).

and negatively on the real interest rate gap, $r_t - \bar{r}_t$, according to the following aggregate demand relation:

$$x_t = x_{t+1|t} - \sigma(r_t - \bar{r}_t),$$

which follows from a first-order condition for optimal consumption choice. The aggregate demand relation can be solved forward to period $t + T$:

$$x_t = x_{t+T|t} - \sigma\sum_{\tau=0}^{T-1}\left(r_{t+\tau|t} - \bar{r}_{t+\tau|t}\right).$$

This expression shows that the current output gap depends positively on the expected output gap T periods ahead, $x_{t+T|t}$, and negatively on the sum of the current and expected future real interest rate gaps, $r_{t+\tau|t} - \bar{r}_{t+\tau|t}$, for the next T periods. I assume that the horizon T is chosen such that the economy is expected to be back to normal by then, in the sense that the output gap is expected to be approximately equal to zero, $x_{t+T|t} \approx 0$. The current output gap then depends only on the sum of the current and expected future real interest rate gaps for the next T periods. If the current output gap is negative (the economy is in recession), the reason is that the sum of the current and expected future real interest rate gaps is too large—that is, the current and expected real interest rates are too high relative to the corresponding neutral interest rates.

Under the assumption that the economy is expected to be back to normal T periods ahead, the current output gap can be written as

$$x_t \approx -\sigma\sum_{\tau=0}^{T-1}\left(i_{t+\tau|t} - \pi_{t+1+\tau|t} - \bar{r}_{t+\tau|t}\right)$$

$$= -\sigma\sum_{\tau=0}^{T-1}i_{t+\tau|t} + \sigma\left(p_{t+T|t} - p_t\right) + \sigma\sum_{\tau=0}^{T-1}\bar{r}_{t+\tau|t},$$

where the first equality uses the definition of the real interest rate, and the second equality uses the fact that the sum of future inflation equals the total change in the (log) price level. I also assume that the economy is expected to be in or close to a liquidity trap during the next T periods, so that the expected instrument rates for that period are approximately zero, $i_{t+\tau|t} \approx 0$ ($0 \leq \tau \leq T - 1$). Then the first term on the right-hand side is approximately zero. For a given current price level p_t (I assume that the current price level is sticky), the output gap depends only on the expected price level T periods ahead, $p_{t+T|t}$, and the sum of the expected neutral interest rates during the next T periods. If the output gap is negative, so that the economy is in a recession, this is for two reasons: the sum of the current and expected future neutral interest rates, $\sum_{\tau=0}^{T-1} \bar{r}_{t+\tau|t}$, is too small, and the sum of the current and expected future real interest rates, $\sum_{\tau=0}^{T-1} r_{t+\tau|t} \approx -\left(p_{t+T|t} - p_t\right)$, is too large. That is, the expected future price level, $p_{t+T|t}$, is too low. It follows that the real interest rate can be lowered and the negative output gap reduced or eliminated if the central bank can induce private sector expectations of a higher future price level.

However, this paper is mostly about reducing the negative output gap by inducing private sector expectations of *lower future instrument rates*. Thus, in the case when the expected future instrument rates during the next T periods are not exactly zero but positive, they can perhaps be reduced further toward zero. However, these rates are already low, and therefore what can be gained from reducing them is small. Furthermore, it may be possible to induce the private sector to expect instrument rates close to zero *after* period T as well, after the liquidity trap is over. In the above framework, this would amount to creating expectations of a positive rather than a zero output gap T periods ahead, $x_{t+T|t} > 0$, which would reduce the current negative output gap. It seems likely that any such attempt to lower expectations of future instrument rates toward zero, when these expectations are already low to start with, will have very small, second-order effects on the current output gap.

In contrast, there is potentially a large first-order effect on the output gap from increasing expectations of the future price level. This is where I wish the focus of this paper had been.

How Can the Central Bank Affect Expectations of the Future Price Level?

The insight that the solution to the problem of a liquidity trap involves affecting private sector expectations of the future price level is due to Paul Krugman.[3] Krugman also noted that this principal solution immediately encounters a practical problem, namely, a credibility problem, in that it is not easy for a central bank to purposely affect such expectations.

3. Krugman (1998).

In particular, a central bank that has built a reputation for consistent low-inflation policy finds it difficult to convince the private sector that it has suddenly changed its mind and wants the price level to increase substantially.

EXPANDING THE MONEY SUPPLY. One possible way to affect expectations of the future price level is by increasing the money supply: what the paper refers to as increasing the *size* of the central bank's balance sheet. As Krugman noted, this is effective only if the private sector perceives the increase in the money supply to be *permanent*. Unfortunately, there is no mechanism through which a modern central bank can commit itself to a particular future money supply.

We can see this in the above framework. Let us assume that the horizon T is chosen such that the liquidity trap is expected to be over and interest rates are expected to be positive beginning in period $t + T$: $i_{t+T|t} > 0$. To a first approximation, we may take demand for the monetary base to be proportional to nominal GDP when interest rates are positive. This implies (disregarding any constant)

$$p_{t+T|t} \approx m_{t+T|t} - y_{t+T|t},$$

where $m_{t+T|t}$ denotes the expected (log) monetary base T periods ahead. That is, as an approximation, the expected future price level is directly related positively to the expected future monetary base and negatively to the expected future output level. If the central bank could affect private sector expectations of the future monetary base, it would, all else equal, also affect private sector expectations of the future price level to the same extent.

Unfortunately, it is not easy for a central bank to directly affect expectations of the future monetary base. The Japanese liquidity trap and the Bank of Japan's response to it provide an unusually clear-cut example. In March 2001 the Bank of Japan instituted its new policy of "quantitative easing," which consisted of a dramatic expansion of the monetary base. By the summer of 2004, the monetary base had increased by more than 60 percent. Suppose that the private sector believes this expansion to be permanent. The private sector would then believe that, some time in the future (for concreteness, say, in four years) when the Japanese liquidity trap is over, nominal GDP will have risen by more than 60 percent. Suppose that the private sector believes that Japanese real GDP in the next four years will rise by only some 10 to 15 percent. The private sector would then believe that, four years hence, the price level will be some

40 to 45 percent higher than today. If this were the case, either the yen would depreciate by some 40 to 45 percent, or Japanese long-term interest rates would rise substantially, or some combination of the two would occur. In fact, neither has occurred. The obvious conclusion is that the private sector does not believe that the expansion of the monetary base is permanent. The quantitative easing has not affected price-level expectations. It appears to be a dramatic failure.

AN INFLATION TARGET OR A PRICE-LEVEL TARGET. An inflation target or, better, a price-level target would be a fine solution, *if* it were credible. However, merely announcing the target would not be enough: the announcement would have to be combined with statements and actions that make it credible. This seems to be a particular problem for central banks like the Federal Reserve and the Bank of Japan, since they have clearly demonstrated over many years their notorious aversion to any numerical target or other explicit commitment.

FISCAL POLICY. A fiscal expansion—an increase in the fiscal deficit— may or may not be expansionary and increase aggregate demand, depending on the composition of the fiscal expenditure, the degree of Ricardian equivalence, and so forth. Typically, Ricardian equivalence does not seem to hold, and a fiscal deficit is expansionary; however, private sector behavior may be closer to Ricardian equivalence in a crisis, with a fiscal deficit that is perceived to be unsustainable and an expected imminent fiscal consolidation through increased taxes, reduced spending, or both. Japan has certainly tried to implement an expansionary fiscal policy, but this, too, has failed to free Japan from the liquidity trap, although it has certainly led to a dramatic deterioration of Japan's public finances.

A money-financed rather than debt-financed fiscal expansion is often proposed as a remedy for a liquidity trap. But often it is not understood that, for a given fiscal deficit, and aside from any debt-induced inflation incentives for government-controlled (rather than independent) central banks, both money and debt financing work through exactly the same mechanism discussed above in regard to expanding the money supply. Money financing of a fiscal expansion will affect expectations of the future price level only to the extent that it is interpreted as a permanent expansion of the money supply. Again, since there is no mechanism by which the central bank can commit to a future money supply, current money financing of a deficit does not exclude the possibility that the money supply will be reduced in the future. Money financing of a fiscal expansion hence provides no separate mechanism by which to affect expectations of the future price level.

EMPIRICAL ASSESSMENT OF POLICY ALTERNATIVES IN A LIQUIDITY TRAP. In line with the above discussion, the empirical assessment of alternative policies in a liquidity trap should focus on their impact on price-level expectations. An obvious problem is that there are very few examples of this approach being taken, and so a case study approach seems the only feasible one. The "Rooseveltian Resolve" of 1933–34 seems a good case to examine from this point of view, with its devaluation, its new commitment to end deflation and reflate the economy, and its associated impression of a regime change.[4] An examination of price expectations data from this period would prove interesting. Generally, it seems more relevant and revealing to look at price expectations data than interest rate expectations data when assessing alternative policies in a liquidity trap. In particular, one may want to look at data on the effect of central bank communication on price-level expectations.

THE FOOLPROOF WAY. In several recent papers,[5] I have promoted what I call the "Foolproof Way" as an effective policy to escape from a liquidity trap. The Foolproof Way involves, first, the announcement and implementation of a price-level target; second, a currency depreciation and peg consistent with the price-level target; and, third, an exit strategy, to be undertaken when the price-level target has been reached, in which the currency is floated and inflation targeting or price-level targeting is instituted.

In terms of the above framework, the idea is to induce private sector expectations of a higher future price level, such that the real interest rate falls and the economy expands out of the liquidity trap. Let the price-level target for period $t + T$, $\hat{p}_t$, be such that price-level expectations satisfying

$$(1) \qquad p_{t+T|t} = \hat{p}_{t+T|t},$$

and zero instrument rates during the next $T - 1$ periods would be adequate to achieve the desired fall in the real interest rate and increased stimulus of the economy. Price-level expectations and exchange rate expectations will be related according to

$$(2) \qquad p_{t+T|t} = s_{t+T|t} + p^*_{t+T|t} - q_{t+T|t},$$

4. This episode is discussed by Bernanke (2000).
5. Svensson (2001, 2003, 2004); Jeanne and Svensson (2004).

where s_t denotes the (log) exchange rate, p_t^* denotes the (log) foreign price level, and q_t denotes the (log) real exchange rate. I assume that the horizon T is chosen such that the economy is expected to be back to normal by then, and in particular that it is chosen such that the real exchange rate is expected to be back to its natural (neutral, potential) level, $\bar{q}_{t+T|t}$, and hence can be treated as exogenous from the perspective of current monetary policy. I also assume that the foreign price level can be taken as exogenous. Under these assumptions the expected future price level and the expected future exchange rate are directly related and move together.

By interest parity, the current exchange rate is related to the expected future exchange rate and the interest rate differential between the home and the foreign interest rate, $i_t - i_t^*$, by

$$s_t = s_{t+1|t} - \left(i_t - i_t^*\right) = s_{t+T|t} - \sum_{\tau=0}^{T-1} i_{t+\tau|t} + \sum_{\tau=0}^{T-1} i_{t+\tau|t}^*$$

where the second equality follows from solving forward T periods. By equation 2, we get

$$s_t = p_{t+T|t} - \sum_{\tau=0}^{T-1} i_{t+\tau|t} + \dots,$$

where the exogenous terms have been left out. The expectation that future instrument rates will approximately equal zero implies that the current exchange rate is directly related to and moves together with the expected future price level. An increase in the expected future price level corresponds to an equal current depreciation of the currency. The exchange rate peg of the Foolproof Way implements the exchange rate consistent with the future price-level target and the zero instrument rates.[6] If the Foolproof Way and its price-level target are immediately credible, price-level expectations will rise to fulfill equation 1, and the currency will, by equation 2, depreciate by the same amount, and the peg will not be binding. Otherwise, the peg forces private sector price-level expectations to be consistent with the price-level target.

Many comments on the Foolproof Way, including in this paper, have suggested that a potential improvement in the trade balance due to currency depreciation under the peg may be problematic for the trading

---

6. The peg may need to incorporate a rate of crawl to be exactly consistent with a zero home instrument rate. A constant peg would imply a home instrument rate equal to the foreign short-term interest rate, but the practical difference is small.

partners. However, any effects on the trade balance will be exactly the same as would result from a credible price-level target without any peg, or a lower instrument rate, if that were not prevented by the ZLB. The truth is that any expansionary monetary policy implies a real depreciation and thus a trade balance effect. Furthermore, any net effect on the trade balance from expansionary monetary policy will consist of income and substitution effects of opposite signs. In a liquidity trap and a deep recession, the income effect on the trade balance may be particularly strong and actually improve the trade balance for the trading partners. Finally, nothing prevents the trading partners from conducting their own expansionary monetary policy to counteract any contractionary effect from the Foolproof Way. In this way, an optimal world monetary expansion might be achieved.[7]

Changing the Composition of the Central Bank Balance Sheet

The paper also discusses changes in the composition of the central bank balance sheet as a policy alternative in the vicinity of the ZLB.[8] The purpose of such a policy is to affect various risk premiums through portfolio balance effects. For example, consider the relation between the interest rate on a nominal discount bond with a maturity of T periods, i_t^T, and the instrument rate,

$$i_t^T = (1/T)\sum_{\tau=0}^{T-1} i_{t+\tau|t} + \varphi_t^T.$$

Here φ_t^T denotes a term premium, which may depend on the relative supply of maturity-T government bonds, denoted B_t^T. If initially i_t^T is positive, by changing the composition of its assets so as to increase the proportion of maturity-T bonds and reduce the proportion of Treasury bills,

7. See Svensson (2004) for an analysis of the international effects of the Foolproof Way. One possible problem with the Foolproof Way is that the central bank may have an incentive to renege in the future through an unanticipated currency appreciation, so as to achieve low inflation ex post. However, Jeanne and Svensson (2004) show—starting from the fact that a currency appreciation reduces the home-currency value of foreign exchange reserves, and given the strong aversion toward negative central bank capital revealed by central bank officials and noted by central bank commentators—that a central bank can manage its capital so as to create a commitment not to appreciate the currency in the future.

8. Note that the management of central bank capital so as to create a commitment not to appreciate the currency, discussed in Jeanne and Svensson (2004), is an example of a policy that changes the composition of central bank capital (see note 6).

the central bank can reduce the relative supply of maturity-T bonds and lower the term premium, thereby lowering i_t^T toward zero. It is possible in principle for central banks to lower the interest rate on longer-term bond rates somewhat this way. The paper reports some very interesting empirical results on the Federal Reserve's attempts to affect long-term interest rates. But it is not clear that such attempts will have a substantial effect on the current output gap. The impact is probably one of a few basis points, or at most a few tens of basis points, on long-term bond rates that are probably already low. Compared with changes in price-level expectations, it seems to be a second-order effect.[9] Although the paper's empirical results are very interesting and the analysis is well done, it seems clear that we are talking about rather small effects.

Conclusion

In conclusion, it seems obvious that, in the face of a liquidity trap, monetary policy should focus on policy alternatives that are capable of affecting expectations of the future price level rather than just affecting expectations of future interest rates. The effect of changing price-level expectations and related exchange rates seems much more powerful than that of changing long-term nominal interest rates or expectations of future short-term interest rates that are already close to zero. Obviously, there is no bound on prices or exchange rates similar to that on nominal interest rates. Therefore I would like to see more theoretical and empirical research on policies in a liquidity trap that focus on affecting price-level expectations.

General discussion: Robert Gordon agreed with Lars Svensson on the importance of distinguishing between the effects of monetary policy on expectations about future interest rates and its effects on expectations about the future price level. But he disagreed with the view that there is a direct connection between monetary policy statements or actions and expectations about the price level in an economy like the United States. In his view the output gap and supply shocks such as changes in oil prices or exchange rates are the major factors affecting inflation, and they do so

---

9. In the simple analytical framework used in this comment, it is not clear whether i_t^T or $\sum_{\tau=0}^{T-1} i_{t+\tau|t}$ matters more for the output gap. A more elaborate model, one that does not use first-order approximations, is needed to answer that question.

with long and variable lags. In order for statements or actions by the central bank to affect expectations of the future price level, they have to alter expectations of these variables. Even before the emergence of modern financial markets, the monetary base, the instrument directly controlled by policy, was not reliably related to either the money supply or nominal output and prices. The classic example is 1938–39, during the administration of Franklin Roosevelt, when the monetary base tripled in the United States as gold flowed in from Europe. Although the increase in the money supply was substantial, it was far less in percentage terms than the increase in the monetary base, and there was no jump in the price level. The Japanese experience in the face of a liquidity trap in 2001 was similar.

Lars Svensson agreed that a liquidity trap is an extreme situation and that in those circumstances it would be difficult for any central bank to affect expectations by announcing a price-level target. But, he argued, the exchange rate is a much more effective means of affecting price-level expectations. Furthermore, the exchange rate, unlike the nominal short-term interest rate, has no zero bound. Olivier Blanchard remarked that a currency devaluation would increase costs for some firms, which would lead to an immediate increase in some prices and quickly affect expectations of the future price level. Gordon expressed his doubts, observing that, following the 1992 breakup of the European Exchange Rate Mechanism, the pass-through of the exchange rate change to domestic price levels was far from complete.

Several Panel participants pursued the question of whether communications are effective during a liquidity trap. Robert Lawrence found the evidence on the efficacy of such nonconventional monetary policy mechanisms in normal times quite compelling, but he thought it risky to assume the same results in the unusual circumstances of a liquidity trap. This could be why such policies have not worked very well in Japan. Adam Posen echoed Lawrence's concern that announcement effects may not work in a zero-interest-rate environment; he and Kenneth Kuttner had written a paper that reported little impact of statements by the Bank of Japan. William Nordhaus wondered whether one reason Japan has not had success is the lack of a unified central bank with a highly credible leader. John Leahy was also impressed with the evidence on the effectiveness of central bank communication, but he emphasized that the communications studied in the present paper were about monetary instruments over which the Federal Reserve has clear control. It is not obvious how much impact the Federal Reserve could have when commenting about variables, such as the inflation rate, that are not under its direct control. Posen, reminding the Panel that a fiscal expansion brought an end to the Great Depression, suggested analyzing the effects of coordinated monetary and fiscal actions near the zero lower bound. Statements about a coordinated monetary and fiscal policy in such circumstances were likely to be more effective than statements about either one separately. Nordhaus found the results on communications both interesting and persuasive. He thought they were consistent with a 2003 paper by Ray Fair in the *Journal of International Money and Finance,* which estimated the responses of stocks, bonds, and the exchange rate to unexpected announcements in official releases of various economic indicators. Of these "data shocks," those in employment reports had the largest effect on interest rates. However, Nordhaus questioned the authors' interpretation of the United States going off the gold standard as an example of quantitative easing, arguing that Roosevelt's action was essentially an exchange rate event. Ben Bernanke replied that that devaluation could indeed be interpreted as a case of quantitative easing, because it freed up the money supply rather than changing relative prices.

References

Adam, Klaus, and Roberto M. Billi. 2004. "Optimal Monetary Policy under Commitment with a Zero Bound on Nominal Interest Rates." Working paper. Frankfurt: European Central Bank (May).

Akerlof, George A., William T. Dickens, and George L. Perry. 1996. "The Macroeconomics of Low Inflation." *BPEA*, no. 1: 1–59.

Andres, Javier, David Lopez-Salido, and Edward Nelson. 2003. "Tobin's Imperfect Asset Substitution in Optimizing General Equilibrium." Presented at the James Tobin Symposium, sponsored by the Journal of Money, Credit, and Banking and the Federal Reserve Bank of Chicago, November 14–15.

Ang, Andrew, and Monika Piazzesi. 2003. "A No-Arbitrage Vector Autoregression of Term Structure Dynamics with Macroeconomic and Latent Variables." *Journal of Monetary Economics* 50: 745–87.

Ang, Andrew, Monika Piazzesi, and Min Wei. 2003. "What Does the Yield Curve Tell Us about GDP Growth?" Working Paper 10672. Cambridge, Mass.: National Bureau of Economic Research (October).

Auerbach, Alan J., and William G. Gale. 2000. "Perspectives on the Budget Surplus." *National Tax Journal* 53, no. 3, part 1: 459–72.

Auerbach, Alan, and Maurice Obstfeld. 2004. "The Case for Open Market Purchases in a Liquidity Trap." Working paper. University of California, Berkeley (May).

Baba, Naohiko, and others. 2004. "Japan's Deflation, Problems in the Financial System, and Monetary Policy." Paper presented at a Bank for International Settlements conference on Understanding Low Inflation and Deflation, Brunnen, Switzerland, June 19.

Benhabib, Jess, Stephanie Schmitt-Grohé, and Martin Uribe. 2002. "Avoiding Liquidity Traps." *Journal of Political Economy* 110, no. 3: 535–63.

Bernanke, Ben S. 2000. "Japanese Monetary Policy: A Case of Self-Induced Paralysis?" In *Japan's Financial Crisis and Its Parallels to U.S. Experience,* edited by Adam Posen and Ryoichi Mikitani. Special Report 13. Washington: Institute for International Economics.

_____. 2002. "Deflation: Making Sure 'It' Doesn't Happen Here." Remarks before the National Economists' Club, Washington, November 21 (www.federalreserve.gov/boarddocs/speeches/2002/20021121/default.htm).

_____. 2003. "Some Thoughts on Monetary Policy in Japan." Speech to the Japan Society of Monetary Economics, Tokyo, May 31 (www.federalreserve.gov/boarddocs/speeches/2003/20030531/default.htm).

Bernanke, Ben, and Kenneth Kuttner. Forthcoming. "Why Does Monetary Policy Affect the Stock Market?" *Journal of Finance.*

Bernanke, Ben, and Vincent Reinhart. 2004. "Conducting Monetary Policy at Very Low Short-Term Interest Rates." *American Economic Review* 94, no. 2: 85–90.

Blinder, Alan. 2000. "Monetary Policy at the Zero Lower Bound: Balancing the Risks: Summary Panel." *Journal of Money, Credit, and Banking* 32, no. 4: 1093–99.

Bolder, David J. 2001. "Affine Term-Structure Models: Theory and Implementation." Working Paper 2001-15. Ottawa: Bank of Canada.

Bomfim, Antulio N. 2003. "Interest Rates as Options: Assessing the Markets' View of the Liquidity Trap." Working paper. Washington: Board of Governors of the Federal Reserve System (July).

Brainard, William C., and James Tobin. 1968. "Pitfalls in Financial Model-Building." *American Economic Review* 58, no. 2: 99–122.

Clouse, James, and others. 2003. "Monetary Policy When the Nominal Short-Term Interest Rate Is Zero." *Topics in Macroeconomics* 3, no. 1, article 12 (www.bepress.com/bejm/topics/vol3/iss1/art12).

Coenen, Günter, Athanasios Orphanides, and Volker Wieland. 2004. "Price Stability and Monetary Policy Effectiveness When Nominal Interest Rates Are Bounded at Zero." *Advances in Macroeconomics,* 4, no. 1, article 1 (www.bepress.com/bejm/advances/vol4/iss1/art1).

Cox, John C., Jonathan E. Ingersoll, Jr., and Stephen A. Ross. 1985. "A Theory of the Term Structure of Interest Rates." *Econometrica* 53, no. 2: 385–407 (March).

Duffie, Darrell, and Rui Kan. 1996. "A Yield-Factor Model of Interest Rates." *Mathematical Finance,* 6, no. 4: 379–406.

Eggertsson, Gauti, and Michael Woodford. 2003a. "The Zero Bound on Interest Rates and Optimal Monetary Policy." *BPEA,* no. 1: 139–211.

———. 2003b. "Optimal Monetary Policy in a Liquidity Trap." Working Paper 9968. Cambridge, Mass.: National Bureau of Economic Research (September).

Eichengreen, Barry J. 1992. *Golden Fetters: The Gold Standard and the Great Depression, 1919–1939.* New York: Oxford University Press.

Eichengreen, Barry, and Peter Garber. 1991. "Before the Accord: U.S. Monetary-Financial Policy, 1945–51." In *Financial Markets and Financial Crisis,* edited by R. Glenn Hubbard. University of Chicago Press.

Feldstein, Martin. 1997. "The Costs and Benefits of Going from Low Inflation to Price Stability." In *Reducing Inflation: Motivation and Strategy,* edited by Christina Romer and David Romer. University of Chicago Press.

Fischer, Stanley. 1996. "Why Are Central Banks Pursuing Long-Run Price Stability?" In *Achieving Price Stability.* Kansas City: Federal Reserve Bank of Kansas City.

Fisher, Mark, Douglas W. Nychka, and David Zervos. 1995. "Fitting the Term Structure of Interest Rates with Smoothing Splines." Finance and Economics Discussion Paper 95-1. Washington: Board of Governors of the Federal Reserve System.

Friedman, Benjamin M., and Kenneth N. Kuttner. 1998. "Indicator Properties of the Paper-Bill Spread: Lessons from Recent Experience." *Review of Economics and Statistics* 80, no. 1: 34–44.

Friedman, Milton. 1969. *The Optimum Quantity of Money and Other Essays.* Chicago: Aldine.

Fujiki, Hiroshi, and Shigenori Shiratsuka. 2002. "Policy Duration Effect under the Zero Interest Rate Policy in 1999–2000: Evidence from Japan's Money Market Data." *Monetary and Economic Studies* 20, no. 1: 1–31.

Gürkaynak, Refet, Brian Sack, and Eric Swanson. Forthcoming. "The Sensitivity of Long-Term Interest Rates to Economic News: Evidence and Implications for Macroeconomic Models." *American Economic Review.*

Hodrick, Robert J. 1992. "Dividend Yields and Expected Stock Returns: Alternative Procedures for Inference and Measurement." *Review of Financial Studies* 5, no. 3: 357–86.

Holland, Thomas E. 1969. " 'Operation Twist' and the Movement of Interest Rates and Related Economic Time Series." *International Economic Review* 10, no. 3: 260–65.

Hutchinson, William K., and Mark Toma. 1991. "The Bond Price Support Program as a Change in Policy Regimes: Evidence from the Term Structure of Interest Rates." *Journal of Money, Credit, and Banking* 23, no. 3: 367–82.

Jeanne, Olivier, and Lars E. O. Svensson. 2004. "Credible Commitment to Optimal Escape from a Liquidity Trap: The Role of the Balance Sheet of an Independent Central Bank." Working paper. Princeton University (July). (www.princeton.edu/~svensson/papers/js.pdf).

Kimura, Takeshi, and others. 2002. "The Effect of the Increase in Monetary Base on Japan's Economy at Zero Interest Rates: An Empirical Analysis." IMES Discussion Paper Series 2002-E-22. Tokyo: Bank of Japan (December).

Kohn, Donald L., and Brian P. Sack. 2003. "Central Bank Talk: Does It Matter and Why?" Finance and Economics Discussion Series 2003-55. Washington: Board of Governors of the Federal Reserve System (August).

Krugman, Paul. 1998. "It's Baaack! Japan's Slump and the Return of the Liquidity Trap." *BPEA,* no. 2: 137–87.

Kuttner, Kenneth N. 2001. "Monetary Policy Surprises and Interest Rates: Evidence from the Fed Funds Futures Market." *Journal of Monetary Economics* 47, no. 3: 523–44.

Longstaff, F. A., and E. S. Schwartz. 1992. "A Two-Factor Interest Rate Model and Contingent Claims Evaluation." *Journal of Fixed Income* 2, no. 3: 16–23.

Marumo, Kohei, and others. 2003. "Extracting Market Expectations on the Duration of the Zero Interest Rate Policy from Japan's Bond Prices." Financial Markets Department Working Paper 03-E-2. Tokyo: Bank of Japan (July).

Meltzer, Allan H. 1999. "Comments: What More Can the Bank of Japan Do?" Bank of Japan, *Monetary and Economic Studies* 17, no. 3: 189–91.

————. 2001. "Monetary Transmission at Low Inflation: Some Clues from Japan in the 1990s." Bank of Japan, *Monetary and Economic Studies* 19, S-1: 13–34.

Modigliani, Franco, and Richard Sutch. 1966. "Innovations in Interest Rate Policy." *American Economic Review* 56, no. 1/2: 178–97.

————. 1967. "Debt Management and the Term Structure of Interest Rates: An Empirical Analysis of Recent Experience." *Journal of Political Economy* 75, no. 4, part 2: 569–89.

Nagayasu, Jun. 2004. "The Term Structure of Interest Rates and Monetary Policy during a Zero Interest Rate Period." Bank of Japan, *Monetary and Economic Studies* 22, no. 2: 19–43.

Okina, Kunio, and Shigenori Shiratsuka. 2004. "Policy Commitment and Expectation Formation: Japan's Experience under Zero Interest Rates." *North American Journal of Economics and Finance* 15, no. 1: 75–100.

Phelps, Edmund S. 1972. *Inflation Policy and Unemployment Theory.* London: Macmillan.

Reifschneider, David, and John C. Williams. 2000. "Three Lessons for Monetary Policy in a Low-Inflation Era." *Journal of Money, Credit, and Banking* 32, no. 4, part 2: 936–66.

Reinhart, Vincent, and Brian Sack. 2000. "The Economic Consequences of Disappearing Government Debt." *BPEA*, no. 2: 163–209.

Roley, V. Vance. 1982. "The Effect of Federal Debt-Management Policy on Corporate Bond and Equity Yields." *Quarterly Journal of Economics* 97, no. 4: 645–68.

Romer, Christina D. 1992. "What Ended the Great Depression?" *Journal of Economic History* 52, no. 4: 757–84.

Rudebusch, Glenn D., and Tao Wu. 2003. "A Macro-Finance Model of the Term Structure, Monetary Policy, and the Economy." Working Paper 2003-17. Federal Reserve Bank of San Francisco (September).

Ruge-Murcia, Francisco J. 2002. "Some Implications of the Zero Lower Bound on Interest Rates for the Term Structure and Monetary Policy." Cahier 06-2002. Université de Montreal.

Sargent, Thomas J., and Neil Wallace. 1975. " 'Rational' Expectations, the Optimal Monetary Instrument, and the Optimal Money Supply Rule." *Journal of Political Economy* 83, no. 2: 241–54.

Shirakawa, Masaaki. 2002. "One Year under 'Quantitative Easing.' " IMES Discussion Paper 2002-E-3. Tokyo: Bank of Japan (April).

Summers, Lawrence. 1991. "Panel Discussion: How Should Long-Term Monetary Policy Be Determined?" *Journal of Money, Credit, and Banking* 23, no. 3, part 2: 625–31.

Svensson, Lars E. O. 2001. "The Zero Bound in an Open Economy: A Foolproof Way of Escaping from a Liquidity Trap." Bank of Japan, *Monetary and Economic Studies* 19, S-1: 277–312.

———. 2003. "Escaping from a Liquidity Trap and Deflation: The Foolproof Way and Others." *Journal of Economic Perspectives* 17, no. 4: 145–66.

———. 2004. "The Magic of the Exchange Rate: Optimal Escape from a Liquidity Trap in Small and Large Open Economies." Working paper. Princeton University. (www.princeton.edu/~svensson/papers/mag.pdf[July].)

Takeda, Yosuke, and Yasuhide Yajima. 2002. "How the Japanese Government Bond Market Has Responded to the Zero Interest Rate Policy." Tokyo: NLI Research Institute (www.nli-research.co.jp/eng/resea/econo/eco020903.pdf [December 2004]).

Temin, Peter, and Barrie Wigmore. 1990. "The End of One Big Deflation." *Explorations in Economic History* 27 (October): 483–502.

Tobin, James. 1963. "An Essay on Principles of Debt Management." In Commission on Money and Credit, *Fiscal and Debt Management Policies* (cowles.econ.yale.edu/P/cp/p01b/p0195.pdf).

———. 1969. "A General Equilibrium Approach to Monetary Theory." *Journal of Money, Credit, and Banking* 1, no. 1: 15–29.

———. 1974. *The New Economics: One Decade Older.* Princeton University Press.

Toma, Mark. 1992. "Interest Rate Controls: The United States in the 1940s." *Journal of Economic History* 52, no. 3: 631–50.

Vasicek, Oldrich. 1977. "An Equilibrium Characterization of the Term Structure." *Journal of Financial Economics* 5: 177–88.

Woodford, Michael. 2003. *Interest and Prices: Foundations of a Theory of Monetary Policy.* Princeton University Press.

WILLIAM G. GALE
Brookings Institution

PETER R. ORSZAG
Brookings Institution

Budget Deficits, National Saving, and Interest Rates

ECONOMIC ANALYSIS OF the aggregate effects of fiscal policy dates back at least to the work of David Ricardo. Modern academic interest was reinvigorated by the work of Robert Barro and others and by the emergence of large U.S. federal budget deficits in the 1980s and early 1990s.[1] The result was a substantial amount of research, which is summarized in several excellent surveys.[2] The rapid but short-lived transition to budget surpluses in the late 1990s, followed by the sharp reversal in budget outcomes since 2000, has raised interest in this topic again.

Economists tend to view the aggregate effects of fiscal policy from one of three perspectives. To sharpen the distinctions among them, it is helpful to consider a deficit induced by a lump-sum tax cut today followed by a lump-sum tax increase in the future, holding the path of government purchases and marginal tax rates constant. Under the Ricardian equivalence hypothesis proposed by Barro, such a deficit will be fully offset by an increase in private saving, as taxpayers recognize that the tax is merely postponed, not canceled. The offsetting increase in private saving means that the deficit will have no effect on national saving, interest rates,

We thank Christopher House for exceptionally helpful comments and discussions; Emil Apostolov, Matt Hall, Brennan Kelly, and Melody Keung for outstanding research assistance; Alan Auerbach, Robert Cumby, William Dickens, Douglas Elmendorf, Eric Engen, Laurence Kotlikoff, Thomas Laubach, William Nordhaus, David Pattison, Maria Perozek, Frank Russek, John Seater, Matthew Shapiro, and David Wilcox for comments; and Eric Engen, Jane Gravelle, and Thomas Laubach for sharing data.

1. Barro (1974).
2. See Barro (1989), Barth and others (1991), Bernheim (1987, 1989), Elmendorf and Mankiw (1999), and Seater (1993).

exchange rates, future domestic production, or future national income. A second model, the small open economy view, suggests that budget deficits do reduce national saving but, at the same time, induce increased capital inflows from abroad that finance the entire reduction. As a result, domestic production does not decline and interest rates do not rise, but future national income falls because of the added burden of servicing the increased foreign debt. A third model, which we call the conventional view, likewise holds that deficits reduce national saving but that this reduction is at least partly reflected in lower domestic investment. In this model, budget deficits partly crowd out private investment and partly increase borrowing from abroad; the combined effect reduces future national income and future domestic production. The reduction in domestic investment in this model is brought about by an increase in interest rates, thus establishing a connection between deficits and interest rates.

We emphasize throughout this paper that the relationship between deficits and national saving is central to the analysis of the economic effects of fiscal policy. National saving, which is the sum of private and government saving, finances national investment, which is the sum of domestic investment and net foreign investment.[3] The accumulation of assets, whether located in the United States or abroad, associated with national saving means that the capital stock owned by Americans rises. The returns to those additional assets raise the income of Americans in the future.

An increase in the budget deficit reduces national saving unless it is fully offset by an increase in private saving. If national saving falls, national investment and future national income must fall as well, all else equal. Therefore, to the extent that budget deficits reduce national saving, they reduce future national income. This reduction occurs even if there is no increase in domestic interest rates. In that case the reduction in national saving associated with budget deficits manifests itself solely in increased borrowing from abroad (the outcome under the small open economy view). This is the sense in which the effect of deficits on interest rates and exchange rates (which distinguishes the small open economy view from the conventional view) is subsidiary to the question of the

---

3. Domestic investment represents the accumulation of assets in a country by both its own residents and foreigners. Net foreign investment is the accumulation of assets abroad by residents less the accumulation of assets in the home country by foreigners. The sum of the two is just the accumulation of assets, by residents, in the home country and abroad. This sum must equal national saving.

effect on national saving (to which the Ricardian view gives a different answer than the other two).

A key objective of this paper is to generate tests of the empirical effects of budget deficits on national saving and interest rates and therefore to help distinguish among the three models empirically. We test the Ricardian view against the small open economy and conventional views by estimating the effect on national saving of budget deficits associated with tax reductions, after controlling for government purchases, transfers, marginal tax rates, and other factors. Our empirical results imply that an increase in the budget deficit substantially reduces national saving: specifically, after controlling for other factors, a one-dollar increase in the deficit reduces national saving by between 50 and 80 cents. This suggests that the Ricardian view is not a good approximation to reality.

We then test the small open economy view against the conventional view by examining whether deficits affect interest rates. Our results suggest that the emergence of larger projected budget deficits raises long-term interest rates in the United States. Specifically, we find that a sustained increase in the projected unified deficit equal to 1 percent of GDP raises interest rates by 25 to 35 basis points,[4] and a sustained increase of that magnitude in the projected primary deficit (the unified deficit excluding interest payments) raises interest rates by 40 to 70 basis points. Indeed, despite a rancorous public debate, there appears to be a surprising degree of convergence in recent estimates of the effects of fiscal policy on interest rates: results from a variety of econometric studies imply that an increase in the unified deficit of 1 percent of GDP, sustained over ten years, would raise interest rates by 30 to 60 basis points. This estimated relationship between deficits and interest rates not only provides further evidence against the Ricardian view, but also implies that the conventional view is a better description of reality for the United States than the small open economy view.

A second objective of the paper is to apply these findings to an analysis of recent and proposed or expected future fiscal policy actions. Under plausible assumptions described below, the unified deficit over the next decade will average about 3.5 percent of GDP. Our estimates imply that such deficits will reduce national saving over that period by between 2 and 3 percent of GDP. Therefore, after ten years, assets held by Americans will be

---

4. Except where stated otherwise, "deficit" refers to the unified deficit, which includes the deficit or surplus in Social Security and Medicare and net interest payments.

lower, by 20 to 30 percent of GDP, than they otherwise would be; with a rate of return on capital in the range of 6 percent, this implies that national income will be between 1 and 2 percent lower on an ongoing basis by 2015. This suggests that current fiscal policy trends will exert a significant drag on future economic performance and living standards. In addition, our estimated interest rate effects imply that making the 2001 and 2003 tax cuts permanent would raise interest rates by enough to raise the cost of capital for new investment even after taking account of the direct effects of the tax cuts, which means that long-term investment and economic growth would fall.

The first section of the paper describes recent historical patterns and current projections for the federal debt, deficits, and their components. The second section provides a framework for evaluating fiscal policy by comparing the three models identified above and by discussing several other ways in which deficits can affect economic performance. The third section provides a preliminary empirical analysis, whose results generally support the conventional view, and gives a sense of the magnitude of the effects of fiscal policy under the conventional approach in a simplified model. The fourth section examines the effects of deficits on aggregate consumption, and the fifth section explores the links between deficits and interest rates. We conclude by discussing some of the implications of our findings.

Fiscal Policy: Trends and Projections

The federal budget deficit in any year can be measured in a variety of ways; the most appropriate measure is likely to depend on the particular model or application of interest. The most widely used measure, the unified budget balance, is fundamentally a cash-flow metric that includes both the Social Security and the non–Social Security components of the federal budget. To a first approximation, the unified balance shows the extent to which the federal government borrows or lends in credit markets during the year.[5] For some purposes it is more informative to examine the primary budget balance, which excludes net interest payments. Another

---

5. The unified budget is not recorded entirely on a cash-flow basis, and so the unified deficit does not precisely match the increase in debt held by the public. For example, only the subsidy cost of direct loan transactions is now recorded in the unified budget. The government must, however, finance the full value of the loan. This factor causes the unified budget deficit to be smaller than the increase in debt held by the public.

Figure 1. Actual and Standardized Federal Budget Balance, 1962–2004

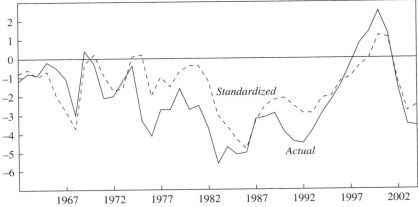

Percent of potential GDP

Sources: Congressional Budget Office, "The Cyclically Adjusted and Standardized Budget Measures" (September 2004).

measure, the standardized budget balance, adjusts the unified budget for the business cycle and certain special items.[6] We focus primarily on these traditional cash-flow measures. In particular, although we recognize the importance of the implicit debt created by promises of future government benefits, we do not incorporate these promises directly into our analysis, in part because historical time series of this accrued debt are not generally available, and in part because it is unclear how the market and households value this implicit debt relative to the government's explicit debt.[7]

Figure 1 shows the surplus or deficit in the federal unified budget and in the standardized budget, both since 1962, as reported by the Congressional Budget Office (CBO).[8] Both measures clearly show an increase in the deficit relative to GDP in the early and mid-1980s, a dramatic correction

6. These include losses due to deposit insurance, receipts from auctions of licenses to use the electromagnetic spectrum, timing adjustments, and the contributions of the United States' allies for Operation Desert Storm (the 1991 Gulf war; Congressional Budget Office, "The Cyclically Adjusted and Standardized Budget Measures," September 2004).

7. Auerbach and others (2003) discuss the relationship among the cash-flow measures, accrual accounting, generational accounting, and other ways of measuring the fiscal status of the government.

8. CBO, "The Cyclically Adjusted and Standardized Budget Measures," September 2004.

Figure 2. **Federal Budget Balance, Projected 2004–14[a]**

Percent of GDP

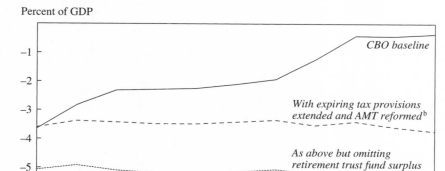

Source: Authors' calculations using Congressional Budget Office, "The Budget and Economic Outlook: An Update" (September 2004), and the TPC Microsimulation Model.
  a. Debt service is imputed using the CBO interest matrix.
  b. Assumes that the 2001 and 2003 tax cuts are made permanent and other expiring tax provisions (except the 2002 tax cuts) extended, and that the AMT is indexed for inflation and dependent exemptions are allowed under the AMT.

over the course of the 1990s, and an equally dramatic deterioration since 2000. In fiscal 2004 the unified deficit was 3.6 percent of potential GDP, and the standardized deficit about 2.5 percent. As the figure shows, deficits of this magnitude are large relative to historical norms. Even so, the current budget situation would not be a concern if future fiscal prospects were auspicious. Unfortunately, those prospects are in fact dismal.

The top line in figure 2 shows the CBO's baseline projections for the deficit in the unified budget as of September 2004.[9] The projections assume that the 2001 and 2003 tax cuts expire as scheduled. Summing the annual projections results in a ten-year baseline unified budget deficit of $2.3 trillion, or 1.5 percent of cumulative GDP over that period, for fiscal 2005 to 2014, with the deficits shrinking over time.

This baseline projection is intended to provide a benchmark for legislative purposes. It is explicitly *not* intended to be a projection of actual or likely budget outcomes or a measure of the financial status of the federal government.[10] Thus adjustments to the baseline are required to generate a

9. CBO, "The Economic and Budget Outlook," January 2004.

more plausible budget scenario and to develop more meaningful measures of the government's financial situation.[11] One concern is that the baseline assumes that all temporary tax provisions expire as scheduled, even though most have been routinely extended in the past. Traditionally, this concern only applied to a small set of policies—such as tax credits for work opportunity or for research and experimentation—that have existed for years, are narrow in scope, and have relatively minor budget costs, and for which extensions occur as a matter of routine. In recent years, however, the distortion created by assuming that all temporary tax provisions will expire as scheduled has grown dramatically, because all of the provisions of the tax cuts in each of the years 2001 through 2004 are scheduled to expire by the end of the decade. These "temporary" provisions are quite different in nature and scope from the other expiring provisions. Whether they will be extended is a major fiscal policy choice, not a matter of routine.[12]

A second concern is that revenue from the alternative minimum tax (AMT) grows dramatically under the baseline, a development that few observers regard as plausible.[13] Finally, the baseline uses cash-flow accounting, which is appropriate for many programs, but which can distort the financial status of programs whose liabilities increase substantially outside the projection period.[14]

Adjusting for these factors has an enormous impact on the ten-year budget projections. Figure 2 shows that, if the 2001, 2002, and 2003 tax cuts are made permanent, if the other expiring tax provisions are extended, and if the AMT problem is resolved (by indexing the AMT for inflation and allowing dependent exemptions, which would still leave 5 million

10. CBO, "The Economic and Budget Outlook," January 2004.

11. See Auerbach and others (2003) for an extended discussion of these issues.

12. See Gale and Orszag (2003b) for further discussion of the expiring provisions, and Gale and Orszag (2004a) on the effects of making the tax cuts permanent.

13. See Burman, Gale, and Rohaly (2003) for discussion of AMT projections and trends.

14. Another concern is that the baseline holds real discretionary spending constant over time. In a growing economy with an expanding population and evolving security needs, this assumption is not credible. But the September 2004 projections contain offsetting biases for discretionary spending that roughly cancel out. In particular, the baseline includes the recent supplemental spending authority for military expenditures in Iraq, which is unlikely to persist for an entire decade. Removing the supplemental and adjusting the spending level for population results in a ten-year outlay total that is about the same as that in the baseline, and so we simply adopt the official baseline figures for discretionary spending.

Figure 3. Public Debt, 1950–2014[a]

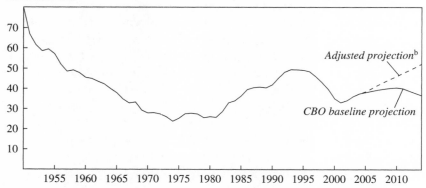

Percent of GDP

Source: Authors' calculations using Congressional Budget Office, "The Budget and Economic Outlook: An Update" (September 2004), OMB, and the TPC Microsimulation Model.
  a. Debt service is imputed using the CBO interest matrix.
  b. Assumes that the 2001 and 2003 tax cuts are made permanent and other expiring tax provisions (except the 2002 tax cuts) extended, and that the AMT is indexed for inflation and dependent exemptions are allowed under the AMT.

households paying the AMT in 2014), then the adjusted unified budget deficit would remain at approximately 3.5 percent of GDP over the decade and would be 3.7 percent of GDP (almost $700 billion) in 2014.[15]

One way to gauge the implications of the adjusted unified baseline is to examine the implied ratio of public debt to GDP, as is done in figure 3. Under the adjusted baseline, the debt-GDP ratio would rise steadily throughout the decade and by 2014 would equal 52 percent, well above the most recent high of 49 percent in 1992, and the highest level since 1956. The debt-GDP ratio would continue to rise thereafter.

The ratio of marketable public debt to GDP tells only part of the long-term budget story, however. Social Security, Medicare part A (the hospital insurance program), and government employee pension programs are projected to run surpluses over the next decade but face shortfalls in the long term. One way to control for these effects is to examine the ten-year

15. These figures include the cost of extending the bonus depreciation provision as specified in the 2003 tax law. Some ambiguity surrounds whether this temporary measure will be extended; its extension was not proposed in the administration's fiscal 2005 budget. If this provision were not extended past its sunset at the end of 2004, the deficit over the decade would be about 3 percent of GDP.

horizon while separating the retirement trust funds from the rest of the budget. For example, the bottom line in figure 2 shows that, omitting the retirement trust funds, the rest of the budget would face deficits of 5.1 percent of GDP over the decade (and 5.3 percent of GDP in 2014) under the assumptions above.

An alternative way to incorporate the entitlement programs is to extend the time horizon of the analysis so that future shortfalls are included. To do this, we report estimates of the fiscal gap, defined as the immediate and permanent increase in taxes or reduction in noninterest expenditure that would be required to establish the same debt-GDP ratio in the long run as holds currently.[16] In an article co-written with Alan Auerbach, we estimate that, under adjustments similar to those made in figure 2, the nation faces a long-term fiscal gap in 2004 of 7.2 percent of GDP through 2080 and 10.5 percent of GDP on a permanent basis.[17] Jagadeesh Gokhale and Kent Smetters have made similar projections, as has the Bush administration.[18]

The main drivers of the fiscal gap, under the above assumptions, are the revenue losses from making the 2001 and 2003 tax cuts permanent and the growth in spending for Medicare, Medicaid, and Social Security. The recent tax cuts, if extended and not eroded over time by the AMT, would cost roughly 2 percent of GDP over the long term.[19] To help put these figures in context, over the next seventy-five years the actuarial deficit in Social Security is 0.7 percent of GDP under the Social Security trustees' assumptions, and 0.4 percent of GDP under new projections issued by the CBO.[20] The deficit in Medicare part A is 1.4 percent of GDP over the next

16. See Auerbach (1994). Over an infinite planning horizon, the requirement is equivalent to assuming that the debt-GDP ratio does not explode. Alternatively, the adjustments set the present value of all future primary surpluses equal to the current value of the national debt, where the primary surplus is the difference between revenue and noninterest expenditure.

17. Auerbach, Gale, and Orszag (2004). In perhaps more familiar terms, the primary deficit would be 4.1 percent of GDP in 2030, 5.5 percent in 2060, and 5.8 percent by 2080; the unified deficit would rise much faster because of accruing interest payments: it would be 13 percent of GDP in 2030, 37 percent by 2060, and 64 percent by 2080. Public debt would be 139 percent of GDP in 2030, 505 percent in 2060, and 942 percent in 2080.

18. Gokhale and Smetters (2003); Office of Management and Budget, *Budget of the United States Government: Fiscal Year 2005 Budget.*

19. Gale and Orszag (2004a).

20. CBO, "The Outlook for Social Security," June 2004. The actuarial deficit in Social Security over an infinite horizon amounts to 1.2 percent of GDP over that horizon under the trustees' assumptions.

Figure 4. Entitlement Expenditure under Current Law, 2003 and Projected 2004–80

Percent of GDP

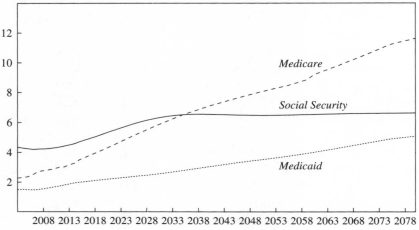

Source: Auerbach, Gale, and Orszag (2004).

seventy-five years under the trustees' assumptions.[21] Thus, extending the tax cuts would reduce revenue over the next seventy-five years by an amount about as large as the entire shortfall in the Social Security and Medicare part A trust funds over the same period.

Even if the tax cuts are not made permanent, however, the fiscal gap would be 5.1 percent of GDP through 2080 and 8.2 percent on a permanent basis. A primary reason is substantial projected increases in entitlement costs. Figure 4 shows the projected increases in Social Security, Medicare (this time including not only part A but also part B, supplementary Medicare insurance, and part D, the new prescription drug benefit), and federal Medicaid costs as a share of GDP over the long term.[22] The projected retirement of the baby boomers, ongoing increases in life expectancy, and growth in health care costs per beneficiary in excess of growth in GDP per capita combine to drive federal expenditure on these three programs from 8.1 per-

21. Unlike with Social Security, the CBO has not issued its own fully independent actuarial analysis of Medicare's long-term finances.
22. Auerbach, Gale, and Orszag (2004). Medicaid is not wholly a federal liability; rather, it is financed in part by the states.

cent of GDP in 2004 to a projected 10.2 percent by 2015, 13.3 percent by 2025, and 22.7 percent by 2075.[23] Figure 4 also shows that the vast majority of the growth occurs in the health-related programs, not in Social Security. Indeed, after about 2030, Social Security costs are roughly stable relative to GDP. The health-related programs not only are projected to increase in cost much more dramatically than Social Security but are also much more difficult to reform.

To be sure, substantial uncertainty surrounds these short- and long-term budget projections. Much of the problem stems from the fact that the surplus or deficit is the difference between two large quantities, revenue and spending. Small percentage errors in either can cause large percentage changes in the difference between them. Furthermore, small differences in growth rates sustained for extended periods can have surprisingly large economic effects. Variations in assumed health care cost inflation, in particular, can have a substantial effect on the projections.[24] Nonetheless, almost all studies that have examined the issue suggest that, even if major sources of uncertainty are accounted for, serious long-term fiscal imbalances will remain.[25]

The Economic Effects of Budget Deficits

We categorize the effects of budget deficits into two types. What we here call the "traditional" effects are those described in terms of changes in the usual macroeconomic aggregates, such as consumption, saving, and investment, resulting from the linkages among them as described in macroeconomics textbooks. The Ricardian view, the small open economy view, and the "conventional" view of deficits all address these kinds of effects. The "nontraditional" effects include the effects of weakened investor confidence in a country's economic leadership due to increased deficits, the possible threshold effect of a sudden change in investor perceptions of

23. Although it is clear that entitlement spending is a major factor in generating long-term fiscal shortfalls, it is not straightforward to determine how much of the fiscal gap is due to these programs, because to a large extent they are supposed to be funded from general revenue. Auerbach, Gale, and Orszag (2004) examine different ways of decomposing the long-term fiscal gap.
24. CBO, "The Long-Term Budget Outlook," December 2003.
25. For example, see Lee and Edwards (2001) and Shoven (2002).

the sustainability of a country's deficits, and those effects that go beyond the strictly economic realm, such as the effect of a country's debtor or creditor status on its international power and influence.

Traditional Models

Figure 5 summarizes the three "traditional" views of deficits, at least as they apply to a deficit created by changes in the timing of a lump-sum tax, holding the path of government purchases constant, as described earlier. Under Ricardian equivalence, private saving rises in response to the deficit by the same amount that government saving falls (that is, by the same amount that the deficit rises); national saving is therefore constant, and no further adjustments are required or expected.[26]

If private saving rises by less than the full amount that public saving falls, then national saving falls, and further adjustments are required to bring national saving and the sum of domestic and net foreign investment back into balance.[27] If the flow of capital from overseas is infinitely elastic, the entire quantity adjustment occurs through increased capital inflows. In this case net foreign investment declines, but the domestic capital stock remains constant. With no change in the domestic capital stock, domestic output (GDP) is likewise constant. Americans' claims on that output, however, decline because the increased borrowing from abroad must be repaid in the future. In other words, the obligation to repay effectively creates a mortgage against future national income; as a result, future gross *national* product declines even though gross *domestic* product is constant.[28] Because the capital inflow in this example is assumed to be infinitely elastic, inter-

26. Barro (1974).

27. The effects described in response to a change in the deficit would all occur simultaneously. Our ordering of the discussion is intended merely to provide a way of thinking about the channels through which deficits affect the economy. It does not imply or require that the effects occur in any particular order over time.

28. The distinction between domestic investment and net foreign investment is of secondary importance in determining national income (GNP), although it clearly affects domestic income (GDP). Elmendorf and Mankiw (1999, p. 1637) note that, "As long as the returns to wealth are the same at home and abroad, the location of the . . . [change in] wealth does not affect our income. . . . Tomorrow's national output and income depend on today's national saving, wherever this saving is ultimately invested." They also note several caveats to this statement, including differences in the tax implications of investment abroad relative to investment at home, and implications for income distribution.

Figure 5. Theoretical Responses to a Change in the Budget Deficit

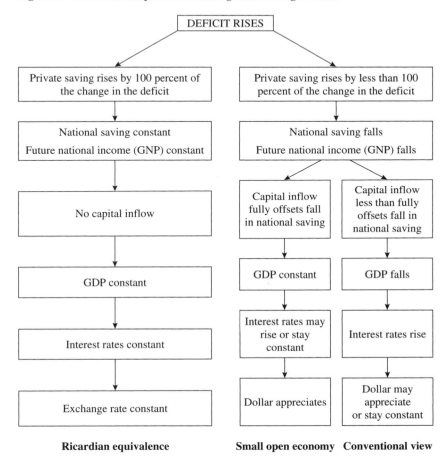

est rates do not change. Even so, larger deficits reduce future national income (GNP). We refer to this scenario as the small open economy view.

A third possibility is that the supply of international capital is not infinitely elastic. In this case, if national saving falls in response to an increased budget deficit, the relative price and quantity adjustments are different than under the small open economy model, but the end result—a decline in future national income—remains the same. In the absence of perfect capital mobility, the reduction in national saving implies a shortage of funds to finance investment, given existing interest rates and exchange rates. That imbalance puts upward pressure on interest rates, as firms compete for the limited pool of funds to finance investment. The increase in interest rates serves to reduce domestic investment. In a closed economy, the entire adjustment to the reduction in national saving would occur through reduced domestic investment. In an open economy with imperfect capital mobility, the decline in national saving and the resulting rise in interest rates induce some combination of a decline in domestic investment and a decline in net foreign investment (that is, an increase in capital inflows). These changes must be sufficient to ensure that the change in national investment equals the change in national saving. Following Douglas Elmendorf and Gregory Mankiw, we refer to this scenario as the conventional view.[29]

Nontraditional Effects

Beyond their traditional effects on national saving, future national income, and interest rates, deficits can affect the economy in other ways. For example, increased deficits may cause investors to gradually lose confidence in U.S. economic leadership. As Edwin Truman emphasizes,[30] a substantial fiscal deterioration over the longer term may cause "a loss of confidence in the orientation of US economic policies." Such a loss in confidence could then put upward pressure on domestic interest rates, as investors demand a higher risk premium on dollar-denominated assets. The costs of current account deficits—which are in part induced by large budget deficits—may even extend beyond the economic costs narrowly defined. Benjamin Friedman notes that, "World power and influence have historically accrued to creditor countries. It is not coincidental that America emerged as a world power simultaneously with our transition from a debtor nation . . . to a creditor supplying investment capital to the rest of the world."[31]

Both the traditional models and the analysis of nontraditional effects focus on gradual negative effects from reduced national saving. This focus may be too limited, however, in that it ignores the possibility of much more sudden and severe adverse consequences.[32] In particular, the

29. Elmendorf and Mankiw (1999).
30. Truman (2001).
31. Friedman (1988, p. 76).
32. Rubin, Orszag, and Sinai (2004).

traditional analysis of budget deficits in large advanced economies does not seriously entertain the possibility of explicit default, or of implicit default through high inflation.[33] If market expectations regarding the avoidance of default were to change and investors had difficulty seeing how the policy process could avoid extreme measures, the consequences could be much more sudden and severe than traditional estimates suggest. The role of financial market expectations in this type of scenario is central. One of the principal ways in which such a "hard landing" could be triggered is if investors begin to doubt whether a country will maintain its strong historical commitment to avoiding high inflation in order to reduce the real value of the public debt. As Laurence Ball and Mankiw note,

> We can only guess what level of debt will trigger a shift in investor confidence, and about the nature and severity of the effects. Despite the vagueness of fears about hard landings, these fears may be the most important reason for seeking to reduce budget deficits . . . as countries increase their debt, they wander into unfamiliar territory in which hard landings may lurk. If policymakers are prudent, they will not take the chance of learning what hard landings in G-7 countries are really like.[34]

Although we do not explicitly incorporate nontraditional effects in our analysis below, they serve as an important reminder of why budget deficits, especially chronic deficits, could exert large adverse effects on U.S. economic performance. Our focus on traditional effects is certainly justifiable in the context of a historical analysis of postwar data from the United States. That does not imply, however, that ignoring such issues is appropriate when examining the likely impacts of future deficits. The nation has never before faced the prospect of deficits that are large, sustained, and indeed likely to grow over many decades.

---

33. The traditional view also suggests that either the exchange rate would stay constant or the currency would appreciate in response to the inflow of capital from abroad. The sign of the exchange rate change, however, is unclear in the presence of changes in a country-specific risk premium. If that premium increases as a country's net international indebtedness (or flow of new international borrowing) increases, the country's currency could depreciate. In other words, although nontraditional effects are likely to accentuate the impact of deficits on interest rates, they may alter even the sign of the exchange rate dynamics.

34. Ball and Mankiw (1995, p. 117).

Figure 6. Net National Saving and Net Federal Saving, 1950–2003

Percent of net national product

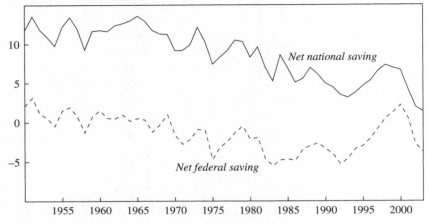

Source: Bureau of Economic Analysis, National Income and Product Accounts.

Preliminary Evidence and Benchmark Calculations

The first part of this section sets up the later analysis of deficits, national saving, and interest rates by providing prima facie evidence of the relationships among them that are consistent with the conventional view but hard to reconcile with the small open economy view or the Ricardian view. The second part then provides some benchmark calculations that give a sense of the magnitudes involved.

A Preliminary Examination of the Data

Figure 6 shows net national saving and net federal government saving as shares of net national product (NNP) since 1950.[35] Federal saving has fluctuated significantly over time, and this variation is visibly correlated

---

35. Net national saving is defined as gross saving minus depreciation of the capital stock and is taken from the National Income and Product Accounts, table 5.1, line 2. Net federal saving is defined as gross federal saving minus depreciation on the federal government's physical capital stock and is taken from the same table, line 11.

Figure 7. Net Domestic Investment and Net National Saving, 1950–2003

Percent of net national product

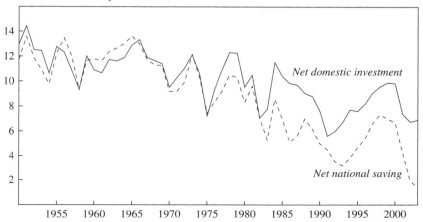

Source: Bureau of Economic Analysis, National Income and Product Accounts.

with swings in national saving. The correlation is especially apparent in the last two decades. The two series both rise moderately in the mid-1980s, decline from the late 1980s to the early 1990s, rise significantly during the 1990s, and then decline again over the past few years. Over the whole period, a regression of national saving on federal saving (each expressed as a share of NNP) yields a coefficient of 1.02 ($t = 7$), and an equivalent first-differences regression (regressing changes in the national saving–NNP ratio on changes in the federal saving–NNP ratio) yields a coefficient of 0.86 ($t = 9$).[36]

Figure 7 shows net national saving and net domestic investment since 1950, again as shares of NNP.[37] The two series follow very similar patterns over time. Domestic investment has declined by less than national saving over the past twenty years and has exceeded national saving in every year since the early 1980s. The difference is reflected in chronic current account

36. Both regressions include a constant term, as do those mentioned in the next two paragraphs.

37. Net domestic investment is equal to gross investment minus depreciation of the capital stock and is taken from the National Income and Product Accounts, table 5.1, line 31.

deficits (not shown) and a substantial decline in the nation's net international investment position.[38] Over the past few years, the decline in national saving has been much sharper than the decline in net domestic investment. Between 1998 and 2003, national saving declined by 6 percent of NNP, with about half of the decline made up by increased capital inflows, and half by reduced net domestic investment. A regression of the net domestic investment–NNP ratio on the net national saving–NNP ratio yields a coefficient of 0.57 ($t = 15$). When the regression is performed on first differences of the two measures, the coefficient is 0.83 ($t = 10$).[39]

Figure 8 plots annual observations of the projected five-year-ahead real ten-year interest rate on Treasury bonds against the CBO's projections of the unified federal deficit as a share of GDP five years ahead.[40] Figure 9 shows similar observations for real forward long-term rates and projections of the publicly held debt. Both figures show a clear association between projected fiscal policy outcomes and forward long-term real interest rates. A regression of the two series in figure 8 implies that an increase in the projected deficit by 1 percent of GDP is associated with an increase in the forward rate of about 27 basis points ($t = 5$).

Figures 6 through 9 suggest a very simple story: Increases in current federal budget deficits significantly reduce net national saving. This reduction in national saving is reflected partly in increased borrowing from abroad and partly in reduced net domestic investment. Increases in projected future federal deficits raise long-term interest rates, which explains how reductions in national saving serve to reduce domestic investment. These patterns are consistent with the conventional view, but not with the Ricardian or the small open economy view. A primary goal of the paper is to see how robust these simple relationships are to more formal analysis.

38. The current account, as defined by the "net lending" series published by the Bureau of Economic Analysis, ran a small surplus in 1991, in part because of capital account transactions related to the Gulf war and in part because of a large statistical discrepancy. On a current-cost basis, the United States has gone from being the world's largest creditor nation in 1980, with a net international investment position (NIIP) of 13 percent of GDP, to the world's largest debtor nation, with an NIIP of about −22 percent of GDP at the end of 2003. On a market-value basis, the NIIP was 7 percent of GDP in 1982, falling to −24 percent at the end of 2003 (Bureau of Economic Analysis, National Income and Product Accounts, table 1.1.5, 2004).

39. The positive correlation between domestic saving and domestic investment mirrors the findings of a long line of research initiated by Feldstein and Horioka (1980).

40. The data in the figure are described in more detail later in the paper.

Figure 8. Forward Ten-Year Real Treasury Rates and Projected Deficits, 1976–2004[a]

Interest rate (percent a year)

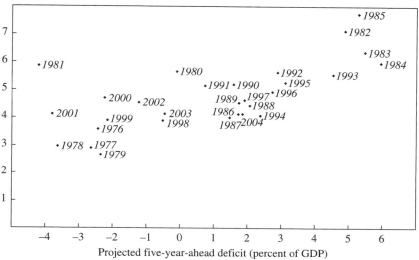

Projected five-year-ahead deficit (percent of GDP)

Source: Laubach (2003).
a. Projected deficits as constructed by Laubach (2003).

The Magnitude of Conventional Effects in Two Simplified Models

To generate some intuition about the potential magnitudes involved in the conventional approach, we examine the impact of budget deficits in two simplified models. Before turning to these models, however, we must first address a key issue: If fiscal policy does influence interest rates, does it do so through changes in government deficits (what we call the "flow perspective") or through changes in the government debt (the "stock perspective")? According to Eric Engen and Glenn Hubbard,[41] government debt rather than deficits should affect the level of interest rates. However, since many models (including the IS-LM model widely taught to undergraduates) imply that budget deficits affect interest rates, we take a broader view. Throughout this paper we leave open the possibility that either the stock perspective or the flow perspective may be valid. In this section we there-

41. Engen and Hubbard (2004).

Figure 9. Forward Ten-Year Real Treasury Rates and Projected Debt, 1976–2004ª

Interest rate (percent a year)

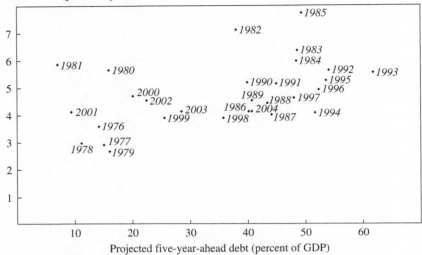

Projected five-year-ahead debt (percent of GDP)

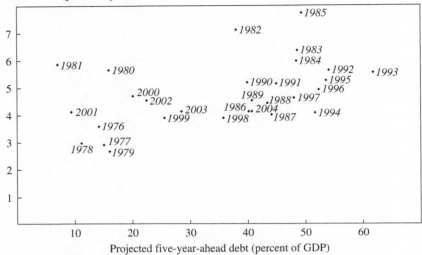

Source: Laubach (2003).
a. Projected debt as constructed by Laubach (2003).

fore undertake two related calibration exercises. One focuses on the impact of the deficit in a Solow model of economic growth, and the other on the impact of debt in a highly stylized steady-state exercise.

First, we follow Matthew Shapiro and examine the effects of sustained budget deficits in the context of the Solow growth model.[42] Following Mankiw,[43] we assume that the economy's growth rate (the sum of the rate of population growth and that of output per worker) is equal to 3 percent a year, the depreciation rate is 4 percent a year, and the capital share of output is 30 percent. We also assume that the initial gross national saving rate is 17.5 percent of output.[44] This level for the saving rate could, for example, reflect a private gross saving rate of 20 percent of output and a unified budget deficit of 2.5 percent, which are the values we assume for

42. Shapiro (2004).
43. Mankiw (2000a, p. 123).
44. Mankiw assumes a capital-output ratio of 2.5 and then solves for the saving rate. The implied saving rate is 17.5 percent.

Table 1. Steady-State Effects of an Increased Budget Deficit in the Solow Growth Model
Percent except where stated otherwise

Parameter	Assumed initial value	*Value in new steady state following increase in deficit of 1 percent of output, offset by private saving as indicated*		
		Offset = 25 percent	*Offset = 0 percent*	*Offset = 50 percent*
Capital share of output	30.0	30.0	30.0	30.0
Annual depreciation rate	4.0	4.0	4.0	4.0
Annual GDP growth rate	3.0	3.0	3.0	3.0
National saving as share of GDP	17.5	16.75	16.5	17.0
Private saving as share of GDP	20.0	20.25	20.0	20.5
Budget deficit as share of GDP	2.5	3.5	3.5	3.5
Income per capita	1.48	1.45	1.44	1.46
Capital-output ratio	2.5	2.39	2.36	2.43
Marginal product of capital	12.0	12.5	12.7	12.4

Source: Authors' calculations.

illustrative purposes. These assumptions generate an initial steady state with a capital-output ratio of 2.5 and a gross marginal product of capital of 12 percent, which are reasonable values for the United States (table 1).

Now assume that the unified budget deficit rises by 1 percent of output on a sustained basis.[45] Suppose that one-quarter of this decline in public saving is offset by an increase in private saving.[46] With this response, private saving rises to 20.25 percent of output, and the national saving rate declines to 16.75 percent. Given the reduction in national saving, output per capita in the new steady state is reduced by 1.9 percent. The marginal product of capital is 54 basis points higher. If we assume that the change

45. Note that this simplified model does not impose a government budget constraint. As a result, we do not have to specify how the tax cut is paid for.

46. This private saving response is somewhat larger than might be expected based on the data patterns in figure 6, but it is within the range of the econometric estimates we report below. It is also roughly consistent with the calculations undertaken by the Council of Economic Advisers (*Economic Report of the President,* 2003) in the Bush administration, which reports that a one-dollar increase in the deficit reduces the domestic capital stock by about 60 cents. The Council's scenario could occur, for example, if a one-dollar increase in the deficit causes private saving to rise by 25 cents (the effect we assume) and international capital flows offset an additional 15 cents of the decline in national saving. Dennis and others (2004) make similar assumptions about private saving and capital flow offsets in modeling the macroeconomy. See Feldstein and Horioka (1980) and Dornbusch (1991) for analyses of the relationship between capital inflows and national saving.

in the interest rate at which government borrows is equal to the change in the marginal product of capital, the implication is that the increase in the unified budget deficit raises the interest rate by 54 basis points.

These results provide one way of calibrating the traditional effects of changes in the budget deficit. Under our base case assumptions, holding other factors constant, a sustained increase in the unified deficit of 1 percent of GDP reduces output by about 2 percent and raises interest rates by about 50 basis points. If half of the decline in public saving, rather than one-quarter, is offset by an increase in private saving, long-term output per capita would decline by 1.2 percent and interest rates would rise by 35 basis points. If there is no private saving response, output per capita would fall by 2.5 percent, and the marginal product of capital would rise by 73 basis points. (Table 1 summarizes these results.)

The Solow model exercise underscores the somewhat arbitrary nature of choosing between the stock and flow perspectives described above: In the steady state of the Solow model, deficits and debt are linked, making it difficult to assert that one variable rather than the other is the one that influences interest rates. Nonetheless, since our Solow analysis was presented in terms of the flow variable (the deficit), we also undertake a closely related exercise framed in terms of the stock variable (government debt). In steady state the debt-GDP ratio is equal to the unified deficit–GDP ratio divided by the GDP growth rate.[47] Assuming a 3 percent growth rate as in the Solow model exercise above, an increase in the unified deficit-GDP ratio of 1 percent of GDP would thus raise the steady-state debt–GDP ratio by approximately 33 percentage points.

To map this increase in the debt-GDP ratio into a change in income and interest rates, we follow the basic contours of the "debt fairy" calculation in Ball and Mankiw.[48] First, as in the Solow model above, we assume that the initial steady state for the economy involves a capital-output ratio of 2.5. The change in the ratio depends on how much of the debt increase is offset by increased private capital accumulation; we assume a 25 percent offset. (Because of depreciation, the 25 percent capital offset is a slightly different concept from the 25 percent saving off-

47. If the unified deficit is a constant share k of GDP, then $(rD + p)/Y = k$, where r is the interest rate, D is government debt, p is the primary budget balance, and Y is GDP. A constant debt-GDP ratio requires that D grow at rate g, or that $(rD + p)/D = g$, where g is the growth rate of Y. Therefore, in a steady state with a constant debt-GDP ratio, $D/Y = k/g$.
48. Ball and Mankiw (1995).

set assumed in the Solow model, and so the results presented here differ slightly from the Solow model results.) The reduction in capital is thus equal to 25 percent (= 33×0.75) of initial GDP. Assuming a marginal product of capital equal to 12 percent, the reduction in the capital stock causes income to decline by about 3 percent. Second, to map the change in the capital-output ratio into a change in the marginal product of capital, a specific form of the aggregate production function is necessary. With a Cobb-Douglas production function, the percentage increase in the marginal product of capital is equal to the percentage decline in the capital-output ratio. The capital-output ratio falls by 7 percent, from 2.50 to 2.32. The marginal product of capital would thus rise by 7 percent, from 12.0 to 12.8. Finally, we again assume that the change in the long-term government borrowing rate is equal to the change in the marginal product of capital. The result is that income declines by 3 percent, and steady-state long-term interest rates increase by about 80 basis points.

Since these two exercises are quite closely related despite their different framing in terms of deficits and debt, it is not surprising that the results are basically similar. A sustained increase in the unified deficit equal to 1 percent of GDP reduces income by 2 to 3 percent and raises long-term interest rates by roughly 50 to 80 basis points under the base case assumptions.[49]

To be sure, it is challenging to move from these simplified models to real-world results. For one thing, the models assume a closed economy, whereas the U.S. economy is large and open. One would therefore expect capital inflows to mitigate the interest rate and domestic production effects to some degree, even though the effect on national income should be largely unaffected by the assumption of a closed economy. In our view, however, these exercises not only help to calibrate the potential magnitude of the effects of deficits and debt on income and interest rates, but also underscore the shortcomings in ruling out the stock (debt) or the flow (deficit) perspective a priori.

Another key consideration is that the results above consider only the effects of increased budget deficits or debt per se. A full analysis of the effects of public policies on economic growth should take into account not only the effects of increased deficits and debt, but also the direct effects of the increases in spending programs or reductions in taxes that cause them. The effects of fiscal policies on both economic performance and interest

---

49. As noted in the text, the small differences reflect the treatment of depreciation.

rates depend not only on the deficit but also on the specific elements of the policies generating that deficit. For example, a dollar spent on public investment projects would increase the unified budget deficit by one dollar, but the net effect on future income would depend on whether the return on those investment projects exceeded the return on the private capital that would have instead been financed by the national saving crowded out by the deficit. Similarly, a deficit of 1 percent of GDP caused by reducing marginal tax rates will generally have different implications for both national income and interest rates than a deficit of 1 percent of GDP caused by increasing government purchases of goods and services. We return to this issue in the concluding section.

Deficits and Consumption

Our goal in this section is to measure the effects of fiscal policy on consumption and thus to distinguish the Ricardian view from the other two views. A wide variety of research tends to reject various *indirect* implications of Ricardian equivalence. For example, previous studies have generally found that motives for bequests are neither universal nor purely altruistic, that consumer spending responds to temporary tax cuts, that only current and not anticipated changes in income affect consumption (although there is mixed evidence on this point), and that aggregate consumption is sensitive to the age distribution of the population.[50]

We focus on a different set of tests: those using aggregate time-series data to examine the impact of tax revenue on consumption, holding other factors constant. Despite the numerous rejections of Ricardian equivalence in the indirect tests noted above, the time has come to revisit the aggregate time-series effects of fiscal policy on consumption, for several reasons. First, these analyses provide a direct test of whether the timing of tax collections affects the economy, controlling for other factors. Second, the aggregate time-series tests measure the *magnitude* of the effects in question. This is particularly important because virtually no one claims that Ricardian equivalence is literally true. Rather, the controversy is over the extent to which Ricardian equivalence is a good approximation

---

50. See, for example, the discussions in Bernheim (1987), Elmendorf and Mankiw (1999), and Seater (1993).

of the aggregate impact of fiscal policies. The indirect tests noted above can be helpful in distinguishing whether the literal implications of Ricardian equivalence hold, but they are often uninformative about the quantitative importance of any particular rejection of the theory. Third, there has been little work on these issues using data beyond the early 1990s. The past ten years, however, have witnessed dramatic shifts in fiscal policy in both directions (figures 1 and 6). These shifts have raised the prominence of policy concerns about budget deficits and should provide useful variation from an econometric perspective. Fourth, despite the rejection of many of the indirect implications of Ricardian equivalence noted above, some lines of research using aggregate time-series data have proved more favorable to the Ricardian view. This may be due to problems that are unique to time-series analysis, but it may also be that Ricardian equivalence is more robust—in particular as a working approximation—than the indirect tests suggest.

Previous Research

The authors of earlier literature surveys have noted the wide variety of research findings from studies of aggregate consumption and fiscal policy and emphasize the daunting econometric problems inherent in such studies, but they come to different conclusions about what the literature shows. Robert Barro, and Elmendorf and Mankiw, conclude that the literature is inconclusive.[51] John Seater concludes that, once the studies are corrected for econometric problems, Ricardian equivalence is corroborated, or at least cannot be rejected.[52] Douglas Bernheim concludes that, once the studies are normalized appropriately, Ricardian equivalence should be rejected.[53]

Previous studies of the effects of fiscal policy on consumption have taken three general approaches. A variety of studies undertake reduced-form analysis of consumption and saving patterns in the United States and other countries.[54] Like figures 6 and 7 above, these studies generally appear to support non-Ricardian interpretations of the data.

51. Barro (1989); Elmendorf and Mankiw (1999).
52. Seater (1993).
53. Bernheim (1989).
54. See, for example, Summers (1985), Carroll and Summers (1987), Poterba and Summers (1986, 1987), and Serres and Pelgrin (2003).

A second, and by far the largest, strand of the literature specifies consumption functions and then tests for the effects of fiscal policy given the consumption function.[55] Perhaps the best-known research in this area is that by Roger Kormendi and Philip Meguire, who find no evidence of non-Ricardian effects.[56]

A third strand of the literature focuses on Euler equation tests. David Aschauer examines the effects of fiscal policy assuming utility maximization and rational expectations, but his model does not nest a non-Ricardian specification.[57] Fred Graham and Daniel Himarios nest Ricardian and non-Ricardian views in a model that builds on work by Fumio Hayashi; they find non-Ricardian results using a nonlinear instrumental variables estimation procedure.[58] Paul Evans and Iftekhar Hasan estimate an empirical

55. Feldstein (1982); Seater and Mariano (1985); Kormendi (1983).
56. Kormendi (1983); Kormendi and Meguire (1986, 1990, 1995). A comprehensive review of the literature following Kormendi (1983) is beyond the scope of this paper, but some highlights include the following. Barth, Iden, and Russek (1986) update the data, correct some data problems, and obtain results broadly similar to those of Kormendi (1983). Modigliani and Sterling (1986) argue that Kormendi's results are flawed because of data problems, a failure to distinguish between temporary and permanent taxes, and inappropriate first-differencing of the data. They develop an aggregate consumption function derived from the life-cycle model that contains Ricardian equivalence as a special case. Their empirical results show strongly non-Ricardian results. Kormendi and Meguire (1986) note significant problems with how Modigliani and Sterling have defined temporary taxes. They show that imposing the condition that taxes and transfers have effects of equal magnitude and opposite sign (as Modigliani and Sterling do) is not supported by the data, and that when that restriction is relaxed, taxes and government debt continue to have Ricardian effects. Feldstein and Elmendorf (1990) work within the Kormendi framework and evaluate the effects of removing the war years, extending the sample, introducing other specification changes, and instrumenting for endogenous explanatory variables. After reproducing Kormendi's estimates, they find that their extensions fundamentally alter the findings, and they obtain very strong non-Ricardian results. Kormendi and Meguire (1990), however, show that Feldstein and Elmendorf's results obtain only as the joint consequence of using what Kormendi and Meguire view as the wrong deflators and failing to incorporate the improved definitions of variables that came out of the 1986 exchanges. Graham (1995) makes two adjustments to the Kormendi and Meguire framework, extended to 1991. He allows state and local variables to have different effects than federal variables. He also claims that theory suggests that labor and capital income should have distinct effects, and he proposes a decomposition of aggregate income and taxes into those due to labor and those due to capital. His reestimates suggest some non-Ricardian results, but not for tax revenue. Kormendi and Meguire (1995) challenge the decomposition of income into labor and capital and show that an alternative definition generates Ricardian results. Meguire (1998, 2003) continues research in this vein.
57. Aschauer (1985); see also Bernheim (1987) and Graham and Himarios (1991).
58. Graham and Himarios (1991); Hayashi (1982).

version of a model due to Olivier Blanchard, which nests Ricardian and non-Ricardian alternatives, and obtain results consistent with Ricardian equivalence.[59] Graham and Himarios correct several data and econometric problems in Evans' work and find strong non-Ricardian effects.[60]

The relative value of the consumption function and Euler equation approaches is a recurring theme in the literature. The advantage of using the Euler equation approach is that Ricardian equivalence requires a combination of utility maximization and rational expectations that the Euler equation can explicitly incorporate. The disadvantage is that Euler equation models can (and do) fail for reasons unrelated to Ricardian equivalence, and Ricardian equivalence can fail in ways that do not affect the Euler equation.[61] Marjorie Flavin argues that the consumption function approach is fundamentally inconsistent with Ricardian equivalence and therefore cannot be used to test the theory.[62] On the other hand, the strongest evidence in favor of Ricardian equivalence comes from the consumption function studies by Kormendi and Meguire.[63] Rather than attempt to resolve this debate, we estimate both consumption function and Euler equation models. We also show that the two specifications are closely related, so that the differences between the resulting estimated equations may not be large, even though the conceptual frameworks are quite different.

Specifying the Consumption Function

Our specification of the consumption function replicates, updates, and extends the work by Kormendi and Meguire and their critics. Kormendi specifies an aggregate consumption function of the following form:[64]

$$(1) \qquad C_t = \alpha_0 + \alpha_{11}Y_t + \alpha_{12}Y_{t-1} + \alpha_2 GS_t + \alpha_3 W_{t-1} + \alpha_4 TR_t \\ + \alpha_5 TX_t + \alpha_6 RE_t + \alpha_7 GINT_t + \alpha_8 GB_{t-1} + \varepsilon_t,$$

where t indexes time periods; C is a measure of consumption; Y is net national product; GS is government purchases of goods and services; W is a measure of private net worth, not including government debt; TR is government transfer payments; TX is tax revenue; RE is corporate retained

---

59. Evans (1988, 1993); Evans and Hasan (1994); Blanchard (1985).
60. Graham and Himarios (1996).
61. Bernheim (1987),
62. Flavin (1987).
63. Kormendi (1983); Kormendi and Meguire (1986, 1990).
64. Kormendi (1983).

earnings; *GINT* is government interest payments; and *GB* is the value of outstanding government debt.[65]

RICARDIAN AND NON-RICARDIAN HYPOTHESES. Although equation 1 is not specified in a structural manner, Kormendi argues that this framework nests both Ricardian and non-Ricardian hypotheses.[66] The Ricardian view is that consumption depends on current wealth, expected future income, and the burdens imposed by government purchases. If current and lagged NNP serve as proxies for future income, then the expected coefficients on NNP and lagged NNP should be between zero and one. Likewise, in this formulation, the coefficient on wealth represents the marginal propensity to consume out of wealth. Current government purchases are included as a proxy for expected future government purchases. The non-Ricardian view embodied in the equation is that consumption depends on disposable income, wealth, and government bonds. Note that disposable income is given by $Y + TR - TX - RE + GINT$.

The central tests between the Ricardian and the non-Ricardian view have to do with the coefficients on current taxes and current transfers. Ricardian equivalence implies that $\alpha_4 = \alpha_5 = 0$, that is, that transfers and taxes should not affect consumption, given the path of government purchases. The values of these coefficients, if they are not zero, provide a quantitative measure of the extent to which Ricardian equivalence fails as a description of reality. The coefficients on the two variables may be different from each other if transfers and taxes generally accrue to groups with different consumption patterns.

Ricardian equivalence also implies that $\alpha_8 = 0$, that is, that consumers do not treat government bonds as net wealth. Although this channel for non-Ricardian effects has attracted an enormous amount of attention over the past several decades, it is unlikely to prove useful in distinguishing Ricardian and non-Ricardian views, for several reasons. First, it is unlikely to be the major channel through which non-Ricardian effects occur. James Poterba and Lawrence Summers, as well as Evans, show that, if Ricardian equivalence is violated solely because forward-looking, life-cycle consumers treat government bonds completely as net worth, the effects of fis-

---

65. National saving equals NNP less government purchases and private consumption. Therefore, because the regression controls for NNP and government purchases, the effect of tax revenue on national saving is simply the inverse of the effect of tax revenue on consumption.

66. Kormendi (1983).

cal policy on short-run consumption are likely to be small.[67] In addition, as discussed further below, there are both data and conceptual problems with interpreting the government bond and wealth variables. As a result, we do not emphasize this channel for testing between the different models.[68]

Unfortunately, the coefficient on government spending does not provide a test of Ricardian equivalence. Ricardian equivalence is a statement about how variations in the timing of taxation affect private consumption, holding expected government purchases constant. It has no necessary implications for the effects of government purchases on private consumption, since the items the government purchases could be substitutes or complements for private consumption.[69] Thus, although it is important to control for expected government purchases, the coefficient on the purchases variable does not provide information that can test the theory.[70]

DATA. All of the variables are first transformed into real per capita levels.[71] To deal with stationarity issues, Kormendi and Meguire, and Martin Feldstein and Elmendorf, estimate regressions in first differences of the levels of the variables and in first differences of their ratios to NNP per capita.[72] Following John Campbell and Mankiw,[73] we also adjust for stationarity a third way, by dividing the first differences in the levels by lagged NNP per capita.[74]

---

67. Poterba and Summers (1987); Evans (1991).

68. The coefficients on government interest payments and retained earnings should be zero under Ricardian equivalence, but this test is not particularly interesting, because these coefficients should also be zero under other hypotheses. For example, the view that households pierce the corporate veil suggests that retained earnings should not affect consumption. Likewise, if government interest payments accrue mainly to high-income households who tend to save the funds, they will not affect consumption.

69. Kormendi (1983) obtains a negative coefficient on government purchases and interprets this finding as evidence in favor of Ricardian equivalence. Kormendi and Meguire (1990), however, acknowledge that the coefficient on government spending is essentially uninformative in testing Ricardian and non-Ricardian views.

70. There is an inconsistency in the specification in that current levels of government purchases are intended to proxy for permanent levels, but current levels of taxes and transfers are intended to represent levels that may well be altered in the future.

71. Details of the data construction may be found at www.brookings.edu/es/commentary/journals/bpea-macro/2004_2_bpea.consumptiondata.pdf or obtained from the authors on request.

72. Kormendi and Meguire (1990); Feldstein and Elmendorf (1990).

73. Campbell and Mankiw (1990).

74. Campbell and Mankiw (1990) divide by lagged disposable income rather than NNP, but the difference is unimportant empirically in our specifications. We divide by NNP in order to maintain consistency with the first-difference-in-ratios specification.

We use two measures of consumption. The first is the one developed by Kormendi: expenditure on nondurables and services, plus 10 percent of current durable expenditures, plus 30 percent of the existing stock of durable goods, all per capita.[75] The second measure is nondurables plus services, a more common measure used in many studies of aggregate consumption.[76]

The wealth variable used by Kormendi and Meguire and others in this literature is an amalgam of different series, with several extrapolations. We instead use data on household wealth from the Federal Reserve Board's Flow of Funds reports. We use household rather than private sector net worth, because the household measure includes the market value of corporate equities held by households, whereas the private sector measure instead uses book values of corporate equity. Since we want to capture the influence of wealth on consumption, we believe that the market value of equities is the more appropriate measure to include. Note, however, that the data for private sector bonds are reported on a book-value basis in the Flow of Funds accounts.

For data on the market value of federal government bonds, we use information from the Federal Reserve Bank of Dallas. For state debt we use the same methodology as Seater,[77] but we include more recent data. Generally, the data under the new definitions track the data under the old definitions very closely for the years in which values of both are present.[78]

With these adjustments, we have nearly the same specification employed by Kormendi and Meguire.[79] In earlier work we almost exactly replicate their results for earlier time periods dating from as far back as 1931 up to 1992.[80]

EXTENDING THE KORMENDI-MEGUIRE APPROACH. Our analysis here focuses on three extensions of this framework. First, we extend the sample

75. Kormendi (1983).

76. Graham (1992) and Graham and Himarios (1996) discuss the importance of alternative consumption measures in testing Ricardian equivalence.

77. Seater (1981).

78. The data from the Federal Reserve Bank of Dallas appear to have been derived using the same procedures as those developed in Cox (1985). The market value of state debt is calculated by multiplying the outstanding par value of state and local bonds (taken from the *Statistical Abstract of the United States*) by the ratio of market to par value for municipal bonds (taken from Standard and Poor's, 2003).

79. Kormendi (1983); Kormendi and Meguire (1986, 1990, 1995).

80. Gale and Orszag (2003c).

period to 2002. The added ten years of data provide valuable variation in fiscal policy and national saving.

Second, we alter the treatment of government taxes and transfers. In the Kormendi-Meguire specification, all government variables (taxes, transfers, purchases, interest payments, and debt) represent combined values for federal, state, and local governments. But federal and state fiscal variables are likely to have different effects on aggregate consumption. Perhaps most important, the states collect a significant share of their revenue through consumption taxes; this revenue would be expected to vary *positively* with consumption, whereas revenue from other taxes would be expected, at least in non-Ricardian theory, to vary negatively. In addition, the states face balanced budget rules. The cyclical dynamics of changes in state taxes or spending may therefore be different than for federal taxes or spending, which implies that the behavioral response to such changes might be different. The balanced budget rules also imply that state debt may be paid off at a different rate than federal debt, which again could influence behavior. Likewise, to the extent that state and local taxes are capitalized into local real estate prices, they are likely to have different effects than federal taxes.[81] For all of these reasons, testing for differences in the effects of federal and state taxes is a reasonable specification check.

Third, in some specifications we include as control variables estimates of marginal tax rates on labor income and capital income. Not controlling for marginal tax rates may bias the coefficient on tax revenue. Changes in tax revenue that also entail changes in tax rates create both substitution and income effects for current consumers. Even in a Ricardian world, changes in marginal tax rates will induce shifts in consumption and labor supply behavior. Therefore, in order to isolate the effects of changes in tax revenue, a control for tax rates is required. Several authors emphasize the potential importance of the confounding effects of not controlling for marginal tax rates;[82] its importance is buttressed by the work of Kenneth Judd and of Alan Auerbach and Laurence Kotlikoff, who show that the

---

81. Another issue is that state and federal governments typically allocate their purchases of goods and services differently: a large share of federal purchases goes to defense, whereas state purchases are dedicated more to education, police, and health care. Finally, mobility across states is much higher than emigration out of the United States; the basic Ricardian story does not hold when individuals (and their offspring) can escape the future burden of taxation by moving.

82. Barro (1989); Bernheim (1989); Plosser (1987b).

short-term dynamics of tax cuts are strongly affected by private responses to marginal tax incentives.[83] Despite all of these considerations, however, almost all previous studies of Ricardian equivalence omit marginal tax rates from their regressions; an exception is the study by Seater and Roberto Mariano, and even they omit corporate tax rates.[84]

For the marginal tax rate on labor income we use a measure constructed by the Treasury Department, which represents the combined marginal tax rate due to income and payroll taxes on a four-person family with twice the median income, all of which comes from wages. (We use twice median income, rather than median income, to capture the fact that significantly more than half of all earnings accrue to those who earn more than the median.) Our capital income tax rate is the average, economy-wide, marginal effective tax rate on new capital investment.[85] An advantage of these series is that most of the variation in them stems from legislative changes in tax rules rather than from changes in macroeconomic aggregates.

Consumption Function Results

Table 2 shows ordinary least squares (OLS) results for the specification described above. We estimate regressions for three time periods, two measures of consumption, three transformations of the dependent and independent variables, and three specifications of the explanatory variables.

The first panel of table 2 reports results from regressions that follow the Kormendi and Meguire specification of explanatory variables.[86] The first three columns report estimates of equations in which the variables are entered as first differences of their levels; the second column of this group shows that, when the sample is restricted to 1954–92, consumption does not respond to changes in taxes in a statistically significant fashion. This finding replicates and confirms the basic Kormendi and Meguire estimates. The first column, however, shows that merely updating the data through 2002 alters the conclusion, even with no further changes in specification. In this regression the coefficient on the tax variable implies that, controlling for other factors, between 27 and 39 percent of a tax cut is spent in the year it occurs; the Ricardian benchmark would be zero, and the pure Keynesian

---

83. Judd (1985, 1987a, 1987b); Auerbach and Kotlikoff (1987). In contrast, Seater (1993) suggests that any bias arising from the omission of marginal tax rates is not important.
84. Seater and Mariano (1985).
85. These data are from Gravelle (2004).
86. Kormendi and Meguire (1990).

Table 2. Consumption Function OLS Estimates of the Effects of Taxes on Aggregate Consumption[a]

Dependent variable	Variables entered as first differences of levels			Variables entered as ratios to NNP per capita			Variables entered as first differences of levels, scaled to NNP per capita		
	1956–2002	1954–92	1954–2000	1956–2002	1954–92	1954–2000	1956–2002	1954–92	1954–2000
Regressions using Kormendi-Meguire specification of independent variables									
Kormendi measure of consumption[b]	-0.39	-0.14	-0.23	-0.22	-0.09	-0.19	-0.24	-0.14	-0.23
	(-0.14)	(0.16)	(0.17)	(0.13)	(0.15)	(0.14)	(0.12)	(0.14)	(0.13)
Expenditure on nondurables and services[c]	-0.27	-0.15	-0.23	-0.18	-0.10	-0.18	-0.21	-0.15	-0.22
	(0.12)	(0.16)	(0.16)	(0.13)	(0.15)	(0.14)	(0.12)	(0.14)	(0.13)
As above but entering federal taxes and state and local taxes separately[d]									
Kormendi measure of consumption	-0.46	-0.21	-0.30	-0.28	-0.17	-0.26	-0.31	-0.25	-0.31
	(0.13)	(0.16)	(0.16)	(0.12)	(0.15)	(0.13)	(0.11)	(0.12)	(0.12)
Expenditure on nondurables and services	-0.34	-0.23	-0.29	-0.25	-0.20	-0.26	-0.27	-0.27	-0.31
	(0.11)	(0.16)	(0.14)	(0.11)	(0.14)	(0.12)	(0.11)	(0.12)	(0.12)
As above but also including marginal tax rates[d]									
Kormendi measure of consumption	-0.46	-0.15	-0.26	-0.34	-0.22	-0.30	-0.34	-0.24	-0.33
	(0.14)	(0.15)	(0.17)	(0.13)	(0.14)	(0.13)	(0.12)	(0.13)	(0.13)
Expenditure on nondurables and services	-0.34	-0.18	-0.27	-0.30	-0.25	-0.30	-0.30	-0.26	-0.32
	(0.12)	(0.15)	(0.15)	(0.12)	(0.15)	(0.13)	(0.11)	(0.14)	(0.13)

Source: Authors' regressions using data from Bureau of Economic Analysis, National Income and Product Accounts; Gravelle (2004); Department of the Treasury; Federal Reserve; U.S. Census Bureau; and Standard and Poor's.

a. Table reports regression coefficients on the tax revenue variable in equation 1 in the text. Numbers in parentheses are robust standard errors.
b. Real consumption per capita of nondurables and services, plus 10 percent of expenditure on durable goods, plus 30 percent of the stock of durable goods (Kormendi, 1983).
c. Real expenditure per capita on nondurables and services multiplied by the sample-period mean ratio of total consumption expenditure to nondurable and services expenditure.
d. Coefficients are for the effect of federal taxes only. Data on marginal tax rates on capital and labor are unavailable before 1956.

benchmark would be close to 100 percent. These conclusions are not particularly sensitive to the starting point for the data (results not shown), but they are sensitive to the ending date: the third column shows that the statistical significance of the tax coefficient depends on whether 2001 and 2002 are included. This sensitivity to the last two years of the data is not present when the specification is improved, as shown below. The remaining columns in the first panel report results of different transformations of the dependent variable and show similar although smaller effects.

The middle panel splits the federal and state tax variables, for the reasons noted above. This has several effects on the results. First, the absolute values of the coefficients and the associated *t* statistics on federal taxes are larger than were the corresponding values for all taxes in the first panel. For the period 1954 through 2002, the estimates suggest that between 25 and 46 cents of every dollar in federal tax cuts is consumed in the first year, controlling for other factors. Second, the statistical significance of the results is no longer sensitive to whether the last two years are included. Third, although the results are not shown, the coefficients on the state tax variables are positive, large, and precisely estimated. This buttresses the view that federal and state taxes can have different effects on the economy, and it points out an important source of aggregation bias (between federal and state tax revenue) in previous work on this subject.[87]

The regressions reported in the bottom panel of table 2 again split the tax variables into their federal and state components but also include the variables for marginal tax rates on labor income and capital income. Their inclusion has only a small effect on the estimated coefficients.

Table 3 reports the coefficient estimates for the six regressions in the bottom panel of table 2 that cover the full sample period (1956–2002). Several results are worth highlighting. The coefficients on NNP and lagged NNP are similar to those reported by Kormendi and Meguire.[88] Government purchases enter with a small, positive, statistically insignificant coefficient.[89] The contrast between the effects of federal and state taxes is stark. State taxes enter with a positive coefficient that hovers around 1.0, whereas the

87. The results are similar when all the fiscal variables, not just taxes, are split into federal and state components (not shown).

88. Kormendi and Meguire (1990).

89. In Gale and Orszag (2003c) we show that, in earlier periods, the coefficient on the purchases variable is larger and precisely estimated, consistent with other results in the literature.

Table 3. OLS Coefficient Estimates for All Independent Variables in the Consumption Function[a]

Independent variable	Variables measured as first differences of levels		Variables measured as first differences of ratios to NNP per capita		Variables measured as first differences of levels, scaled to NNP per capita	
	Kormendi consumption measure	Nondurables and services expenditure	Kormendi consumption measure	Nondurables and services expenditure	Kormendi consumption measure	Nondurables and services expenditure
Current-period NNP	0.36 (0.08)	0.33 (0.07)	3.41 (0.96)	3.05 (0.92)	0.27 (0.06)	0.31 (0.06)
Lagged NNP	0.13 (0.05)	0.08 (0.04)	0.08 (0.04)	0.07 (0.03)	0.04 (0.04)	0.03 (0.04)
Government purchases	0.15 (0.15)	0.10 (0.12)	0.11 (0.11)	0.07 (0.10)	0.08 (0.10)	0.06 (0.10)
Federal taxes	−0.46 (0.14)	−0.34 (0.12)	−0.34 (0.13)	−0.30 (0.12)	−0.34 (0.12)	−0.30 (0.11)
State and local taxes	0.88 (0.49)	0.99 (0.41)	0.85 (0.37)	1.00 (0.35)	0.92 (0.37)	0.98 (0.35)
Government transfers	0.76 (0.29)	0.52 (0.25)	0.56 (0.19)	0.55 (0.18)	0.26 (0.26)	0.25 (0.24)
Government interest paid	0.08 (0.31)	0.15 (0.26)	0.06 (0.26)	0.24 (0.25)	−0.06 (0.27)	0.09 (0.25)

(continued)

Table 3. OLS Coefficient Estimates for All Independent Variables in the Consumption Function[a] *(continued)*

Independent variable	Variables measured as first differences of levels		Variables measured as first differences of ratios to NNP per capita		Variables measured as first differences of levels, scaled to NNP per capita	
	Kormendi consumption measure	Nondurables and services expenditure	Kormendi consumption measure	Nondurables and services expenditure	Kormendi consumption measure	Nondurables and services expenditure
Lagged government debt	-0.03	-0.03	-0.03	-0.02	-0.02	-0.02
	(0.02)	(0.02)	(0.02)	(0.02)	(0.02)	(0.02)
Lagged wealth	0.02	0.02	0.01	0.01	0.01	0.01
	(0.01)	(0.01)	(0.01)	(0.01)	(0.01)	(0.01)
Corporate retained earnings	0.10	0.06	0.08	0.06	0.01	0.00
	(0.16)	(0.14)	(0.15)	(0.14)	(0.00)	(0.00)
Marginal tax rate on capital[b]	1.03	1.08	0.06	0.06	0.06	0.07
	(0.65)	(0.55)	(0.03)	(0.03)	(0.03)	(0.03)
Marginal tax rate on labor[b]	-1.39	-1.45	-0.06	-0.06	-0.06	-0.07
	(0.71)	(0.59)	(0.03)	(0.03)	(0.03)	(0.03)
Constant	0.06	0.07	0.00	0.00	0.00	0.01
	(0.05)	(0.04)	(0.00)	(0.00)	(0.00)	(0.00)

Source: Authors' regressions using data from Bureau of Economic Analysis, National Income and Product Accounts; Gravelle (2004); Department of the Treasury; Federal Reserve; U.S. Census Bureau; and Standard and Poor's.

a. Table reports regression coefficients for all independent variables in the regressions using 1956–2002 data in the bottom panel of table 2. Numbers in parentheses are robust standard errors. Number of observations $N = 47$. All lags are one-period lags. Consumption measures are as defined in table 2.

b. Both the coefficient and the standard error are multiplied by 100.

coefficient on federal taxes is always negative; both coefficients are significantly different from zero. Government transfers raise consumption, and the effect is statistically different from zero in most of the specifications.[90] The marginal tax rate on capital enters with a positive coefficient, whereas the marginal tax rate on labor enters with a negative coefficient. Both effects are plausible and are economically small. Private wealth enters with a small, positive, but imprecisely estimated effect, and government bonds with a small, negative, but imprecisely estimated effect.[91]

In summary, these results demonstrate that, within the framework that supporters of Ricardian equivalence have viewed as providing the most credible evidence in their favor, updated data and an improved specification reveal robust non-Ricardian effects: in these specifications about 30 to 46 cents of every dollar in federal tax cuts is spent in the same year.

Nevertheless, there are significant concerns with this set of specifications. Most notably, the equations are not derived explicitly from a well-defined economic model, and many of the key explanatory variables are likely to be endogenous. Although one can use instrumental variables techniques to address concerns about endogeneity, such an effort raises special problems in the consumption function approach,[92] and the specification contains a very large number of potentially endogenous variables. For these reasons we turn to Euler equations, which we estimate in both OLS and instrumental variables forms.

Specifying the Euler Equation

This section develops an Euler equation specification that nests Ricardian and non-Ricardian alternatives. In the standard specification, under the permanent-income hypothesis, consumers adjust their consumption in each

---

90. In the regressions that exclude the marginal tax rates, the transfers coefficient is always large, positive, and statistically significant.

91. We examined several alternative specifications, none of which affected the results in any important way. First, to account for the fact that Ricardian consumers should care about expected future government purchases, not just current purchases, we performed regressions using data on future government purchases, or with CBO projections of five-year-ahead government spending, instead of current values. Second, we adjusted the government bond variable to include only domestically held bonds. Third, we explored alternative definitions of taxes and transfers, by changing the classification of nontax payments from a revenue item to a negative transfer payment and changing the classification of federal transfers to states from a government purchase to a transfer.

92. See Flavin (1987).

period so that the marginal utility of consumption follows a random walk.[93] With a few simplifying assumptions, consumption itself follows a random walk (with drift), which implies that the change in consumption is given by

$$(2) \qquad \Delta C_t = \alpha + \varepsilon_t,$$

where ε_t is a forecast error that is uncorrelated with all information in periods $t - 1$ and before but may be correlated with current-period information.

Our goal is to expand on the model in equation 2 to account explicitly for Ricardian consumers and for consumers who exhibit any of a variety of types of non-Ricardian behavior. Campbell and Mankiw specify a model in which a share λ of all disposable income YD goes to rule-of-thumb consumers who immediately consume the resources.[94] The remainder of income accrues to "farsighted" consumers, who behave according to equation 2. This generates a consumption equation of the form

$$(3) \qquad \Delta C_t = \alpha + \lambda \Delta YD_t + (1 - \lambda)\varepsilon_t.$$

Blanchard develops a model of farsighted, life-cycle consumers that also contains Ricardian equivalence as a special case (where consumers have an infinite horizon).[95] Based on Blanchard, Evans, and Graham and Himarios,[96] the model implies that aggregate consumption can be written as

$$(4) \qquad \Delta C_t = \alpha + \beta_1 \Delta W_{t-1} + \beta_2 \Delta B_{t-1} + v1_t,$$

where W is private net worth and B is the real outstanding stock of government bonds. As Evans shows,[97] life-cycle consumers will generate *negative* values for β_1 and β_2. In the limiting case of Ricardian equivalence, β_1 and β_2 are zero, and the equation collapses to equation 2. Thus, if proportions μ_1 and μ_2 of private wealth and government bonds, respectively, are held by life-cycle consumers, and the remaining shares by Ricardian consumers, equations 3 and 4 can be combined to allow for both groups of consumers:

$$(5) \qquad \Delta C_t = \alpha + \lambda \Delta YD_t + \gamma_1 \Delta W_{t-1} + \gamma_2 \Delta B_{t-1} + v2_t,$$

where $\gamma_i = \beta_i \mu_i$.

93. Hall (1978).
94. Campbell and Mankiw (1989, 1990).
95. Blanchard (1985).
96. Blanchard (1985); Evans (1988); Graham and Himarios (1996).
97. Evans (1988).

Finally, Ricardian consumers should not be influenced by changes in disposable income or past changes in wealth, but they may be affected by changes in expectations regarding future government purchases (although, as noted above, the sign of the effect is not clear). Moreover, for all groups, with the possible exception of strict rule-of-thumb consumers, changes in the marginal tax rates on capital and labor (*MTRK* and *MTRL,* respectively) may affect consumption choices. These considerations generate an Euler specification of the following form:

$$(6) \qquad \Delta C_t = \alpha + \lambda \Delta YD_t + \gamma_1 \Delta W_{t-1} + \gamma_2 \Delta B_{t-1} + \varphi_1 \Delta GS_t$$
$$+ \varphi_2 \Delta MTRK_t + \varphi_3 \Delta MTRL_t + u_t,$$

where *GS* is again government purchases and the error term u_t is uncorrelated with all variables in earlier time periods.

This Euler equation has a number of interesting properties. First, it allows for the presence of both rule-of-thumb consumers and life-cycle consumers, and it contains Ricardian equivalence as the special case where $\lambda = \gamma_1 = \gamma_2 = 0$.[98] Thus the equation allows for testing of Ricardian equivalence in a utility-maximizing framework that nests both Ricardian and several non-Ricardian hypotheses and shows the quantitative importance of any deviations from Ricardian equivalence.

Second, with a little transformation the equation is not that different from the consumption function specification developed by Kormendi (equation 1). In the notation used earlier in the paper, disposable income can be written as $YD = NNP - TX - RE + TR + GINT$. When that expression is substituted into equation 6 and the coefficients on each component of disposable income are allowed to vary, the resulting equation differs from equation 1 only in that equation 1 contains a lagged NNP term and equation 6 includes marginal tax rate terms.

To isolate the effects of federal taxes on consumption, we decompose the disposable income term in equation 6 into pretax income (*YP*), federal taxes (*TXF*), and state and local taxes (*TXSL*). This yields equation 7, which we estimate by OLS and instrumental variables in the next section:

$$(7) \qquad \Delta C_t = \alpha + \lambda_1 \Delta YP_t + \lambda_2 \Delta TXF_t + \lambda_3 \Delta TXSL_t + \gamma_1 \Delta W_{t-1}$$
$$+ \gamma_2 \Delta B_{t-1} + \varphi_1 \Delta GS_t + \varphi_2 \Delta MTRK_t + \varphi_3 \Delta MTRL_t + u_t.$$

---

98. These restrictions derive directly from the Campbell and Mankiw (1989, 1990) and Blanchard (1985) models.

Euler Equation Results

Table 4 presents estimates of equation 7 for the period 1956–2002.[99] The top panel presents the results of OLS regressions, for comparison with table 2. The results using first differences of levels and those using first differences scaled by lagged income are somewhat smaller than those in table 2 and suggest that between 22 and 39 cents of each dollar in federal tax cuts is consumed in the year the tax cuts occur. The results using the first difference in ratios are substantially larger, suggesting that between 50 and 70 cents per dollar of tax cuts is consumed in the first year. Thus the results show no obvious bias relative to the findings in table 2.

These results, of course, still suffer from endogeneity problems. We therefore follow Campbell and Mankiw in using lagged values of the right-hand-side variables as instruments for their current value, and lagged values of consumption itself as an instrument for current income.[100] In models where agents are forward-looking, lagged consumption will help to predict current income but is not correlated with the stochastic component of current consumption. For reasons discussed by Robert Hall, Campbell and Mankiw, and others,[101] we avoid using once-lagged variables as instruments and instead use variables that are lagged twice and three times.

The middle panel of table 4 reports instrumental variables estimates in which all of the current-period variables are treated as endogenous except for private sector wealth and government bonds, which are measured at the end of the previous period and are treated as exogenous. All of the regressions report negative effects of tax revenue on consumption. Most of the effects are statistically significant, ranging between 32 and 64 cents per dollar of tax cuts. The regressions that control for marginal tax rates usually produce larger (in absolute value) effects of tax cuts on consumption.

---

99. Given the lags and the choice of instruments, the availability of the tax rate variables restricts consideration to samples starting in 1956. When the tax rate variables are dropped, regressions with samples that begin earlier in the 1950s are possible. These regressions yield results very similar to those of regressions without marginal tax rates where the sample begins in 1956.

100. Campbell and Mankiw (1989, 1990).

101. Hall (1988); Campbell and Mankiw (1989).

Table 4. Euler Equation OLS and Instrumental Variables Estimates of the Effects of Taxes on Aggregate Consumption[a]

Dependent variable	Variables entered as first differences of levels		Variables entered as first differences of ratios to NNP per capita		Variables entered as first differences of levels, scaled to NNP per capita	
	Marginal tax rate excluded	Marginal tax rate included	Marginal tax rate excluded	Marginal tax rate included	Marginal tax rate excluded	Marginal tax rate included
OLS estimates						
Kormendi consumption measure	-0.38 (0.15)	-0.39 (0.16)	-0.70 (0.19)	-0.56 (0.14)	-0.25 (0.11)	-0.27 (0.11)
Expenditure on nondurables and services	-0.27 (0.11)	-0.26 (0.11)	-0.65 (0.17)	-0.50 (0.13)	-0.22 (0.11)	-0.22 (0.09)
Sample period	1954–2002	1956–2002	1954–2002	1956–2002	1954–2002	1956–2002
Instrumental variables, current explanatory variables endogenous						
Kormendi consumption measure	-0.51 (0.23)	-0.64 (0.20)	-0.56 (0.28)	-0.38 (0.31)	-0.30 (0.22)	-0.45 (0.18)
Expenditure on nondurables and services	-0.32 (0.18)	-0.41 (0.16)	-0.51 (0.26)	-0.29 (0.31)	-0.22 (0.20)	-0.32 (0.16)
Sample period	1957–2002	1959–2002	1957–2002	1959–2002	1957–2002	1959–2002
Instrumental variables, all explanatory variables endogenous						
Kormendi consumption measure	-0.62 (0.40)	-0.98 (0.41)	-0.75 (0.43)	-0.61 (0.50)	-0.44 (0.35)	-0.73 (0.34)
Expenditure on nondurables and services	-0.42 (0.35)	-0.85 (0.44)	-0.70 (0.41)	-0.53 (0.53)	-0.51 (0.39)	-0.71 (0.36)
Sample period	1957–2002	1959–2002	1957–2002	1959–2002	1957–2002	1959–2002

Source: Authors' regressions using data from Bureau of Economic Analysis, National Income and Product Accounts; Gravelle (2004); Department of the Treasury; Federal Reserve; U.S. Census Bureau; and Standard and Poor's.
a. Table reports regression coefficients on the tax revenue variable in equation 1 in the text. Numbers in parentheses are robust standard errors. Consumption measures are as defined in table 2.

The bottom panel of table 4 reports the effects on consumption when all right-hand-side variables, including the lagged value of private sector wealth and government bonds, are treated as endogenous. These results uniformly show a larger (in absolute value) effect of tax revenue on consumption. Six of the twelve regressions generate statistically significant effects, with coefficients ranging from 71 to 98 cents in added consumption per dollar of taxes cut. All six have p-values below .10, and in three the p-value is below .05. The other six regressions also show large effects (44 to 62 cents on the dollar) but are estimated less precisely.

Table 5 reports the coefficients on all regressors for the six instrumental variables regressions in table 4 that include marginal tax rates as explanatory variables. Before-tax income and federal tax revenue usually enter as important determinants of aggregate consumption. Most of the other variables do not. In particular, marginal tax rates have much smaller and less significant effects in this specification than in the consumption function specification. Government bonds have negative coefficients when they are not instrumented and positive coefficients when they are, but in neither case are the estimates statistically different from zero. Likewise, private sector wealth enters with a small, positive, but usually statistically insignificant coefficient. The state and local tax variable generally enters positively but is estimated imprecisely. The fact that standard errors are larger across the board is not unexpected in instrumental variables estimates, and they serve to highlight the generally statistically significant and economically substantial effects of federal taxes on consumption.

Discussion

The results just presented establish that changes in tax revenue can have significant negative effects on contemporaneous changes in consumption when government purchases, marginal tax rates, and other factors are controlled for. The implications of these findings for Ricardian equivalence merit additional discussion. Define a Ricardian *consumer* as one who would have a zero marginal propensity to consume (MPC) out of a current tax cut if all of the following assumptions hold: all taxes are lump-sum, the tax cut is coupled with a future lump-sum tax increase of equivalent present value on the consumer or the consumer's heirs; the future income of the consumer and his or her heirs is known; and government purchases are unaffected.

Table 5. Instrumental Variables Coefficient Estimates for All Independent Variables in the Euler Equation[a]

Independent variable	Variables entered as first differences of levels		Variables entered as first differences of ratios to NNP per capita		Variables entered as first differences of levels, scaled to NNP per capita	
	Kormendi consumption measure	Nondurables and services expenditure	Kormendi consumption measure	Nondurables and services expenditure	Kormendi consumption measure	Nondurables and services expenditure
Current independent variables endogenous						
Before-tax income	0.41	0.36	0.94	0.89	0.41	0.41
	(0.17)	(0.14)	(0.27)	(0.25)	(0.13)	(0.13)
Government purchases	0.25	0.20	0.11	0.04	0.12	0.11
	(0.29)	(0.24)	(0.27)	(0.28)	(0.20)	(0.19)
Federal taxes	-0.64	-0.41	-0.38	-0.29	-0.45	-0.32
	(0.20)	(0.16)	(0.31)	(0.31)	(0.18)	(0.16)
State and local taxes	0.22	0.74	-0.16	0.09	0.48	0.83
	(0.80)	(0.66)	(0.85)	(0.87)	(0.54)	(0.52)
Lagged government debt	-0.02	-0.02	-0.01	-0.01	-0.01	-0.01
	(0.03)	(0.02)	(0.04)	(0.04)	(0.02)	(0.02)
Lagged wealth	0.03	0.01	0.00	0.00	0.01	0.01
	(0.01)	(0.01)	(0.01)	(0.01)	(0.01)	(0.01)
Marginal tax rate on capital[b]	2.60	1.50	0.00	-0.10	0.10	0.10
	(1.60)	(1.30)	(0.10)	(0.10)	(0.10)	(0.10)
Marginal tax rate on labor[b]	-0.70	-0.90	0.00	-0.10	0.00	0.00
	(1.40)	(1.10)	(0.10)	(0.10)	(0.10)	(0.00)
Constant	0.16	0.12	0.00	0.00	0.01	0.01
	(0.06)	(0.05)	(0.00)	(0.00)	(0.00)	(0.00)

(continued)

Table 5. Instrumental Variables Coefficient Estimates for All Independent Variables in the Euler Equation[a] (continued)

Independent variable	Variables entered as first differences of levels		Variables entered as first differences of ratios to NNP per capita		Variables entered as first differences of levels, scaled to NNP per capita	
	Kormendi consumption measure	Nondurables and services expenditure	Kormendi consumption measure	Nondurables and services expenditure	Kormendi consumption measure	Nondurables and services expenditure
All explanatory variables endogenous						
Before-tax income	0.52	0.49	0.89	0.84	0.48	0.51
	(0.26)	(0.27)	(0.29)	(0.28)	(0.18)	(0.20)
Government purchases	0.16	0.09	0.12	0.07	0.09	0.07
	(0.40)	(0.40)	(0.31)	(0.33)	(0.25)	(0.28)
Federal taxes	−0.98	−0.85	−0.61	−0.53	−0.73	−0.71
	(0.41)	(0.44)	(0.50)	(0.53)	(0.34)	(0.36)
State and local taxes	0.36	0.65	0.09	0.34	0.47	0.76
	(1.04)	(1.06)	(0.98)	(1.00)	(0.69)	(0.76)
Lagged government debt	0.04	0.09	0.05	0.07	0.02	0.04
	(0.11)	(0.11)	(0.11)	(0.11)	(0.08)	(0.08)
Lagged wealth	0.04	0.03	0.01	0.01	0.03	0.03
	(0.02)	(0.02)	(0.03)	(0.03)	(0.02)	(0.02)
Marginal tax rate on capital[b]	2.50	1.30	0.00	−0.10	0.10	0.10
	(2.30)	(2.30)	(0.10)	(0.10)	(0.10)	(0.10)
Marginal tax rate on labor[b]	0.60	0.80	0.00	0.00	0.00	0.00
	(2.30)	(2.30)	(0.10)	(0.10)	(0.10)	(0.10)
Constant	0.11	0.07	0.00	0.00	0.01	0.00
	(0.10)	(0.10)	(0.00)	(0.00)	(0.00)	(0.00)

Source: Authors' regressions using data from Bureau of Economic Analysis, National Income and Product Accounts; Gravelle (2004); Department of the Treasury; Federal Reserve; U.S. Census Bureau; and Standard and Poor's.

a. Table reports regression coefficients for all independent variables in the regressions including the marginal tax rate in the bottom two panels of table 4. Numbers in parentheses are robust standard errors. Number of observations $N = 44$. All lags are one-period lags. Consumption measures are as defined in table 2.

b. Both the coefficient and the standard error are multiplied by 100.

It is well established that a Ricardian consumer can have a nonzero MPC out of a tax cut if any of these assumptions is violated. As a result, interpreting our empirical results requires some care. We make two broad points. First, violations of several of the assumptions above can generate nonzero MPCs for Ricardian consumers but seem unlikely to explain our empirical results, which generate MPCs between 50 and 80 percent. Second, the violations that can explain such high MPCs out of tax cuts also generate strongly non-Ricardian effects of *public policies* even if *consumers* are Ricardian in the sense defined above.

On the first point: violations of several of the assumptions may indeed exist in the real world but are unlikely to explain our results. If taxes are distortionary, tax cuts will alter relative prices and hence affect consumption and labor supply through standard substitution effects. However, the marginal propensity to consume out of a temporary tax cut created by distortionary taxes is likely to be either small or negative for Ricardian consumers.[102]

Likewise, the "fiscal rule" that households believe to be operating will affect the MPC, but it is unlikely that uncertainty about fiscal rules can explain our results. If the path of government purchases is held constant and future income is known, but the incidence of the future lump-sum tax is uncertain (in terms of either the timing or who will be affected), a lump-sum tax cut now coupled with a lump-sum tax increase later could lead Ricardian consumers to increase their precautionary saving. That is, they would save not only the tax cut but also an additional amount to account for the increased riskiness of future taxes. This would generate a negative MPC out of the tax cut.[103] Clearly, this cannot explain the MPCs estimated above.

The more likely it is that a tax cut will be financed by reductions in future government purchases, the more likely that the MPC out of a tax cut will be positive for Ricardian consumers, because such a tax cut would imply that the burden of future taxes would also fall—that is, that the tax cut would be permanent. But current tax revenue does not appear to be a

102. Cardia (1997) shows that, in simulation models that would generate Ricardian equivalence but for the presence of distortionary taxes, or distortionary taxes in combination with finite horizons, the estimated MPC out of a tax cut in equations like those estimated in this paper is less than .08. Judd (1987b) shows that, in an infinite-horizon model, the MPC out of a temporary cut in tax rates, coupled with a future increase in tax rates, is negative.

103. Barro (1989); Kormendi (1983); Seater (1993).

good predictor of future government purchases, and so it is unlikely that changing views of government purchases explain our results.[104]

On the second point: simulation models suggest that, if future income is uncertain or if taxes serve a social insurance role in reducing the amplitude of swings in uncertain future income, the MPC out of a tax cut could be within the 50 to 80 percent range that we estimate.[105] In this case consumers are "Ricardian" in the sense defined above, but intergenerational transfers of public resources have long-lasting, strongly non-Ricardian effects on the economy.

A related issue is that our empirical consumption results address only short-term Ricardian equivalence. In some models Ricardian equivalence fails in the short run but holds in the long run.[106] In others, small deviations from short-term Ricardian equivalence grow over time into very large deviations from long-term Ricardian equivalence.[107]

Thus our empirical findings cannot distinguish between the view that consumers are truly non-Ricardian and the view that consumers are Ricardian but that the characteristics of enacted policies do not conform to the assumptions stated above under which Ricardian equivalence holds. In either case, however, our results imply that, controlling for other factors, tax cut–induced deficits reduce national saving, at least in the short run. This is the sense in which we describe our results as "non-Ricardian."

Summary

Our consumption function OLS regressions demonstrate robust non-Ricardian effects even within the basic specification that has previously suggested the strongest support for Ricardian equivalence. When the sample period is extended to cover the most recent years, federal and state tax variables are split, and a marginal tax rate variable is included, the results suggest that about 30 to 46 cents of every dollar in tax cuts is spent in the same year—and the effect is precisely estimated in all specifications that use the full sample period.

The OLS regressions likely suffer from severe simultaneity problems, however. When instrumental variables regressions are used in the Euler

104. Modigliani and Sterling (1986) and Feldstein and Elmendorf (1990) report regressions of current government purchases on lagged values of tax revenue, controlling for other factors, and find no predictive power of tax revenue for future purchases.

105. Barsky, Mankiw, and Zeldes (1986); Feldstein (1988).

106. Smetters (1999); Mankiw (2000b).

107. Auerbach and Kotlikoff (1987).

specification, with twice- and three-times-lagged variables as instruments, the results are generally more strongly non-Ricardian. If we drop the highest and lowest estimates in the bottom panel of table 4, the remaining coefficients from this specification, which is our preferred one, suggest that about 50 to 85 cents of every dollar in tax cuts is spent in the first year; half of the effects are measured precisely. This range is consistent with some previous assessments,[108] but it is inconsistent with the Ricardian prediction of a full offset from private saving, and the difference, as we will discuss further in the concluding section, is economically important.

Deficits and Interest Rates

In this section we present our findings on the effects of deficits and other fiscal measures on long-term interest rates. We begin by reviewing previous research on this issue.

Previous Research

For a number of well-known reasons, the effects of fiscal policy on interest rates have proved difficult to pin down statistically. The issues include the appropriate definitions of deficits and debt, whether deficits or debt should be the variable of interest, how to distinguish expected from unexpected changes in these variables, and the potential endogeneity of many of the key explanatory variables. We discuss several of these issues below.[109] In part because of these statistical issues, the evidence from the empirical literature as a whole is mixed.[110]

---

108. For example, Bernheim (1987) and the CBO ("Description of Economic Models," November 1998) conclude that private saving would rise by between 20 and 50 percent of an increase in the deficit (hence consumption would rise by between 50 and 80 percent of the increase in the deficit). Elmendorf and Liebman (2000) conclude that private saving would offset 25 percent of the increase in the deficit. Gale and Potter (2002) estimate that private saving will offset 31 percent of the decline in public saving caused by the 2001 tax cut.

109. Bernheim (1987), Elmendorf and Mankiw (1999), and Seater (1993) provide comprehensive analyses.

110. Previous analyses reach widely varying conclusions about the effects of deficits on interest rates. For example, Barth and others (1991) survey forty-two studies through 1989, seventeen of which found a "predominately significant, positive" effect of deficits on interest rates (that is, larger deficits raised interest rates); six studies found mixed effects, and

As we noted in our discussion of the stylized models above, we take no a priori view regarding whether interest rates should be affected by deficits or by debt. Below, however, we often refer to the relationship between interest rates and "deficits," in part for simplicity and in part because our results suggest that deficits contain more useful information than debt in explaining interest rates.

PROJECTED DEFICITS AND INTEREST RATES. Our previous contribution to interpreting the literature has been to highlight the key role of using expected deficits rather than current deficits.[111] Almost twenty years ago, Feldstein wrote, "it is wrong to relate the rate of interest to the concurrent budget deficit without taking into account the anticipated future deficits. It is significant that almost none of the past empirical analyses of the effect of deficits on interest rates makes any attempt to include a measure of expected future deficits."[112] Since financial markets are forward-looking, excluding expectations could bias the analysis toward finding no relationship between interest rates and deficits.[113]

Over the past twenty years, many studies have incorporated more accurate information on expectations of *future* sustained deficits. These studies tend to find economically and statistically significant connections between anticipated deficits and current interest rates. In a recent paper we summarize the findings of the studies on this topic reviewed by James Barth and others as well as

---

nineteen found "predominately insignificant or negative" effects. Barth and others (p. 72) conclude that "Since the available evidence on the effects of deficits is mixed, one cannot say with complete confidence that budget deficits raise interest rates. . . . But, equally important, one cannot say that they do not have these effects." Other reviewers of the literature have reached similar conclusions. Elmendorf and Mankiw (1999, p. 1658) note that "Our view is that this literature . . . is not very informative." Bernheim (1989, p. 56) writes that "it is easy to cite a large number of studies that support any conceivable position." Appendix table A-1 updates the Barth and others (1991) survey and shows that, of more than sixty studies, roughly half found a predominantly significant, positive effect and the other half found either no effect or mixed effects.

111. Gale and Orszag (2002, 2003a). One recent study expands the literature along a different dimension: Kiley (2003) examines the relationship between current government debt and the return to capital in the nonfinancial corporate sector. Kiley finds that a 1-percentage-point increase in the debt-GDP ratio is associated with a 10-basis-point increase in the return to capital.

112. Feldstein (1986).

113. Bernheim (1987) notes that, if households perfectly anticipate future deficits, one may well find no empirical relationship between current deficits and interest rates, even though the path of interest rates and economic activity would be substantially different in the absence of the deficits.

several more recent papers.[114] Appendix table A-1 shows that, of nineteen papers that incorporate timely information on projected deficits, thirteen find predominantly positive, significant effects between anticipated deficits and current interest rates, five find mixed effects, and only one finds no effects. The studies that find no significant effect are disproportionately those that do not take expectations into account at all or do so only indirectly through a vector autoregression. Thus, although the literature as a whole, taken at face value, generates mixed results, those analyses that focus on the effects of anticipated deficits tend to find a positive and significant impact on interest rates.

The challenge in incorporating market expectations about future deficits is that such expectations are not directly observable. An important caveat to the literature examining expected deficits, then, is that, to the extent that proxies for expected deficits are imperfect reflections of current expectations, the coefficient on the projected deficit will tend to be biased toward zero because of classical measurement error, and the tendency will be to *underestimate* the effects of deficits on interest rates.

Researchers have used different strategies in the face of this challenge. One approach is to use published forecasts of the deficit as a proxy for market expectations. For example, Elmendorf, using deficit forecasts from Data Resources, Inc., finds that an increase in the projected deficit of 1 percent of GNP raises five-year bond yields by 43 basis points. Matthew Canzoneri, Robert Cumby, and Behzad Diba, using CBO projections, find that "an increase in projected future deficits averaging 1 percent of current GDP is associated with an increase in the long-term interest rate relative to the short-term interest rate of 53 to 60 basis points."[115]

One potential concern with these studies is that the business cycle could be affecting current yields.[116] Thomas Laubach suggests a novel way to resolve this issue:[117] he examines the relationship between projected deficits (or debt) and the level of real *forward* (five-year-ahead)

---

114. Gale and Orszag (2003a); Barth and others (1991).
115. Canzoneri, Cumby, and Diba (2002, p. 365).
116. For example, in a recession the projected unified deficit could increase merely because of the lingering effects from the rise in debt during the downturn; at the same time, the yield curve could steepen as short-term interest rates are depressed by Federal Reserve policy. This could potentially introduce an artificial relationship, actually driven by the business cycle and monetary policy, between the yield spread and the projected unified deficit.
117. Laubach (2003).

long-term interest rates. The underlying notion is that current business cycle conditions should not influence the long-term rates expected to prevail beginning five years from now. Laubach uses CBO and Office of Management and Budget (OMB) deficit and debt projections and finds that a 1-percentage-point increase in the five-year-ahead projected deficit-GDP ratio raises the five-year-ahead interest rate on ten-year Treasury notes by between 24 and 39 basis points, and that a 1-percentage-point increase in the projected debt-GDP ratio raises the same long-term forward rate by between 3.5 and 5.6 basis points.

Following Laubach but controlling for additional variables, Engen and Hubbard use CBO projections and obtain somewhat smaller effects.[118] They find that an increase in the projected deficit equal to 1 percent of GDP raises the five-year-ahead ten-year rate (the same rate Laubach examines) by 18 basis points, and that an increase in the projected debt equal to 1 percent of GDP raises the forward long-term rate by between 2.8 and 3.3 basis points.

For Laubach and for Engen and Hubbard, the deficit-based results are not dissimilar from the debt-based results. Consider, for example, an increase in the budget deficit equal to 1 percent of GDP in each year over the next ten years. By the end of the ten years, such an increase will have raised government debt by roughly 10 percent of GDP. The deficit-based results found by Laubach would suggest about a 30-basis-point increase in interest rates in this scenario, whereas the debt-based results would suggest about a 45-basis-point increase. Likewise, the deficit-based results of Engen and Hubbard would suggest an increase in long-term rates of roughly 20 basis points, and their debt-based results suggest an increase of roughly 30 basis points (ten times the effect for an increase of 1 percent of GDP).

A second approach to incorporating expected deficits involves event analysis of news reports about deficit reduction legislation or budget projections. This approach examines the change in interest rates (or other variables) on the day on which deficit news is released. For example, Elmendorf examines financial market reactions to events surrounding passage of the Gramm-Rudman-Hollings legislation in 1985 and the Budget Enforcement Act of 1990;[119] he concludes that "higher expected government spending and budget deficits raised real interest rates . . . while lower expected spend-

118. Engen and Hubbard (2004).
119. Elmendorf (1996).

ing and deficits reduced real rates."[120] Unfortunately, given the inability to measure market expectations, this approach does not permit a mapping between the size of the unanticipated deficit and the interest rate effect.[121]

Notably, the results of most studies using either of the two approaches to incorporating anticipated deficits are consistent with the range of 20 to 60 basis points for an increase in projected deficits equal to 1 percent of GDP over ten years mentioned by us in a previous paper, and with the range of 30 to 60 basis points proposed by Robert Rubin, Orszag, and Allen Sinai.[122] This range is also consistent with the results of large macroeconometric models.[123] The simplified Solow model and debt calculation discussed

120. The Council of Economic Advisers (*Economic Report of the President,* 1994, p. 78), studying the events surrounding passage of the Omnibus Budget Reconciliation Act of 1993, concluded that event analysis "linking the announcement and enactment of credible budget reduction to changes in the long-term interest rate . . . provides support for the view that the interest rate declines were largely due to budget policy."

121. Several other papers examine interest rate changes surrounding the release of new budget projections. Thorbecke (1993) uses OMB and CBO projections and finds that a $100 billion increase in the deficit (relative to the previously projected level) is associated with an immediate increase in ten-year interest rates of 14 to 26 basis points. Quigley and Porter-Hudak (1994) use CBO and OMB projections and find that a 1 percent increase in the deficit itself (not as a percentage of GDP) raises short-term interest rates by 0.37 to 0.87 basis point. Assuming a baseline deficit of 2 percent of GDP, their result implies that an increase in the deficit of 1 percent of GDP (a 50 percent increase in the deficit) would raise short-term interest rates by 18.5 to 43.5 basis points. Kitchen (1996) uses changes in OMB forecasts and finds a statistically significant but quite modest effect: an increase in the deficit projection of 1 percent of GDP raises ten-year bond yields by 3.4 basis points for one-year budget projections. He finds even smaller effects for multiyear budget projections on long-term interest rates. Calomiris and others (2004) examine announcement effects about previous deficits, rather than announcement effects about future deficits or future legislation. They find no effects on current interest rates of the announcement of the previous month's deficit. Their deficit measure, however, is based on the monthly budget updates provided by the CBO and the Department of the Treasury. These monthly updates are quite noisy and depend on factors such as the timing of defense contract payments. The variation in the monthly data is thus unlikely to provide significant information about the budget outlook.

122. Gale and Orszag (2003a); Rubin, Orszag, and Sinai (2004). Brook (2003) similarly concludes that "most empirical work conducted in the past ten years estimates the impact on US real long-term interest rates of a sustained 1 percentage point decrease in the US fiscal position to be in the range of 20–40 basis points, and the impact on the slope of the yield curve to be in the range of 10–60 basis points."

123. Almost all major macroeconometric models imply an economically significant connection between changes in budget deficits and changes in long-term interest rates. The precise effects depend on a wide variety of factors, including whether the change in the deficit is caused by a change in taxes or a change in spending, how monetary policy reacts,

above generate somewhat larger numbers, but those calculations assume a closed economy. In a large open economy like the United States, the effect of deficits on interest rates would be expected to be somewhat smaller, and this is consistent with the empirical evidence summarized above.

VECTOR AUTOREGRESSIONS. Some of the most frequently cited papers that find no effect of deficits on interest rates, including those by Evans and by Charles Plosser, employ vector autoregressions (VARs).[124] The VARs in these studies are typically based on a very limited number of variables and only on past values of such variables; they ignore information on current and projected deficits that is not reflected in such variables but may be widely known to market participants. As a result, the VAR-based projections have been shown to be inferior to those produced by the OMB or Data Resources, Inc.[125] The implication is that VAR-based projections based on past values of variables are more likely to suffer from measurement error and thus to be biased toward showing no effect of deficits on interest rates.[126]

Despite these limitations, several recent papers have applied the VAR methodology to examining the connection between deficits and interest rates. For example, Canzoneri, Cumby, and Diba include both the federal funds rate and the ten-year bond rate in a structural VAR; they find that the ten-year yield rises by 45 basis points immediately, and by roughly 40 basis points in the long run, in response to an upward spending shock equal to 1 percent of GDP.[127] Engen and Hubbard use a VAR framework that includes *anticipated* deficits to estimate that an increase in the federal deficit equal to 1 percent of GDP causes the real interest rate to rise by 12 basis

---

and how foreign governments react. The results vary widely, in part because different policies are simulated and standardization is difficult, but suggest that a sustained increase in the primary (noninterest) deficit of 1 percent of GDP would raise interest rates by 40 to 50 basis points after one year and 50 to 100 basis points after ten years (see Gale and Orszag, 2002).

124. Evans (1987a, 1987b); Plosser (1982, 1987a).

125. Bernheim (1987); Cohen and Garnier (1991); Elmendorf (1993).

126. These studies have also been criticized on other grounds. For example, the tests appear to have very little power and in some cases are even unable to reject the hypothesis that expected inflation has no effect on nominal interest rates, and the results are not robust to changes in sample period or specification. For further discussion see Bernheim (1987) and Elmendorf and Mankiw (1999). A recent study by Kormendi and Protopapadakis (2004) shares the characteristic of estimating the effects on interest rates of a deficit measure that depends only on past values of the explanatory variables.

127. Canzoneri, Cumby, and Diba (2002).

points.[128] Qiang Dai and Thomas Philippon estimate a structural VAR that uses information provided by no-arbitrage restrictions on the yield curve.[129] They conclude that a 1-percent-of-GDP increase in the unified deficit raises ten-year bond yields by 41 basis points. Silvia Ardagna, Francesco Caselli, and Timothy Lane, using data from a panel of sixteen advanced industrial countries over several decades, show in a VAR that a 1-percent-of-GDP increase in the primary deficit leads to a cumulative increase in interest rates of almost 150 basis points over ten years.[130] They also show that the initial, static effect of such an increase is in the neighborhood of 10 basis points.

Specification

To examine these issues we follow Laubach and Engen and Hubbard and undertake reduced-form regressions of the following generic form:[131]

$$i_t = \alpha + \beta f_t + \Gamma \mathbf{Z} + \varepsilon_t,$$

where i is a measure of the interest rate, f is a measure of fiscal policy, and $\mathbf{Z}$ is a vector of control variables.[132]

Our primary interest is in the coefficient β, which estimates the effect of the fiscal policy variable on interest rates. We examine the role of several such variables, each expressed as a share of GDP, at different time periods: federal publicly held debt, the unified deficit, the primary deficit, and primary outlays and revenue.

Since it is conceivable that both stock and flow measures of fiscal policy matter, and that the effect of a change in one fiscal variable could depend on the level of the other, we include both debt and deficits in some of the regressions.[133] The regressions that separate primary outlays and revenue provide insight to the extent that, as noted in the discussion of Ricardian equiva-

---

128. Engen and Hubbard (2004).
129. Dai and Phillippon (2004).
130. Ardagna, Caselli, and Lane (2004).
131. Laubach (2003); Engen and Hubbard (2004).
132. Details of the variable definitions and sources used in these regressions may be found at www.brookings.edu/es/commentary/journals/bpea-macro/2004_2_bpea_interest data.pdf or obtained from the authors on request.
133. Ardagna, Caselli, and Lane (2004, p. 4) include both debt and deficits in their model, for similar reasons: ". . . in theory, the relationship between fiscal policy and interest rates may be mediated by either variable. . . . Furthermore, even if one were specifically interested in the effects of only one of these variables, it would still make sense to control for the other. For example, given the current stock of debt, including the deficit may help [control] for the expected future path of the debt itself."

lence above, changes in outlays could have different effects on national saving and thus on interest rates than changes in revenue.[134] We undertake several different versions of our generic regression, all of them using data from 1976 to 2004:

—*Effects of projected fiscal policy on forward interest rates.* Our preferred specifications examine the relationship between forward long-term interest rates and projected fiscal variables. This specification comes closest to eliminating the confounding effect of current macroeconomic conditions on both interest rates and deficits: most projections assume that the economy will be operating at full employment within a relatively short projection period into the future. In these specifications, i_t reflects the simple average of one-year-forward interest rates from five to fourteen years ahead, calculated from the yield curve for zero-coupon bonds.[135] This provides a forward ten-year interest rate. The fiscal policy measures f_t are measured five years ahead, as a share of projected GDP in that year, and are taken from the CBO baseline projections.

—*Effects of projected fiscal policy on current interest rates.* In these regressions, i_t is the current ten-year constant-maturity Treasury yield rather than the forward yield. The fiscal measures are the same as above.

—*Effects of current fiscal policy on current interest rates.* In these regressions we examine the relationship between current long-term rates and current rather than projected fiscal policy outcomes. The fiscal measures are all for the current year.

We perform (but do not always report) each regression using both real and nominal values of the variables. We compute the real interest rate by adjusting the nominal rate for the long-term inflationary expectations series incorporated in the Federal Reserve Board's FRB/US macroeconomic model.[136] In the regressions explaining the nominal interest rate, the inflationary expectations series is included as an explanatory variable. In

---

134. Ricardian equivalence is a statement about the effects of variations in the timing of lump-sum tax payments, holding constant both the path of transfers and government purchases. Our regressions separate tax revenue from purchases and transfers.

135. These variables and some of the other data used in this study come from Thomas Laubach and Eric Engen. The forward interest rate is computed from the zero-coupon yield curve as of the last trading day for the month of the CBO projection.

136. Since 1991:3, this series is based on that of the Survey of Professional Forecasters published by the Federal Reserve Bank of Philadelphia. An appendix to Laubach (2003) describes this series before 1991:3.

both cases the variable measures expected inflation over the subsequent twelve-month period.

All regressions include a constant term and an estimate of the GDP growth rate. The equations using projected fiscal policy include the growth rate projected by the CBO five years ahead. The equations using current fiscal policy measures include the current growth rate.

We include several additional control variables, since macroeconomic conditions can affect the level of interest rates associated with any given fiscal policy outcome. We include a dummy variable for periods when the economy is in recession (as determined by the Business Cycle Dating Committee of the National Bureau of Economic Research); the variable is both entered on its own and interacted with the fiscal measures. The purpose of this dummy and interaction term is to examine whether, even when controlling for projected GDP growth, future fiscal policy outcomes have a different effect on interest rates during a recession than during a recovery.[137]

Following Laubach and Engen and Hubbard,[138] we include a measure of the equity premium, which is intended to control for changes in risk aversion, which in turn could affect interest rates. The measure is defined as dividend income, from the National Income and Product Accounts, divided by the market value of corporate equities held by households, from the Federal Reserve's Flow of Funds accounts, plus the trend growth rate in real GDP, minus the real yield on ten-year Treasury notes.[139] We follow Engen and Hubbard in controlling for Federal Reserve holdings (in the debt equations) and purchases (in the deficit equations) of Treasury securities as a share of GDP, as a way of controlling for monetary policy.[140] We also follow Engen and Hubbard in including an oil price variable.[141]

Finally, Engen and Hubbard include a dummy variable for changes in defense spending, defined as the defense dummy variable constructed by

---

137. Rubin, Orszag, and Sinai (2004) raised such a possibility.

138. Laubach (2003); Engen and Hubbard (2004).

139. Laubach (2003).

140. The results were not affected by substituting the federal funds rate or the three-month Treasury rate for Federal Reserve purchases or holdings of Treasury securities.

141. Engen and Hubbard (2004) cite evidence in Barro and Sala-i-Martin (1991) and Barro (1991) that real oil prices can affect real interest rates. We include the spot price for West Texas Intermediate crude oil, adjusted by the GDP deflator. This oil price series is slightly different from that in Engen and Hubbard (2004). The empirical results are unaffected by this difference.

Figure 10. Defense Spending, 1976–2003

Percent of GDP

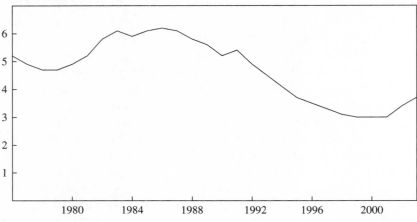

Source: CBO.

Valerie Ramey and Shapiro, augmented to include the military buildup in 2002.[142] We are skeptical that this variable is capturing significant shifts in defense spending, however. The Engen-Hubbard indicator variable is set equal to 1 only in 1980 and 2002. Yet increases in defense spending as a share of GDP were larger in 1981, 1982, 1983, and 2003 than in 1980 (figure 10). Another concern is that a sustained defense buildup should have lasting effects on interest rates, not a one-year effect as their dummy variable implies. Moreover, the decline in defense spending following the collapse of the Soviet Union might also rightfully be considered a noteworthy event in trends in defense spending.[143] For these reasons we use actual defense spending as a share of GDP as a control variable, rather than the dummy variable.

Because some of the regression results suggested evidence of first-order autocorrelation in the error term, we use robust standard errors when esti-

---

142. Ramey and Shapiro (1998).
143. It is also worth noting that, in Ramey and Shapiro (1998, figure 6d), the effect on interest rates of a defense spending shock in their model dies out after five years, so that there ought not be an impact on the five-year ahead, ten-year interest rate in the first place.

mation is undertaken using OLS; we also present the results using maximum likelihood to estimate a first-order autoregressive model.[144]

Results

PROJECTED FISCAL POLICY AND FORWARD INTEREST RATES. Table 6 reports results of OLS regressions in which the real forward (five-year-ahead) long-term interest rate is the dependent variable. The findings leave two broad impressions. First, a robust, economically and statistically significant relationship is observed between forward long-term real interest rates and projected fiscal imbalances. Second, the R^2 statistics show that there is more information in the projected deficit variables than in the projected debt variables.

We begin with the simplest formulations (columns 6-1 through 6-4), which include only the projected fiscal policy measure and the projected GDP growth rate as control variables. An increase five years out in the projected debt of 1 percent of GDP (column 6-1) raises the real forward long-term interest rate by 4.9 basis points. An increase in the projected unified deficit equal to 1 percent of GDP (column 6-2) raises the forward long-term real interest rate by 29 basis points. An increase in the projected primary deficit of 1 percent of GDP (column 6-3) is associated with a still-larger impact on the forward long-term rate of 40 basis points. When revenue and primary outlays are entered separately, a projected reduction in revenue of 1 percent of GDP five years out is estimated to raise the forward long-term rate by 42 basis points, and a projected increase in outlays of the same magnitude and timing raises the forward long-term rate by 37 basis points. All of these estimates are significantly different from zero.

Adding a recession dummy and a term interacting the dummy with the fiscal policy variable (columns 6-5 through 6-8) raises the estimated coefficients on the fiscal variables slightly: the coefficient on the projected primary deficit, for example, rises from 40 to 45 basis points. The coefficients on the terms interacting the recession dummy and the projected fiscal measures suggest that a given fiscal projection has a smaller (in absolute value) effect on interest rates during a recession than during a period of full

---

144. Estimation is undertaken using the "arima" command in the STATA statistical software package.

Table 6. OLS Estimates of the Effects of Projected Fiscal Variables on Real Forward Ten-Year Treasury Rates[a]

Independent variable	Regression											
	6–1	6–2	6–3	6–4	6–5	6–6	6–7	6–8	6–9	6–10	6–11	6–12
Fiscal variables												
Projected debt/GDP	0.049 (0.016)				0.056 (0.018)				0.038 (0.012)			
Projected deficit/GDP		0.293 (0.068)				0.315 (0.070)				0.282 (0.072)		
Projected primary deficit/GDP			0.395 (0.100)				0.445 (0.091)				0.388 (0.099)	
Projected revenue/GDP				−0.424 (0.203)				−0.531 (0.130)				−0.292 (0.133)
Projected primary outlays/GDP				0.370 (0.113)				0.391 (0.141)				0.430 (0.219)
Recession dummy and interactions												
Recession dummy					2.913 (0.554)	1.615 (0.396)	1.128 (0.484)	−6.731 (4.350)	0.870 (1.031)	0.897 (0.344)	0.719 (0.334)	6.555 (6.634)
Recession dummy × projected debt/GDP					−0.043 (0.025)				−0.012 (0.023)			
Recession dummy × projected deficit/GDP						−0.178 (0.109)				−0.099 (0.053)		
Recession dummy × projected primary deficit/GDP							−0.258 (0.147)				−0.152 (0.075)	
Recession dummy × projected revenue/GDP								0.380 (0.127)				0.030 (0.157)
Recession dummy × projected primary outlays/GDP								0.057 (0.173)				−0.356 (0.229)

Control variables

	(1)	(2)	(3)	(4)	(5)	(6)	(7)	(8)	(9)	(10)	(11)	(12)
Oil price									0.048	0.023	0.015	0.023
									(0.017)	(0.019)	(0.020)	(0.022)
Equity premium[b]									−0.283	−0.293	−0.338	−0.377
									(0.161)	(0.134)	(0.143)	(0.175)
Defense spending/GDP									−0.041	−0.079	0.012	−0.028
									(0.179)	(0.141)	(0.148)	(0.195)
Federal Reserve holdings of Treasuries									−0.208			
									(0.345)			
Federal Reserve purchases of Treasuries										−0.743	−0.690	−0.602
										(0.755)	(0.741)	(0.821)
Projected GDP growth rate	0.555	0.278	0.185	0.204	0.296	0.034	−0.053	−0.001	0.152	0.346	0.363	0.311
	(0.438)	(0.300)	(0.289)	(0.264)	(0.406)	(0.233)	(0.205)	(0.208)	(0.585)	(0.521)	(0.526)	(0.554)
Constant	1.335	3.666	4.809	5.767	1.629	4.168	5.377	7.880	3.522	4.261	4.999	2.586
	(1.593)	(0.806)	(0.799)	(4.878)	(1.687)	(0.689)	(0.494)	(3.684)	(2.276)	(0.924)	(0.880)	(5.275)
Adjusted R^2	.213	.436	.408	.386	.463	.642	.641	.636	.679	.779	.773	.758

Source: Authors' regressions using data from CBO; Laubach (2003); OMB: Bureau of Economic Analysis, National Income and Product Accounts; Financial Forecast Center; National Bureau of Economic Research; Federal Reserve.

a. Sample period for all regressions is 1976–2004. All projected variables are five-year projections. Numbers in parentheses are robust standard errors. Number of observations $N = 29$.

b. Dividend component of national income as a percentage of the market value of corporate equity held (directly or indirectly) by households, minus the real ten-year Treasury yield, plus the real GDP growth rate projected five years ahead. The value of the premium in the quarter prior to the release of the projections is used.

employment. Four of the five interaction terms have p-values below .12, and one of these is significant at the 1 percent level. This suggests that the effect of a projected deficit on forward long-term rates may be smaller if the economy is *currently* in recession than if it is not. This presents a puzzle, since it is unclear why a current recession should affect the relationship between the two future variables.[145]

Adding the other control variables (monetary policy, defense spending, the oil price, and the equity premium; columns 6-9 through 6-12) reduces the estimated coefficients on the fiscal variables slightly: The coefficient on the projected primary imbalance, for example, declines to 39 basis points (column 6-11). The interaction between the recession dummy and projected unified or primary deficits remains statistically and economically significant (columns 6-10 and 6-11). Many of the additional control variables enter with the expected sign, but few are statistically significant other than the equity premium, which enters negatively.[146] The coefficient on real oil prices is positive and significant in the debt equation (column 6-9), but it is not statistically significant in the others. The coefficient on Federal Reserve open-market purchases is negative but not statistically significant. Defense spending enters with a negative coefficient, but it is not statistically significant.

Running the same regressions using the *nominal* forward long-term rate as the dependent variable and including inflationary expectations as a right-hand-side variable (table 7) generates similar fiscal effects. The coefficient on the projected primary deficit, for example, ranges between 33 and 46 basis points. The results in tables 6 and 7 underscore a robust, statistically significant connection between forward long-term interest rates and projected fiscal policy outcomes.

Table 8 includes *both* projected debt and projected primary deficit variables in the same regressions. To avoid double counting, we use projected debt as a share of GDP at the end of year $t + 4$ and primary budget mea-

(text continues on page 164)

---

145. Rubin, Orszag, and Sinai (2004) hypothesize, based mostly on Rubin's experience with real-world financial markets, that "it is possible during economic downturns that financial markets do not focus on long-term fiscal issues; if this is the case, the effect of the fiscal deterioration on long-term interest rates will manifest itself only as the economy recovers." We have not evaluated whether arbitrage based on this evidence would generate expected profits after taking into account trading costs and other factors.

146. The same result is observed in Laubach (2003) and Engen and Hubbard (2004).

Table 7. OLS Estimates of the Effects of Projected Fiscal Variables on Nominal Forward Ten-Year Treasury Rates[a]

Independent variable	Regression											
	7-1	7-2	7-3	7-4	7-5	7-6	7-7	7-8	7-9	7-10	7-11	7-12
Fiscal variables												
Projected debt/GDP	0.035								0.038			
	(0.019)								(0.011)			
Projected deficit/GDP		0.250			0.056	0.351				0.281		
		(0.096)			(0.020)	(0.085)				(0.073)		
Projected primary deficit/GDP			0.329				0.464				0.384	
			(0.127)				(0.112)				(0.098)	
Projected revenue/GDP				-0.400				-0.527				-0.229
				(0.180)				(0.126)				(0.123)
Projected primary outlays/GDP				0.245				0.398				0.458
				(0.147)				(0.256)				(0.238)
Recession dummy and interactions												
Recession dummy					2.874	1.850	1.201	-6.515	1.243	0.988	0.750	9.254
					(0.691)	(0.491)	(0.512)	(6.437)	(1.168)	(0.432)	(0.347)	(7.462)
Recession dummy × projected debt/GDP					-0.042				-0.021			
					(0.026)				(0.030)			
Recession dummy × projected deficit/GDP						-0.206				-0.105		
						(0.122)				(0.057)		
Recession dummy × projected primary deficit/GDP							-0.271				-0.149	
							(0.160)				(0.074)	
Recession dummy × projected revenue/GDP								0.375				-0.037
								(0.130)				(0.159)
Recession dummy × projected primary outlays/GDP								0.050				-0.430
								(0.254)				(0.263)

(continued)

Table 7. OLS Estimates of the Effects of Projected Fiscal Variables on Nominal Forward Ten-Year Treasury Rates[a] (*continued*)

Independent variable	Regression											
	7-1	7-2	7-3	7-4	7-5	7-6	7-7	7-8	7-9	7-10	7-11	7-12
Control variables												
Oil price									0.052	0.027	0.017	0.031
									(0.018)	(0.020)	(0.020)	(0.021)
Equity premium[b]									−0.244	−0.275	−0.330	−0.370
									(0.136)	(0.134)	(0.142)	(0.168)
Defense spending/GDP									0.055	0.011	0.051	0.056
									(0.275)	(0.230)	(0.235)	(0.259)
Federal Reserve holdings of Treasuries									−0.367			
									(0.412)			
Federal Reserve purchases of Treasuries										−0.786	−0.707	−0.615
										(0.702)	(0.733)	(0.804)
Projected GDP growth rate	−0.169	−0.078	−0.248	−0.265	0.273	0.274	0.042	0.011	0.228	0.393	0.372	0.335
	(0.598)	(0.443)	(0.385)	(0.378)	(0.525)	(0.370)	(0.333)	(0.378)	(0.635)	(0.551)	(0.552)	(0.594)
Expected inflation[c]	1.327	1.184	1.236	1.275	1.012	0.858	0.940	0.989	0.809	0.878	0.949	0.847
	(0.172)	(0.194)	(0.179)	(0.165)	(0.151)	(0.153)	(0.149)	(0.225)	(0.278)	(0.209)	(0.203)	(0.228)
Constant	2.740	4.057	5.088	7.874	1.678	3.939	5.340	7.671	4.103	3.989	4.883	0.668
	(1.907)	(0.875)	(0.722)	(3.774)	(1.851)	(0.739)	(0.506)	(5.871)	(2.050)	(1.157)	(1.123)	(6.100)
Adjusted R^2	.813	.854	.853	.851	.854	.906	.903	.900	.914	.941	.938	.935

Source: Authors' regressions using data from CBO; Laubach (2003); OMB; Bureau of Economic Analysis, National Income and Product Accounts; Financial Forecast Center; National Bureau of Economic Research; Federal Reserve.
a. Sample period for all regressions is 1976–2004. All projected variables are five-year projections. Numbers in parentheses are robust standard errors. Number of observations $N = 29$.
b. Defined as in table 6.
c. As constructed by Laubach (2003).

Table 8. Further OLS Estimates of the Effects of Projected Fiscal Variables on Real Forward Ten-Year Treasury Rates[a]

Independent variable	Regression					
	8-1	*8-2*	*8-3*	*8-4*	*8-5*	*8-6*
Fiscal variables						
Projected debt/GDP	−0.034	−0.038	−0.042	−0.046	−0.016	−0.017
	(0.028)	(0.033)	(0.028)	(0.030)	(0.027)	(0.043)
Projected primary deficit/GDP	0.541		0.648		0.475	
	(0.176)		(0.156)		0.177	
Projected revenue/GDP		−0.528		−0.661		−0.400
		(0.212)		(0.179)		(0.275)
Projected primary outlays/GDP		0.582		0.665		0.559
		(0.233)		(0.224)		(0.386)
Recession dummy and interactions						
Recession dummy			1.036	−5.343	1.315	4.925
			(1.366)	(4.138)	(0.825)	(7.757)
Recession dummy × projected debt/GDP			−0.005	−0.008	−0.016	−0.013
			(0.028)	(0.022)	(0.019)	(0.020)
Recession dummy × projected primary deficit/GDP			−0.349		−0.163	
			(0.195)		(0.156)	
Recession dummy × projected revenue/GDP				0.397		0.083
				(0.179)		(0.268)
Recession dummy × projected primary outlays/GDP				−0.026		−0.280
				(0.208)		(0.279)
Control variables						
Oil price					0.003	0.005
					(0.020)	(0.034)
Equity premium[b]					−0.354	−0.380
					(0.152)	(0.187)
Defense spending/GDP					0.077	0.015
					(0.143)	(0.167)
Federal Reserve purchases of Treasuries					−0.628	−0.561
					(0.749)	(0.844)
Projected GDP growth rate	−0.133	−0.186	−0.446	−0.501	0.307	0.305
	(0.440)	(0.426)	(0.277)	(0.315)	(0.601)	(0.620)
Constant	7.235	6.547	8.429	8.676	5.947	3.337
	(2.347)	(4.848)	(1.852)	(3.994)	(2.127)	(5.651)
Adjusted R^2	.416	.393	.662	.664	.761	.738

Source: Authors' regressions using data from CBO; Laubach (2003); OMB; Bureau of Economic Analysis, National Income and Product Accounts; Financial Forecast Center; National Bureau of Economic Research; Federal Reserve.

a. Regressions are similar to those in table 6 except that at least two fiscal variables (one of which is projected debt) are included in each equation. Sample period for all regressions is 1976–2004. All projected variables are five-year projections except the debt-GDP ratio, which is a four-year projection. Numbers in parentheses are robust standard errors. Number of observations $N = 29$.

b. Defined as in table 6.

sures in year $t + 5$.[147] In this "horse race" between stocks and flows, the deficit variables dominate. Indeed, the coefficient on the projected debt variable becomes statistically insignificant (and slightly negative), and the estimated effect of the projected deficit *increases:* whereas in table 6 we found an effect of 29 to 45 basis points for a 1-percent-of-GDP change in the projected primary variable (primary deficit, primary outlays, or revenue), table 8 shows an effect of 40 to 67 basis points once the analysis controls for projected debt-GDP ratios. The recession interaction is statistically significant in one of the regressions (column 8-4, for the interaction with revenue), but insignificant in the others. Of the other variables, only the equity premium remains statistically significant. The inclusion of both debt and deficit variables produces similar results when, as in table 7, the nominal forward interest rate is used as the dependent variable and inflationary expectations are included on the right-hand side (results not shown).

Table 9 shows results for the same specification as in table 8 but using a first-order autoregressive moving average (ARMA) model for the estimation, because some of the results (in particular, when the additional control variables are included) suggest autocorrelated errors. In these regressions the coefficient on the projections of the primary deficit, primary outlays, and revenue ranges between 44 and 67 basis points. Again, the coefficients on the debt variables are generally small, negative, and statistically insignificant, and some of the recession interaction terms are significant. We highlight the specification in column 9-5 as something of a central estimate and will use it as a baseline for our sensitivity analysis below. In that specification a 1-percent-of-GDP increase in the primary deficit projected five years in the future raises current forward rates by 53 basis points, controlling for a wide variety of other explanatory factors.[148]

PROJECTED FISCAL POLICY AND CURRENT LONG-TERM RATES. Table 10 shows regressions of the *current* real ten-year interest rate on projected future fiscal variables. In the specifications that include (besides GDP

(text continues on page 69)

---

147. Using projected debt at the end of $t + 5$ and the deficit in $t + 5$ would double-count the deficit in $t + 5$. Likewise, using debt at the end of $t + 4$ and the unified deficit in $t + 5$ would effectively double-count interest payments in $t + 5$, since they are already implied by the debt level at the end of $t + 4$.

148. Estimates of the specifications in tables 6 through 9 in first-difference form led to similar coefficient estimates and large standard errors.

Table 9. ARMA Estimates of the Effects of Projected Fiscal Variables on Real Forward Ten-Year Treasury Rates[a]

Independent variable	Regression					
	9-1	9-2	9-3	9-4	9-5	9-6
Fiscal variables						
Projected debt/GDP	−0.029	−0.038	−0.047	−0.047	−0.013	−0.010
	(0.031)	(0.034)	(0.026)	(0.026)	(0.017)	(0.019)
Projected primary deficit/GDP	0.455		0.673		0.534	
	(0.225)		(0.169)		(0.113)	
Projected revenue/GDP		−0.442		−0.672		−0.508
		(0.219)		(0.171)		(0.154)
Projected primary outlays/GDP		0.564		0.669		0.489
		(0.227)		(0.201)		(0.213)
Recession dummy and interactions						
Recession dummy			0.770	−5.549	0.512	1.688
			(1.511)	(3.597)	(0.854)	(4.807)
Recession dummy × projected debt/GDP			0.003	−0.003	0.013	0.015
			(0.033)	(0.029)	(0.021)	(0.022)
Recession dummy × projected primary deficit/GDP			−0.385		−0.330	
			(0.231)		(0.159)	
Recession dummy × projected revenue/GDP				0.423		0.295
				(0.213)		(0.180)
Recession dummy × projected primary outlays/GDP				−0.051		−0.368
				(0.243)		(0.245)
Control variables						
Oil price					−0.010	0.003
					(0.020)	(0.029)
Equity premium[b]					−0.447	−0.448
					(0.118)	(0.118)
Defense spending/GDP					0.029	0.032
					(0.063)	(0.085)
Federal Reserve purchases of Treasuries					−0.330	−0.297
					(0.545)	(0.585)
Projected GDP growth rate	−0.150	−0.250	−0.484	−0.506	0.775	0.734
	(0.429)	(0.407)	(0.213)	(0.259)	(0.560)	(0.565)
Constant	6.941	5.388	8.748	8.871	5.365	5.448
	(2.346)	(4.761)	(1.701)	(3.375)	(1.332)	(3.147)
AR(1) coefficient	0.331	0.346	−0.100	−0.061	−0.587	−0.588
	(0.308)	(0.280)	(0.210)	(0.214)	(0.239)	(0.232)
Wald χ^2	52.409	56.816	419.014	71,263.451	2,751.599	39,603.831

Source: Authors' regressions using data from CBO; Laubach (2003); OMB; Bureau of Economic Analysis, National Income and Product Accounts; Financial Forecast Center; National Bureau of Economic Research; Federal Reserve.

a. Sample period for all regressions is 1976–2004. All projected variables are five-year projections except the debt-GDP ratio, which is a four-year projection. Numbers in parentheses are semirobust standard errors. Number of observations $N = 29$.

b. Defined as in table 6.

Table 10. OLS Estimates of the Effects of Projected Fiscal Variables on Real Current Ten-Year Treasury Rates[a]

Independent variable	Regression											
	10-1	10-2	10-3	10-4	10-5	10-6	10-7	10-8	10-9	10-10	10-11	10-12
Fiscal variables												
Projected debt/GDP	0.035 (0.019)				0.045 (0.020)				0.017 (0.020)			
Projected deficit/GDP		0.255 (0.097)				0.274 (0.076)				0.175 (0.100)		
Projected primary deficit/GDP			0.319 (0.152)				0.360 (0.109)				0.169 (0.155)	
Projected revenue/GDP				-0.331 (0.326)				-0.378 (0.279)				-0.006 (0.246)
Projected primary outlays/GDP				0.308 (0.158)				0.346 (0.208)				0.280 (0.228)
Recession dummy and interactions												
Recession dummy					4.393 (0.826)	2.579 (0.746)	2.141 (0.907)	-9.671 (9.527)	1.680 (1.133)	1.211 (0.786)	1.195 (0.658)	10.028 (8.171)
Recession dummy × projected debt/GDP					-0.063 (0.040)				-0.027 (0.031)			
Recession dummy × projected deficit/GDP						-0.192 (0.210)				-0.029 (0.086)		
Recession dummy × projected primary deficit/GDP							-0.224 (0.282)				0.038 (0.132)	
Recession dummy × projected revenue/GDP								0.329 (0.276)				-0.234 (0.262)
Recession dummy × projected primary outlays/GDP								0.344 (0.320)				-0.250 (0.248)

Control variables

	(1)	(2)	(3)	(4)	(5)	(6)	(7)	(8)	(9)	(10)	(11)	(12)
Oil price									0.046 (0.026)	0.034 (0.033)	0.039 (0.034)	0.047 (0.042)
Equity premium[b]									−0.437 (0.163)	−0.494 (0.177)	−0.506 (0.178)	−0.567 (0.185)
Defense spending/GDP									−0.139 (0.301)	0.075 (0.218)	0.170 (0.212)	0.076 (0.222)
Federal Reserve holdings of Treasuries									−0.985 (0.344)			
Federal Reserve purchases of Treasuries										−2.008 (0.538)	−1.941 (0.566)	−1.809 (0.724)
Projected GDP growth rate	0.783 (0.508)	0.662 (0.410)	0.558 (0.408)	0.566 (0.400)	0.386 (0.410)	0.267 (0.279)	0.177 (0.277)	0.167 (0.356)	0.462 (0.664)	0.697 (0.658)	0.514 (0.659)	0.473 (0.730)
Constant	0.510 (1.817)	1.887 (1.123)	2.914 (1.143)	3.321 (7.498)	0.973 (1.792)	2.714 (0.897)	3.770 (0.769)	4.396 (7.498)	7.418 (2.573)	2.654 (0.911)	3.059 (0.945)	−1.652 (5.919)
Adjusted R^2	.028	.181	.135	.100	.410	.498	.464	.478	.755	.781	.763	.751

Source: Authors' regressions using data from CBO; Laubach (2003); OMB; Bureau of Economic Analysis, National Income and Product Accounts; Financial Forecast Center; National Bureau of Economic Research; Federal Reserve.
a. Sample period for all regressions is 1976–2004. All projected variables are five-year projections. Numbers in parentheses are robust standard errors. Number of observations $N = 29$.
b. Defined as in table 6.

growth) only fiscal variables or only fiscal and recession variables (columns 10-1 through 10-8), the coefficients on the fiscal variables tend to be somewhat smaller than when the forward long-term rate is used (table 6) but are still statistically significant. For example, the coefficient on the projected primary deficit is either 32 or 36 basis points. The coefficients become smaller and statistically insignificant when the additional control variables are included: the coefficient on the primary deficit falls to 17 basis points.

Notably, Federal Reserve holdings or purchases of Treasury securities, which did not affect forward long-term rates in tables 6 through 9, have an economically significant and statistically precise effect on current long-term rates in table 10 (and in tables 11 through 13). This suggests that different factors may affect current long-term rates than affect forward rates.

When current nominal long-term rates are used as the dependent variable (table 11), projected unified deficits and projected primary deficits each enter with a statistically significant coefficient of about 20 basis points in the regressions that include all of the control variables (columns 11-10 and 11-11, respectively). When current real rates are used and both the projected debt and projected primary deficit variables are included (table 12), the estimated coefficient on the latter increases to over 50 basis points in the specifications that include only fiscal variables or only fiscal and recession variables, but this effect disappears in the regressions that include all the control variables. The results are similar when nominal rates are used and when an AR(1) model is estimated (results not shown).

EFFECTS OF CURRENT FISCAL POLICY ON CURRENT LONG-TERM RATES. Table 13 presents regressions of the real current long-term interest rate on *current* fiscal variables. The fiscal variables are generally not statistically significant in these specifications, and they remain insignificant when the nominal rate is used, when an AR(1) model is estimated, and when both debt and deficit variables are entered simultaneously (results not shown).

Sensitivity Analysis

Table 14 presents results of our sensitivity analysis on the risk measure and the state-of-the-economy measure. The equity premium variable raises

(text continues on page 176)

Table 11. OLS Estimates of the Effects of Projected Fiscal Variables on Current Nominal Ten-Year Treasury Rates[a]

Independent variable	Regression											
	11-1	11-2	11-3	11-4	11-5	11-6	11-7	11-8	11-9	11-10	11-11	11-12
Fiscal variables												
Projected debt/GDP	0.002 (0.022)				0.025 (0.024)				0.019 (0.017)			
Projected deficit/GDP		0.108 (0.120)				0.203 (0.111)				0.178 (0.082)		
Projected primary deficit/GDP			0.133 (0.157)				0.251 (0.142)				0.217 (0.117)	
Projected revenue/GDP				−0.268 (0.255)				−0.587 (0.222)				−0.272 (0.254)
Projected primary outlays/GDP				−0.025 (0.188)				−0.105 (0.341)				0.161 (0.214)
Recession dummy and interactions												
Recession dummy					3.115 (1.122)	2.122 (0.831)	1.727 (0.897)	−22.057 (9.284)	0.649 (0.850)	0.778 (0.432)	0.817 (0.328)	−1.307 (9.465)
Recession dummy × projected debt/GDP					−0.041 (0.038)				−0.002 (0.022)			
Recession dummy × projected deficit/GDP						−0.138 (0.208)				0.001 (0.064)		
Recession dummy × projected primary deficit/GDP							−0.150 (0.271)				0.010 (0.093)	
Recession dummy × projected revenue/GDP								0.569 (0.215)				0.046 (0.271)
Recession dummy × projected primary outlays/GDP								0.706 (0.332)				0.063 (0.281)

(continued)

Table 11. OLS Estimates of the Effects of Projected Fiscal Variables on Current Nominal Ten-Year Treasury Rates[a] (continued)

Independent variable	11-1	11-2	11-3	11-4	11-5	11-6	11-7	11-8	11-9	11-10	11-11	11-12
						Regression						
Control variables												
Oil price									0.035	0.014	0.012	0.011
									(0.021)	(0.025)	(0.027)	(0.034)
Equity premium[b]									−0.545	−0.578	−0.606	−0.595
									(0.169)	(0.161)	(0.171)	(0.195)
Defense spending/GDP									−0.404	−0.351	−0.295	−0.275
									(0.293)	(0.181)	(0.189)	(0.203)
Federal Reserve holdings of Treasuries									−0.544			
									(0.500)			
Federal Reserve purchases of Treasuries										−1.804	−1.739	−1.758
										(0.794)	(0.804)	(0.794)
Projected GDP growth rate	−0.883	−0.569	−0.660	−0.693	−0.388	−0.200	−0.364	−0.526	0.252	0.475	0.397	0.373
	(0.646)	(0.586)	(0.520)	(0.480)	(0.669)	(0.573)	(0.516)	(0.498)	(0.670)	(0.610)	(0.610)	(0.658)
Expected inflation[c]	1.753	1.637	1.666	1.739	1.398	1.277	1.340	1.623	1.527	1.579	1.608	1.642
	(0.227)	(0.268)	(0.250)	(0.229)	(0.249)	(0.268)	(0.253)	(0.300)	(0.249)	(0.200)	(0.196)	(0.256)
Constant	3.741	3.240	3.700	8.984	2.573	3.161	3.980	16.428	5.814	3.948	4.454	6.400
	(2.033)	(1.159)	(0.948)	(5.489)	(2.151)	(1.066)	(0.783)	(8.615)	(3.048)	(1.002)	(0.930)	(7.141)
Adjusted R^2	.809	.818	.817	.819	.843	.858	.854	.874	.940	.957	.954	.949

Source: Authors' regressions using data from CBO; Laubach (2003); OMB; Bureau of Economic Analysis, National Income and Product Accounts; Financial Forecast Center; National Bureau of Economic Research; Federal Reserve.
a. Sample period for all regressions is 1976–2004. All projected variables are five-year projections. Numbers in parentheses are robust standard errors. Number of observations $N = 29$.
b. Defined as in table 6.
c. As constructed by Laubach (2003).

Table 12. Further OLS Estimates of the Effects of Projected Fiscal Variables on Real Current Ten-Year Treasury Rates[a]

Independent variable	Regression					
	12-1	*12-2*	*12-3*	*12-4*	*12-5*	*12-6*
Fiscal variables						
Projected debt/GDP	−0.052	−0.062	−0.037	−0.050	0.019	0.017
	(0.039)	(0.041)	(0.033)	(0.031)	(0.028)	(0.037)
Projected primary deficit/GDP	0.541		0.527		0.085	
	(0.276)		(0.194)		(0.198)	
Projected revenue/GDP		−0.504		−0.479		0.026
		(0.344)		(0.344)		(0.348)
Projected primary outlays/GDP		0.660		0.655		0.209
		(0.312)		(0.281)		(0.304)
Recession dummy and interactions						
Recession dummy			3.677	−6.378	4.129	9.496
			(2.272)	(9.464)	(1.102)	(9.220)
Recession dummy × projected debt/GDP			−0.050	−0.056	−0.076	−0.072
			(0.047)	(0.026)	(0.022)	(0.024)
Recession dummy × projected primary deficit/GDP			−0.162		0.304	
			(0.309)		(0.174)	
Recession dummy × projected revenue/GDP				0.180		−0.422
				(0.352)		(0.335)
Recession dummy × projected primary outlays/GDP				0.419		0.128
				(0.248)		(0.248)
Control variables						
Oil price					0.024	0.026
					(0.033)	(0.049)
Equity premium[b]					−0.547	−0.585
					(0.200)	(0.207)
Defense spending/GDP					0.238	0.147
					(0.228)	(0.242)
Federal Reserve purchases of Treasuries					−2.199	−2.100
					(0.656)	(0.787)
Projected GDP growth rate	0.073	−0.081	−0.251	−0.493	0.745	0.741
	(0.559)	(0.495)	(0.342)	(0.474)	(0.837)	(0.903)
Constant	6.611	4.615	6.654	4.636	1.868	−1.993
	(3.199)	(7.500)	(2.347)	(8.649)	(2.297)	(7.340)
Adjusted R^2	.146	.119	.488	.537	.785	.767

Source: Authors' regressions using data from CBO; Laubach (2003); OMB; Bureau of Economic Analysis, National Income and Product Accounts; Financial Forecast Center; National Bureau of Economic Research; Federal Reserve.

a. These regressions are similar to those in table 6 except that at least two fiscal variables (one of which is projected debt) are included in each equation. Sample period for all regressions is 1976–2004. All projected variables are five-year projections except the debt-GDP ratio, which is a four-year projection. Numbers in parentheses are robust standard errors. Number of observations $N = 29$.

b. Defined as in table 6.

Table 13. OLS Estimates of the Effects of Current-Period Fiscal Variables on Real Current Ten-Year Treasury Rates[a]

Independent variable	13-1	13-2	13-3	13-4	13-5	13-6	13-7	13-8	13-9	13-10	13-11	13-12
Fiscal variables												
Debt/GDP	-0.029				0.034				-0.010			
	(0.031)				(0.023)				(0.027)			
Deficit/GDP		0.165				0.113				0.020		
		(0.115)				(0.114)				(0.145)		
Primary deficit/GDP			0.086				-0.005				-0.062	
			(0.111)				(0.108)				(0.137)	
Revenue/GDP				0.940				0.667				0.205
				(0.114)				(0.287)				(0.288)
Primary outlays/GDP				0.878				0.583				0.269
				(0.173)				(0.334)				(0.460)
Recession dummy and interactions												
Recession dummy					8.161	4.968	2.834	-23.329	3.776	2.411	0.336	-14.988
					(1.590)	(2.306)	(1.374)	(11.876)	(1.874)	(2.231)	(1.177)	(14.676)
Recession dummy × debt/GDP					-0.161				-0.088			
					(0.040)				(0.039)			
Recession dummy × deficit/GDP						-0.748				-0.515		
						(0.791)				(0.535)		
Recession dummy × primary deficit/GDP							-0.050				0.249	
							(2.052)				(0.929)	
Recession dummy × revenue/GDP								-0.440				-0.118
								(0.859)				(0.949)
Recession dummy × primary outlays/GDP								1.667				0.909
								(1.106)				(1.044)

Control variables

	(1)	(2)	(3)	(4)	(5)	(6)	(7)	(8)	(9)	(10)	(11)	(12)
Oil price									0.041	0.057	0.066	0.041
									(0.023)	(0.020)	(0.020)	(0.032)
Equity premium[b]									-0.410	-0.478	-0.432	-0.459
									(0.111)	(0.124)	(0.130)	(0.162)
Defense spending/GDP									-0.022	0.316	0.338	0.244
									(0.271)	(0.297)	(0.249)	(0.292)
Federal Reserve holdings of Treasuries									-1.087			
									(0.301)			
Federal Reserve purchases of Treasuries										-1.612	-1.523	-1.620
										(0.629)	(0.709)	(0.736)
GDP growth rate	-0.283	-0.293	-0.294	-0.086	0.086	-0.009	0.071	0.048	0.014	-0.059	-0.028	0.007
	(0.179)	(0.171)	(0.180)	(0.139)	(0.173)	(0.187)	(0.203)	(0.223)	(0.109)	(0.128)	(0.138)	(0.140)
Constant	6.100	4.617	5.045	-29.049	2.108	3.499	3.484	-19.215	9.752	3.096	2.476	-5.023
	(1.450)	(0.685)	(0.636)	(5.000)	(1.091)	(0.689)	(0.754)	(10.761)	(2.598)	(1.126)	(1.318)	(11.283)
Adjusted R^2	.090	.123	.081	.453	.351	.287	.245	.422	.771	.739	.731	.726

Source: Authors' regressions using data from CBO; Laubach (2003); OMB; Bureau of Economic Analysis, National Income and Product Accounts; Financial Forecast Center; National Bureau of Economic Research; Federal Reserve.

a. Sample period for all regressions is 1976–2004. All fiscal variables are current-period variables. Numbers in parentheses are robust standard errors. Number of observations $N = 29$.

b. Defined as in table 6.

Table 14. ARMA Estimates of Effects on Interest Rates Using Alternative Controls for Economic Activity and Risk

Independent variable	Regression											
	14-1	14-2	14-3	14-4	14-5	14-6	14-7	14-8	14-9	14-10	14-11	14-12
Projected debt/GDP	-0.013	-0.051	-0.184	0.009	-0.018	-0.069	-0.226	0.000	-0.019	-0.067	-0.216	0.001
	(0.017)	(0.020)	(0.045)	(0.023)	(0.021)	(0.017)	(0.052)	(0.018)	(0.023)	(0.020)	(0.055)	(0.018)
Projected primary deficit/GDP	0.534	0.520	1.334	0.224	0.438	0.573	1.336	0.238	0.428	0.572	1.340	0.241
	(0.113)	(0.123)	(0.299)	(0.110)	(0.169)	(0.173)	(0.433)	(0.099)	(0.156)	(0.174)	(0.420)	(0.103)
Recession dummy	0.512				0.275				0.127			
	(0.854)				(1.125)				(1.204)			
Recession dummy × projected debt/GDP	0.013				0.005				0.007			
	(0.021)				(0.023)				(0.025)			
Recession dummy × projected primary deficit/GDP	-0.330				-0.215				-0.217			
	(0.159)				(0.183)				(0.183)			
GDP gap		-0.809				-0.912				-0.911		
		(0.209)				(0.305)				(0.302)		
GDP gap × projected debt/GDP		0.021				0.023				0.023		
		(0.005)				(0.006)				(0.006)		
GDP gap × projected primary deficit/GDP		-0.112				-0.120				-0.120		
		(0.022)				(0.033)				(0.033)		
Unemployment rate			-0.955				-1.164				-1.132	
			(0.315)				(0.454)				(0.464)	
Unemployment rate × projected debt/GDP			0.026				0.032				0.030	
			(0.006)				(0.008)				(0.008)	

	(1)	(2)	(3)	(4)	(5)	(6)	(7)	(8)	(9)	(10)	(11)	(12)
Unemployment rate × projected primary deficit/GDP	-0.447 (0.118)		-0.154 (0.034)				-0.155 (0.049)				-0.155 (0.048)	
Equity premium[b]	-0.271 (0.086)		-0.274 (0.101)	-0.283 (0.144)								
Dividend/market value					-0.043 (0.129)	0.022 (0.085)	0.079 (0.096)	0.080 (0.120)				
Projected GDP growth rate	0.775 (0.560)	-0.424 (0.327)	-0.372 (0.429)	0.008 (0.575)	-0.603 (0.270)	-1.267 (0.212)	-1.187 (0.324)	-0.767 (0.298)	-0.647 (0.231)	-1.243 (0.190)	-1.112 (0.281)	-0.736 (0.280)
Federal Reserve purchases of Treasuries	-0.330 (0.545)	-1.200 (0.347)	-1.313 (0.402)	-0.879 (0.596)	-0.846 (0.596)	-1.217 (0.485)	-1.241 (0.566)	-0.903 (0.680)	-0.766 (0.542)	-1.273 (0.398)	-1.429 (0.469)	-1.040 (0.596)
Oil price	-0.010 (0.020)	0.057 (0.008)	0.056 (0.011)	0.052 (0.013)	0.042 (0.013)	0.075 (0.012)	0.072 (0.013)	0.065 (0.010)	0.043 (0.013)	0.076 (0.009)	0.076 (0.011)	0.069 (0.009)
Defense spending/GDP	0.029 (0.063)	-0.005 (0.068)	-0.120 (0.073)	-0.007 (0.103)	-0.070 (0.089)	-0.073 (0.086)	-0.199 (0.085)	-0.121 (0.102)	-0.084 (0.095)	-0.069 (0.088)	-0.182 (0.085)	-0.094 (0.105)
Constant	5.365 (1.332)	8.281 (1.334)	13.470 (2.366)	4.445 (1.827)	7.284 (1.485)	10.287 (1.075)	16.110 (2.794)	5.905 (1.323)	7.254 (1.529)	10.234 (1.166)	15.815 (2.843)	5.949 (1.239)
AR(1) coefficient	-0.587 (0.239)	-0.530 (0.213)	-0.512 (0.224)	-0.218 (0.261)	-0.183 (0.253)	-0.423 (0.227)	-0.373 (0.201)	-0.050 (0.197)	-0.155 (0.212)	-0.432 (0.204)	-0.409 (0.191)	-0.105 (0.183)
Wald χ^2	2,751.599	889.574	1,315.638	259.491	703.087	499.778	342.81	247.073	588.278	505.274	408.035	219.635

Source: Authors' regressions using data from CBO; Laubach (2003); OMB: Bureau of Economic Analysis, National Income and Product Accounts; Financial Forecast Center; National Bureau of Economic Research; Federal Reserve.
a. Sample period for all regressions is 1976–2004. All projected variables are five-year projections except the debt-GDP ratio, which is a four-year projection. Numbers in parentheses are semirobust standard errors. Number of observations $N = 29$.
b. Defined as in table 6.

a number of issues. A change in the ratio of the dividend yield to market
value could imply either a change in the return on all assets or a shift in
preferences for stocks versus bonds. In addition, the equity premium variable includes a measure of the previous period's long-term interest rates,
which might create endogeneity problems.[149] We therefore examine the
effects of dropping the interest rate component of the equity premium—
and thus entering the dividend–market value ratio in lieu of the equity
premium—and of omitting both risk variables. The recession dummy
also raises some concerns, since it is discontinuous and takes the value
of 1 only in 1980, 1981, 1982, and 1991.[150] To explore other options, we
perform regressions using the GDP gap, the unemployment rate, or no
control for the current state of the economy.[151]

Column 14-1 in table 14 reproduces the estimates from the regression
reported in column 9-5 of table 9, which includes both the recession
dummy and the equity premium. The next two columns use alternative
measures of the state of the economy, and column 14-4 uses none. Columns
14-5 through 14-8 repeat the first four specifications using the dividend
yield instead of the equity premium, and columns 14-9 through 14-12
include no risk measure. (Thus, column 14-12 includes no control for either
risk or the state of the economy.) In all twelve specifications, projected primary
deficits in year $t + 5$ have positive, precisely estimated, and substantial
impacts on forward long-term rates; in contrast, projected ratios of public
debt to GDP never show a positive significant effect. Controlling for the
GDP gap (columns 14-2, 14-6, and 14-10) generates fiscal policy effects
similar to those using the recession measure. Controlling for the unemployment rate (columns 14-3, 14-7, and 14-11) generates very large effects
of deficits on interest rates. Not controlling for the state of the economy
(columns 14-4, 14-8, and 14-12) generates much smaller effects of fiscal

149. Laubach (2003) uses as an instrument for the equity premium variable the previous
period's value of the term and finds that it does not affect his results.
150. The 2001 recession began in March and ended in November and thus did not overlap with either the January 2001 or January 2002 CBO forecasts.
151. The last specification follows that of Laubach (2003) and Engen and Hubbard
(2004). It is appropriate to note, however, that our goal in including the recession variable is
not just to control for the state of the economy, but also to explore whether the effects of
future projected fiscal policy outcomes were systematically different in a recession, perhaps
because participants in financial markets have shorter horizons during such periods. Controlling for smoother measures, such as the GDP gap or the unemployment rate, may not provide as clean a test of that hypothesis.

policy on interest rates. This suggests that, even when one examines forward long-term rates, it is important to control for the current state of the economy. Alternative specifications of the risk variable do not affect the impact of projected fiscal policy on interest rates.

Table 15 examines the sensitivity of the results across time periods and fiscal policy measures. Dropping the years after 2000 allows an analysis that is independent of the Bush tax cuts and the recent recession. Dropping the years before 1981 is interesting, because Christopher House shows that, during the 1981–2004 period, the actual deficit in year t is closely correlated with the projection in that year of the deficit in year $t + 5$.[152] This raises two key questions: First, to what extent are the results in tables 6 through 9 for the whole period due to potentially unusual patterns in the 1976–81 period? Second, are the central results for projected fiscal policy in those tables merely masking the fact that *current* deficits affect future interest rates and that projected deficits happen to proxy well for current deficits during this period?[153]

To address the first question, column 15-1 of table 15 again repeats the results from column 9-5 in table 9, and columns 15-2 and 15-3 show results of the same specification for different sample periods. The effect of projected fiscal policy on forward rates is similar in each of the three sample periods: between 42 and 57 basis points for each 1-percent-of-GDP change in the projected primary deficit.[154] This shows that the effects of projected fiscal policy reported in tables 6 through 9 are not due just to the inclusion of data for the 1976–81 period.[155]

152. See the comment by House following this paper.

153. The correlation between the deficit in period t and the deficit in period $t + 5$ that is predicted in period t (both measured as a share of GDP) is 0.6 for the 1981–2004 period and 0.5 for 1976–2004. In contrast, the correlation between the actual deficit in period $t + 5$ and the period $t + 5$ deficit predicted in period t is negative (between −.3 and −.5) in both periods. A regression of the projected five-year-ahead deficit on the current deficit yields a coefficient of about 0.8 ($t = 5$) in each of the subperiods. A regression of the projected five-year-ahead deficit on the actual outcome yields a coefficient less than 0.1 in absolute value. See Cohen and Follette (2003) for a discussion of the difficulties in projecting fiscal variables beyond a year or two.

154. This finding is consistent with Laubach's (2003) finding that his results are not sensitive to subperiods within the overall 1976–2004 sample period.

155. Note that the overall relationship between interest rates and fiscal policy could evolve over time for a wide variety of reasons, including increasing openness of the economy (which would tend to make the relationship weaker) and a broader use of government debt to hedge mortgage-backed securities (which could tend to make the relationship stronger).

Table 15. ARMA Estimates of Effects on Interest Rates Using Alternative Time Periods and Including Current Fiscal Measures[a]

	Regression and sample period														
	15-1	15-2	15-3	15-4	15-5	15-6	15-7	15-8	15-9	15-10	15-11	15-12	15-13	15-14	15-15
Independent variable	1976–2004	1976–2000	1981–2004	1976–2004	1976–2000	1981–2004	1976–2004	1976–2000	1981–2004	1976–2004	1976–2000	1981–2004	1976–2004	1976–2000	1981–2004
Projected debt/GDP	-0.013 (0.017)	0.013 (0.020)	-0.002 (0.023)							-0.010 (0.017)	0.004 (0.027)	-0.042 (0.019)	-0.011 (0.019)	0.013 (0.044)	-0.023 (0.045)
Projected primary deficit/GDP	0.534 (0.113)	0.424 (0.109)	0.566 (0.181)							0.311 (0.160)	0.293 (0.181)	0.480 (0.127)	0.464 (0.149)	0.372 (0.215)	0.647 (0.249)
Current deficit/GDP				0.349 (0.078)	0.372 (0.075)	0.452 (0.073)				0.206 (0.099)	0.170 (0.108)	0.412 (0.095)			
Standardized current deficit/GDP							0.309 (0.164)	0.423 (0.223)	0.303 (0.173)				0.084 (0.106)	0.051 (0.236)	0.120 (0.206)
Recession dummy × projected debt/GDP	0.013 (0.021)	-0.010 (0.023)	-0.006 (0.023)							0.404 (0.277)	0.332 (0.328)	-0.076 (0.032)	-0.950 (1.490)	-1.079 (2.143)	0.108 (0.052)
Recession dummy × proj. primary deficit/GDP	-0.330 (0.159)	-0.192 (0.152)	-0.224 (0.180)							-0.039 (0.180)	-0.020 (0.179)	-0.060 (0.120)	1.759 (3.148)	2.086 (4.507)	-0.485 (0.203)
Recession dummy × current deficit/GDP				-0.293 (0.379)	-0.319 (0.388)	0.342 (0.279)				-7.045 (4.755)	-5.979 (5.582)	1.045 (0.362)			
Recession dummy × standardized deficit/GDP							-0.124 (0.537)	-0.207 (0.562)	0.658 (0.446)				12.990 (20.286)	14.499 (29.196)	-1.526 (0.889)

Recession dummy	0.512	1.397	1.727	1.257	1.288	-1.430	0.692	0.872	-0.916	13.922	12.319	—[b]	17.946	20.530	—[b]
	(0.854)	(0.927)	(0.988)	(1.595)	(1.637)	(1.142)	(1.043)	(1.126)	(0.777)	(8.577)	(9.920)		(26.370)	(37.774)	
Projected GDP growth rate	0.775	0.987	1.752	-0.192	-0.233	0.310	-0.405	-0.400	-0.499	0.477	0.619	0.902	0.722	0.893	1.454
	(0.560)	(0.549)	(0.499)	(0.385)	(0.423)	(0.390)	(0.457)	(0.499)	(0.579)	(0.555)	(0.584)	(0.396)	(0.539)	(0.637)	(0.600)
Federal Reserve purchases of Treasuries	-0.330	-1.033	-0.725	-0.543	-0.682	-0.360	-0.637	-0.980	-0.299	-0.476	-0.904	-0.164	-0.469	-1.042	-0.501
	(0.545)	(0.584)	(0.722)	(0.341)	(0.381)	(0.298)	(0.672)	(0.762)	(0.821)	(0.414)	(0.551)	(0.408)	(0.592)	(0.614)	(0.803)
Oil price	-0.010	-0.010	-0.050	0.051	0.053	0.042	0.064	0.065	0.084	0.013	0.011	-0.036	-0.002	0.000	-0.051
	(0.020)	(0.018)	(0.027)	(0.015)	(0.015)	(0.017)	(0.022)	(0.023)	(0.025)	(0.028)	(0.029)	(0.020)	(0.028)	(0.028)	(0.028)
Equity premium[c]	-0.447	-0.450	-0.570	-0.476	-0.457	-0.760	-0.331	-0.301	-0.418	-0.541	-0.513	-0.922	-0.467	-0.459	-0.658
	(0.118)	(0.123)	(0.127)	(0.154)	(0.171)	(0.149)	(0.160)	(0.166)	(0.233)	(0.129)	(0.138)	(0.121)	(0.112)	(0.151)	(0.212)
Defense spending/GDP	0.029	0.052	0.053	-0.208	-0.257	-0.076	-0.076	-0.218	-0.102	-0.123	-0.096	-0.123	-0.025	0.013	0.026
	(0.063)	(0.068)	(0.066)	(0.091)	(0.084)	(0.081)	(0.143)	(0.151)	(0.126)	(0.083)	(0.108)	(0.093)	(0.091)	(0.197)	(0.078)
Constant	5.365	3.693	3.763	5.579	5.814	5.196	5.036	5.464	5.001	5.669	4.777	7.817	5.302	3.716	5.585
	(1.332)	(1.547)	(1.678)	(0.526)	(0.535)	(0.523)	(0.650)	(0.571)	(0.961)	(1.350)	(2.134)	(1.501)	(1.448)	(3.603)	(3.645)
AR(1) coefficient	-0.587	-0.572	-0.651	-0.428	-0.415	-0.677	-0.308	-0.314	-0.393	-0.585	-0.529	-0.847	-0.595	-0.563	-0.712
	(0.239)	(0.232)	(0.250)	(0.195)	(0.199)	(0.187)	(0.285)	(0.292)	(0.313)	(0.202)	(0.235)	(0.118)	(0.238)	(0.278)	(0.282)
No. of observations	29	25	24	29	25	24	29	25	24	29	25	24	29	25	24
Wald χ^2	2,751.599	1,707.171	1,742.58	396.423	437.69	516.704	294.717	297.645	163.839	1,520,000	3,150,000	1,724.856	22,338.964	19,077.866	1,008.725

Source: Authors' regressions using data from CBO; Laubach (2003); OMB; Bureau of Economic Analysis, National Income and Product Accounts; Financial Forecast Center; National Bureau of Economic Research; Federal Reserve.

a. All projected variables are five-year projections except the debt-GDP ratio, which is a four-year projection. Numbers in parentheses are semirobust standard errors.

b. Variable omitted from the regression because of collinearity.

c. Defined as in table 6.

The rest of table 15 addresses the second question. Columns 15-4 through 15-6 replace the projected fiscal policy controls with the current unified deficit, and columns 15-7 through 15-9 do the same using the current standardized deficit. These regressions show positive and significant effects of *current* deficits on *forward* long-term rates, with effects ranging between 30 and 45 basis points for a 1-percent-of-GDP change in the current deficit. These effects are almost as large as the effects of projected fiscal policy shown in columns 15-1 through 15-3, and they highlight the concern raised by House that current deficits may be driving the results that have been attributed to projected fiscal policy.

Columns 15-10 through 15-15 include *both* projected and current deficits. Column 15-12 shows that, for 1981–2004, the period highlighted by House, *current* deficits have a substantial effect on *forward* rates— 41 basis points per percentage point of GDP—even when projected deficits are controlled for. This is an interesting and unexpected result, but it should not detract from the finding that the impact of *projected* primary deficits on *forward* rates is still substantial: 48 basis points per percentage point of GDP, compared with 53 basis points in column 15-1. Thus table 15 shows that, even though current deficits and the five-year-ahead projection of deficits move largely in tandem during the 1981–2004 period, projected deficits still have a large and independent effect on forward long-term rates, even after controlling for current deficits. This in turn implies that the results in tables 6 through 9, linking projected fiscal policy and long-term forward rates, are in no way an artifact of the tight relationship between current deficits and the projected five-year-ahead deficit between 1981 and 2004, nor are projected deficits merely a proxy for current deficits.[156]

Table 16 shows that the heightened sensitivity of interest rates to both current and projected deficits in the 1981–2004 period also holds in regressions that examine the effects of projected fiscal policy on current long-

156. Other results in table 15 are also of interest. When we control for projected deficits, a 1-percent-of-GDP increase in the current deficit raises forward long-term rates by about 20 basis points in the 1976–2004 or the 1976–2000 period (columns 15-10 and 15-11, respectively). A 1-percent-of-GDP increase in the projected primary deficit in year $t + 5$ raises forward rates by about 30 basis points. Columns 15-13 through 15-15 control for the current standardized deficit instead of the current unified deficit. In stark contrast to columns 15-7 through 15-9, the current standardized deficit appears to have no effect on forward long-term interest rates across any of the time periods, once projected deficits are included. Controlling for the standardized deficit raises the estimated impact of the projected primary deficit by 10 to 15 basis points, compared with the results that control for the current unified deficit.

Table 16. ARMA Estimates of the Effects of Projected and Current-Period Fiscal Variables on Real Current Ten-Year Treasury Rates[a]

	Regression and sample period					
	16-1	16-2	16-3	16-4	16-5	16-6
Independent variable	1976–2004	1976–2000	1981–2004	1976–2004	1976–2000	1981–2004
Fiscal variables						
Projected debt/GDP	0.028	0.004	−0.024			
	(0.035)	(0.029)	(0.015)			
Projected primary	0.096	0.226	0.764			
deficit/GDP	(0.152)	(0.125)	(0.121)			
Current-period debt/GDP				0.001	−0.034	−0.003
				(0.091)	(0.049)	(0.027)
Current-period primary				−0.019	0.127	0.336
deficit/GDP				(0.215)	(0.194)	(0.155)
Recession dummy and interactions						
Recession dummy	4.360	3.330	6.966	3.677	1.967	3.811
	(1.117)	(1.178)	(0.877)	(1.456)	(1.468)	(1.202)
Recession dummy × projected debt/GDP	−0.083	−0.060	−0.120			
	(0.028)	(0.025)	(0.017)			
Recession dummy × projected primary deficit/GDP	0.311	0.173	−0.097			
	(0.145)	(0.122)	(0.077)			
Recession dummy × current-period debt/GDP				−0.119	−0.074	−0.111
				(0.046)	(0.039)	(0.028)
Recession dummy × current-period primary deficit/GDP				1.308	0.772	0.911
				(1.262)	(0.943)	(0.440)
Projected GDP growth rate	0.982	0.765	2.137			
	(1.080)	(0.887)	(0.403)			
Current GDP growth rate				0.025	−0.112	0.055
				(0.170)	(0.170)	(0.077)
Federal Reserve purchases of Treasuries	−2.815	−2.487	−2.694	−1.638	−1.565	−1.808
	(1.547)	(0.904)	(0.494)	(1.389)	(0.808)	(0.666)
Control variables						
Oil price	0.019	0.023	−0.090	0.043	0.046	0.036
	(0.034)	(0.032)	(0.026)	(0.052)	(0.034)	(0.020)
Equity premium[b]	−0.540	−0.506	−1.005	−0.468	−0.601	−1.121
	(0.163)	(0.158)	(0.098)	(0.471)	(0.260)	(0.223)
Defense spending/GDP	0.169	0.071	0.334	0.398	0.071	0.263
	(0.188)	(0.170)	(0.076)	(0.355)	(0.317)	(0.126)
Constant	1.507	3.451	4.785	2.760	6.658	5.660

(*continued*)

Table 16. ARMA Estimates of the Effects of Projected and Current-Period Fiscal Variables on Real Current Ten-Year Treasury Rates[a] *(continued)*

	Regression and sample period					
	16-1	*16-2*	*16-3*	*16-4*	*16-5*	*16-6*
Independent variable	*1976– 2004*	*1976– 2000*	*1981– 2004*	*1976– 2004*	*1976– 2000*	*1981– 2004*
	(2.371)	(2.231)	(0.996)	(5.596)	(3.911)	(1.922)
AR(1) coefficient	−0.258	−0.106	−0.844	0.191	0.302	−0.196
	(0.561)	(0.369)	(0.168)	(0.753)	(0.404)	(0.417)
No. of observations	29	25	24	29	25	24
Wald χ^2	1,461.312	7,677.126	9,711.773	398.419	287.23	6,623.901

Source: Authors' regressions using data from CBO; Laubach (2003); OMB; Bureau of Economic Analysis, National Income and Product Accounts; Financial Forecast Center; National Bureau of Economic Research; Federal Reserve.

a. All projected variables are five-year projections except the debt-GDP ratio, which is a four-year projection. Numbers in parentheses are semirobust standard errors.

b. Defined as in table 6.

term rates (similar to tables 10 through 12) and the effects of current fiscal policy on current long-term rates (similar to table 13). During the period since 1981, a 1-percent-of-GDP increase in projected deficits raises current long-term rates by 76 basis points, and a 1-percent-of-GDP increase in the current primary deficit raises current long-term rates by 33 basis points. These results imply much stronger effects of projected and current fiscal policy on current interest rates for this shorter period than tables 10 through 13 suggest for the whole 1976–2004 period.

Summary

In the preferred specifications (tables 8 and 9), which allow both debt and deficits to affect interest rates, the estimated effect on forward long-term rates from a 1-percent-of-GDP shift in projected primary budget variables ranges between 40 and 70 basis points, depending on the specification and on whether the fiscal variable is the primary deficit, or revenue and primary outlays separately. Our effects are larger than those found by Laubach and by Engen and Hubbard,[157] because we include both projected debt and projected deficits as variables, and because we include measures of whether the economy is currently in recession. The results show that the effects of projected deficits are *larger* when projected debt is included, and

157. Laubach (2003); Engen and Hubbard (2004).

that the effect of a given future deficit tends to be larger if the economy is currently not in a recession than if it is.

In sharp contrast, the projected debt-GDP ratio never exerts a positive and significant effect on future interest rates when it is entered in a regression that also includes projected deficits. The projected deficit thus seems a more informative measure than projected debt. This is reflected in table 6, where the deficit-only equations had significantly higher R^2s than the debt-only equations, and most strikingly in tables 8, 9, 14, 15, and 16, where, when both variables are entered, deficits have large effects and the debt has virtually none.

Our estimates of the effect of an increase in the projected unified budget deficit are somewhat smaller——25 to 35 basis points for each 1-percent-of-GDP increase—than that of an increase in the primary deficit. This should be expected, since a shift of 1 percent of GDP in the primary deficit would represent a more dramatic change than a shift of 1 percent of GDP in the unified deficit. Finally, our results when debt is entered in the equation by itself suggest that an increase in the projected debt by 1 percent of GDP raises long-term rates by between 3 and 6 basis points.

All of the estimates above may understate the true effects for at least two reasons. First, as Rubin, Orszag, and Sinai note,[158] and as discussed earlier in the paper, the effects would be larger if sustained deficits cause investors to lose confidence in the ability of policymakers to avoid a fiscal crisis. Second, because the projected fiscal policy variables are only approximations of investors' true expectations, the regressions may suffer from classical measurement error, which would bias the coefficient on projected deficits toward zero.

Conclusion

The empirical evidence presented in this paper indicates that federal budget deficits reduce national saving and raise long-term interest rates. Reasonable rules of thumb based on our estimates are that each 1-percent-of-GDP increase in current deficits reduces national saving by 0.5 to 0.8 percent of GDP, that each 1-percent-of-GDP increase in projected future unified deficits raises forward long-term interest rates by 25 to 35 basis points, and that each 1-percent-of-GDP increase in projected

158. Rubin, Orszag, and Sinai (2004).

future primary deficits raises forward long-term interest rates by 40 to 70 basis points.

These findings carry substantial implications. First, both the consumption and the interest rate results reject the Ricardian view of the world. Second, the interest rate results reject the small open economy view, at least as it applies to the U.S. economy.

Third, the results suggest that the sustained fiscal deficits now facing the United States will impose significant economic costs. Under the assumptions we have described, the unified budget deficit over the next decade is projected to average about 3.5 percent of GDP. Our results suggest that these deficits will reduce annual national saving by 2 to 3 percent of GDP. As a result, by the end of the decade, the assets owned by Americans will be roughly 20 to 30 percent of GDP less than they would be if the unified budget were balanced over the next decade. With a rate of return on capital of 6 percent, those missing assets will reduce national income by 1 to 2 percent in 2015 and each year thereafter.[159] Our results also suggest that the increase in unified deficits will raise interest rates by 80 to 120 basis points.

Fourth, our results suggest that making the 2001 and 2003 tax cuts permanent would raise the cost of capital for new investment, reduce long-term investment, and reduce long-term economic growth. Tax cuts have offsetting effects on the cost of new investment, with marginal tax rate cuts reducing, and higher interest rates from deficits increasing, the cost of capital. Gale and Samara Potter show that, if the 2001 tax cut were to raise interest rates by 50 basis points, the cost of capital would rise for corporate equipment and structures, noncorporate equipment and structures, and owner-occupied housing.[160] By 2014 the 2001 tax legislation, if extended past its official sunset, would increase the public debt by just over $3.4 trillion,[161] or about 19 percent of projected GDP in 2014. This implies an interest rate increase of 57 basis points using the Engen and Hubbard estimates,[162] and an even larger increase using our estimates. From an alternative perspective, making the 2001 tax cut permanent would reduce

159. The assumption of a 6 percent rate of return is intended to be conservative, understating the effects. If, for example, the rate of return were instead 12 percent, as assumed in our benchmark calculation, the loss of national income would be 2 to 4 percent in 2015 and each year thereafter.

160. Gale and Potter (2002).

161. This estimate is based on Joint Committee on Taxation (2001, 2002, 2003) revenue figures for the original legislation, CBO estimates of the costs of extensions, and CBO interest rate matrix calculations for debt service costs.

162. Engen and Hubbard (2004).

revenue by about 1.7 percent of GDP on a permanent basis (assuming the tax cuts are not effectively supplanted by the alternative minimum tax). Using our estimates for primary deficits, this implies that interest rates will rise by 70 and 120 basis points. Both sets of estimates imply that the 2001 tax cut will end up *reducing* long-term investment. It might be thought that the 2003 tax cut would have more beneficial effects on investment, since it focused on dividend and capital gains tax cuts. In recent work, however, we show that the net effect of making the 2001 *and* the 2003 tax cuts permanent would be to raise the cost of capital once the interest rate effects are taken into account—even under the Engen-Hubbard estimates.[163] These findings imply that making the tax cuts permanent would reduce the long-term level of investment, which is consistent with a negative effect on national saving and on future living standards.

Finally, after 2014 the budget outlook grows steadily worse as costs associated with federal retirement and health programs mount. Under reasonable projections and in the absence of policy changes, the nation thus faces a long period of sustained large budget deficits. In this context the negative long-term effects of deficits presented in this paper, substantial though they are, may provide an unduly auspicious perspective on the adverse consequences of fiscal deficits.

163. Gale and Orszag (2004b).

APPENDIX

Table A-1. Findings of Empirical Studies of Budget Deficits and Interest Rates

Type of study	Predominantly positive, significant effect	Mixed effect	Predominantly insignificant effect
Impact of expected or anticipated deficit			
Before 1985 1985–94	Makin and Tanzi (1984) Feldstein (1986) Wachtel and Young (1987) Bovenberg (1988) Thomas and Abderrezak (1988a) Thomas and Abderrezak (1988b) Barth and Bradley (1989) Thorbecke (1993) Elmendorf (1993)	Sinai and Rathjens (1983) Kim and Lombra (1989) Cohen and Garnier (1991) Quigley and Porter-Hudak (1994)	Bradley (1986)
1995–present	Elmendorf (1996) Kitchen (1996) Canzoneri, Cumby, and Diba (2002) Laubach (2003)	Engen and Hubbard (2004)	
No. of studies	13	5	1
VAR-based dynamics Before 1985 1985–1994	Miller and Russek (1991)		Plosser (1982) Evans (1985) Evans (1987a) Evans (1987b) Plosser (1987a) Evans (1989)
1995–present	Tavares and Valkanov (2001) Dai and Phillippon (2004) Ardagna, Caselli, and Lane (2004)	Mountford and Uhlig (2000) Perotti (2002) Engen and Hubbard (2004)	
No. of studies	4	3	6

Impact of current deficit or debt		
Before 1985		
Feldstein and Eckstein (1970)	Echols and Elliott (1976)	Feldstein and Chamberlain (1973)
Kudlow (1981)	Dewald (1983)	Canto and Rapp (1982)
Carlson (1983)		Frankel (1983)
Hutchison and Pyle (1984)		Hoelscher (1983)
Muller and Price (1984)		Makin (1983)
		Mascaro and Meltzer (1983)
		Motley (1983)
		Tatom (1984)
		U.S. Treasury (1984)
1985–1994		
Barth, Iden, and Russek (1985)	Tanzi (1985)	Giannaros and Kolluri (1985)
de Leew and Hollaway (1985)	Zahid (1988)	Kolluri and Giannaros (1987)
Hoelscher (1986)	Coorey (1992)	Swamy and others (1988)
Cebula (1987)		
Cebula (1988)		
Cebula and Koch (1989)		
Cebula and Koch (1994)		
1995–present		
Miller and Russek (1996)		Calomiris and others (2004)
Kitchen (2002)		
Kiley (2003)		
Cebula (2000)		
No. of studies		
16	5	13
Total no. of studies		
33	13	20

Comments and Discussion

Eric M. Engen: Government debt and deficits matter. Although some politicians may argue that deficits do not affect the politics of public policy or voters' behavior, government borrowing does affect the economy. The disagreements among economists concerning government debt and deficits are primarily over the channels through which the effects occur and the magnitude of those effects.

In this paper, William Gale and Peter Orszag review past and expected future federal government borrowing and present a theoretical summary of some of the different ways in which government debt can affect the economy. They also contribute to the body of research on the economic effects of government debt by providing new empirical estimates of two channels through which these effects operate. First, they estimate the degree to which private domestic saving may rise coincidently with increased government borrowing. Second, they estimate the effect of federal government debt and deficits on interest rates. My discussion will focus first on their empirical analyses of the two channels and then turn to their more general discussion of the economic effects of government debt.

The first part of the authors' empirical analysis estimates both an aggregate consumption function and an Euler equation specification for changes in aggregate household consumption spending. In both specifications they estimate the impact of changes in debt-financed government taxes while controlling for government spending, (lagged) government debt, marginal tax rates on capital and labor, and other economic factors. This empirical analysis contributes to the literature that studies whether households are more Keynesian or more Ricardian in their reactions to government borrowing, that is, whether households view government bonds issued because of a tax cut as net wealth or as future tax obligations.

The authors' results, using several different empirical specifications, imply that households are neither purely Keynesian nor purely Ricardian. In most of their regressions they find that, in the short run, a statistically significant portion of a debt-financed tax cut is saved, but their estimates of that response cover a fairly broad range. In their aggregate consumption function specifications, with federal spending held constant, a one-dollar decrease in federal tax payments is estimated to increase consumption spending in the short run by 30 to 46 cents, implying that households offset 54 to 70 percent of the increase in federal borrowing by saving more. The Euler equation estimates yield a much broader range of results, which depend crucially on whether changes in consumption are measured in levels or as a ratio to net national product, whether controls for marginal tax rates are included, and whether explanatory variables are treated as endogenous. In these estimates, with federal spending held constant, a one-dollar decrease in federal tax payments is estimated to increase consumption spending in the short run in the range of 22 to 98 cents, implying that household saving offsets anywhere from 2 to 78 percent of the increase in federal borrowing.

Although Gale and Orszag state that their preferred estimates suggest that increases in private saving offset a much narrower 20 to 50 percent of the increase in federal borrowing from a tax cut, it is difficult a priori to rule out any of their specifications, and readers may have their own preferences.[1] Despite the authors' improvements over many previous econometric analyses of this issue, their broad range of estimates provides little assurance that this analysis advances the consensus on the *short-run magnitude* of this effect, even if we can safely rule out that households do not

1. Recent analysis of the deficit-financed tax rebates in 2001 by Johnson, Parker, and Souleles (2004) using household-level spending data suggests that about 50 to 70 percent of these tax rebates were spent, on average, in the following two quarters. The results of this short-run, household-level analysis of the 2001 tax rebate are consistent with the authors' preferred range of estimates from their aggregate spending analysis. However, this deficit-financed tax cut was implemented during a recession, and so it is not clear whether the results of this study are more generally comparable to the effect of deficit-financed tax cuts in the many nonrecession periods covered by Gale and Orszag's aggregate data. Shapiro and Slemrod (2003) also investigate the effects of the 2001 tax rebate, and, although they do not use the more detailed household-level spending data used in Johnson, Parker, and Souleles (2004), they find qualitatively similar results.

appear to be purely Keynesian or purely Ricardian. Moreover, as the authors note in discussing their results, these estimates do not address the potential *long-run* effect of deficit-financed tax cuts on private saving, which could differ from the short-run effect.

The second part of Gale and Orszag's empirical analysis investigates the effects of federal government debt and deficits on interest rates. Their empirical research here is similar to recent studies by Thomas Laubach and by Glenn Hubbard and myself.[2] In general, their estimates of the effect of the federal debt or deficit on the level of the real interest rate are fairly similar to what these other recent studies find. Although the specifications vary to some degree from paper to paper, all three find that a 1-percentage-point increase in the Congressional Budget Office's five-year-ahead projection of federal *debt* relative to GDP increases the real five-year-ahead ten-year Treasury rate by about 2 to 5 basis points. All three studies estimate that a 1-percentage-point increase in the CBO's five-year-ahead projection of the federal *deficit* relative to GDP increases the real five-year-ahead ten-year Treasury rate in a somewhat broader range, from 25 to 38 basis points. The relative similarity of the results across these three papers stands in marked contrast to the incredibly wide range of empirical estimates reported in the earlier literature.

Where the papers part company, however, is over which specification— one that regresses the *level* of the interest rate on the *level* of federal debt, or one that regresses it on the *change* in federal debt (that is, the level of the deficit)—is potentially more informative and more consistent with the current state of macroeconomic analysis of this issue. Gale and Orszag believe that the specification using the deficit is more informative. They suggest that, if the change in the deficit is perceived by financial markets as essentially permanent, or at least persistent, then the deficit specification better captures the effects of this perception. Gale and Orszag basically interpret these results in a manner consistent with Laubach's reconciliation of the differences between the debt-based and the deficit-based approach. Hubbard and I, in contrast, view the former (that is, the specification relating the level of federal debt to the level of the interest rate) as both more informative and more consistent with the current state of macroeconomic theory. Moreover, we offer a different explanation for reconciling the different empirical results.

2. Laubach (2003); Engen and Hubbard (2004).

The specification used most often in previous studies of this issue has been one that regresses the level of the interest rate on the deficit. This specification comes from the relationship implied by a Keynesian IS-LM framework. However, as Gregory Mankiw wrote in his review of the state of macroeconomics over a decade ago, "The IS-LM model rarely finds its way into scholarly journals: some economists view the model as a relic of a bygone age and no longer bother to teach it. The large-scale macroeconometric models are mentioned only occasionally at academic conferences, often with derision."[3] Instead intertemporal models based on a production function in which the interest rate is ultimately determined by the level of the capital stock, and thus by the level of federal debt, are much more conventional in current macroeconomic analysis.[4] Examples include the Solow growth model, the Ramsey-Cass-Koopmans model, and the Diamond model as discussed in David Romer's graduate macroeconomics text;[5] the overlapping-generations models presented in Olivier Blanchard and Stanley Fischer's macroeconomics text;[6] and the general equilibrium model used in the widely cited book on fiscal policy by Alan Auerbach and Laurence Kotlikoff.[7] In all of these types of macroeconomic models, the interest rate is determined by the marginal product of capital and is a function of the level of the capital stock, which in turn is determined by federal government debt rather than just the deficit. Thus Hubbard and I suggest that the econometric specification that relates the level of government debt to the level of the interest rate is more consistent with the current state of macroeconomic theory than one that relates the level of the deficit to the level of the interest rate.[8]

Gale and Orszag as well as Laubach suggest that the specification using the deficit is still informative if changes in the federal deficit are perceived by financial market participants to be very persistent. Indeed, if so, this could help explain the larger interest rate effect estimated when the deficit is used. However, if projected deficits are persistent, this information should also be reflected in a measure of projected federal debt, which

3. Mankiw (1990, p. 1646).
4. Engen and Hubbard (2004) discuss such a model. This is the case even if other features of the model yield more Keynesian, rather than classical, results. See Mankiw (1992).
5. Romer (1996).
6. Blanchard and Fischer (1989).
7. Auerbach and Kotlikoff (1987).
8. Engen and Hubbard (2004).

includes not only the deficit projection for a particular year but also projections for earlier years.

An alternative explanation for this difference in the estimated interest rate effects is suggested in my paper with Hubbard. Because the Congressional Budget Office's projections of federal deficits are closely correlated with their projections of federal debt (the correlation coefficient is .89 with both projections expressed as a percentage of GDP), the coefficient estimate on the smaller deficit component also picks up the effect of previously accumulated government debt, and the coefficient estimate is larger than when total government debt is used. Thus the larger interest rate effect estimated using the deficit specification may reflect not the implied persistence of deficit projections by financial market participants, but rather a misspecified model.

Gale and Orszag's discussion of the potential effects of government borrowing makes many other interesting and thoughtful points concerning government debt that are beyond the scope of my comments here. However, I will conclude with two related points about the overall picture for future fiscal policy and federal borrowing in the United States that the paper does not emphasize. First, much of the emphasis in this paper on these future developments focuses on the recent tax cuts. However, future government borrowing will in all likelihood be determined more by what happens with spending on Social Security, Medicare, and Medicaid. Moreover, the history of federal tax policy in the United States shows that whereas legislation to adjust taxes is passed frequently, and that tax increases are not uncommon, entitlement reform occurs far less frequently. Particularly rare are changes in entitlements that reduce rather than increase their projected growth.

Second, federal borrowing is not the only feature of fiscal policy that has macroeconomic impacts. Both the level and the structure of government taxes and spending can also have significant effects. If the fiscal gap is closed in the years ahead by raising taxes, particularly taxes on labor and capital, the negative effect on the economy will likely be much greater than if the fiscal gap were closed by reforming entitlement spending. The type and mix of policies ultimately used to reduce the fiscal gap are at least as important as reducing the expected future government borrowing associated with current fiscal policy.

Christopher L. House: How do budget deficits affect the economy? This is the central question in this paper by William Gale and Peter Orszag, and, not surprisingly, it is a difficult question to answer. Moreover, since the deficit is simply spending minus revenue, the answer to this question seems to require answers to two other questions: How do taxes affect the economy? And how does government spending affect the economy? To isolate the effects of deficits, Gale and Orszag cast their question in terms of Ricardian equivalence.

Ricardian equivalence says that, if the government cuts taxes today but commits itself to increase future taxes by an amount equal to the capitalized value of the tax cut, there should be no effect on economic activity. A tax change that has no effect on the present discounted value of taxes—that is, a policy that changes only the timing of tax collection—is very special. Here I will refer to such a tax cut as a *Ricardian tax cut*. Ricardian tax cuts are the only tax cuts that leave a consumer's permanent income unchanged, and thus a deficit caused by a Ricardian tax cut has no effect on the economy. Of course, Ricardian equivalence holds only under certain conditions: consumers must be rational and forward looking, they must have access to loan markets, taxes cannot be distortionary, and so on. However, the basic message of Ricardian equivalence is clear: there is no direct connection between deficits and economic activity.

To assess whether Ricardian equivalence is a good approximation for policy analysis in the real world, Gale and Orszag examine two statistical relationships: the reaction of aggregate consumption to tax changes, and the relationship between deficits and interest rates. Ricardian equivalence says that neither consumption nor the real interest rate should respond to deficits caused by a Ricardian tax cut.

To examine the relationship between aggregate consumption and budget deficits, Gale and Orszag estimate a consumption function of the form

(1) $$\Delta C_t = \beta_0 + \beta_1 \Delta Y_t + \beta_2 \Delta T_t + \beta_3 \Delta G_t + \ldots + e_t,$$

where Δ is the difference operator ($\Delta x = x_t - x_{t-1}$). Because they include government spending ΔG_t in the regression, the coefficient on government revenue ΔT_t gives the partial correlation between government surpluses and consumption. They find that the coefficient on ΔT_t is negative and statistically significant. An increase in taxes of 1 percent of GDP is associated with a reduction in consumption of between 0.5 and 0.8 percent of GDP. The systematic reaction of consumption to variations in taxes, controlling for government spending, appears to be prima facie evidence against the Ricardian view.

There are two challenges to a causal interpretation of regression estimates of equation 1, however. The first is that Ricardian equivalence applies only to Ricardian tax cuts. Tax changes that affect permanent income will typically cause changes in consumption when they occur. In other words, even if the world were Ricardian, there would be no reason to expect the coefficient on ΔT_t to be zero.

The second problem, not wholly unrelated to the first, is that the right-hand-side variables are endogenous. Omitted variables that are correlated with both ΔT_t and ΔC_t (and thus in the error) may cause the estimated coefficients to be biased from their true structural values.

It is instructive to consider an idealized environment in which equation 1 flows directly from maximizing behavior and in which Ricardian equivalence is known to hold. For specificity, suppose that in each period a consumer maximizes lifetime utility $\sum_{t=0}^{\infty} \beta^t u(C_t)$ subject to a budget constraint

$$C_t + \left[A_{t+1}/(1+r) \right] = Y_t - T_t + A_t,$$

where A denotes the consumer's current real assets. Income (Y) and taxes (T) are uncertain but depend on a set of forecasting variables $\mathbf{X}_t$, which could include lagged values of Y, T, and so forth. The solution to this optimization problem is a state-dependent consumption function $C = c(Y, T, \mathbf{X}, A)$. That C depends on Y, T, and A is not surprising. Because it forecasts future levels of after-tax income, $\mathbf{X}$ also influences C.

Although the precise form of the consumption function depends on the form of the utility function, the stochastic process for income and so forth, we can approximate it to obtain a linear equation similar to equation 1:

(2) $\Delta C_t = c_0 + c_y \Delta Y_t + c_T \Delta T_t + c_x \Delta \mathbf{X}_t + c_a \Delta A_t.$

If this consumer is a representative consumer, this is the aggregate consumption function, c_y is the aggregate marginal propensity to consume (MPC) out of current income Y, and c_T, the coefficient that Gale and Orszag focus on, is the aggregate MPC from a tax cut. The standard Keynesian assumption is that c_y is between zero and 1 and that $c_T = -c_y$.

Ricardian equivalence holds in this setting. Faced with a Ricardian tax cut, the consumer will not alter his or her consumption spending at all. Importantly, however, this does not imply that c_T is zero. In fact, it is almost certainly not zero. Only if *all* tax changes were Ricardian would $c_T = 0$. Any change in taxes that signals a permanent change in after-tax income would cause the consumer to rationally alter his or her spending.

In reality, many tax changes have this property. For instance, consumption should react to a "peace dividend" like that at the end of the cold war. Such a tax change is associated with projected reductions in future government spending and thus might have an effect on the consumer's permanent income. Tax cuts intended to "starve the beast"—that is, that reduce revenue in order to force reductions in spending—might also be perceived to have a permanent impact on the consumer's after-tax income. The tax cuts of 2001 and 2003 are intended to be permanent. Even if they are not, there is no implicit or explicit plan to recover the forgone revenue with higher future taxes. If people believe that the budget will be balanced in part through spending cuts, consumption should increase.

In general, the sign of c_T depends not on whether Ricardian equivalence holds, but rather on the relationship between current tax changes and future tax changes. If current tax changes always come with the assurance of offsetting future tax changes (that is, if the projected path of government spending is unchanged) then $c_T = 0$. Otherwise $c_T \neq 0$. In particular, $c_T < 0$ is entirely consistent with Ricardian behavior. At a basic level, the problem is whether the regression adequately controls for future changes in government spending. Although equation 1 includes current and lagged government purchases, it is not clear whether this is enough to test Ricardian equivalence.

The second issue with the estimation of equation 1 is the endogeneity problem. Unless all of the relevant **X** variables are included in the regression, it is likely that the OLS coefficients will be biased. If all of the relevant variables in **X** were known, the estimated equation would fit perfectly and the correct structural parameters could be estimated.

To deal with the endogeneity problem, Gale and Orszag use an instrumental variables procedure that builds on the approach taken by Robert Hall and by John Campbell and Gregory Mankiw.[1] Campbell and Mankiw's procedure takes advantage of the fact that, under fairly general conditions, the permanent income hypothesis (PIH) implies that the change in consumption from one period to the next is uncorrelated with past information. Put differently, consumption does not respond to *anticipated* changes in dispos-

1. Hall (1978); Campbell and Mankiw (1989).

able income. Thus, for consumers who obey the PIH (Ricardian consumers), any lagged variable that is correlated with current taxes is a valid instrument.

The basic approach considers an environment with both forward-looking (Ricardian) consumers and "rule-of-thumb" consumers.[2] The forward-looking consumers behave according to the PIH, whereas the rule-of-thumb consumers are assumed to simply consume their disposable income ($c = y - T$). If λ is the fraction of rule-of-thumb consumers, it is easy to show that aggregate consumption obeys

$$\Delta C_t = \lambda[\Delta Y_t - \Delta T_t] + v_t,$$

where $\text{Cov}(Z_{t-1}, v_t) = 0$ for any lagged variable Z_{t-1}. Thus any Z_{t-1} is potentially a valid instrument. The identification problem from this approach is quite subtle, however. Although lagged variables are valid instruments, they do not identify the aggregate MPC. Instead they identify λ, the fraction of non-Ricardian agents. The aggregate MPC out of taxes is the sum of the MPC for the Ricardian agents (what I called c_T above) and the MPC for the rule-of-thumb consumers, which is 1 by assumption. The aggregate MPC, which is what Gale and Orszag care about, is then

$$\text{MPC} = (1 - \lambda)c_T + \lambda.$$

Thus λ is equal to the aggregate MPC only if $c_T = 0$, which brings us back to the first point: even if Ricardian equivalence holds, the MPC out of taxes is not generally zero; only if *all* tax changes were Ricardian would $c_T = 0$.

A natural question then arises as to whether one can use lagged variables as instruments for a model with only Ricardian (that is, PIH) consumers. Unfortunately, the answer to this question is no. Although these are valid instruments, they are not useful. The PIH says that $E_t(\Delta C_{t+1}) = 0$ and that $\text{Cov}(\Delta C_{t+1}, Z_t) = 0$. If an instrumental variables regression of the change in consumption on the change in income yields a nonzero coefficient, the PIH can be rejected. Unfortunately, the validity of the instruments must also be rejected, since they rely directly on the PIH being true.

Empirically addressing whether the economy is Ricardian appears to require a special instrument—specifically, it requires an instrument for a Ricardian tax cut. Put differently, to know how consumers respond to changes in the timing of taxes, one must observe their reaction to such policies.

---

2. In addition to the rule-of-thumb consumers considered by Campbell and Mankiw, Gale and Orszag include "life cycle" consumers, following Blanchard (1985).

The second type of evidence that Gale and Orszag examine is the statistical correlation between real interest rates and budget deficits. They make no claim that their results are causal or structural; rather they confine themselves to investigating whether a strong statistical relationship exists between deficits and interest rates. To answer this question they consider a variety of regressions of real interest rates on measures of the deficit as a percentage of GDP. The regressions include cyclical indicators and other covariates.

Their main finding is that one gets very different answers depending on whether real interest rates are regressed on *current* deficits or on expected *future* deficits. They find that expected future deficits have a strong positive correlation with real interest rates, whereas current actual deficits do not. Although the partial correlation between current deficits and real interest rates is positive, it is typically not statistically significant. This finding has intuitive appeal. Interest rates are inherently forward looking and, as a result, undoubtedly incorporate expectations about future pressures in the lending market. This explanation is particularly appealing if the deficit forecasts contain significant information beyond the simple correlation of deficits at time t with deficits at time $t + k$.

The interpretation that the authors' finding is due to the forward-looking nature of interest rates is quite plausible. Moreover, several alternative explanations can be ruled out. For instance, since high current interest rates would increase future interest payments, one might expect that reverse causality could lead to such a finding. Gale and Orszag show, however, that their finding remains intact if they use the primary deficit instead (that is, if they exclude debt service). Another possibility is that the CBO's budget forecasts are systematically optimistic, and thus a projected future deficit is indicative of a much larger current deficit. A simple examination of the dynamic relationship between current and future deficits reveals that, although this effect may be present to some extent, it cannot explain the authors' results.

There are two reasons to doubt the "forward looking" interpretation. First, from a purely numerical point of view, the main difference between current deficits and projected deficits, and thus the main difference between the two regression results, comes from only a handful of observations. Projected deficits and current actual deficits track each other closely for most of the sample period. However, early in the sample (from 1976 to 1981), there are a few sharp differences between the CBO's deficit projections and the current deficit. If those observations are dropped from the sample, the correlation between current deficits and real interest rates is comparable to the correlation between projected deficits and real interest rates.

Second, an essential component of the "forward looking" interpretation is the notion that CBO forecasts are informative about future budget deficits. Surprisingly, the sample correlation between projected deficits and actual realized future deficits is negative. Put differently, one might do better by guessing the opposite of the CBO forecast. It is important not to overstate this negative correlation, however. Like the contemporaneous correlation between projected deficits and current deficits, much of the negative correlation comes from only a few observations.

Neither of these observations invalidates Gale and Orszag's basic finding, but both suggest that the interpretation of the correlation must be made with care. In the end, Gale and Orszag have only a limited amount of data on which to base their conclusion. Whether their finding is due to the fact that interest rates are forward looking and thus anticipate expected future borrowing is ultimately not clear.

It should be emphasized that, even if the world were Ricardian, there would still be good reasons to be concerned about deficits. Properly managed budget deficits increase the efficiency of the economy by smoothing distortionary tax rates over time.[3] The government should borrow when spending is above average or revenue is below average. When spending is low or revenue is high, the government should save. If, however, because of poor planning or a lack of political willpower, the government does the opposite, it will find itself in the undesirable position of having to raise taxes dramatically just when it most needs the revenue.

In a non-Ricardian world, the inefficiencies associated with poorly managed government debt are magnified. In addition to suffering inefficient variations in distortionary tax rates, firms may be forced to abandon economically viable investment projects so that the government's spending can be financed.

On the whole, although it is far from conclusive, the evidence presented by Gale and Orszag casts doubt on the Ricardian view of government budget debt and deficits. Taken literally, the paper says that an increase in deficit financing of 1 percent of GDP reduces national saving by roughly half of a percent of GDP and raises interest rates by roughly 30 basis points. Eco-

3. Barro (1979).

nomically, these are *very* substantial effects. If Gale and Orszag are correct, we should indeed be worried about the current path of the federal budget.

General discussion: Benjamin Friedman emphasized that the authors' coefficient estimates relating the real interest rate to the debt-GDP ratio might appear to be small but in fact implied substantial effects of deficits on capital formation. He reminded the Panel that fiscal policy during the Reagan administration raised the debt-GDP ratio by approximately 25 percentage points, which, given the paper's estimates, corresponds to a 75-basis-point increase in real interest rates. Such an increase would be quite large both by historical standards and compared with the curvature of the production function. If, in equilibrium, the real marginal product of capital corresponds to the real interest rate, then the former will also be increased by 75 basis points, which would require a very large reduction in capital intensity unless the elasticity of substitution is much smaller than usually assumed. Friedman also pointed out that the latest CBO baseline projection of future deficits, which implies only a small increase in the debt-GDP ratio and thus a small impact on real interest rates, is misleading. After making the authors' adjustments to the CBO baseline projection, the implied future debt-GDP ratio is much larger, and the estimated impact on real interest rates is substantial. Referring to Christopher House's comment on the paper, Friedman pointed out that there is no practical difference between, on the one hand, a world where tax cuts will be undone as assumed in the Ricardian model but the behavior of consumers is not Ricardian and, on the other, a world where behavior is Ricardian but the tax cuts are not undone. Therefore, when one is thinking about the effects of actual U.S. fiscal policy, this distinction is unimportant.

Some panelists questioned whether the results reported in the paper should be expected to hold during periods of fiscal stress. Lars Svensson noted that Ricardian equivalence would not normally hold, but he cited the Swedish example of the early 1990s, when consumption dropped and saving increased dramatically in the face of a large fiscal deficit. He reasoned that people then viewed the fiscal situation as unsustainable and, fearing that it would soon lead to a reduction of benefits or an increase in taxes, started saving for that rainy day. Under such circumstances, Ricardian equivalence may be more likely. Austan Goolsbee argued that the effect of the fiscal position on interest rates would not be linear in a crisis and so could not be inferred from the authors' estimates. The experience of countries that have fallen into fiscal crisis shows that there is little effect on interest rates until the sustainability of the debt comes into question, at which point interest rates increase dramatically. He thought it was important to understand why the large debts and deficits in the United States in the 1940s and in Japan in recent years had so little effect on interest rates, and under what circumstances that might change. Goolsbee also pointed out that projections of future deficits make assumptions about several important factors, such as income growth and the rate of return on equities, that are also important to current consumption. He suggested that, rather than use such projections, the effects of future revenue growth be estimated using the tax rates called for in legislation as instruments.

Olivier Blanchard was skeptical of the paper's Euler equation tests of Ricardian equivalence. In the end, such a test involves regressing the change in consumption on the change in income, the change in taxes, and some other factors that usually are not significant. However, the change in taxes is likely to proxy for the change in spending, so that it is hard to interpret its coefficient. For this and other reasons, he found it hard to believe the results of such a test. Blanchard noted that several papers have found effects on consumption from the timing of tax payments, but such results are of limited use if one is interested in the effects of large deficits on the economy over many years. The high correlation between national saving and federal saving that is apparent in the authors' figure 6 does not imply causality, because so many factors affect both public and private saving. However, the relation might be tested using an instrument that, under the assumption of Ricardian equivalence, would not affect national saving except through public saving. Candidates for such an instrument might be fiscal rules such as Gramm-Rudman-type spending caps or a variable identifying the political party in power.

References

Ardagna, Silvia, Francesco Caselli, and Timothy Lane. 2004. "Fiscal Discipline and the Cost of Public Debt Service: Some Estimates for OECD Countries." Working Paper 10788. Cambridge, Mass.: National Bureau of Economic Research (September).

Aschauer, David A. 1985. "Fiscal Policy and Aggregate Demand." *American Economic Review* 75: 117–27.

Auerbach, Alan J. 1994. "The U.S. Fiscal Problem: Where We Are, How We Got Here, and Where We're Going." In *NBER Macroeconomics Annual,* edited by Stanley Fischer and Julio Rotemberg. Cambridge, Mass.: National Bureau of Economic Research.

Auerbach, Alan J., and Laurence Kotlikoff. 1987. *Dynamic Fiscal Policy.* Cambridge, U.K.: Cambridge University Press.

Auerbach, Alan J., William G. Gale, and Peter R. Orszag. 2004. "Sources of the Fiscal Gap." *Tax Notes* 103, no. 8: 1049–59.

Auerbach, Alan J., and others. 2003. "Budget Blues: The Fiscal Outlook and Options for Reform." In *Agenda for the Nation,* edited by Henry Aaron, James Lindsey, and Pietro Nivola. Brookings.

Ball, Laurence, and N. Gregory Mankiw. 1995. "What Do Budget Deficits Do?" In *Budget Deficits and Debt: Issues and Options.* Kansas City, Mo.: Federal Reserve Bank of Kansas City.

Barro, Robert J. 1974. "Are Government Bonds Net Worth?" *Journal of Political Economy* 82, no. 6: 1095–1117.

———. 1979. "On the Determination of the Public Debt." *Journal of Political Economy,* 87, no. 5: 940–71.

———. 1989. "The Ricardian Approach to Budget Deficits." *Journal of Economic Perspectives* 3, no. 2: 37–54.

———. 1991. "World Interest Rates and Investment." Working Paper 3849. Cambridge, Mass.: National Bureau of Economic Research (September).

Barro, Robert J., and Xavier Sala-i-Martin. 1991. "World Real Interest Rates." Working Paper 3317. Cambridge, Mass.: National Bureau of Economic Research (April).

Barsky, Robert B., N. Gregory Mankiw, and Stephen P. Zeldes. 1986. "Ricardian Consumers with Keynesian Propensities." *American Economic Review* 76, no. 4: 676–91.

Barth, James R., and Michael D. Bradley. 1989. "Evidence on Real Interest Rate Effects of Money, Debt, and Government Spending." *Quarterly Review of Economics and Business* 29, no. 1: 49–57.

Barth, James R., George Iden, and Frank S. Russek. 1985. "Federal Borrowing and Short Term Interest Rates: Comment." *Southern Economic Journal* 52, no. 2: 554–59.

_____. 1986. "Government Debt, Government Spending, and Private Sector Behavior: Comment." *American Economic Review* 76, no. 5: 1158–67.

Barth, James R., and others. 1991. "The Effects of Federal Budget Deficits on Interest Rates and the Composition of Domestic Output." In *The Great Fiscal Experiment,* edited by Rudolph G. Penner. Washington: Urban Institute Press.

Bernheim, B. Douglas. 1987. "Ricardian Equivalence: An Evaluation of Theory and Evidence." In *NBER Macroeconomics Annual,* Vol. 2, edited by Stanley Fischer. Cambridge, Mass.: National Bureau of Economic Research and MIT Press.

_____. 1989. "A Neoclassical Perspective on Budget Deficits." *Journal of Economic Perspectives* 3, no. 2: 55–72.

Blanchard, Olivier J. 1985. "Debt, Deficits, and Finite Horizons." *Journal of Political Economy* 93, no. 2: : 223–47.

Blanchard, Olivier J., and Stanley Fischer. 1989. *Lectures on Macroeconomics.* MIT Press.

Bovenberg, A. Lans. 1988. "Long-Term Interest Rates in the United States." International Monetary Fund *Staff Papers* 35, no. 2: 382–90.

Bradley, Michael D. 1986. "Government Spending or Deficit Financing: Which Causes Crowding Out?" *Journal of Economics and Business* 38, no. 3: 203–14.

Brook, Anne-Marie. 2003. "Recent and Prospective Trends in Real Long-Term Interest Rates: Fiscal Policy and Other Drivers." OECD Economics Department Working Paper 367. Paris: OECD (September 29).

Burman, Leonard E., William G. Gale, and Jeffrey Rohaly. 2003. "The Expanding Role of the Alternative Minimum Tax." *Journal of Economic Perspectives* 17, no. 2: 173–86.

Calomiris, Charles W., and others. 2004. "Do Budget Deficit Announcements Move Interest Rates?" Washington: American Enterprise Institute (December).

Campbell, John Y., and N. Gregory Mankiw. 1989. "Consumption, Income, and Interest Rates: Reinterpreting the Time Series Evidence." In *NBER Macroeconomics Annual,* edited by Olivier Blanchard and Stanley Fischer. MIT Press.

_____. 1990. "Permanent Income, Current Income and Consumption." *Journal of Business and Economic Statistics* 8, no. 3: 265–79.

Canto, Victor A., and Donald Rapp. 1982. "The 'Crowding Out' Controversy: Arguments and Evidence." Federal Reserve Bank of Atlanta *Economic Review* (August): 33–37.

Canzoneri, Matthew B., Robert E. Cumby, and Behzad T. Diba. 2002. "Should the European Central Bank and the Federal Reserve Be Concerned about Fiscal Policy?" Presented at the Federal Reserve Bank of Kansas City's symposium on "Rethinking Stabilization Policy," Jackson Hole, Wyo., August.

Cardia, Emanuela. 1997. "Replicating Ricardian Equivalence Tests with Simulated Series." *American Economic Review* 87, no. 1: 65–79.

Carlson, Jack. 1983. "The Relationship between Federal Deficits and Interest Rates." Statement before the Joint Economic Committee (October 21).

Carroll, Chris, and Lawrence H. Summers. 1987. "Why Have Private Savings Rates in the United States and Canada Diverged?" *Journal of Monetary Economics* 20: 249–79.

Cebula, Richard J. 1987. *The Deficit Problem in Perspective.* Lexington, Mass.: D. C. Heath.

_____. 1988. "Federal Government Budget Deficits and Interest Rates: A Brief Note." *Southern Economic Journal* 55, no.1: 206–10.

_____. 2000. "Impact of Budget Deficits on Ex Post Real Long-Term Interest Rates." *Applied Economics Letters* 7: 177–79.

Cebula, Richard J., and James V. Koch. 1989. "An Empirical Note on Deficits, Interest Rates, and International Capital Flows." *Quarterly Review of Economics and Business* 29, no. 3: 121–27.

_____. 1994. "Federal Budget Deficits, Interest Rates, and International Capital Flows: A Further Note." *Quarterly Review of Economics and Finance* 34, no. 1: 117–20.

Cohen, Darrel, and Glenn Follette. 2003. "Forecasting Exogenous Fiscal Variables in the United States." Finance and Economics Discussion Series. Washington: Board of Governors of the Federal Reserve System (November 5).

Cohen, Darrel, and Olivier Garnier. 1991. "The Impact of Forecasts of Budget Deficits on Interest Rates in the United States and Other G-7 Countries." Washington: Division of Research and Statistics, Federal Reserve Board.

Coorey, Sharmini. 1992. "The Determinants of U.S. Real Interest Rates in the Long Run." In *The United States Economy: Performance and Issues,* edited by a staff team headed by Yusuke Horiguchi. Washington: International Monetary Fund.

Cox, W. Michael. 1985. "The Behavior of Treasury Securities Monthly, 1942-1984." *Journal of Monetary Economics* 16: 227–40.

Dai, Qiang, and Thomas Philippon. 2004. "Government Deficits and Interest Rates: A No-Arbitrage Structural VAR Approach." New York University (March 14).

De Leeuw, Frank, and Thomas M. Holloway. 1985. "The Measurement and Significance of the Cyclically Adjusted Federal Budget and Debt." *Journal of Money, Credit, and Banking* 17, no. 2: 232–42.

Dennis, Robert, and others. 2004. "Macroeconomic Analysis of a 10 Percent Cut in Income Tax Rates." Washington: Congressional Budget Office (May).

De Serres, Alain, and Florian Pelgrin. 2003. "The Decline in Private Saving Rates in the 1990s in OECD Countries: How Much Can Be Explained by Non-Wealth

Determinants?" OECD Economics Department Working Paper 344. Paris: OECD.

Dewald, William G. 1983. "Federal Deficits and Interest Rates: Theory and Evidence." Federal Reserve Bank of Atlanta *Economic Review* (January): 20–29.

Dornbusch, Rudiger. 1991. "National Saving and International Investment: Comment." In *National Saving and Economic Performance,* edited by B. Douglas Bernheim and John B. Shoven. University of Chicago Press.

Echols, Michael E., and Jan Walter Elliott. 1976. "Rational Expectations in a Disequilibrium Model of the Term Structure." *American Economic Review* 66, no.1: 28–44.

Elmendorf, Douglas W. 1993. "Actual Budget Deficits and Interest Rates." Department of Economics, Harvard University (March).

————. 1996. "The Effects of Deficit Reduction Laws on Real Interest Rates." Finance and Economics Discussion Series 1996–44. Washington: Board of Governors of the Federal Reserve (October).

Elmendorf, Douglas W., and Jeffrey B. Liebman. 2000. "Social Security Reform and National Saving in an Era of Budget Surpluses." *BPEA*, no. 2: 1–71.

Elmendorf, Douglas W., and N. Gregory Mankiw. 1999. "Government Debt." In *Handbook of Macroeconomics,* Vol. 1C, edited by John B. Taylor and Michael Woodford. Amsterdam: Elsevier Science.

Engen, Eric M., and R. Glenn Hubbard. Forthcoming. "Federal Government Debt and Interest Rates." In *NBER Macroeconomics Annual,* edited by Mark Gertler and Kenneth Rogoff. MIT Press.

Evans, Paul. 1985. "Do Large Deficits Produce High Interest Rates?" *American Economic Review* 75, no. 1: 68–87.

————. 1987a. "Interest Rates and Expected Future Budget Deficits in the United States." *Journal of Political Economy* 95, no. 11: 34–58.

————. 1987b. "Do Budget Deficits Raise Nominal Interest Rates? Evidence from Six Countries." *Journal of Monetary Economics* 20: 281–300.

————. 1988. "Are Consumers Ricardian?" *Journal of Political Economy* 96, no. 5: 983–1004.

————. 1989. "A Test of Steady-State Government-Debt Neutrality." *Economic Inquiry* 27 (January): 39–55.

————. 1991. "Is Ricardian Equivalence a Good Approximation?" *Economic Inquiry* 29, no. 4: 626–44.

————. 1993. "Consumers Are Not Ricardian: Evidence from Nineteen Countries." *Economic Inquiry* 31(October): 534–48.

Evans, Paul, and Iftekhar Hasan. 1994. "Are Consumers Ricardian? Evidence for Canada." *Quarterly Review of Economics and Finance* 34, no. 1: 25–40.

Feldstein, Martin S. 1982. "Government Deficits and Aggregate Demand." *Journal of Monetary Economics* 9: 1–20.

_____. 1986. "Budget Deficits, Tax Rules, and Real Interest Rates. " Working Paper 1970. Cambridge, Mass.: National Bureau of Economic Research (July).

_____. 1988. "The Effects of Fiscal Policies When Incomes Are Uncertain: A Contradiction to Ricardian Equivalence." *American Economic Review* 78, no. 1: 14–23.

Feldstein, Martin S., and Gary Chamberlain. 1973. "Multimarket Expectations and the Rate of Interest." *Journal of Money, Credit, and Banking* 4, no. 4: 873–902.

Feldstein, Martin S., and Otto Eckstein. 1970. "The Fundamental Determinants of the Interest Rate." *Review of Economics and Statistics* 52, no. 4: 363–75.

Feldstein, Martin, and Douglas W. Elmendorf. 1990. "Government Debt, Government Spending, and Private Sector Behavior Revisited: Comment." *American Economic Review* 80, no. 3: 589–99.

Feldstein, Martin S., and Charles Horioka. 1980. "Domestic Savings and International Capital Flows." *Economic Journal* 90, no. 358: 314–29.

Flavin, Marjorie. 1987. "Comment." In *NBER Macroeconomics Annual*, edited by Stanley Fischer. Cambridge, Mass.: National Bureau of Economic Research and MIT Press.

Frankel, Jeffrey A. 1983. "A Test of Portfolio Crowding-Out and Related Issues of Finance." Working Paper 1205. Cambridge, Mass.: National Bureau of Economic Research (September).

Friedman, Benjamin. 1988. *Day of Reckoning: The Consequences of American Economic Policy Under Reagan and After.* Random House.

Gale, William G., and Peter R. Orszag. 2002. "The Economic Effects of Long-Term Fiscal Discipline." Discussion Paper. Washington: Urban-Brookings Tax Policy Center (December 17).

_____. 2003a. "Economic Effects of Sustained Budget Deficits." *National Tax Journal* 56: 463–85 (September).

_____. 2003b. "Sunsets in the Tax Code." *Tax Notes* 99, no. 10: 1553–61.

_____. 2003c. "Effects of Fiscal Policy on Aggregate Consumption and Saving: A Re-evaluation of Ricardian Equivalence." Brookings (December; also presented at the American Economic Association Meeting, San Diego, January 2004).

_____. 2004a. "Economic Effects of Making the 2001 and 2003 Tax Cuts Permanent." *International Tax and Public Finance.* Forthcoming.

_____. 2004b. "Tax Cuts, Interest Rates, and the User Cost of Capital." Brookings.

Gale, William G., and Samara R. Potter. 2002. "An Economic Evaluation of the Economic Growth and Tax Relief Reconciliation Act of 2001." *National Tax Journal* 55, no. 1: 133–86.

Giannaros, Demetrios S., and Bharat R. Kolluri. 1985. "Deficit Spending, Money, and Inflation: Some International Empirical Evidence." *Journal of Macroeconomics* 7, no. 3: 401–17.

Gokhale, Jagadeesh, and Kent Smetters. 2003. *Fiscal and Generational Imbalances: New Budget Measures for New Budget Priorities.* Washington: AEI Press.

Graham, Fred C. 1992. "On the Importance of the Measurement of Consumption in Tests of Ricardian Equivalence." *Economic Letters* 38, no. 4: 431–34.

———. 1995. "Government Debt, Government Spending, and Private-Sector Behavior: Comment." *American Economic Review* 85, no. 5: 1348–56.

Graham, Fred C., and Daniel Himarios. 1991. "Fiscal Policy and Private Consumption: Instrumental Variables Tests of the 'Consolidated Approach.'" *Journal of Money, Credit and Banking* 23, no. 1: 53–67.

———. 1996. "Consumption, Wealth, and Finite Horizons: Tests of Ricardian Equivalence." *Economic Inquiry* 34: 527–44.

Gravelle, Jane G. 1994. *The Economic Effects of Taxing Capital Income.* MIT Press.

———. 2004. "Historical Effective Marginal Tax Rates on Capital Income." Congressional Research Service Report for Congress. Washington: Congressional Research Service (January 12).

Hall, Robert E. 1978. "Stochastic Implications of the Life Cycle–Permanent Income Hypothesis." *Journal of Political Economy* 86: 971–87.

———. 1988. "Intertemporal Substitution in Consumption." *Journal of Political Economy* 96: 339–57.

Hayashi, Fumio. 1982. "The Permanent Income Hypothesis: Estimation and Testing by Instrumental Variables." *Journal of Political Economy* 90: 895–916.

Hoelscher, Gregory P. 1983. "Federal Borrowing and Short Term Interest Rates." *Southern Economic Journal* 50 (October): 319–33.

———. 1986. "New Evidence on Deficits and Interest Rates." *Journal of Money, Credit, and Banking* 18, no. 1: 1–17.

Hubbard, R. Glenn, and Kenneth L. Judd. 1986. "Liquidity Constraints, Fiscal Policy, and Consumption." *BPEA*, no. 1: 1–59.

Hutchison, Michael, and David H. Pyle. 1984. "The Real Interest Rate/Budget Deficit Link: International Evidence, 1973-1982." Federal Reserve Bank of San Francisco *Economic Review* (Fall): 26–35.

Johnson, David S., Jonathan A. Parker, and Nicholas S. Souleles. 2004. "The Response of Consumer Spending to the Randomized Income Tax Rebates of 2001." Bureau of Labor Statistics, Princeton University, and University of Pennsylvania (February).

Joint Committee on Taxation. 2001. "Estimated Budget Effects of the Conference Agreement for H.R.: 1836[1]." Document JCX-51-01. Washington (May 26).

_____. 2002. "Estimated Revenue Effects of the 'Job Creation and Worker Assistance Act of 2002.'" Document JCX-13-02. Washington (March 6).

_____. 2003. "Estimated Budget Effects of the Conference Agreement for H.R. 2.: The Jobs and Growth Tax Relief Reconciliation Act of 2003." Document JCX-55–03. Washington (May 22).

Judd, Kenneth L. 1985. "Short Run Analysis of Fiscal Policy in a Simple Perfect Foresight Model." *Journal of Political Economy* 93, no. 2: 298–319.

_____. 1987a. "The Welfare Cost of Factor Taxation in a Perfect Foresight Model." *Journal of Political Economy* 95, no. 4: 675–709.

_____. 1987b. "Debt and Distortionary Taxation in a Simple Perfect Foresight Model." *Journal of Monetary Economics* 20, no. 5: 1–72.

Kiley, Michael T. 2003. "The Effect of Government Debt on the Return to Capital." Washington: Board of Governors of the Federal Reserve (December).

Kim, Sun-Young, and Raymond E. Lombra. 1989. "Why the Empirical Relationship between Deficits and Interest Rates Appears So Fragile." *Journal of Economics and Business* 41, no. 3: 241–51.

Kitchen, John. 1996. "Domestic and International Financial Market Responses to Federal Deficit Announcements." *Journal of International Money and Finance* 15, no. 2: 239–54.

_____. 2002. "A Note on Interest Rates and Structural Federal Budget Deficits." Washington: House Budget Committee (October).

Kolluri, Bharat R., and Demetrios S. Giannaros. 1987. "Budget Deficits and Short-term Real Interest Rate Forecasting." *Journal of Macroeconomics* 9, no. 1: 109–25.

Kormendi, Roger. 1983. "Government Debt, Government Spending, and Private Sector Behavior." *American Economic Review* 73, no. 5: 994–1010.

Kormendi, Roger C., and Philip Meguire. 1986. "Government Debt, Government Spending, and Private Sector Behavior: Reply." *American Economic Review* 76, no. 5: 1180–87.

_____. 1990. "Government Debt, Government Spending, and Private Sector Behavior: Reply and Update." *American Economic Review* 80, no. 3: 604–17.

_____. 1995. "Government Debt, Government Spending, and Private Sector Behavior: Reply." *American Economic Review* 85, no. 5: 1357–61.

Kormendi, Roger C., and Aris Protopapadakis. 2004. "Budget Deficits, Current Account Deficits, and Interest Rates: The Systematic Evidence on Ricardian Equivalence." Center for Society and Economy, Business School, University of Michigan.

Kudlow, Lawrence. 1981. "Statement before the Senate Budget Committee: Statistical Appendix" (October 20).

Laubach, Thomas. 2003. "New Evidence on the Interest Rate Effects of Budget Deficits and Debt." Washington: Board of Governors of the Federal Reserve System (May).

Lee, Ronald, and Ryan Edwards. 2001. "The Fiscal Impact of Population Change." In *Seismic Shifts: The Economic Impact of Demographic Change,* edited by Jane Sneddon Little and Robert K. Triest. Conference Series 46. Federal Reserve Bank of Boston.

Makin, John H. 1983. "Real Interest, Money Surprises, Anticipated Inflation and Fiscal Deficits." *Review of Economics and Statistics* 65, no. 3: 374–84.

Makin, John H., and Vito Tanzi. 1984. "Level and Volatility of U.S. Interest Rates: Roles of Expected Inflation, Real Rates and Taxes." In *Taxation, Inflation, and Interest Rates,* edited by Vito Tanzi. Washington: International Monetary Fund.

Mankiw, N. Gregory. 1990. "A Quick Refresher Course in Macroeconomics." *Journal of Economic Literature* 28, no. 4: 1645–60.

————. 1992. "The Reincarnation of Keynesian Economics." *European Economic Review* 36: 559–65.

————. 2000a. *Macroeconomics.* New York: Worth Publishers.

————. 2000b. "The Savers-Spenders Theory of Fiscal Policy." *American Economic Review* 90 (*Papers and Proceedings*), no. 2: 120–25.

Mascaro, Angelo, and Allen H. Meltzer. 1983. "Long- and Short-Term Interest Rates in a Risky World." *Journal of Monetary Economics* 12, no. 4: 485–518.

Meguire, Philip. 1998. "Comment: Social Security and Private Savings." *National Tax Journal* 51, no. 2: 339–58.

————. 2003. "Social Security and Personal Saving: 1971 and Beyond." *Empirical Economics* 28, no. 1: 115–39.

Miller, Stephen M., and Frank S. Russek. 1991. "The Temporal Causality between Fiscal Deficits and Interest Rates," *Contemporary Policy Issues* 9: 12–23.

————. 1996. "Do Federal Deficits Affect Interest Rates? Evidence from Three Econometric Methods." *Journal of Macroeconomics* 18, no. 3: 403–28.

Modigliani, Franco, and Arlie G. Sterling. 1986. "Government Debt, Government Spending, and Private Sector Behavior: Comment." *American Economic Review* 76, no. 5: 1168–79.

Motley, Brian. 1983. "Real Interest Rates, Money and Government Deficits." Federal Reserve Bank of San Francisco *Economic Review* (Summer): 31–45.

Mountford, Andrew, and Harald Uhlig. 2000. "What Are the Effects of Fiscal Policy Shocks?" London: Centre for Economic Policy Research (October).

Muller, Patrice, and Robert Price. 1984. "Public Sector Indebtedness and Long-Term Interest Rates." Paper presented at the World Bank/Brookings Institution Workshop on "International Consequences of Budgetary Deficits in the OECD," Washington, September.

Perotti, Roberto. 2002. "Estimating the Effects of Fiscal Policy in OECD Countries." Presented at the International Seminar on Macroeconomics (ISOM), Frankfurt, June.

Plosser, Charles I. 1982. "Government Financing Decisions and Asset Returns." *Journal of Monetary Economics* 9, no. 3: 325–52.

_____. 1987a. "Fiscal Policy and the Term Structure." *Journal of Monetary Economics* 20, no. 6: 343–67.

_____. 1987b. "Comment." In *NBER Macroeconomics Annual*, edited by Stanley Fischer. Cambridge, Mass.: National Bureau of Economic Research and MIT Press.

Poterba, James M., and Lawrence H. Summers. 1986. "Finite Lifetimes and the Crowding Out Effects of Budget Deficits." Working Paper 1955. Cambridge, Mass.: National Bureau of Economic Research (June).

_____. 1987. "Recent US Evidence on Budget Deficits and National Savings." Working Paper 2144. Cambridge, Mass.: National Bureau of Economic Research (February).

Quigley, Michael Regan, and Susan Porter-Hudak. 1994. "A New Approach in Analyzing the Effect of Deficit Announcements on Interest Rates." *Journal of Money, Credit, and Banking* 26, no. 4: 894–902.

Ramey, Valerie A., and Matthew D. Shapiro. 1998. "Costly Capital Reallocation and the Effects of Government Spending." Carnegie Rochester Conference Series on Public Policy 48 (June): 145–94.

Romer, David. 1996. *Advanced Macroeconomics.* McGraw Hill.

Rubin, Robert E., Peter R. Orszag, and Allen Sinai. 2004. "Sustained Budget Deficits: Longer-Run U.S. Economic Performance and the Risk of Financial and Fiscal Disarray." Paper presented at the AEA-NAEFA Joint Session, Allied Social Science Associations Annual Meetings, The Andrew Brimmer Policy Forum, "National Economic and Financial Policies for Growth and Stability," San Diego, January 4.

Seater, John J. 1981. "The Market Value of Outstanding Government Debt, 1919-1975." *Journal of Monetary Economics* 8 (July): 85–101.

_____. 1993. "Ricardian Equivalence." *Journal of Economic Literature* 31, no. 1: 142–90.

Seater, John J., and Roberto S. Mariano. 1985. "New Tests of the Life-Cycle and Tax-Discounting Hypotheses." *Journal of Monetary Economics* (March): 195–215.

Shapiro, Matthew. Forthcoming. "Comment." In *NBER Macroeconomics Annual,* edited by Mark Gertler and Kenneth Rogoff. MIT Press.

Shapiro, Matthew D., and Joel Slemrod. 2003. "Did the 2001 Tax Rebate Stimulate Spending? Evidence from Taxpayer Surveys." In *Tax Policy and the Economy,* Vol. 17, edited by James Poterba. MIT Press.

Shoven, John B. 2002. "The Impact of Major Life Expectancy Improvements on the Financing of Social Security, Medicare and Medicaid." In *Creating Methuselah: Molecular Medicine and the Problems of an Aging Society,* edited by Henry J. Aaron and William B. Schwartz. Brookings.

Sinai, Allen, and Peter Rathjens. 1983. "Deficits, Interest Rates, and the Economy." *Data Resources U.S. Review* (June): 1.27–1.41.

Smetters, Kent. 1999. "Ricardian Equivalence: Long-Run Leviathan." *Journal of Public Economics* 73, no. 3: 395–421.

Summers, Lawrence H. 1985. "Issues in National Savings Policy." Working Paper 1710. Cambridge, Mass.: National Bureau of Economic Research.

Swamy, P. A. V. B., Bharat R. Kolluri, and Rao N. Singamsetti. 1988. "What Do Regressions of Interest Rates on Deficits Imply?" Finance and Economics Discussion Series 3. Washington: Division of Research and Statistics, Board of Governors of the Federal Reserve (January).

Tanzi, Vito. 1985. "Fiscal Deficits and Interest Rates in the United States, An Empirical Analysis, 1960-1984." International Monetary Fund *Staff Papers* 32, no. 4: 551–76.

Tatom, John A. 1984. "A Perspective on the Federal Deficit Problem." Federal Reserve Bank of St. Louis *Review* 66, no. 6: 5–17.

Tavares, Jose, and Rossen Valkanov. 2001. "The Neglected Effect of Fiscal Policy on Stock and Bond Returns." Anderson School, University of California, Los Angeles (October).

Thomas, Lloyd B., Jr., and Ali Abderrezak. 1988a. "Anticipated Future Budget Deficits and the Term Structure of Interest Rates." *Southern Economic Journal* 55, no. 1: 150–61.

_____. 1988b. "Long-Term Interest Rates: The Role of Expected Budget Deficits." *Public Finance Quarterly* 16, no. 3: 341–56.

Thorbecke, Willem. 1993. "Why Deficit News Affects Interest Rates." *Journal of Policy Modeling* 15, no. 1: 1–11.

Truman, Edwin M. 2001. "The International Implications of Paying Down the Debt." Policy Brief Number 01v7. Washington: Institute for International Economics.

United States Department of the Treasury. 1984. *The Effects of Deficits on Prices of Financial Assets: Theory and Evidence.* Washington (March).

Wachtel, Paul, and John Young. 1987. "Deficit Announcements and Interest Rates." *American Economic Review* 77, no. 5: 1007–12.

Zahid, Khan H. 1988. "Government Budget Deficits and Interest Rates: The Evidence Since 1971, Using Alternative Deficit Measures." *Southern Economic Journal* 54, no. 3: 725–31.

MARTIN NEIL BAILY
Institute for International Economics and McKinsey Global Institute

ROBERT Z. LAWRENCE
Harvard University and Institute for International Economics

What Happened to the Great U.S. Job Machine? The Role of Trade and Electronic Offshoring

The loss of manufacturing jobs and hundreds of thousands of service jobs over the past few years, and the threat of the loss of millions more to offshore outsourcing, is a clear call to our business and political leaders that our trade policies simply are not working. At the least, not in the national interest.[1]

THE BUSINESS CYCLE recovery of the past few years has been an unusual one. In particular, payroll employment since the trough of the 2001 recession has been remarkably weak compared with previous recessions—a point illustrated in figure 1.[2] The decline in payroll employment from the peak in March 2001 to the trough in November of the same year was modest, but employment continued to fall for the next twenty-one months, ending up just over a million jobs below the trough before starting to

We are grateful to the participants at the Brookings Panel meeting and to Mac Destler, Jeffrey Frankel, Catherine Mann, and Edwin Truman for helpful comments. Thanks also to Sunil Patel of NASSCOM for comments. Jacob Kirkegaard, Katharina Plück, and Magali Junowicz provided substantial assistance in the preparation of this paper. Vivek Agrawal of McKinsey and Company provided additional assistance with respect to the McKinsey case study on Indian offshoring. We have benefited greatly from the assistance of Macroeconomic Advisers in preparing our simulations of the future impact of offshoring, but the simulations reported using their model should not be taken as predictions by that organization.

1. Lou Dobbs, "A Home Advantage for U.S. Corporations," *CNN Friday,* August 27, 2004.

2. This now-familiar figure originated at the Council of Economic Advisers in the 1980s, where it was given considerable play "for obvious reasons," as Michael Mussa has remarked—job growth after the early 1980s recession was very strong indeed.

211

Figure 1. Total Nonfarm Payroll Employment before and after Business Cycle Troughs

Index (trough = 100)

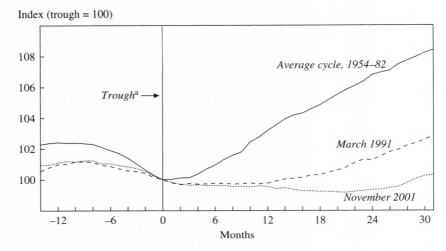

Source: Bureau of Labor Statistics, Current Employment Survey Statistics, July 2004.
a. As identified by the Business Cycle Dating Committee of the National Bureau of Economic Research.

recover. This contrasts with most previous recessions, in which job growth following the trough was strong. The aftermath of the previous recession, that of 1990–91, was also characterized by relatively weak job performance, as figure 1 also shows. But the jobs picture since 2001 has been much weaker even than that "jobless recovery."

In many press reports and in the minds of many Americans, much of the weakness in the labor market is the fault of foreign competition. As the quotation above indicates, there is uneasiness that manufacturing and services sector jobs have been, or will be, moved abroad. Partly because of technological change and partly because of trade agreements, so the argument goes, U.S. workers now have to compete against a huge low-wage global labor pool, and the sustained weakness in employment since 2000 is a sign that this competition is undermining the great U.S. job machine.

Most economists dismiss these concerns as showing a misunderstanding of how international trade works and of the ability of the U.S. economy to reemploy workers displaced by trade. Indeed, most economists would argue that, over the long run, the United States will have to reduce its trade deficit, and that this could create more opportunities for blue-collar workers in export industries. Similarly, the more services the United States imports, the larger U.S. exports of both goods and other services will eventually have to be to pay for them. But economists' reassurances on this point have not carried a lot of weight in the popular debate—or even at times in the policy debate.

Putting the role of trade in the U.S. economy in perspective is not simply a matter of setting the record straight. Misperceptions on the part of workers may discourage them from acquiring the skills they need in order to get good jobs. Misperceptions on the part of voters and elected officials can lead to bad policies. In this paper, therefore, we try to put trade and electronic offshoring concerns in the right perspective, in a way that is easily understandable. We estimate the size of the first-round job dislocation that trade and electronic offshoring may have caused between 2000 and 2003.[3] The approach we use, and several assumptions we make along the way, have the effect of exaggerating the impact on trade and offshoring on the U.S. labor market. Nevertheless, the results show that the weakness in U.S. payroll employment since 2000 has not been caused by a flood of imports of either goods or services. It should certainly not be attributed to any trade agreements the United States has signed.[4] Rather, the weakness of employment is primarily the result of inadequate growth of domestic demand in the presence of strong productivity growth.

The paper also goes beyond this basic result in several ways and makes the following additional findings: First, to the extent that trade did cause a loss of manufacturing jobs, it was the weakness of U.S. exports after 2000 and not the strength of imports that was responsible—the share of imports in the U.S. market actually declined. Second, the weakness in U.S. exports was primarily the result of a strong dollar. The world market for manufactured exports continued to grow after 2000, but the United States

3. The use of the terms "offshoring" and "outsourcing" to refer to a wide variety of (often overlapping) activities has created considerable confusion. In this paper we use the term "electronic offshoring" to refer to imports of electronically transmitted services. For a discussion of these terms and one set of definitions, see Bhagwati, Panagariya, and Srinivasan (forthcoming).

4. The North American Free Trade Agreement (NAFTA), in particular, has borne the brunt of allegations that trade agreements are responsible for large job losses. Yet NAFTA came into effect in 1995, and the subsequent five years saw very robust employment growth. Hence whatever NAFTA's employment effects may have been, it is simply implausible to blame it for unemployment in 2001 and beyond.

lost market share. Third, the impact on U.S. employment of services sector offshoring to India in 2000–03 was very small compared with the aggregate changes in services sector employment during that period. Fourth, focusing more narrowly on the U.S. technology sector, there has been a loss of lower-paid programming jobs, much of which can be attributed to offshoring to India. But the employment picture for computer services occupations as a whole has actually been surprisingly strong in the last few years, especially if one allows for the unsustainable, domestic demand-driven surge in employment in 2000. Fifth, trade is also unlikely to be a major source of additional manufacturing jobs in the future: even if the United States eliminates its merchandise trade deficit over the next decade, the net addition to manufacturing employment is likely to be modest. Sixth and finally, although some have predicted that over 3 million U.S. service jobs will be offshored via information technology through 2015, and simulations from a macroeconomic model suggest that offshoring of this magnitude will be large enough to have appreciable effects on the macroeconomy, the nature of those effects depends crucially on how that offshoring is modeled. If offshoring is modeled as a decline in the price at which the United States can buy foreign services, then U.S. GDP, real compensation of employees, and real profits will all be higher in 2015 as a result of services offshoring. If instead offshoring is modeled simply as an increase in the quantity of services imports at today's prices, the welfare benefits will be smaller because more exports are needed to pay for these. Nonetheless, again, a relatively modest number of jobs are generated in manufacturing to produce these exports. All told, our analysis suggests that trade is neither the major source of the current troubles facing U.S. manufacturing workers nor a potential solution to their problems in the future.

The Pattern of Employment Change

This section uses detailed data broken down by industry and occupation to review which sectors of the economy have lost jobs in recent years and which types of workers lost them. We find that the job losses were overwhelmingly concentrated in the manufacturing sector, and that major services industries that had been consistent job creators over the 1990s stopped creating jobs after 2000, and indeed lost significant numbers of jobs in some cases. The loss of manufacturing jobs and the erosion of the job-creating capabilities of private sector service industries played into popular fears that trade and offshoring are driving the outcome.

Job Changes by Major Sector

Our ability to make consistent comparisons across industries over time is limited because of the changeover from the Standard Industrial Classification (SIC) to the North American Industry Classification System (NAICS) in 1997. A recent major revision to the occupational classifications makes comparisons across occupations similarly problematic. Nevertheless, the patterns in the available data are striking. Figure 2 shows annual average employment changes by broad industry grouping (based on NAICS definitions) from 1990 to 2000 and from 2000 to 2003, calculated from payroll data from establishments. Private sector employment declined after 2000 at a rate of 880,000 a year, or 2.64 million in total. Government employment meanwhile rose by more than 200,000 a year, so that the total decline in payroll employment for the three years was 1.86 million. Employment in the manufacturing sector was very hard hit indeed, declining at a rate of over 900,000 a year, for a total of 2.8 million jobs lost over the three years, more than the decline in total private sector employment. The sectors with the largest employment gains after 2000 were health and education (more the former than the latter) and the government sector (which includes employment in public educational institutions).

The other large sources of the post-2000 decline by industry were professional and business services and wholesale and retail trade, where employment fell at rates of 223,000 and 232,000 jobs a year, respectively. These two sectors' contribution to the overall swing in labor market conditions is even greater than their post-2000 job losses indicate. Unlike manufacturing, both sectors were large contributors to the job gains of the 1990s, and they then flipped to large losses after 2000. If one compares the size of the swings in employment performance before and after 2000, manufacturing remains the largest contributor to the shift in the employment picture, but professional and business services is close behind, and the contribution of wholesale and retail trade is large also. The information sector likewise went from being a solid employment creator in the 1990s to an employment loser after 2000. Besides data processing ser-

Figure 2. Employment Gains and Losses by Sector, 1990–2000 and 2000–03[a]

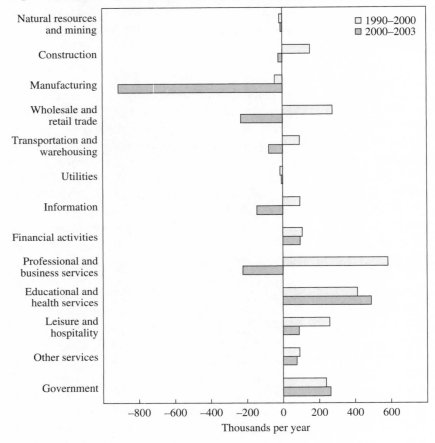

vices and telecommunications providers, this sector also includes many industries that are less about information technology (IT) than about information itself (media and publishing companies, for example).

In summary, the shift in employment performance after 2000 was widespread across the major nongovernment sectors of the economy, as is to be expected in a general business cycle downturn. However, much of the action was in the three large sectors of manufacturing, professional and business services, and wholesale and retail trade. Manufacturing is notable for the very large job losses it suffered, and the other two are notable because they went from being big job gainers to job losers.[5]

Job Changes by Occupation

The Bureau of Labor Statistics conducts an establishment survey that reports employment by occupation by industry (the Occupational Employment Statistics, or OES data). These data are not in the form of annual averages, because in November 2002 the survey frequency was shifted from once a year to twice a year. Because of classification changes, consistent data are available only since 1999. Figure 3 shows the breakdown of the total job decline from the fourth quarter of 2000 to the second quarter of 2003. The total job loss in this survey is comparable to, although a bit smaller than, the job loss in the regular establishment survey. Figure 3 also shows the mean annual wage of each group.

By far the largest employment decline by occupation occurred among production workers. Given what happened in the manufacturing sector, this is not a great surprise. About three-quarters of the decline in production occupations occurred among workers employed in the manufacturing sector. Private sector services saw a decline of 437,000 production workers, notably in the areas of administrative support and waste management, professional and technical services, and wholesale trade. The data provide much detail within the category of production workers, but no obvious pattern emerges—declines occurred more or less across the board. The largest job decline was in team assemblers, followed by electrical and electronic equipment assemblers.

---

5. One important qualification is necessary. Within the professional and business services sector, the two industries that had the largest employment gains before 2000 and the largest employment losses after 2000 were the employment services industry and the computer systems design and related services industry. Both of these subindustries provide intermediate services for other industries across the economy. We examine the computer services sector later in the paper. The biggest mover in the employment services industry is temporary help services, which provides employees to a range of other industries. This subindustry alone accounted for about a quarter of the job gains in the professional and business services sector before 2000 and about 58 percent of the job losses after. Thus the employment weakness was not quite as concentrated in three big sectors as appears from the industry employment data. Job losses in other industries were attributed back to the business services sector as temporary employees were released.

Figure 3. Changes in Employment by Occupation, 2000–03

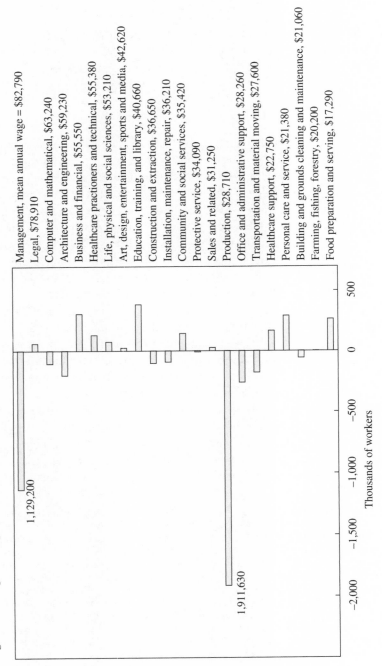

Management, mean annual wage = $82,790
Legal, $78,910
Computer and mathematical, $63,240
Architecture and engineering, $59,230
Business and financial, $55,550
Healthcare practioners and technical, $55,380
Life, physical and social sciences, $53,210
Art, design, entertainment, sports and media, $42,620
Education, training, and library, $40,660
Construction and extraction, $36,650
Installation, maintenance, repair, $36,210
Community and social services, $35,420
Protective service, $34,090
Sales and related, $31,250
Production, $28,710
Office and administrative support, $28,260
Transportation and material moving, $27,600
Healthcare support, $22,750
Personal care and service, $21,380
Building and grounds cleaning and maintenance, $21,060
Farming, fishing, forestry, $20,200
Food preparation and serving, $17,290

1,129,200

1,911,630

−2,000   −1,500   −1,000   −500   0   500

Thousands of workers

Source: Bureau of Labor Statistics, Occupational Employment Statistics (OES).

Somewhat surprisingly, the occupational category that suffered the second-largest number of job losses was managers—the highest-paid category. The biggest losses occurred for general and operational managers, chief executives, financial managers, administrative services managers, and human resource managers. Few subcategories showed gains, and those that did were mostly education and social services managers and legislators. The breakdown of managerial job losses by industry shows that the largest losses occurred in private services (713,000 jobs lost at mean annual earnings of $174,000 in 2003), followed by manufacturing (334,000 at $92,000).

The employment declines in the two broad occupational categories of managers and production workers more than account for the total job loss in the establishment data.[6] When the downturn hit, it seems that companies got rid of many of their production workers and managers. This is consistent with firms deciding to shut down whole operations and lines of business that were no longer profitable once the boom ended.[7]

To summarize this section, the manufacturing sector is extensively involved in international trade. It is therefore not surprising that many observers have found it plausible to assign imports a major role in the loss of production jobs between 2000 and 2003. Traditionally, business services activities have been overwhelmingly driven by domestic economic activity and seen as much less susceptible to cyclical fluctuations. But the change in the fortunes of well-paid workers in this sector during this period may have created an environment of uncertainty in which new trends could be seen as having highly ominous implications.

6. The total job loss in the OES occupational data is slightly smaller than that over the same period from the payroll data. The OES sample is from a separate survey with fewer respondents.

7. There is a significant discrepancy between the occupational decomposition from the OES and that from the Current Population Survey (CPS) data. The sharp decline in employment of managers that is evident in the OES establishment data does not appear in the CPS data; in fact, the CPS data show a modest increase in employment in this occupational category from 2000 to 2003. The number of managers in the CPS is nearly twice that in the OES data, in part because the self-employed and small farmers often describe themselves as managers. Significant "grade inflation" also appears elsewhere in the CPS data: experienced sales clerks are often described as assistant managers, for example. The drop in production worker employment, however, shows up strongly in both data sources. The CPS also shows a significant decline in administrative and office support jobs, which is much less pronounced in the OES data.

Figure 4. Manufacturing Employment[a]

Millions of workers

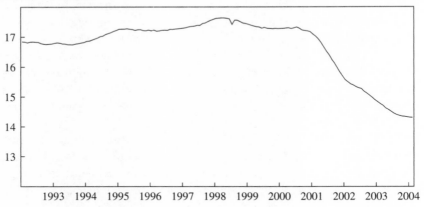

Source: Bureau of Labor Statistics, Current Employment Survey Statistics.
a. As defined in NAICS, seasonally adjusted.

The Impact of Trade on the Manufacturing Sector

> The recession has bludgeoned the nation's factories in the past three years, with a record 36 consecutive months of job losses totaling 2.7 million. Low demand at home and abroad, coupled with a flood of imports, have slowed production.[8]

In this section we use input-output tables of the U.S. economy to estimate the direct impact of trade on employment in U.S. manufacturing between 2000 and 2003. First, however, we place the recent employment performance in historical perspective, explain why the manufacturing trade deficit has been viewed as an important causal factor in the employment decline, and use GDP data to show that the performance of exports—not imports—is the more important part of the recent employment story.

The manufacturing share of U.S. employment has been declining for at least half a century. This is not unique to the United States, however; it is typical of developed economies and even characteristic of many developing economies. The basic reason is that although demand for the output of the manufacturing sector has grown about as rapidly as GDP, it has not

---

8. Liz Austin (Associated Press), "Commerce Secretary Announces New Position of Assistant Secretary for Manufacturing," *Detroit News,* September 3, 2003.

grown fast enough to offset the relatively rapid productivity growth in the sector.[9] As a result, the relative demand for manufacturing workers has declined.[10]

Some observers explain the recent job loss in manufacturing by pointing to the relatively rapid manufacturing productivity growth of recent years, but between 2000 and 2003 this factor did not play a dominant role. Over that period the share of manufacturing in nonfarm payrolls fell from 13.1 percent to 11.1 percent—a drop of 15 percent. But the 12 percent increase in nonfarm output per worker-hour between 2000 and 2003 was only 3 percentage points less than the increase in manufacturing labor productivity. This leaves 80 percent (12 percentage points of the 15 percent) of the decline in manufacturing's employment share to be explained by other factors.[11]

Moreover, the concerns were more about absolute job loss than about manufacturing's declining share. As figure 4 illustrates, in the decade of the 1990s, the absolute level of employment in manufacturing remained fairly stable. In fact, between 1993 and 1998 manufacturing payrolls increased from 16.8 million to 17.6 million, almost regaining their 1989 peak of 18 million. They then declined modestly to 17.3 million by 2000. Thereafter, however, manufacturing employment fell precipitously. Between 2000 and 2003 payroll employment in manufacturing fell 16.2 percent—the largest slump in manufacturing employment in postwar history.[12]

Table 1 ranks major industries (as identified by three-digit NAICS categories) by the size of their employment declines between 2000 and 2003. Although the job losses were concentrated among producers of capital

9. The demand for manufactured output depends on both the income and price elasticities. Rapid productivity growth could, of course, be associated with an increasing employment share in the sector if the demand for manufactured goods were sufficiently elastic, but it is not. See *Economic Report of the President*, 2004, for a discussion.

10. The declining share of employment in manufacturing has not been consistently associated with a declining share of manufacturing output in GDP. Measured in chained 1996 dollars, the share of manufacturing output in overall GDP did decline from 17.3 percent in 2000 to 16.1 percent in 2002. But this occurred after manufacturing's share had risen from 15.8 percent of GDP in 1992 to peak at 17.6 percent in 1998.

11. According to Bureau of Labor Statistics estimates, output per hour in the nonfarm business sector and in manufacturing increased by 11.7 percent and 14.8 percent, respectively, between 2000 and 2003.

12. The largest previous decline was from 19.4 million to 16.7 million between 1979 and 1983.

Table 1. Changes in Employment and Trade Balance by Manufacturing Industry, 2000–03

Industry	Employment, 2000 (thousands of workers)	Change in employment, 2000–03 (Thousands of workers)	Percent	Change in value added, 2000–03 (percent)	Change in value added per employee, 2000–03 (percent)	Change in exports, 2000–03 (percent)	Change in imports, 2000–03 (percent)	Change in trade balance, 2000–03 (billions of dollars)
Computer and electronic products	1,863.50	−531.30	−28.5	−13.54	20.95	−23.56	−15.16	−8.09
Machinery	1,452.60	−312.20	−21.5	−9.53	15.23	−16.46	−2.26	−12.98
Fabricated metal products	1,761.70	−290.50	−16.5	−11.66	5.78	−11.12	7.51	−4.67
Apparel and leather and allied products	537.00	−195.00	−36.3	−23.48	20.15	−27.20	5.88	−8.03
Textile mills and textile product mills	581.50	−166.20	−28.6	−23.47	7.15	2.01	15.74	−2.08
Motor vehicles, bodies, and trailers, and parts	1,283.46	−164.15	−12.8	3.12	18.25	−20.10	−6.82	−5.80
Primary metals	611.60	−147.00	−24.0	−20.79	4.27	−11.04	−22.78	7.62
Electrical equipment, appliances, and components	587.70	−136.50	−23.2	−10.76	16.24	−15.23	6.68	−6.85
Plastics and rubber products	940.30	−134.50	−14.3	−7.09	8.42	−6.80	17.89	−4.34
Printing and related support activities	801.00	−130.90	−16.3	−9.25	8.48	−2.23	12.02	−0.62
Furniture and related products	676.10	−106.80	−15.8	−9.53	7.44	−15.82	25.82	−4.51
Other transportation equipment	737.74	−94.35	−12.8	−1.18	13.31	−13.39	1.47	−7.17
Paper products	599.30	−89.00	−14.9	−15.27	−0.49	−9.23	−3.48	−0.81
Miscellaneous manufacturing	734.10	−82.20	−11.2	−0.09	12.51	20.24	15.48	−3.83
Chemical products	975.20	−79.30	−8.1	8.18	17.76	13.40	36.28	−15.33
Nonmetallic mineral products	553.60	−66.10	−11.9	−3.06	10.09	−21.63	−2.61	−1.38
Food and beverage and tobacco products	1,762.70	−58.10	−3.3	7.81	11.48	−0.42	26.65	−7.53
Wood products	593.50	−56.90	−9.6	2.35	13.20	−19.63	7.74	−2.18
Petroleum and coal products	122.10	−9.70	−7.9	−7.01	1.02	6.98	9.59	−1.81

Sources: Current Employment Survey, Bureau of Labor Statistics; U.S. International Trade Commission; Bureau of Economic Analysis.

goods and apparel, every three-digit industry saw its payrolls fall. The bursting of the high-technology bubble resulted in the loss of more than half a million jobs in the industry that produces computers and electronic products—fully 28.5 percent of the industry's 2000 employment. Other large declines occurred in machinery (312,000 jobs lost, or 21.5 percent) and fabricated metal products (290,000, or 16.5 percent). Apparel and leather (195,000 jobs lost, or 36.3 percent) and textile product mills (166,200, or 28.6 percent) were severely affected. Table 1 also shows the change in value added by industry and in value added per employee—important drivers of employment change whose role will be featured in the later analysis.

To many observers, trade was the obvious culprit for these job losses. The United States has run increasing deficits in manufacturing trade since 1992. These deficits have been both large relative to the size of the sector and growing. The growth in the deficit has been particularly pronounced since 1997, when U.S. exports stagnated in the aftermath of the Asian financial crisis while U.S. imports increased rapidly as the economy boomed. As a result, between 1997 and 2000 the trade deficit in manufactured goods more than doubled, from $136 billion to $317 billion. As table 2 indicates, between 2000 and 2003 the trade balance in manufacturing declined by an additional $86.1 billion, predominantly because exports fell by $62.3 billion (8.8 percent), although imports also increased, by $23.6 billion (2.3 percent).

Table 1 illustrates that declining trade balances were widespread across industries between 2000 and 2003. Only one of the nineteen industries in manufacturing—primary metals—avoided a decline in its trade balance over the period. The sectors with the largest declines were chemical products ($15.3 billion), machinery ($13.0 billion), computers ($8.1 billion), apparel ($8.0 billion), and food ($7.5 billion). Export performance was particularly weak: exports fell in fifteen of the nineteen industries. The largest percentage declines were in apparel (down $3 billion, or 27.2 percent), computers ($46 billion, or 23.6 percent), and motor vehicles ($8 billion, or 20.1 percent). Other large declines were in machinery (down $15 billion) and other transportation (which includes aircraft; down $6.5 billion).

How do these deficits compare with overall manufacturing output? Figure 5 shows the manufacturing trade deficit as a percentage of manufacturing output, with output measured in two different ways. The first

Table 2. Selected Indicators of the Macroeconomy and Manufacturing, 2000–03

Indicator	2000	2003	Change, 2000–03	Change, 2000–03 (percent)
Output (billions of dollars)				
GDP	9,817.0	10,987.9	1,170.9	11.9
Manufacturing	1,426.2	1,392.8	–33.4	–2.3
Employment (millions of workers)				
Nonfarm business sector	131.8	129.9	–1.9	–1.4
Manufacturing	17.3	14.5	–2.8	–16.2
Manufacturing productivity				
Output per hour (index, 1992 = 100)	134.2	154.6	20.4	15.2
Merchandise trade (billions of dollars)				
Exports	784.3	726.4	–57.9	–7.4
Imports	1,243.5	1,282.0	38.5	3.1
Balance	–459.2	–555.6	–96.4	21.0
Manufacturing trade (billions of dollars)				
Exports	707.2	644.9	–62.3	–8.8
Imports	1,024.4	1,048	23.6	2.3
Balance	–317.0	–403.1	–86.1	27.2

Sources: Bureau of Labor Statistics; Bureau of Economic Analysis, National Income and Product Accounts, June 17, 2004, revision; U.S. International Trade Commission.

measure is value added in the industry—the contribution to GDP that originates in the sector. On this basis the manufacturing trade deficit was equal to 28.3 percent of manufacturing output in 2003, up from 21.3 percent in 2000. The second measure is the gross output of the sector—how much manufacturing sells outside the sector, whether to U.S. buyers or overseas.[13] Calculated on this basis, the trade deficit is not as large a factor in the overall manufacturing picture: it equaled 15.6 percent of gross output in 2003, up from 11.9 percent in 2000.

Although these comparisons give somewhat different results, the size of the deficit and its pervasiveness across sectors make it easy for Ameri-

13. The Bureau of Economic Analysis (BEA) estimates this figure by adding up the output of all manufacturing establishments and then estimating what fraction of that output consists of sales to other parts of the same sector. These intrasector sales are then netted out, and the remainder is the gross output of the sector.

Figure 5. Manufacturing Trade Deficit as a Fraction of Manufacturing Value Added and Gross Output, 1989–2003

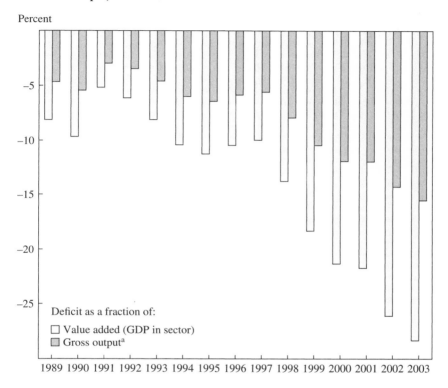

Percent

Deficit as a fraction of:

☐ Value added (GDP in sector)
▨ Gross output[a]

1989 1990 1991 1992 1993 1994 1995 1996 1997 1998 1999 2000 2001 2002 2003

Sources: Bureau of Economic Analysis, National Income and Product Accounts; Bureau of Labor Statistics; authors' calculations
a. Adjusted to remove intramanufacturing transactions.

cans to believe that trade played a major role in the manufacturing reces-sion. In particular, as the quotation above suggests, many saw imports as the principal culprit. But do the data support this view?

We focus on imports first. Changes in domestic spending will generally be reflected in changes in imports, and thus imports tend to act as a stabi-lizer for domestic employment. When domestic spending falls or grows slowly, for example, some of the impact will occur abroad. Fewer U.S. jobs will therefore be lost than if the economy were self-contained. Con-versely, in the presence of imports, fewer domestic jobs will be created when domestic demand is growing rapidly. Thus one benchmark in assessing the impact of imports is whether or not they are rising faster than domestic spending. In general, if imports were a major independent cause of job loss, one might expect to see them outpacing domestic spending; if they were simply responding to shifts in domestic spending, they would rise at the same pace; and if they were acting to stabilize employment where spending was weak, they would rise more slowly than spending.

Table 3 provides some perspective on the role of goods in U.S. GDP. It is important to note that these data measure final sales of goods. In addition to manufacturing value added, therefore, they include distribution margins and primary commodity inputs, issues we will deal with later. Nonetheless, they provide important insights into this question. Between 2000 and 2003, measured in 2000 chain-weighted dollars, the volume of merchandise imports grew by 5.1 percent, a pace that was actually slower than U.S. domestic spending on goods for domestic use (consumption, investment, and government spending), which increased by 6.6 percent. In 2000 dollars, therefore, the share of imports in U.S. domestic spending on goods actually *fell* from 31.8 percent to 31.4 percent. (In current dollars there was a slightly larger decline in the import share.)

The export story is different. Here one benchmark is the share of exports in domestic goods output. Between 2000 and 2003, goods output *increased* by 3.8 percent, but the volume of merchandise exports actually *declined* by 8.0 percent. This led to a decline in the share of goods exports in goods output from 23 percent to 20 percent. Together with the import data, these data suggest that falling exports detracted from employment, and not that a rising share of imports led to disproportionate unemployment.

Although highly suggestive, measures such as these may fail to accurately indicate the size of the trade effects on the manufacturing sector, because they include value added in other sectors.[14] Trade flows operate on the demand for labor in manufacturing in complex ways. First, manufactured exports are not produced entirely within the manufacturing sector: manufactured goods also embody value added from other sectors, such as services and primary commodities. Second, and conversely, trade in non-manufactured goods and services will embody manufactured goods. And third, many goods produced in the United States contain imported components. Ignoring this could lead to an overstatement of U.S. employment

---

14. On the one hand, the ratio of the trade balance to value added will *overstate* the contribution of trade to manufacturing, because the components in the numerator, which

Table 3. Output and Absorption of Goods in the National Income Accounts, 2000–04

Item	2000	2003	2004	Change, 2000-03 (percent)
In billions of chain-weighted 2000 dollars				
GDP	9,817.0	10,381.3	10,697.5	5.7
Total output of goods	3,449.3	3,581.8	3,784.8	3.8
Merchandise imports	1,243.5	1,307.3	1,394.1	5.1
Merchandise exports	784.3	721.7	767.2	−8.0
Domestic use of goods[a]	3,908.5	4,167.4	4,411.7	6.6
Imports as share of domestic goods market (percent)[b]	31.8	31.4	31.6	−1.4
Exports as share of domestic production (percent)[c]	22.7	20.1	20.3	−11.4
In billions of current dollars				
GDP	9,817.0	11,004.0	11,557.9	12.1
Total output of goods	3,449.3	3,564.5	3,779.4	3.3
Merchandise imports	1,243.5	1,282.0	1,435.7	3.1
Merchandise exports	784.3	726.4	800.4	−7.4
Domestic use of goods	3,908.5	4,120.1	4,414.7	5.4
Imports as share of domestic goods market (percent)	31.8	31.1	32.5	−2.2
Exports as share of domestic production (percent)	22.7	20.4	21.2	−10.4

Source: Bureau of Economic Analysis, National Income and Product Accounts, August 27, 2004, revision.
a. Total goods output plus merchandise imports, minus merchandise exports, which is equal to the sum of consumption, investment, and government use.
b. Merchandise imports divided by goods for domestic use.
c. Merchandise exports divided by total output of goods.

due to exports. Similarly, displacement due to imports could be overstated, because imports may displace domestic products that themselves contain imported intermediates. In the analysis that follows, we try to account for these effects by linking trade flows with domestic production using input-output tables and by making adjustments to reflect imported components.

The Basic Relationship between Trade and Employment

We start by clarifying some basic relationships and concepts. In this analysis we are interested in the relative importance of trade and domestic

are measures of the value of manufactured trade, will also include value contained in these products from other sectors (primary commodity inputs and services). On the other hand, the ratio of the trade balance to gross output could *understate* the impact, to the degree that the denominator includes the value of nonmanufactured goods inputs.

use in the shifts in U.S. manufacturing employment between 2000 and 2003. But, in addition to these demand-side variables, manufacturing productivity growth plays a major role. We can decompose changes in employment into three elements: changes due to changes in productivity, changes due to changes in trade (exports and imports), and changes due to changes in domestic use. Taking productivity as given, we can then ascribe employment changes to trade and domestic use.

Start from the identity:

$$(1) \qquad\qquad V_i = Q_i \,/\, E_i,$$

where V is value added per worker, Q is output, E is employment, and i indexes industries. With lowercase letters indicating percentage changes, this gives (approximately)

$$(2) \qquad\qquad e_i = q_i - v_i.$$

A second key identity links domestic production to trade and domestic use. We know that in an open economy $Y = C + I + G + X - M$. Defining domestic use D as $C + I + G$, we get the identity $Y = D + X - M$. For each industry, therefore,

$$(3) \qquad\qquad Q_i = D_i + X_i - M_i.$$

Note that, in this formulation, when we say that output in an industry is "due to" domestic use and trade, we do not mean that it is due *only* to domestic use of and trade in the products made by that industry. For example, when an automobile is exported from the United States, it will embody inputs such as steel, aluminum, computers, and so forth that have been produced in other industries. The impact of exports from one industry on production in all other industries must therefore be correctly attributed. Similarly, when an import replaces a domestic product, it reduces demand not only in the industry in which the product is made but also in the sectors that produce inputs for that product. A complete accounting of the role of trade and domestic demand should incorporate these indirect effects.

Equation 3 implies that

$$(4) \qquad\qquad q_i = w_d d_i + w_x x_i - w_m m_i.$$

In other words, the rate of change of output equals the sum of the weighted rates of change in value added due to domestic use and due to exports minus the weighted rate of change of value added due to imports. The weights reflect base-year (year zero) shares; that is, $w_d = D_0/Q_0$, $w_x = X_0/Q_0$, and $w_m = M_0/Q_0$. Substituting equation 4 into equation 2, and using the fact that $w_d + w_x - w_m = 1$, gives

$$(5) \qquad e_i = w_d(d_i - v_i) + w_x(x_i - v_i) - w_m(m_i - v_i).$$

In words, the percentage change in employment is equal to the weighted average of the percentage changes in the differences between the growth rate of labor productivity and value added due to domestic use, value added due to exports, and value added attributable to imports. This expression indicates, for example, that for employment due to exports to remain unchanged, the growth rate in value added due to exports (x_i) must be equal to the growth rate in labor productivity (v_i). If value added due to exports increases more slowly than productivity growth, exports will contribute negatively to employment. A similar relation holds for domestic demand, whose growth rate must exceed that of productivity if domestic demand is to contribute positively to employment.

Since imports enter negatively into equation 5, the opposite condition holds for imports. If the value added attributable to imports increases less rapidly than productivity growth, this will contribute positively to domestic employment. Imports are assumed to displace employment in domestic import-competing industries. However, productivity is continually rising in these industries, which means that, for a given level of imports, the number of jobs displaced goes down over time. It would take progressively fewer and fewer U.S. workers to make a given quantity of manufactured goods being imported. Only if imports rise faster than productivity will the number of U.S. jobs being displaced by imports rise over time.

We emphasize that equation 5 is an ex post identity and that the elements in equation 5 are all endogenous variables. Decomposing employment changes using this identity provides an ex post accounting of the relative importance of these variables in shifting employment; it does not explain what has caused these variables to change. Productivity, trade flows, and domestic demand are interrelated in complex ways. Their movements may reflect independent causes or interactions among them. For example, rapid U.S. productivity growth could lead to relatively lower U.S. prices, more U.S. exports, fewer imports, and more domestic use. However, rapid U.S. productivity growth could also lead to higher U.S. incomes and more demand for *both* domestic products and imports. Similarly, rapid increases in imports could stimulate domestic productivity growth, and increases in domestic demand could lead to more imports and fewer exports.

In addition, it is dangerous to imply that increased imports and larger trade deficits necessarily come at the expense of domestic employment. The clearest way to see this is to imagine that the economy is at full employment, as it was in 2000. In that case it is not possible for domestic supply to meet a further increase in demand. The ability to trade allows national spending to exceed national income, and so the increase in national spending leads to a larger trade deficit, but there is no job loss due to imports. Yet a mechanical decomposition might lead to the claim of jobs lost due to imports.

In sum, these estimates can be helpful in providing a perspective on the relative importance of domestic demand and trade in manufacturing employment. But it is important to be cautious in drawing causal implications from these results.

Our Approach

It is relatively straightforward to obtain measures of employment and labor productivity (e_i and v_i in equation 5). The real work comes in estimating the changes due to exports (x_i) and imports (m_i). Once these are obtained, changes due to domestic use (d_i) can be derived as a residual. In this study we estimate these effects due to trade using the summary U.S. input-output tables for 1997, the most recent year for which data are available at a sufficiently disaggregated level. The total-requirements version of this table is structured as a matrix, with over 130 industries listed by row and over 130 commodities by column. The values in the table are coefficients reporting the gross output required from the indicated industry to produce one dollar of the indicated commodity for final use. The coefficients reflect both direct and indirect requirements. For example, producing an automobile requires a host of inputs—these are the direct requirements. But to produce these inputs, another set of inputs is required, and yet another set to produce these inputs, and so on—these are the indirect requirements. The coefficients in the matrix capture all of these effects.

As an example, for each dollar of final delivery of motor vehicles, the largest total requirement is output of 99.8 cents by the motor vehicle manufacturing industry. In addition, 53.3 cents of output is required from the industry titled "motor vehicle body, trailer and parts manufacturing," 13.1 cents from wholesale trade, 6.9 cents from electrical equipment manufacturing, 5.7 cents from plastics, and so on. All told, 288.8 cents are required from the economy as a whole to produce a dollar's worth of motor vehicles delivered to final demand. (This figure exceeds one dollar because it captures the value of all components along the value chain as well as final output.) To obtain our estimates, we go through five calculations.

VALUE ADDED. First, since we are interested in estimating value added by industry, we multiply each of the matrix coefficients by the 1997 ratio of value added to gross output for each industry. This provides us with estimates of the direct and indirect value added required from each industry to produce a dollar of final demand. For motor vehicles, for example, the ratio of value added to output was 0.156. Thus the 99.8 cents' worth of final demand for motor vehicles was associated with 15.6 cents of value added in motor vehicles.[15]

AGGREGATION. To make our work tractable and intelligible, we then aggregate these value-added coefficients to provide estimates at the three-digit NAICS level, which, for example, divides manufacturing into nineteen industries. We aggregate the commodities by weighting the coefficients in the columns comprising parts of the three-digit sector by the share of each commodity in the total commodity output of that sector.[16] We then sum the coefficients in the rows that make up each three-digit

---

15. Let IO = total requirements table and IOv = total value added requirements table.

v = vector of the ratio of value added to gross output by industry (from the 1997 input-output use table)

go = vector of gross output (from the 1997 input-output use table):

    (1) $v = va/go$

    (2) $IOv = v * IO$

16. If C_{ij} are the coefficients of the matrix IO, we need to obtain new coefficients C_{ik}, for a matrix IO3d with three-digit industry requirements. We first collapse the number of columns using growth outputs in the industry subsectors as weights. We obtain $C_{ik} = (c_{i1}*go_1 + c_{i2}*go_2 + \cdots + c_{iJ}*go_J)/(go_1 + go_2 + \cdots + go_J)$, with $j = 1, 2, \cdots, J$ and $go_1 + go_2 + \cdots + go_J = go_k$. Then we aggregate these C_{ik} for all *is* in each three-digit industry.

industry. This results in a matrix that estimates direct and indirect value added at the three-digit level.

VALUE ADDED DUE TO TRADE. Under the assumption that the intersectoral relationships between 2000 and 2003 are the same as those of 1997, we then use three-digit NAICS trade data to estimate the value added in each three-digit manufacturing industry that is embodied in merchandise trade in 2000, 2002, and 2003. We obtain separate estimates for exports and imports.[17]

CORRECTING FOR IMPORTED COMPONENTS. These value-added components are upper-bound estimates of the effects due to exports and imports, because the requirements table is derived under the assumption that all inputs are produced domestically. To account for imported components used as intermediate inputs, we adjust the requirements by assuming that imported inputs are purchased in proportion to their share in the domestic market, where the domestic market is defined for each industry as the sum of gross output and imports.[18] (We will also report our aggregate results without making this correction.)

EMPLOYMENT. The final step involves estimating the employment content of value added. We assume that productivity in each U.S. industry is the same whether the production is for export, to replace imports, or to serve other domestic demand. This implies that the relative allocations of employment to exports, import substitution, and domestic use, within each industry, are the same as the relative allocations of value added.

Data on value added per employee for manufacturing industries are available for 2000 and 2002. To correspond to the trade data, which are in current dollars, we use current-dollar value added per employee. Neither real nor nominal value added per employee is available by industry for 2003, and so we estimate the 2003 figure by multiplying the 2002 data by the growth in the industry-level industrial production index and the industry producer price index between 2002 and 2003. Dividing industry value added due to exports and imports by value added per worker provides us with estimates of industry employment "due to" exports and imports.

17. $X * IO3d = vaX$ (total value added of exports)

$M * IO3d = vaM$ (total value added of imports).

18. $adjvaX = vaX * \{1 - [m/(go + m)]\}$ (total value added of exports adjusting by imported inputs) and $adjvaM = vaM * [m/(go + m)]$ (total value added of imports adjusting by imported inputs).

Finally, we estimate employment due to domestic use as a residual—the difference between actual employment and employment due to trade.

In addition to the caveats given earlier, we note that input-output co-efficients allow for no substitution possibilities among inputs and no changes in input requirements over time. Furthermore, among products, the analysis assumes that final demands always substitute between particular imports and the output of the domestic industry that manufactures products similar to those imports, rather than between particular imports and products of some other industry.

Results

Trade plays an important role in manufacturing employment. In 2000 production for export accounted for 3.43 million manufacturing jobs, or 20 percent of manufacturing employment. Each dollar of exports was associated with 48 cents of manufacturing value added, with the rest coming from imported inputs and other domestic sectors. Each million dollars in exports, therefore, required 5.2 jobs in manufacturing. On average, these jobs were associated with high levels of labor productivity. Output per employee engaged in export production was $91,700, considerably higher than either the $80,700 in manufacturing as a whole or the $84,600 for domestic production that replaces imports.

Between 2000 and 2003, productivity growth in manufacturing was remarkably rapid. Our estimated measure of nominal value added per employee increased by 15.3 percent over the three years, just about the same as the official measure of (real) output per worker-hour in manufacturing estimated by the Bureau of Labor Statistics. We estimate that production for export accounted for 3.43 million jobs in 2000. In 2000 value added per employee in U.S. manufacturing was $80,700. We estimate that by 2003 this had increased to $93,100. Had demand remained constant, manufacturing employment would have fallen by 2.64 million—only slightly less than the actual total loss of 2.74 million jobs between 2000 and 2003. Thus one way to interpret the data is to say that the decline is entirely "due to" domestic productivity growth. Taking output as given, in other words, productivity improvements caused all the job loss.

However, an alternative approach is to see how domestic use and trade contributed to the decline, taking productivity growth as given—an analysis we are now in a position to undertake. As equation 5 indicates, given productivity growth, a sufficient condition for aggregate employment to have remained constant would have been for value added due to domestic demand, exports, and imports to rise by 15.3 percent each. Instead value added due to domestic demand and imports increased by just 0.3 percent and 2.4 percent, respectively, while value added due to exports actually fell by 11.1 percent. The result was the precipitous 15.9 percent slump in employment.

Our estimates point to the failure of domestic demand growth to match productivity growth as the major source of the decline. We attribute 88 percent of the drop, or some 2.5 million jobs, to the slow growth in domestic demand (table 4); we attribute only 12 percent, or some 314,000 jobs, to trade. Although the employment decline attributable to exports played a major role, accounting for 28 percent of the drop, or 742,000 jobs, imports actually *offset* this fall by 429,000 jobs and thus had a positive effect as judged by this baseline. This positive effect arises partly because of rapid productivity growth and partly because of the slow growth of imports, the manufacturing job content of U.S. imports (which have a negative impact on employment) was actually 8.8 percent lower than in 2000.[19]

Imports mitigated the job loss in manufacturing over 2000–03, but not because of an exogenous downward shock to imports. There is no evidence that the United States was suddenly able to compete more effectively against foreign producers. The slow growth of imports was due to the slow growth in overall U.S. demand, which affected both domestic suppliers of manufactured goods and foreign suppliers.

In the above estimates we have adjusted the input-output coefficients to take account of imported inputs. This has the effect of reducing the estimated impact of trade flows by reducing the domestic value added due to exports and that due to imports. When we do not make these adjustments, therefore, we get somewhat larger effects due to trade and thus smaller effects due to domestic demand, but qualitatively the results are the same. Using this approach, the net impact of trade on manufacturing job loss rises from 314,000 to 341,000.[20]

---

19. Between 2000 and 2003, value added per employee due to exports and imports increased by 13.7 percent and 12.3 percent, respectively, both somewhat less than the increase in value added in manufacturing as a whole.

20. Without the import correction, between 2000 and 2003, 951,000 jobs are lost because of lower exports and 611,000 jobs are gained because of lower imports.

Table 4. Sources of Change in Manufacturing Employment, 2000–03

Millions of workers

Year	Total	Exports	Imports	Trade[a]	Domestic use[b]
2000	17.175	3.434	–4.944	–1.510	18.685
2002	14.899	2.739	–4.372	–1.633	16.532
2003	14.324	2.691	–4.515	–1.824	16.148
Change, 2000–03	–2.851	–0.742	0.429	–0.314	–2.537

Sources: Bureau of Labor Statistics, Current Employment Survey; Bureau of Economic Analysis, Input-Output Tables; authors' calculations.

a. Difference between previous two columns.

b. Number of U.S. workers who would have been employed if all imports had been replaced by domestic production.

Table 5 presents the decomposition at a more disaggregated level. The second and third columns again document the very large shrinkage in manufacturing employment over this period, with the largest percentage declines experienced by apparel (36.3 percent), textiles (28.6 percent), computers and electronic products (28.5 percent), primary metals (24.0 percent), and electrical equipment (23.2 percent). In all of these industries domestic use was, by a large measure, the major source of the loss, ranging from 112 percent in the case of apparel (where, surprisingly, trade actually had a positive impact) to 87 percent of the decline in electrical equipment. The effects of sluggish domestic demand (and rapid productivity growth) were devastating for the apparel sector. Together these induced a jobs decline equal to 40.6 percent of 2000 employment. Large declines were also experienced by computers and electronic products (28.7 percent), textiles (24.2 percent), primary metals (23.4 percent), and electrical equipment (20.2 percent).

By contrast, the net job losses due to trade in most industries were relatively small. The noteworthy exceptions were chemical products and plastics, in which the losses due to trade were 17.1 percent and 10.9 percent of 2000 employment, respectively. In all other sectors, net losses due to trade were less than 4.5 percent of 2000 employment. In both chemicals and plastics the dominant source of the declines was exports. Losses due to reduced exports in chemicals and plastics equaled 15.9 percent and 10.5 percent of 2000 employment, respectively. Employment due to exports also subtracted from employment in computer products (down 14.8 percent) and primary metals (8.2 percent), but imports actually helped stabilize employment in computers (15.0 percent), apparel (7.9 percent), and primary metals (7.6 percent).

Table 5. Sources of Change in Manufacturing Employment and Share of Employment Producing for Export, 2000–03

Industry	Employment, 2000 (thousands of workers)	Change in employment, 2000–03		Contributions to percentage change in employment, 2000–03 (percentage points)				Employment share due to exports (percent)	
		Thousands of workers	Percent	Production for domestic use	Production for trade Exports	Imports	Total	2000	2003
Computer and electronic products	1,863.5	−531.3	−28.5	−28.7	−14.8	15.0	0.2	41.3	37.0
Machinery	1,452.6	−312.2	−21.5	−17.5	−8.1	4.1	−4.0	30.0	27.9
Fabricated metal products	1,761.7	−290.5	−16.5	−13.5	−3.6	0.6	−3.0	20.7	20.4
Apparel and leather and allied products	537.0	−195.0	−36.3	−40.6	−3.6	7.9	4.3	9.6	9.4
Textile mills and textile product mills	581.5	−166.2	−28.6	−24.2	−2.9	−1.6	−4.4	24.4	30.1
Motor vehicles, bodies, and trailers, and parts	1,283.5	−164.1	−12.8	−11.6	−2.8	1.7	−1.2	9.0	7.1
Primary metals	611.6	−147.0	−24.0	−23.4	−8.2	7.6	−0.6	49.2	54.0
Electrical equipment, appliances, and components	587.7	−136.5	−23.2	−20.2	−6.8	3.8	−3.0	24.9	23.6
Plastics and rubber products	940.3	−134.5	−14.3	−3.4	−10.5	−0.5	−10.9	27.3	19.7
Printing and related support activities	801.0	−130.9	−16.3	−15.3	−1.2	0.1	−1.1	9.0	9.3
Furniture and related products	676.1	−106.8	−15.8	−11.9	−0.9	−3.0	−3.9	4.3	4.1
Other transportation equipment	737.7	−94.4	−12.8	−8.7	−7.0	2.9	−4.1	29.6	25.9
Paper products	599.3	−89.0	−14.9	−12.6	−1.5	−0.8	−2.3	20.5	22.3
Miscellaneous manufacturing	734.1	−82.2	−11.2	−11.2	0.7	−0.7	−0.0	15.7	18.5
Chemical products	975.2	−79.3	−8.1	9.0	−15.9	−1.2	−17.1	41.3	27.6
Nonmetallic mineral products	553.6	−66.1	−11.9	−10.7	−3.4	2.2	−1.2	13.7	11.7
Food and beverage and tobacco products	1,762.7	−58.1	−3.3	−1.7	−0.8	−0.8	−1.6	8.0	7.5
Wood products	593.5	−56.9	−9.6	−8.1	−2.5	1.0	−1.5	10.6	9.0
Petroleum and coal products	122.1	−9.7	−7.9	−4.2	−0.1	−3.7	−3.8	22.7	24.6
All manufacturing	17,174.7	−2,850.7	−16.6	−13.4	−5.8	2.6	−3.2	22.4	20.0

Sources: Bureau of Labor Statistics, Current Employment Survey; Bureau of Economic Analysis, Input–Output Tables; authors' calculations.

The final two columns of table 5 present our estimates for each industry of the share of employment that depends on exports. In 2000, for manufacturing as a whole, this share was 22.4 percent—almost a quarter of all jobs. Strikingly, the industry with the greatest dependence was primary metals (ferrous and nonferrous): 49.2 percent of all jobs in this industry depended on exports in 2000. This is undoubtedly a surprise to those in industries such as steel who focus on the direct impact of imports and ignore the powerful indirect effects that stem from their own dependence on U.S. exports from metals-using sectors. Indeed, the primary metals industry has become even more dependent on exports, with this share rising to 54 percent in 2003. Moreover, as table 5 also indicates, the negative influence on employment in primary metals during 2000–03 came from the behavior of exports, not imports. Other sectors with a strong dependence on exports in 2000 were computers (where exports supported 41.3 percent of employment), chemical products (41.3 percent), machinery (30.0 percent), and other transportation (which includes aircraft; 29.6 percent). Another interesting result is that export-related employment in textiles increased from 24.4 percent to 30.1 percent from 2000 to 2003.

Over all, the results of this analysis are certainly at odds with the widespread perception that the bulk of job loss in U.S. manufacturing is attributable to a rapid increase in outsourcing. Instead they suggest that the behavior of imports has been, if anything, a stabilizing factor and that the weakness due to trade is attributable to the behavior of exports. Accordingly, we turn now to consider what might explain export behavior.

Understanding the Weakness in U.S. Exports

Lackluster demand for U.S. exports has been another source of weakness in the manufacturing sector over the past three years. Exports have been depressed, in part due to slow growth in other major economies. Since the fourth quarter of 2000, the average annual rates of real GDP growth in the euro area and Japan have been less than half that of the United States. Industrial supplies and capital goods make up the bulk of U.S. goods exports.[21]

The previous section concluded that, on net, trade was not a major cause of the loss of manufacturing jobs but that the weakness in exports,

---

21. *Economic Report of the President, 2004*, p. 55.

by itself, did account for a decline of 742,000 jobs in the sector. Here we ask why U.S. exports were weak.

As the quotation just above indicates, one obvious explanation for the decline in U.S. manufactured exports over 2000–03 is the world growth recession, and the outright recession in major U.S. markets such as continental Europe, that occurred after 2000. If the slowdown in the global economy was matched by a slowdown in global trade, then U.S. exports would have weakened even if the United States had been able to maintain its share of world trade.

Table 6 shows the rates of growth or decline in manufactures exports by the United States and by the rest of the world over 1990–2003.[22] The first column shows that, measured in current dollars, U.S. exports declined over the period 2000–03, after growing very rapidly in the 1990s. The second column shows non-U.S. trade, also measured in current dollars. One can infer from these numbers that the United States actually increased its share of world trade in the 1990s but then suffered a sharp decline in share in 2000–03. Non-U.S. trade dipped only in 2001 and came back very strongly indeed in 2003. Indeed, non-U.S. trade grew about as rapidly after 2000 as it did in the 1990s, indicating that the weakness of U.S. exports was associated with a sharp decline in the U.S. share of world trade.

A problem with measuring non-U.S. trade in dollars is that the growth rates are sensitive to changes in dollar exchange rates. If the dollar rises against the euro, for example, the dollar value of intra-European trade is pushed down, and the growth rate of non-U.S. trade is reduced. The third column of table 6 therefore measures non-U.S. trade in terms of a basket of major currencies other than the dollar.[23] This adjustment raises the estimate of world growth in the 1990s, raises it again in 2001, leaves it little changed in 2002, and lowers it sharply in 2003. It remains the case that non-U.S. trade grows after 2000—indeed, there is now no year in which it falls. The growth rate over the three-year period is lower, however, in the third column than in the second.

One way to avoid the question of which currency to use in measuring the volume of world trade is to use estimates of trade volumes, calculated using

22. The World Trade Organization provides data on world manufactures trade only through 2002. We assume that the growth rate for 2002–03 was the same as the growth in non-oil merchandise trade.

23. The differences between the second and third columns reflect the rates of change in the Federal Reserve's nominal index of major currencies over the years in question.

Table 6. Growth in Manufactures Exports, United States and Rest of World

Percent a year[a]

Period	Growth in U.S. manufactures exports, measured in dollars	Growth in rest-of-world manufactures exports	
		Measured in dollars	Measured by index of major currencies[b]
1990–95	9.16	9.13	7.53
1995–2000	7.58	4.44	8.62
2000–01	−7.17	−3.18	2.61
2001–02	−5.59	5.83	4.21
2002–03	3.11	16.32	2.12
2000–03	−3.32	6.02	2.98

Sources: Data from World Trade Organization, U.S. International Trade Commission, Federal Reserve Board, and authors' calculations.

a. Compound annual growth rates.

b. Federal Reserve's real index of major currencies, which includes the euro, the Canadian dollar, the U.K. pound, the Swiss franc, the Australian dollar, the Swedish krona, and the Japanese yen.

unit value price measures; these data are available from the United Nations *Monthly Bulletin.* There are some questions about the validity of these unit value price measures, but, leaving those concerns aside, the data indicate that an index of the volume of U.S. manufactures exports fell from 100 in 2000 to 87 by 2003. In contrast, the volume of European manufactures exports rose from 100 to 105, and the volume of manufactures exports for all developed economies (including the United States) rose from 100 to 101.

These different figures all suggest that although stronger economic growth in the rest of the world would certainly have increased U.S. exports, it is a mistake to blame much of the U.S. export weakness on a general slowdown in world trade—the reason emphasized by the 2004 *Economic Report of the President* in the quotation above. U.S. exports declined after 2000 even as exports by the rest of the world grew. In short: the biggest export problem that the United States faced after 2000 was the decline in its share of world trade.

Understanding the Decline in the U.S. Export Share after 2000

There are three possible reasons for the decline in the U.S. share of world manufactures exports, each distinct from the other two. The first is that U.S. exports may have been concentrated in commodities for which world demand was growing relatively slowly. For example, U.S. exports of IT goods rose rapidly in the 1990s, but then the technology sector slumped. The second possible reason is that U.S. exports may have gone mainly to countries that had particularly weak demand for imports during the period. And the third is that the United States may have lost competitiveness against other suppliers to the world market.

A standard approach to decomposing the trade data so as to capture the effect of world trade growth and of the three sources of changes in the U.S. share of that growth is as follows:[24] Let V_{ij} be the value of U.S. exports of commodity i to country j in period 1, and V'_{ij} the value of U.S. exports of commodity i to country j in period 2. Then we can define V and V' as follows:

$$V = \sum_i \sum_j V_{ij} = \text{total U.S. exports in period 1}$$
$$V' = \sum_i \sum_j V'_{ij} = \text{total U.S. exports in period 2.}$$

In addition, let r be the percentage increase in total world exports from period 1 to period 2, r_i the percentage increase in world exports of commodity i from period 1 to period 2, and r_{ij} the percentage increase in world exports of commodity i to country j from period 1 to period 2. Then, as Edward Leamer and Robert Stern showed,[25] the change in U.S. exports from period 1 to period 2 can be expressed as follows:

$$V' - V = rV + \sum_i (r_i - r)\left(\sum_j V_{ij}\right) + \sum_i \sum_j (r_{ij} - r_i)V_{ij} + \sum_i \sum_j (V'_{ij} - V_{ij} - r_{ij}V_{ij}).$$

The four terms on the right-hand side of this equation correspond to the four components described above. The first term reflects the change in U.S. exports that would occur if the United States simply maintained a constant share of world trade. The second shows the extent to which U.S. trade changes as a result of the commodity composition of U.S. exports. The third shows the extent to which U.S. trade changes as a result of the country composition of U.S. exports. The final term is then the "competitiveness" term, although, when calculated as a residual, this term also includes the effect of any additional factors not accounted for in the other terms.[26]

24. Richardson (1970, 1971a, 1971b) has made important contributions to the literature, while the discussion here is based on the exposition in Leamer and Stern (1970).

25. Leamer and Stern (1970).

26. In implementing the decomposition we have made an adjustment to the standard model, in line with the approach used earlier. In the equations shown above, world trade

The data required to implement this decomposition were obtained from the United Nations commodity trade database (the COMTRADE data).[27] We carried out the decomposition for the period 2000 to 2003, to match the previous analysis of employment. Unfortunately, not all countries have reported to the United Nations for 2003, and so the trade of some countries is excluded from the analysis. One sign of this is that U.S. merchandise exports as reported below are about 18 percent smaller than the figure shown in table 3. This does not appear to have a significant impact on the findings, however, as we will discuss shortly when exploring the robustness of the results.

The Drop in U.S. Exports from 2000 to 2003

The results of the full decomposition are shown in table 7. U.S. exports declined by $46.2 billion over this period, or about 7.2 percent. Over the same period, however, non-U.S. world merchandise trade expanded by 23.5 percent. If the United States had maintained a constant share of world trade, U.S. exports would also have risen by 23.5 percent, increasing by $151.7 billion rather than declining by $46.2 billion.

To what extent was this decline in export share the result of the particular mix of commodities that the United States sells in world markets? The answer is, not at all. The overall commodity effect was very small and, indeed, actually helped the United States a little, boosting U.S. exports by a trivial 0.6 percent (about $4 billion). Although some products that the United States sells, such as high-technology goods, did not grow as rapidly as overall world trade, others, such as auto parts, automobiles, medical products, and aircraft (including military aircraft and helicopters), grew more rapidly. Overall, then, the commodity effect was almost a wash.

---

includes exports from all countries, including the United States. The "neutral baseline" underlying the first term of the decomposition is that the United States will maintain a fixed share of total world trade. The problem with that approach is that, if U.S. exports fall, this lowers total world exports. So, in this formulation, the drop in U.S. exports is attributed in part to the drop in U.S. exports, a circularity we want to avoid. We therefore calculate non-U.S. world trade as the total exports of all countries except the United States, and we use this as the variable that reflects the changes in world demand by commodity or by country or for total manufactured trade (this procedure affects the values of the *r*s).

27. The data used in the version of this paper presented at the Brookings Panel meeting in September 2004 were different from those shown here, and there are some resulting differences in findings. The UN COMTRADE data became available after the meeting.

Table 7. Sources of the Decline in U.S. Merchandise Exports, 2000–03[a]

Item	Billions of dollars	As share of 2000 exports (percent)
Exports, 2000	645.9	100.0
Exports, 2003	599.7	92.8
Change in exports, 2000–03	46.2	–7.2
Impact on change in exports due to:		
Growth in rest-of-world trade	151.7	23.5
Commodity composition of exports	4.0	0.6
Country composition of exports	–46.2	–7.2
Change in "competitiveness"[b]	–155.7	–24.1

Source: Authors' calculations based on United Nations COMTRADE data.
a. Data differ from those in table 8 because of differences in sources. The COMTRADE data cover about 85 percent of U.S. exports in 2000 and 2003.
b. Calculated as a residual.

To what extent was the decline in market share the result of relatively weak demand in the countries to which the United States sells? This market distribution factor does account for a portion of the U.S. export weakness: it can explain a 7.2 percent ($46.2 billion) decline in U.S. exports.[28] This result is heavily attributable to the importance of U.S. trade with Canada; the important roles of Brazil and Europe as destinations for U.S. exports also contributed. Trade with Mexico was a positive for U.S. exports, however, and so was trade with China.

It is worth summarizing the combined effect of the first three terms in the decomposition. The basic finding is that the drop in U.S. exports was not a result of a drop in world trade, which continued to grow in 2000–03. Trade in the countries to which the United States sells did not grow as rapidly as overall world trade. This softens but does not change the basic conclusion that the drop in U.S. exports was a result of a decline in the U.S. share of trade. That drop in share was in part a reflection of the bursting of the high-technology bubble, but, overall, the problem was not that the United States was trying to sell products that the rest of the world did not want.

That leaves the "competitiveness" term as the key factor that accounts for the drop in U.S. exports. "Loss of competitiveness" is a vague term, however, and could refer to a number of factors. It might reflect new, structural changes in U.S. export markets: for example, the entry of new competitors such as China and India, an improvement in the relative qual-

28. The fact that this decline is almost identical to the total decline is a coincidence and does not hold in any of the variations of the decomposition.

ity of foreign goods, or a change in the sourcing patterns of U.S. multi-national corporations away from the United States toward other foreign locations. However, such structural factors have been at work for some time and seem unlikely to be the main reason for the rather abrupt shift from rapid export growth in the 1990s to export decline in 2001 and 2002.

Any economic time series, of course, contains some random variation, and the "competitiveness" term includes any residual effects not captured in the other terms of the decomposition, as well as any measurement errors. U.S. exports grew unusually rapidly in 2000, perhaps a carryover from export orders placed in the booming 1990s. Some decline, at least in the growth of exports, might well have occurred even with unchanged economic conditions.

Finally, the competitiveness term may reflect the fact that U.S. goods became relatively more expensive because of the behavior of the exchange rate. The dollar strengthened against other major currencies in the late 1990s and continued to do so until early 2002. The lagged effect of the sharp rise in the dollar was a major reason for the export decline in 2000–03, as will be shown shortly.

We tested these results of the decomposition of the U.S. export decline for robustness as follows. As we noted earlier, the calculations in table 6 cover 2000–03 but omit some countries for which trade data are not available. Data for a broader set of countries are available in the COMTRADE database through 2002, and so we repeated the decomposition exercise for the period 2000 to 2002, first using all available countries, and then only the countries for which data exist for 2003. Restricting the sample of countries in this way made virtually no difference to the results of the decomposition for 2000–02, and so we infer that the same restriction in 2003 has not distorted the findings. Second, we excluded various commodities from merchandise trade, such as energy products and items such as gold and "returned goods." We also performed the decomposition for manufactured goods only. These variations again made very little difference to the results, and therefore we have reported the findings for all merchandise trade for comparability with the earlier employment calculations.

The Impact of the Dollar on U.S. Exports

To explore quantitatively the impact of changes in exchange rates, we used a rule-of-thumb framework based on empirical estimates of export equations done by other researchers.[29] We assume that 25 percent of the effect of a change in the real dollar index on U.S. exports occurs in the year after the devaluation, another 50 percent in the following year, and the remaining 25 percent in the third year. The elasticity of U.S. exports to changes in dollar exchange rates is assumed to be either 1.5 or 1.0.

We choose as our dollar index the real effective index of the dollar against major currencies, reported by the Federal Reserve Board. We use this index because it seems reasonable to assume that U.S. exports compete primarily with the exports of other industrial countries. Table 8 shows the impact of the dollar on U.S. merchandise exports from 2000 to 2003, using the lag structure described above and the two alternative elasticities of demand for exports.

The first column of the table again shows the actual values of U.S. merchandise exports in 2000-03, based on official U.S. trade data. The second column shows what exports would have been if the rise in the dollar had not occurred (taking into account the lags). With an assumed elasticity of 1.5, exports would have risen by $96.8 billion between 2000 and 2003, rather than falling by $54.8 billion as they did. The third and fourth columns show the impact on exports of the rise in the dollar, in dollars and as a percentage of the total effect, respectively. The fifth column simply repeats the figures given in table 4, showing the jobs due to exports, including the decline of 742,000 from 3.43 million in 2000 to 2.69 million in 2003. The sixth column recalculates what these numbers would have been had the dollar's exchange rate not changed over the period. Productivity was growing fast enough that the number of jobs due to exports would still have declined, but by only 183,000 instead of 742,000. As the last column indicates, the U.S. economy would have had 559,000 additional jobs due to exports if the dollar had remained unchanged, according to this analysis. This would have eliminated the loss of manufacturing jobs due to trade that we identified above.

A value of 1.5 for the exchange rate elasticity of exports is fairly high. If the true elasticity is smaller, the impact on exports and employment

29. See, for example, Houthakker and Magee (1969), Mahdavi (2000), Marquez (2002), Hooper, Johnson, and Marquez (1998), Mann (1999), Goldstein and Khan (1985), Senhadji and Montenegro (1999), Stone (1979), Yang (1998), and Bailliu and Bouakez (2004). Although there are some outliers, results of most export equations fall within the range of 1.0 to 1.5 for the long-run elasticity with a three-year lag. Most of the estimates are based on prices rather than on the exchange rate, and so we assume 100 percent pass-through of changes in the exchange rate by U.S. exporters.

Table 8. Impact of Exchange Rate Changes on Merchandise Exports and Manufacturing Employment, 2000–03

Year	Merchandise exports (billions of dollars)		Impact of change in dollar exchange rate on merchandise exports[a]		Manufacturing jobs due to exports (millions)		Impact of change in dollar exchange rate on manufacturing jobs[b] (millions)
	Actual	With unchanged dollar	Billions of dollars[a]	Percent	Actual	With unchanged dollar	
Assuming exchange rate elasticity of export demand = 1.5							
2000	784.3	784.3	0.0	0.0	3.434	3.434	0.0
2001	731.2	762.9	–31.7	–4.2	n.a.	n.a.	n.a.
2002	697.3	784.1	–86.8	–11.1	2.739	3.080	–0.341
2003	729.5	881.1	–151.6	–17.2	2.691	3.250	–0.559
Assuming exchange rate elasticity of export demand = 1.0							
2000	784.3	784.3	0.0	0.0	3.434	3.434	0.0
2001	731.2	752.2	–21.0	–2.8	n.a.	n.a.	n.a.
2002	697.3	754.0	–56.7	–7.5	2.739	2.961	–0.223
2003	729.5	827.3	–97.8	–11.8	2.691	3.052	–0.361

Sources: Data from U.S. International Trade Commission, Bureau of Economic Analysis, and Federal Reserve Board, and authors' calculations.
a. Difference between exports with unchanged dollar and actual exports.
b. Difference between export jobs with unchanged dollar and actual exports.

will be proportionally lower. The corresponding calculations for an elasticity of 1.0 are shown in the bottom panel of table 8. According to the last column of that panel, under that assumption there would have been an additional 361,000 jobs due to exports with an unchanged dollar. Again, the job loss due to trade would have been eliminated.

Conclusions

We conclude that the current and lagged effect of the rising dollar was the key reason for the weakness in U.S. exports after 2000. Stronger growth in world trade would have helped U.S. exports, but the evidence presented here indicates that the main factor contributing to this export weakness was a decline in the U.S. share of world exports. The slump in trade in high-technology products lowered U.S. exports after 2000, but this impact was largely offset by the relative strength of demand for the other goods that the United States sells in world markets. A number of alternative explanations for the weakness of U.S. exports have been presented by others. One is that the United States has lost competitiveness to China; a second is that U.S. multinational firms are increasingly sourcing their exports from foreign countries. But our analysis suggests that the impact of the stronger dollar is sufficient to account for most of the erosion in the U.S. share of trade in world markets and for the negative impact of trade on employment.

The competitiveness effect reported in table 7 was $155.7 billion, but that figure was derived from a database that excluded some countries. Simply scaling up that figure to make it comparable to table 8 gives a competitiveness effect of $189.1 billion in 2003. With an elasticity of 1.5 for the exchange rate, the rise in the dollar can explain fully 80 percent of this figure. It is thus by far the most compelling explanation of the weakness of U.S. exports and hence of the loss of manufacturing jobs due to trade.

We have not tried to determine what explains the change in the dollar exchange rate. One plausible explanation is that the rapid growth associated with the technology boom in the 1990s created investment opportunities that attracted capital to the United States. When the boom subsided, however, the lagged effects of the strong dollar on U.S. exports served to compound the difficulties facing U.S. manufactures because of stagnant domestic demand. As private capital flows subsided after 2000, they were replaced to a large extent by foreign government purchases of U.S. assets to keep the dollar high and reduce its rate of decline.

The Impact of Services Sector Offshoring to India on U.S. Jobs

The development of the business services sector in India, geared heavily to exporting to the United States, has added a new layer of concern about the availability of good jobs in this country. The impact of trade on U.S. manufacturing jobs has been a matter of debate for many years, and one popular response has been to promote the benefits of education. Low-skilled manual jobs in manufacturing are being shifted overseas, it is argued, but American workers can still earn high wages provided they increase their level of skill and education. The increase in the return to education over the past twenty years has reinforced this idea.

The rapid growth of services sector offshoring in India has rocked this conventional wisdom.[30] With large numbers of highly motivated, college-educated, English-speaking workers becoming available in India, in part through improved access to telecommunications capabilities, white-collar workers in the United States now feel threatened.

This section explores the extent to which the weakness in job creation in the U.S. services sector during 2000–03, noted at the beginning of this paper, can be attributed to the movement of service jobs to India. Here as in the earlier discussion, we are well aware that, in a full, long-term, general equilibrium analysis there is no reason why an expansion of trade should induce a loss of U.S. jobs in the aggregate. But getting a sense of the number of jobs that may have been shifted from the United States to India is important to putting services sector offshoring in the right perspective.

Gauging the Impact of Offshoring to India

NASSCOM (National Association of Software and Service Companies) is an Indian trade association that tracks the newly emerging busi-

---

30. There is now a large literature on the impact of offshoring: for example, Schultze (2004), Brainard and Litan (2004), Bhagwati, Panagariya, and Srinivasan (forthcoming), Baily and Farrell (2004), Atkinson (2004), and Bardhan and Kroll (2003).

ness services industry in that country.[31] It collects data from Indian companies that provide IT services, such as computer programming, as well as other business services (called business process offshoring or IT-enabled services) such as call centers and back office processing (for banks and insurance companies, for example).

The initial impetus to the development of this industry came in part from General Electric Company, which in the 1990s saw the potential for cost savings from the availability of a skilled low-cost work force. In the past, foreign companies operating in India, and even domestic companies, faced substantial barriers from the country's maze of regulations and lack of infrastructure. Reliable electric power and telecommunications were not readily available, and it took much time and persistence before General Electric was able to start offshoring. The first movers were foreign multinationals like General Electric and the U.K.-based HSBC Group, but the industry has shifted over time so that local companies such as Daksh, Spectramind, Infosys, and Wipro have contributed to the growth in recent years. It remains the case, however, that two-thirds of the industry consists of captive producers (those owned by or affiliated with foreign multinationals, many of them U.S. and British companies).

The first column of table 9 shows that, over the period from NASSCOM's 2000/01 fiscal year to its 2003/04 fiscal year (NASSCOM's fiscal year ends with the first quarter), software employment in India increased by 200,000 workers. Of these, 134,000 were involved in services exported to the United States. On the assumption that this work would have required the same number of employees in the United States—that is, that the productivity of the U.S. and Indian software industries are the same, this implies a transfer of 134,000 U.S. jobs.

The second column of table 9 shows a comparable computation for business process offshoring. Employment in these activities in India increased by 175,500 workers, 140,400 of whom produced services that were exported to the United States. Again assuming a one-for-one job transfer, this means a loss of 140,400 U.S. jobs in this service activity.

The assumption of comparable productivity is a strong one. Some who have studied the Indian industry and visited its facilities report that the

---

31. A description of NASSCOM and a variety of data series are available on the organization's website. This section uses information collected as part of the McKinsey Global Institute (2003) case study of India offshoring.

Table 9. Estimated Number of Jobs Offshored to India, 2001/02–2003/04ᵃ
Thousands

Item	Software	Business process offshoring	Total
Total increase in employment in India	200.0	175.5	375.5
Of which: jobs involved in export to U.S.	134.0	140.4	274.4
U.S. employment loss[b]	134.0	140.4	274.4
Average per year			91.5
Memoranda: average annual change in U.S. services sector employment			
1990–2000			2,137.2
2000–03			327.1

Sources: NASSCOM, Bureau of Labor Statistics data, and authors' calculations.
a. Years are fiscal years ending with the first quarter.
b. Assuming one-for-one substitution.

actual productivity differences are mixed. There is some evidence that call centers in India are more productive than their U.S. counterparts, because they can attract higher-quality employees (college graduates in India versus high school graduates in the United States). Also, the jobs are not well liked by U.S. workers, so that turnover in the U.S. call centers is very high, affecting productivity for the worse.[32] On balance, however, it is likely that productivity would be higher in the United States, because the higher-value-added programming tasks tend to remain onshore, whereas more of the routine code development is carried out in India. Thus the job loss estimates in the table probably exceed the actual losses.

This conclusion is reinforced by two related factors. First, some of the tasks that moved to India would otherwise have been performed by automated IT hardware and software in the United States; hence the jobs would have been lost in any case. Voice response units replacing call center workers are an example. Second, because the services being provided from India are cheaper than equivalent services provided from within the United States, it is likely that a greater quantity of these services are sold than if Indian offshoring were not available, and that these services are performed in a more labor-intensive fashion.

The last column of table 9 compares the estimated total number of services sector jobs offshored to India with the change in total U.S. services

32. See, for example, McKinsey Global Institute (2003).

sector employment. Summing the estimates for the software and business process industries suggests that at most about 275,000 jobs moved to India over the three-year period 2000/01 to 2003/04, for an annual average change of about 91,500 jobs. For the displaced workers the costs of this increase in trade were surely substantial, but a job shift of this size is very small compared with the 2.1 million service jobs created in the United States in a typical year during the 1990s; it is even small compared with the net annual increase from 2000 to 2003, when annual service job creation fell to about 327,000.

Comparing the NASSCOM Data with U.S. Services Trade Data

According to the Bureau of Economic Analysis (BEA), *total* U.S. services trade with India is very small, and indeed the United States actually runs a surplus. Moreover, total U.S. services imports from India actually declined between 2000 and 2002. ("Services trade" refers to private services trade unless stated otherwise.) The BEA data, shown in figure 6, indicate that services imports from India rose fairly strongly from 1995 to 2000, more than doubling in current dollars from about $850 million to $1.90 billion, but subsequently fell back to $1.84 billion in 2002. Services exports to India have been consistently larger than services imports from India, according to the BEA, and have grown very rapidly over time, especially after 1999. Exports in 2002 are reported as $3.28 billion.

The BEA data do not indicate the nature of the services that are traded, but the discrepancy with the NASSCOM data is already clear. According to NASSCOM, IT and business process services exports from India to the United States were around $6 billion in 2002, more than triple the BEA's figure for *total* U.S. services imports from India in that year. There are several reasons why the BEA data may understate imports from India, and why the NASSCOM data may overstate exports to the United States. Most likely both errors are occurring. But, before we dissect this discrepancy, it is worth noting one important inference to be drawn from the BEA data. As already noted, the United States is not simply an importer of services from India; it is also a significant and growing exporter of services to India. As the Indian economy grows, it is likely to provide an increasing market for U.S. services and to contribute to job creation in services industries where the United States has a comparative advantage. The analysis of offshoring presented above leaves out this part of the employment effects of services trade between the two countries.

Figure 6. Private Sector Services Trade between United States and India

Billions of dollars

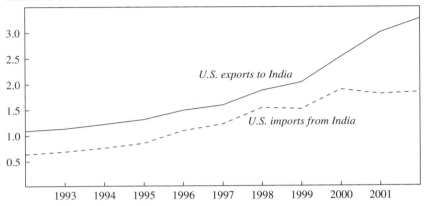

The BEA data are based on company surveys, which may miss a lot of the recent offshoring, since the imports in question may be destined to sectors not traditionally well covered by surveys designed to pick up international trade.[33] In particular, the BEA misses much of the most important part of IT services imports from India, namely, "bundled services"—software sold along with the computer hardware purchased by end-users. The BEA may also classify some services imports as goods imports (for example, if the software is to be used in a packaged software product).[34] In addition, since much of the activity in India is taking place in companies that are subsidiaries of U.S. companies or otherwise affiliated with them, these companies have some discretion about where the disbursements are recorded and at what price.

In general, the data collection and analysis at BEA are very strong, and the U.S. trade data are better and more extensive than data available from most other countries. But BEA has limited resources and can only use the

33. It is inherently easier for Indian statisticians to cover that country's limited number of IT services exporters than it is for the BEA to cover the entire spectrum of potential IT services importers in the U.S. economy, especially at a time when such imports may be going to new sectors.

34. This problem is not large, however: the United States imports less than $10 million worth of Records, Tapes, and Discs (SITC End-use Category 41220) a year.

data available to it from existing surveys, which were not set up to monitor services sector offshoring from India. There is a large overall statistical discrepancy in the international accounts, which makes it evident that not all international transactions are captured. The magnitude and time pattern of the BEA data on services imports from India also seem totally out of line with the rapid growth and development of the IT and business process industries, located in India and serving the U.S. market, which is visible to Indians themselves and to journalists and researchers from the United States.

The most important reason why the NASSCOM data may exaggerate India's exports is that some fraction of the software services provided by companies reporting to NASSCOM is performed by employees who are actually located in the United States—for example, the work of programmers on assignment to and located in the United States may be counted as Indian exports if they are working under contract to a company based in India. NASSCOM itself states on its website that 40 percent of its IT activities are associated with personnel located at the customer's site. BEA Director Steven Landefeld has noted that the payments made to these persons would not be counted as imports to the United States, nor in his view should they be.[35] If this view is correct, we should scale back the numbers given earlier by 40 percent for the IT jobs. The estimate of the software jobs transferred would drop from 134,000 over three years to 80,400.

We chose not to scale back the earlier estimates, however, for the following reasons. First, applying the 40 percent figure for Indian personnel located in the United States seems inconsistent with U.S. visa data reported by the Department of Homeland Security (or the Immigration and Naturalization Service). In particular, the number of Indians on H1-B visas (issued to workers in specialty occupations) in the United States was only 81,000 (47,500 of whom worked in computer-related fields) in 2002, and indeed was *lower* than the level in 2000. The number on L-1 visas (intercompany transfers) was only 20,400 and had also fallen since 2000. On this evidence it seems that the number of Indians transferred to U.S. companies has been falling since 2000, not rising, which makes it very hard to attribute any of the *growth* in employment reported in the NASSCOM employment data to increases in persons working in the

---

35. Steven Landefeld, personal communication with the authors, April 7, 2004.

United States. Perhaps the H1-B and L-1 visa data are missing a lot of people, but we know that entering the United States has become much more difficult since September 2001. Either a lot of employees of Indian companies have green cards or U.S. citizenship, or the 40 percent figure is wrong.[36]

The second reason is that this paper is exploring the decline in U.S. payroll employment. If Indian workers employed by establishments located in India are being assigned to projects located in U.S. companies' domestic facilities, these workers will not show up on the U.S. payroll survey.[37] They are not on the payroll of a U.S. company. From the perspective of understanding U.S. payroll employment, it is appropriate to count these jobs as having been offshored to Indian workers and companies, regardless of how their salaries either are or should be counted in the U.S. balance of trade data.

Finally, and most important, the purpose of this exercise is to show that the offshoring of services sector jobs to India, so far, has been small compared with total services sector employment in the United States. If the NASSCOM data do overstate the magnitude of offshoring, then that conclusion will hold even more strongly. The NASSCOM data on the offshoring of services from the United States then provide an upper bound on the actual value of U.S. services imports and on the number of jobs previously performed in the United States that are now being performed in India.

U.S. Employment in Occupations Likely to Have Been Affected by Offshoring

Given the enormous size of the services sector in the United States (about 110 million workers in 2004), it is not really a surprise to find that services sector offshoring to India so far has not been large in relation to total U.S. services employment. But it is certainly possible that the impact on the U.S. labor market of the growth of the Indian industry has been larger for IT and IT-enabled occupations. Our conclusion is that, yes, offshoring to India has been large enough to have had some impact on IT jobs in the United States. However, we find that employment in the

---

36. Thus far we have not been able to receive clarification from NASSCOM about the validity of the 40 percent figure.

37. This was confirmed by a phone conversation with Bureau of Labor Statistics staff.

IT sector has actually been surprisingly strong in the past few years, especially if one allows for the unsustainable surge in employment in 2000.

Table 10 uses data from the OES, described above, with a focus on employment patterns between 1999 and 2003 in those occupations that may have been affected by offshoring.[38] Looking first at the computer-related services occupations (top panel of table 10), we find only a modest drop in total employment—about 65,500 over 2000–03, or about 2.5 percent.[39] Moreover, as Catherine Mann has pointed out, the employment decline after 2000 followed a huge technology boom in the late 1990s, which culminated in a surge of employment and investment aimed at resolving the Y2K problem.[40] The employment levels reached in 2000 were not sustainable, regardless of what happened to U.S. services trade with India. As one sign of this, employment in computer occupations was actually over 230,000 higher in 2003 than it had been in 1999 (the earliest year for which these data are available). The short time period makes it impossible to be sure of the trends, but the figures for 1999–2003 tentatively suggest an underlying trend toward increasing employment in computer occupations over the period, with a temporary surge in 2000 that was followed by a temporary downward adjustment.

The table does show some shift in the mix of employment within computer occupations. The biggest job losers were computer programmers and computer support personnel, about 139,000 of whom lost jobs over 2000–03. Among computer support personnel there was a large surge in employment between 1999 and 2000, strongly suggesting a Y2K effect. Employment in 2003 remained above the level in 1999.

For computer programmers, however, the decline in employment could have been the result of offshoring to India. Table 10 shows a decline of 99,090 in U.S. computer programming jobs from 2000 to 2003. Our estimate of IT jobs in India in table 9 suggests that as many as 134,000 such jobs were created in India to serve the United States. Our estimate of the

38. The table is adapted from similar tables in Mann (2003) and Kirkegaard (2004). We have benefited from their analysis of high-technology employment.
39. The analysis in this section does not include production workers in the IT hardware industry. We showed above that manufacturing employment in the computer and semiconductor industries fell very sharply after 2000.
40. Mann (2003).

Table 10. Changes in Employment in IT and Low-Wage IT-Enabled Occupations, 1999–2003

Occupation	SOC code	Employment			Change in employment		Percent of total employment in category, 2003	Average annual wage (dollars)
		1999	2000	2003	1999–2003	2000–2003		
IT occupations								
Computer and information scientists, research	15-1011	26,280	25,800	23,210	–3,070	–2,590	0.9	84,530
Computer programmers	15-1021	528,600	530,730	431,640	–96,960	–99,090	16.8	64,510
Computer software engineers, applications	15-1031	287,600	374,640	392,140	104,540	17,500	15.2	75,750
Computer software engineers, systems software	15-1032	209,030	264,610	285,760	76,730	21,150	11.1	78,400
Computer support specialists	15-1041	462,840	522,570	482,990	20,150	–39,580	18.7	42,640
Computer systems analysts	15-1051	428,210	463,300	474,780	46,570	11,480	18.4	66,180
Database administrators	15-1061	101,460	108,000	100,890	–570	–7,110	3.9	61,440
Network and computer systems administrators	15-1071	204,680	234,040	237,980	33,300	3,940	9.2	59,140
Network systems and data communications analysts	15-1081	98,330	119,220	148,030	49,700	28,810	5.7	62,060
Total, IT occupations		2,347,030	2,642,910	2,577,420	230,390	–65,490	100.0	66,072
Low-wage IT-enabled occupations								
Telemarketers	41-9041	485,650	461,890	404,150	–81,500	–57,740	27.9	22,590
Switchboard operators, including answering services	43-2011	248,570	243,100	217,700	–30,870	–25,400	15.0	22,230
Telephone operators	43-2021	50,820	52,150	45,310	–5,510	–6,840	3.1	29,770
Computer operators	43-9011	198,500	186,460	160,170	–38,330	–26,290	11.1	31,870
Data entry keyers	43-9021	520,220	458,720	339,010	–181,210	–119,710	23.4	23,590
Word processors and typists	43-9022	271,310	257,020	191,180	–80,130	–65,840	13.2	28,400
Office machine operators, except computer	43-9071	101,490	86,380	90,470	–11,020	4,090	6.3	23,760
Total, low-wage IT-enabled occupations		1,876,560	1,745,720	1,447,990	–428,570	–297,730	100.0	26,030
Total, IT and low-wage IT-enabled occupations		4,223,590	4,388,630	4,025,410	–198,180	–363,220		46,051

Source: Bureau of Labor Statistics, Occupational Employment Statistics, 1999–May 2003.

shift of jobs to India is probably too high, but nevertheless these figures indicate the possibility that the loss of U.S. programming jobs was the result of a movement of work to India.

As already noted, comparative advantage within the computer programming sector may have led, as trade with India became cheaper and easier, to basic programming tasks being offshored while the higher-end activities continued to expand in the United States. Between 2000 and 2003 there were increases in the employment of computer software engineers (applications and systems) even as employment of computer programmers declined. The same holds even more strongly from 1999 to 2003.

In short, the availability of low-cost programming services from India surely has had an impact on the U.S. software industry. Indeed, one would expect such an impact, because U.S. customers benefit from the effects of the input price reduction generated by the availability of low-cost programmers.

The benefits from increased services trade will be reduced if such trade results in the permanent loss of U.S. human capital. This would occur if trained programmers in the United States were never reemployed or were moved to jobs that did not make use of the programming skills they had acquired. Press accounts provide anecdotal evidence that some U.S. workers have indeed experienced such a loss of human capital. Although this situation is attributable in part to offshoring, there were also misperceptions in the late 1990s about the sustainability of the technology boom.

In addition, the employment data in table 10 suggest that the loss of jobs in the technology sector was actually relatively small over all. Given the slump in the U.S. technology sector and in the *domestic* demand for IT, it is actually very surprising that employment in computer occupations fell so little between 2000 and 2003 and that it remains well above the 1999 employment level.

The bottom panel of table 10 shows that IT-enabled low-wage occupations, such as telemarketers, computer operators, and word processors, experienced substantial employment declines—nearly 300,000 over the 2000–03 period and well over 400,000 from 1999 through 2003. The declines occurred across the board in these occupations, and some were probably due to activities being shifted overseas. In other cases, however, technology was the culprit. For example, employment of word processors has declined in part because most office workers now carry out that function themselves on personal computers instead of using dictation or handwritten material. Similarly, computer operators are not needed in the same numbers because of the shift away from mainframes.

It is noteworthy that wages for these occupations are not very high—in the $10 to $15 an hour range. That is certainly better than the minimum wage, but not so high that alternative jobs at similar pay would be difficult to find in most urban labor markets. Voluntary turnover rates are also fairly high among positions at that level. As discussed previously, this suggests that human capital losses would be limited. We do not wish to minimize the personal cost borne by those whose jobs are shifted overseas, but the adjustment cost of this offshoring to the labor market as a whole should not be very high.

Conclusions

Even under assumptions that may greatly overstate the offshoring of services sector jobs to India, we find that press reports and popular discussion of the issue greatly exaggerate its importance to the U.S. labor market. The evidence so far suggests that the number of jobs transferred to India is tiny relative to total employment in the U.S. services sector. Within computer occupations, we find that the net job loss for computer programmers in the United States is likely attributable to offshoring. However, the surprising fact is how little employment in computer services has fallen in recent years, given the weakness in U.S. domestic demand for technology services.

The Impact of Expected Future Offshoring in Services

One possible rejoinder to this conclusion is that what has happened so far may be minor, but that in the future the offshoring of services sector jobs will affect the U.S. labor market more severely. We explore that possibility next.

The debate over the effects of electronic offshoring in the long run has reflected a variety of concerns. A recent paper by Jagdish Bhagwati, Arvind Panagariya, and T. N. Srinivasan considers the impact of offshoring on welfare.[41] A second issue is the impact of electronic outsourcing on the *structure* of U.S. employment. In the short run the United States may run larger trade deficits as a result of the increase in services sector off-shoring, but over the long run any increase in services imports will have to be paid for by additional net exports—that is, by exporting more goods and services or reducing imports of other goods and services. Thus, although outsourcing could mean fewer services jobs in some sectors, it could also mean more jobs in other sectors that produce tradable goods and services.

In this analysis the first question to be addressed is, How large is out-sourcing likely to be? Although any forecast of the future magnitude of services sector offshoring is subject to great uncertainty, the most fre-quently quoted figures, those compiled by Forrester Research, suggest that 3.4 million U.S. service jobs will be offshored to India and other countries by 2015.[42] These estimates derive from a series of company interviews in both the United States and India. Forrester attempted to assess which U.S. occupations were amenable to offshoring, what skills were available overseas, and what investments were being made or planned to develop capabilities overseas.[43]

The Forrester study finds that 315,000 service jobs had already been offshored by 2003 and that an additional 3.1 million jobs would move off-shore by 2015—hence the estimated total of 3.4 million. By far the largest occupational category affected is office workers, accounting for nearly half of the jobs offshored. But the study further suggests that a range of possible employment categories could be offshored, including computer, business, management, and sales workers, and workers in architecture and the life sciences.[44]

Although one should not place undue confidence in the Forrester num-bers, they are sufficiently interesting for their implications to be explored. Moreover, in different simulation runs, we used some alternative assump-tions about the magnitude of offshoring. The results were roughly linear, so that those who believe that the true number of offshored jobs will be half as great, or twice as great, as our estimates can simply halve or dou-

---

41. Bhagwati, Panagariya, and Srinivasan (fothcoming); Samuelson (2004).
42. McCarthy and others (forthcoming).
43. McCarthy and others (2004, p. 4).
44. McCarthy and others (2004, p. 5).

ble the results reported here to get a first approximation of the impact on the economy.

To formulate the simulations, we worked with Ben Herzon and Joel Prakken of Macroeconomic Advisers (MA) to see how the level of off-shoring predicted by Forrester would affect the economy. The difficult part of this analysis is to capture in a sensible fashion the impact of the "shock" imparted to the economy by the rapid increase in services sector offshoring. We experimented with various approaches and will report the two that, together, provide the most helpful insights. The impact of off-shoring is inferred from the deviations of our "offshoring" simulations from MA's baseline simulation; therefore we begin by offering a sense of what the baseline looks like.

The Baseline Scenario

MA's long-term simulations do not attempt to capture cyclical variations of the economy more than a few quarters out. This is standard practice for such forecasting models, for example those of the Council of Economic Advisers and the Office of Management and Budget, as well as the economic assumptions used by the Congressional Budget Office in its budget forecast-ing. The baseline simulation embodies an implicit Federal Reserve reaction function that ensures that, in the absence of shocks, the economy remains close to full employment, assumed to be consistent with an unemployment rate of around 5.3 percent. The baseline used for this paper uses actual data through the first quarter of 2004 and thus does not reflect the increases in oil prices and the weakening of the U.S. economy that occurred in mid-2004 (what Federal Reserve Chairman Alan Greenspan has referred to as a "soft patch"). In this baseline the U.S. economy continues its cyclical recovery, and the unemployment rate falls to its target range by the end of 2004.

These characteristics of the baseline, together with the gradual, smooth ramp-up of offshoring that is built into the Forrester estimates, mean that for our purposes there is little significant information to be obtained from the quarter-to-quarter changes in the economic variables. We compare the starting point of the baseline (in the first quarter of 2004) with the end point in the fourth quarter of 2015. The variables move relatively smoothly during the intermediate years.

When the MA model is run without adjustments, it predicts continuing large current account deficits for the United States. However, MA's current thinking is that these large deficits are not sustainable and that the dollar will decline substantially over the next ten years or so.[45] The baseline simulation therefore shows a gradual decline in the dollar of around 21 percent and a reduction of the U.S. current account deficit to around $100 billion, or 0.5 percent of the predicted $20 trillion current-dollar U.S. GDP in 2015:4. The downward adjustment of the current account, accompanied by a shift in real net exports from negative to positive, is accomplished without imposing excessively high interest rates, because a substantial reduction in the federal budget deficit is assumed over the same period. The baseline thus builds in a rather smooth resolution of the two big deficit problems facing today's economy.

Table 11 reports the values for a range of variables in the starting and ending quarters of the baseline and their growth rates when appropriate. Over the nearly twelve-year forecast period, real GDP grows at 2.9 percent a year and inflation averages a bit under 2.0 percent a year. Nonfarm payroll employment rises at 0.9 percent a year over the period, and labor productivity growth in the nonfarm business sector is 2.3 percent a year. The decline in the dollar contributes to strong growth of real U.S. nonfarm merchandise exports, at a rate of 7.3 percent a year; real services export growth is similar. Since trend productivity growth in the manufacturing sector is less than 7.3 percent a year, the implied growth of real exports would contribute positively to manufacturing employment in this baseline simulation. The baseline simulation implies that trade will increase manufacturing employment going forward. Real nonpetroleum imports are dampened by the fall in the dollar and grow at 5.6 percent a year. Real petroleum imports (not shown) grow even more slowly. Real services imports in the baseline are also dampened by the dollar decline and by rising prices, and they grow relatively slowly.

The baseline projections can be combined with our estimates of employment due to exports and imports in 2003, reported in table 4, to provide estimates of changes in employment due to trade between 2003 and 2015. To do this, it is necessary to make an assumption about what rate of labor productivity growth in manufacturing would be associated with a 2.3 percent annual average growth rate for nonfarm business out-

45. It is notoriously difficult to model exchange rate determination econometrically; in particular, it is very difficult to capture the downward pressure on the dollar that will likely come about (and in part has already come about) as dollar assets rise as a share of the portfolio of the rest of the world.

Table 11. Characteristics of Baseline Scenario

Item	2004:1	2015:4	Growth rate (percent a year)
Real GDP (billions of chained 2000 dollars)	10,716.0	14,986.1	2.90
Nominal GDP (billions of current dollars)	11,459.6	19,679.2	4.71
Chain PCE deflator (2000 = 100)[a]	106.6	134.0	1.97
Unemployment rate (percent)	5.63	5.28	n.a.
Nonfarm business sector employment (millions)	108.3	120.7	0.93
Output per hour in nonfarm business sector (chained 2000 dollars)	45.80	59.77	2.29
Federal funds rate (percent a year)	1.00	6.33	n.a.
Yield on ten-year Treasury note (percent a year)	4.01	7.11	n.a.
Nominal exchange rate (1997 = 100)[b]	113.30	96.94	n.a.
Current account balance (billions of current dollars)	−575.7	−99.0	n.a.
Net goods and services exports (billions of chained 2000 dollars)	−525.2	210.7	n.a.
Nonfarm merchandise exports (billions of chained 2000 dollars)	717.9	1,642.9	7.30
Total merchandise exports (billions of current dollars)	788.3	2,040.5	8.43
Services exports (billions of chained 2000 dollars)	330.6	736.2	7.05
Nonpetroleum merchandise imports (billions of chained 2000 dollars)	1,244.7	1,807.1	3.22
Total merchandise imports (billions of current dollars)	1,384.5	2,508.3	5.19
Services imports (billions of chained 2000 dollars)	243.1	260.8	0.60
Services imports (billions of current dollars)	278.4	456.3	4.29

Source: Authors' simulations using the Macroeconomic Advisers' model.
a. PCE, personal consumption expenditures.
b. Trade–weighted index of thirty-five currencies against the dollar.

put. Fortunately for our purposes, it turns out that, between 1992 and 2003, annual growth in output per hour in nonfarm business averaged 2.3 percent, exactly the same as assumed in the baseline. Since annual growth in output per worker-hour in manufacturing between 1992 and 2003 averaged 3.9 percent, we assume that the same rate will prevail between 2003 and 2015. This leads us to conclude that, in the baseline, the employment content of exports will increase by 3.4 percent a year (7.3 percent − 3.9 percent), while the employment content of imports will rise at 1.7 percent a year (5.6 percent − 3.9 percent). This level of performance in merchandise trade would boost manufacturing employment by 316,000 by 2015.

Different people have different views about the future path of the U.S. economy. Some have argued that an economic crisis may have to occur before the nation's deficit problems will be resolved. Terrorism or other shocks could disrupt economic growth. Others argue that large U.S. current account or budget deficits, or both, can continue indefinitely. However, the MA baseline looks exactly right for the purpose here. We want to abstract from other economic issues and focus on the impact of offshoring. To what extent services sector offshoring might interact with other shocks we leave to others to determine.

The Macroeconomic Effect of Services Sector Offshoring: Adding More Imports

One simple way to model the impact of services offshoring is to impose on the model an increase in the demand for services imports. We asked MA to adjust the services import equation so as to shift the demand curve outward. Using the Forrester employment data and the U.S. wage-cost numbers as a basis, we estimated what the increase in imports would be, under the assumption that the imported services would cost only half as much as supplying the equivalent services domestically.[46]

If the dollar exchange rate is left unchanged, the increase in imports translates into an increased current account deficit. We judged that a more neutral comparison with the baseline would result from imposing an additional decline in the dollar as a result of the increased offshoring, in order to keep the current account balance the same as in the baseline.

Table 12 summarizes the results of this simulation. The model translates the increase in imports into an immediate negative shock to GDP, which Federal Reserve policy must offset in order to preserve employment. Over time, however, the greater decline in the dollar stimulates exports and slows real import growth. By the end of the simulation run, the dollar is 7.5 below its baseline level, and this has increased real merchandise exports and reduced real merchandise imports. The lower dollar has pushed inflation up a little and pushed up interest rates. With the higher interest rates there is a slight reduction in productivity growth, and real GDP is down very slightly by 2015 compared with the baseline. In

---

46. The 50 percent figure is our estimate based on McKinsey Global Institute (2003). If anything, the cost would be somewhat less than 50 percent—in the 45 to 50 percent range. It is possible that the relative cost calculation would change over time as the foreign industry expands. However, Indian businesses are expanding their operations outside of their current region, to avoid rising labor costs, and other countries are investing in the infrastructure and language training that would allow them to enter the market.

Table 12. Scenario Modeling Impact of Offshoring as Increase in Services Imports

Item	2015:4	Change from baseline 2015:4	Growth rate, 2004:1–2015:4 (percent a year)
Real GDP (billions of chained 2000 dollars)	14,895.7	–90.4	2.8
Nominal GDP (billions of current dollars)	19,535.2	–144.0	4.6
Chain PCE deflator (2000 = 100)[a]	134.8	0.9	2.0
Unemployment rate (percent)	5.2	0.1	n.a.
Nonfarm business sector employment (millions)	120.6	–0.1	0.9
Output per hour in nonfarm business sector (chained 2000 dollars)	59.4	–0.4	2.2
Federal funds rate (percent a year)	6.9	0.6	n.a.
Yield on ten-year Treasury note (percent a year)	7.56	0.45	n.a.
Nominal exchange rate (1997 = 100)[b]	89.4	–7.5	n.a.
Current account balance (billions of current dollars)	–97.7	1.3	n.a.
Net goods and services exports (billions of chained 2000 dollars)	331.1	120.4	n.a.
Nonfarm merchandise exports (billions of chained 2000 dollars)	1,686.0	43.1	7.5
Total merchandise exports (billions of current dollars)	2,177.7	137.1	9.0
Services exports (billions of chained 2000 dollars)	738.9	2.7	7.1
Nonpetroleum merchandise imports (billions of chained 2000 dollars)	1,649.6	–157.4	2.4
Total merchandise imports (billions of current dollars)	2,477.9	–30.4	5.1
Services imports (billions of chained 2000 dollars)	334.7	73.9	2.8
Services imports (billions of current dollars)	630.8	174.5	7.2

Source: Authors' simulations using the Macroeconomic Advisers' model.
a. PCE, personal consumption expenditures.
b. Trade–weighted index of thirty–five currencies against the dollar.

this simulation the increase in services imports generates increased merchandise exports to help pay for them. This in turn requires a real devaluation of the dollar and thus a reduction in the U.S. terms of trade, which also has employment consequences for manufacturing.

Compared with the baseline, the value of merchandise exports increases by $137.1 billion, or 6.7 percent, while the value of merchandise imports falls by 1.2 percent. We estimate that this shift would lead to an additional 335,000 jobs in manufacturing in 2015. This highlights the fact that, once the current account is adjusted, the impact of increased spending on services imports leads to increased employment in manufacturing.

In summary, this simulation run, modeled as a case in which the United States has effectively developed an increased taste for services imports, results in a modest negative for the economy: inflation, productivity, and the terms of trade are all negatively affected. The job displacement happens slowly, based on the Forrester assessment, and this allows Federal Reserve policy to maintain full employment. The MA model is a general equilibrium model, and it predicts that most of the workers displaced from their jobs will find new ones. There is a predicted boost to manufacturing employment, although overall employment is essentially the same in this simulation run as it is in the baseline.

The Macroeconomic Effect of Services Sector Offshoring: A Decline in the Price of Services Imports

The previous simulation is a useful starting point, but it does not reflect the underlying economics of services sector offshoring. What is the underlying shock that triggers the increased offshoring that Forrester predicts? Presumably, it is that improved technology and infrastructure combined with capital and training have lowered the price that the United States pays for services sector imports. As a result, the United States buys more of them. For any given value of the dollar, the decline in import prices improves the U.S. terms of trade.

With offshoring, U.S. companies find they can produce the same level of sales or gross output with fewer domestic workers. Initially, their profitability rises as they sell at the same price domestically with reduced costs (they pay only 50 percent of the cost for the activities they offshore). Over time, however, competition works to lower prices and distributes the benefits back to consumers. Productivity rises within the companies doing the offshoring. They buy more foreign inputs but save labor, and, since they have reduced their costs, their productivity is higher. Productivity rises for the U.S. economy as a whole if the workers and capital displaced by the increased services imports are reemployed in activities that generate more than enough real output to pay for the increase in real services imports.

In order to capture this process, MA adjusted the price of services imports down by an amount large enough to induce an increase in the real quantity of services imports that, in turn, was large enough to displace the number of workers that Forrester predicts will be displaced. In the same quarter in which the increased offshoring takes place, there is a drop in payroll employment and a rise in productivity and corporate profits. Over time, domestic prices fall and Federal Reserve policy acts to restore employment. Domestic workers who are displaced are reabsorbed into the economy, according the normal dynamics built into the MA model.

Table 13 summarizes the results of the simulations. Offshoring of the magnitude suggested by Forrester is enough to add 0.2 percentage point to annual GDP growth and nearly 0.3 percentage point a year to growth in labor productivity in the nonfarm business sector. Real GDP is $384 billion higher by 2015. Total employment and unemployment are essentially the same as in the baseline. The inflation rate has been lowered by 0.25 percentage point a year, even though the dollar is down 4.8 percent.

As one would expect, real services imports are higher in this simulation, but services imports in current dollars are actually slightly lower. The fall in the price of imports means that the United States can buy more real imports for the same dollar cost. The decline in the dollar partially offsets the opening up of the low-cost offshoring opportunity.[47]

Table 13 shows that the values of merchandise exports and imports both rise—by $101.6 billion and $63.5 billion, respectively—relative to the baseline. In this scenario manufacturing employment due to trade increases by 62,000. In both simulations, therefore, more services imports implies more jobs in manufacturing over the long run.

The idea that offshoring could raise U.S. productivity and hence U.S. GDP is not a surprise. That is, after all, what we expect to be the benefit of expanded trade. The magnitude of the increments to these variables, however, is larger than we anticipated. It is not easy to determine how changes in variables play out through the structure of a large macroeconomic model, but it seems that the reason for the "multiplier effect" of offshoring on real GDP is that the Federal Reserve follows a path of lower interest rates in this simulation. It does that because domestic labor is being released as a result of the job displacement and because inflation is lower as a result of the cheaper services imports. In the MA model the lower interest rates have a positive impact on domestic investment, and this contributes to the growth in productivity and hence in GDP.

47. The decline in the dollar increases merchandise exports in these results. That result is plausible enough, but it was not robust across the different model runs. The MA model's price equations capture relative price effects between traded goods and services prices and the price of domestic production. Depending on the specification, these effects can eliminate the increase in merchandise exports.

Table 13. Scenario Modeling Impact of Offshoring as Reduction in Price of Services Imports

Item	2015:4	Change from baseline 2015:4	Growth rate, 2004:1–2015:4 (percent a year)
Real GDP (billions of chained 2000 dollars)	15,369.9	383.8	3.12
Nominal GDP (billions of current dollars)	19,687.5	8.3	4.71
Chain PCE deflator (2000 = 100)[a]	130.2	−3.7	1.72
Unemployment rate (percent)	5.3	0.0	n.a.
Nonfarm business sector employment (millions)	120.7	−0.0	0.93
Output per hour in nonfarm business sector (chained 2000 dollars)	61.7	1.9	2.57
Federal funds rate (percent a year)	5.3	−1.0	15.27
Yield on ten-year Treasury note (percent a year)	6.36	−0.75	3.98
Nominal exchange rate (1997 = 100)[b]	93.2	−3.7	n.a.
Current account balance (billions of current dollars)	−98.5	0.6	n.a.
Net goods and services exports (billions of chained 2000 dollars)	190.5	−20.2	n.a.
Nonfarm merchandise exports (billions of chained 2000 dollars)	1,721.6	78.7	7.73
Total merchandise exports (billions of current dollars)	2,142.2	101.6	8.88
Services exports (billions of chained 2000 dollars)	764.1	27.9	7.39
Nonpetroleum merchandise imports (billions of chained 2000 dollars)	1,824.5	17.4	3.31
Total merchandise imports (billions of current dollars)	2,571.7	63.5	5.41
Services imports (billions of chained 2000 dollars)	350.6	89.8	3.17
Services imports (billions of current dollars)	449.4	−6.9	4.16

Source: Authors' simulations using the Macroeconomic Advisers' model.
a. PCE, personal consumption expenditures.
b. Trade-weighted index of thirty-five currencies against the dollar.

Whether or not the magnitude of the impact on GDP predicted in this simulation is correct, the model is providing a valid lesson. The impact of offshoring that is being captured in the second run is basically the same as that of an opening to trade, such as a reduction in tariffs. And a range of empirical evidence supports the view that trade expansion results in higher GDP.[48]

48. See Cline (2004) for a summary of the evidence and references.

Wages and Profits

The simulation runs on the MA model do not tell us anything about the distribution of wages across different types of workers, but they do make a prediction about total wages (or rather, total compensation of employees) and profits. Table 14 reports the findings. The simulation in which the services import equation was add-factored up showed a negative effect on the economy, and table 14 indicates that this loss is imposed on employees. Real compensation is reduced by nearly $160 billion by 2015, or 1.9 percent. Profits remain essentially unaffected in this simulation.

In contrast, the simulation in which the price of imports is reduced results in benefits to the economy, and these are shared by labor and capital. Real compensation is increased by $209 billion and profits by $142 billion. The increase in profits is much larger in percentage terms (11.4 percent) than the increase in compensation (2.5 percent). Offshoring in this simulation thus shifts the distribution of income toward capital. In this simulation the initial impact of offshoring is to increase profits and displace labor. Over time, however, competition and higher productivity result in lower prices, and that is what increases real compensation. But higher profits are a persistent consequence of the ongoing process of offshoring. It is not surprising to find that, if the U.S. economy becomes more exposed to low-cost labor, the result will be to shift the distribution of income toward capital. Employees as a whole are better off in this simulation, however.

Conclusion

We began by pointing to the large and sustained drop in payroll employment that followed the end of the 1990s boom, and we presented a variety of evidence to suggest that trade and offshoring were not major reasons for this decline. The weakness in U.S. exports did contribute to the job loss, however.

What, then, is the main explanation of the weakness in employment? Charles Schultze has argued that the main cause is rapid productivity growth.[49] We agree that rapid productivity growth may be playing some

---

49. Schultze (2004).

Table 14. Real Compensation of Employees and Corporate Profits under Alternative Scenarios

Billions of 2000 dollars

	Compensation		Profits	
Scenario	*Total*	*Difference from baseline*	*Total*	*Difference from baseline*
Baseline	8,458.2	0.0	1,247.5	0.0
Modeling offshoring as increase in services imports	8,298.7	-159.5	1,249.4	1.9
Modeling offshoring as reduction in services imports prices	8,667.4	209.2	1,389.2	141.7

Source: Authors' simulations using the Macroeconomic Advisers' model.

role, but it is a mistake to place too much emphasis on this factor as a fundamental cause.

In most textbooks an increase in productivity implies an outward shift in the aggregate supply curve, resulting in lower prices and increased output for any given aggregate demand schedule. There is no presumption that employment will fall; indeed, to the extent that increased productivity results in a higher marginal product of labor and wages are sticky, there should be an increase in employment.

In addition, two previous shifts in the productivity trend in the postwar U.S. economy provide evidence on how productivity affects aggregate employment. In the 1970s a decline in productivity growth, combined with the additional adverse supply shock of rising food and energy prices, resulted in a sharp recession, with higher prices and much lower employment. In that episode slower productivity growth contributed to higher inflation and to recession. In the second half of the 1990s, an acceleration of productivity growth was followed by continued strong employment growth and the lowest unemployment rate in a generation. The more rapid growth of aggregate supply was more than balanced by growth in aggregate demand. And, since faster productivity growth contributed to rising real incomes and a rising stock market, the increased supply helped generate increased demand.

In sum, these two earlier instances of changes in the trend rate of productivity growth (after 1973 and after 1995) do not support the hypothesis that faster aggregate productivity growth causes lower employment. At the least, the 1990s show that faster productivity growth does not automatically generate weak employment.

Rapid productivity growth after 2000 did raise the bar, however. It meant that aggregate demand would have had to grow strongly in order to maintain employment growth, and that did not occur. With strongly expansionary monetary and fiscal policies, the recession of 2001 was very mild, and the employment drop was not unusual. The puzzle has been the failure of demand and employment to recover strongly enough after 2001. The reasons for this include the uncertainty resulting from 9/11 and the war in Iraq, the direct effect of higher oil prices, the overhang from the investment boom of the late 1990s, the weakness of the stock market (only partly offset by the recovery in 2003), and, as we have emphasized, the lagged impact of the strong dollar in the aftermath of the Asian financial crisis. The drop in U.S. capital goods investment, and notably the decline in the demand for high-technology products, contributed to the weakness of manufacturing employment. Monetary and fiscal policies, although expansionary, were not powerful enough to offset these negatives. Fiscal policy was more effective at increasing the budget deficit than at spurring demand. Monetary policy was about as expansionary as it could be, and it certainly helped sustain demand for housing and automobiles. But history suggests that low interest rates can have a limited impact on aggregate demand in the presence of business and consumer uncertainty, especially given the lower bound on nominal interest rates.

We do not suggest that the U.S. economy is mired in perpetual job weakness, however. The economy has repeatedly demonstrated its ability to recover, and we expect aggregate demand and employment to increase going forward, barring a new oil shock or major terrorist attack or other calamity.

Since trade and offshoring were not the main reasons for the employment weakness, they should not be the focus of policies to restore employment. Likewise, since imports were not the reason for the job loss, there is not an employment case for trade restrictions to curtail imports.

Instead the best trade-related remedy for manufacturing employment is a lower value of the dollar and a sustained recovery of the world economy—outcomes that are desirable for other reasons as well. In the late 1990s, when domestic demand in the United States was booming, the strong dollar helped relieve pressures on the U.S. labor market by reducing exports and stimulating imports. It would certainly have been inadvisable and inflationary for the United States to have reduced interest rates in an effort to weaken the dollar in 1999 and 2000. However, once the economy fell into a recession, the lagged impact of the strong dollar contributed to labor market weakness.

U.S. policymakers have limited power to affect the exchange rate of the dollar and the strength of the world economy. However, once the overall recovery is well established, a sustained effort to reduce the federal budget deficit would help lower interest rates and reduce the overvaluation of the dollar—and would be good policy in any case. Policies that might ameliorate the adverse effects of job reallocation caused by trade include, in our judgment, trade adjustment assistance programs and opportunities for workers to improve their skill levels.

Comments and Discussion

Frank Levy: About the time I received this paper, my wife and I had to drive our daughter to college. Because her room needed a floor lamp, we ended up at IKEA. The reader can already see where this story is heading. The floor lamp was nice, functional if not high style, and adjustable in height up to about six feet. It was made in China and cost $9.95. I informally sampled other IKEA items and found many had similarly low prices.

I appreciate the distinction between anecdotes and data, but having just seen these extremely low prices, I found this paper by Martin Baily and Robert Lawrence quite timely. The paper draws four principal conclusions:

—The substantial loss of manufacturing jobs since 2000 was primarily a function of weak aggregate domestic demand, not due to a flood of imports.

—To the extent that trade did cause manufacturing job losses, it did so through a sharp decline in exports. This decline can be largely explained by the rise in the dollar, which undercut U.S. competitiveness.

—The outsourcing of service jobs was not particularly large in scale, either in information technology services or in clerical back office work.

—If, however, the Forrester Research predictions of future outsourcing were to come true, the resulting job losses would be substantial. These job losses would not pose a threat to full employment, but, under a variety of assumptions, they would shift the composition of national income away from wages and toward capital.

In this comment I will discuss first the jobs data and then the paper's analysis of the data. I will end by summarizing what the reader should take away from the paper.

To explain the loss of jobs since 2000, it would be helpful first to get a better understanding of exactly what jobs have been lost. This is at issue because the well-known disagreements between the Current Population Survey and the Employment Survey extend below the level of aggregate employment to specific occupations. The two surveys agree, however, on one central point: the loss of production jobs. The authors use the BLS's Occupational Employment Statistics (OES), which indicate that, between the fourth quarter of 2000 and the second quarter of 2003, production employment declined by 1.9 million. Similarly, Current Population Survey figures taken from the BLS website indicate that, between December 2000 and March 2003, production employment declined by about 1.9 million. In other areas there is less agreement.

One potential disagreement, noted by the authors, is with respect to managerial employment. The OES reports that, again over 2000:4–2003:2, employment in "Management Occupations" fell by 1.1 million, or about 14 percent. This is a stunning figure for so short a time. The sum of employment losses in this and a second category, business and financial operations occupations, is about 824,000, or about 7 percent of the aggregated total. The CPS does not report data for managerial employment separately but rather reports data for the combined category "Management, Business and Financial Operations Occupations," and for the same period it shows a *gain* of 458,000 jobs, or about 2 percent.

It is unclear what to make of this discrepancy, but it is worth noting that employment in the CPS combined category is far larger than employment in the two corresponding categories in the OES: roughly 19.6 million workers versus 12.4 million, respectively, in 2000. As the authors note, some of this difference in levels reflects the well-known bias in the household survey due to respondents' tendency to inflate their occupational titles. It is not clear, however, why self-reporting should bias the *change* in these levels, turning a loss into a gain.

A second discrepancy arises in clerical employment (office and administrative support). Here the difference, however, is one of magnitude rather than sign: the OES shows a decline of about 250,000 workers from a base of about 23 million, whereas the CPS shows a decline of about 1 million from a base of about 20.5 million. Although in the end it may not be possible to resolve these differences, it is worth further effort to get a better sense of how labor demand is tilting.

The paper's estimation of the determinants of the decline in manufacturing employment is helpful, in particular the authors' use of input-output
analysis to develop an accounting of how much of the decline is due to each
of various factors. Some points, however, require clarification. The first is
the importance of productivity growth in job losses. As the authors explain,
when employment is considered, the important variable is not productivity
growth as such but rather the difference between the rate of productivity
growth and the rate of growth of demand. In this kind of comparison,
assigning importance to either variable requires external yardsticks. In
drawing their conclusions, the authors should be clearer about what yardsticks they are using. Early in the paper, they argue that rapid productivity
growth is not a primary cause of the manufacturing employment decline:

> Some observers explain the recent job loss in manufacturing by pointing to the rel-
> atively rapid manufacturing productivity growth of recent years, but between 2000
> and 2003 this factor did not play a dominant role. Over that period the share of man-
> ufacturing in nonfarm payrolls fell from 13.1 percent to 11.1 percent—a drop of 15
> percent. But the 12 percent increase in nonfarm output per worker-hour between
> 2000 and 2003 was only 3 percentage points less than the increase in manufacturing
> labor productivity. This leaves 80 percent (12 percentage points of the 15 percent)
> of the decline in manufacturing employment's share to be explained by other factors.

Ultimately, the authors conclude that the problem lies in the slow
growth of domestic demand for manufacturing output. In reaching this
conclusion, they describe productivity growth in manufacturing over
2000–03 as "remarkably rapid," but they adopt what they call an alternative approach: "to see how domestic use and trade contributed to the
decline, taking productivity growth as given." It is this alternative
approach that leads to their conclusion.

The reader needs firmer footing than this in order to understand what is
likely to happen to manufacturing jobs in the future. What rate of growth
of manufacturing demand would have been required to substantially
reduce job losses? What rate of GDP growth would have been required to
produce that growth in manufacturing demand? And how plausible would
such a rate of GDP growth have been? Because, as the authors say, manufacturing productivity did not grow much faster than overall labor productivity, the rate of GDP growth required to limit manufacturing job
losses may have been implausibly high. Fortunately, the simulations at the
end of the paper shed some light on these questions.

Also requiring some elaboration is the reason for the export decline. The authors make a convincing case that the proximate cause of falling exports was loss of international competitiveness—as opposed to, say, slumping demand on the part of our trading partners. The reader wonders, however, whether the loss of competitiveness was also driven by our trading partners switching to Chinese and Indian products: could cheap foreign products have harmed U.S. producers indirectly by outcompeting them in export markets? The authors dismiss this possibility by saying that China and India have been producing exports for a long time. A more detailed look at the question would be welcome.

I found the authors' discussion of services employment to be enlightening, but I would have liked more perspective on the numbers presented. India is not the only country to which both software and business processing services have been outsourced. As Richard Murnane and I were finishing our book on computers, a General Electric appliance technician called to apologize for a glitch in an appointment, saying that GE had just shifted its call center work from India to Costa Rica. (It turned out that the appointment had been made by a software program.) If India was the main source of *growth* in outsourcing during this period, then the focus on NASSCOM data is reasonable. But some clarification on that point is needed.

The discussion of India provides a natural lead-in to my last question: What should the reader take away from this paper? The paper does a very good job at debunking certain assertions in the current debate, but, in this case, debunking those claims is not equivalent to debunking what I see as the underlying problem.

Much of the politics of import competition has centered on the job prospects for less educated workers, often understood as those with no more than a high school diploma. To be sure, software engineers who have lost their jobs to outsourcing do not fit this picture, and, on the other hand, many people with only a high school diploma work in nontradable crafts such as plumbing and carpentry. But, on balance, it is usually the jobs of high school graduates—production workers, call center workers, and others—that are the focus of the outsourcing and offshoring debate.

As the authors note at several points, this means that imports get the blame both for the loss of U.S. jobs they actually cause and for those losses that are in fact due to technological advance. And, as the authors also note, these impacts of trade and technology do overlap to some degree. Murnane and I have argued that tasks that can be adequately described in terms of rules—that is, tasks that do not involve extensive tacit knowledge—are amenable to computerization, but that the same tasks are also amenable to moving offshore, because they can be explained with less risk of misunderstanding.[1] Thus one observes call center work being handled by continuous speech recognition or by Philippine operators reading from scripts; basic tax preparation done by Indian accountants or by TurboTax; fabrication done by robots in the United States or by foreign manufacturers communicating with their U.S. customers through digital design protocols; and so on.

The authors argue that a flood of cheap imports should not be blamed for the current problems in the market for high school graduates. With the caveats already noted, that conclusion seems reasonable, but that is not to say that the demand problems themselves are a fiction. To the contrary, the rapid productivity growth in manufacturing that the authors cite, and the examples they mention in the services sector, suggest that skill-biased technical change is not going away any time soon. They also suggest that the fear for which trade is a surrogate is correct—that many of the jobs recently lost are not coming back, even in the long run. The authors' simulations support this point and make the added point that a sharp increase in labor supply—from both foreign labor and computers—will shift the composition of national income away from labor and toward profits.

Earlier this year, David Autor, Murnane, and I did a back-of-the-envelope projection suggesting that, if the demand shift of the last thirty years continues, half of the labor force in 2020 could have four years of college, yet the college–high school wage premium would be no lower than it is today.[2] At the same time, we know from David Ellwood's careful work that, even under optimistic assumptions, no more than about 35 percent of the labor force is likely to have that much education.[3] In the absence of specific policies to correct this imbalance, the share of the work force receiving low wages is likely to increase, as too many workers without college-level skills will be chasing too few jobs for which they qualify.[4] The projected combination of more jobs paying low wages

---

1. Levy and Murnane (2004).
2. Autor, Murnane, and Levy (2004).
3. Ellwood (2001).
4. Or, as Gary Burtless (1990, p. 30) famously wrote, "Ironically, [less-skilled workers'] labor market position could be improved if the U.S. economy produced *more* not fewer jobs requiring limited skill."

and a shift in national income toward profits suggests that now is a particularly illogical time to consider eliminating taxes on capital income as a basis for tax reform.

In sum, the authors begin their paper the way economists love to begin, with a quote from a noneconomist warning of catastrophe, whose claims the paper then calmly but rigorously proceeds to dismantle. In this case the silly noneconomist may have gotten some of his facts wrong: the labor imbalances of which he speaks may owe more to technology than to trade, and more to factors within countries than between them. But, ultimately, Lou Dobbs may have more logic on his side than this paper admits.

Daniel E. Sichel: The coincidence of the sharp decline in manufacturing employment in recent years and the growing current account deficit has led many in the media to posit a causal link from trade to the employment dropoff. The outsourcing and offshoring of corporate operations, which likewise have received extensive media coverage recently, also are often cited as culprits behind recent job losses. This paper by Martin Baily and Robert Lawrence tackles both of these issues. The first part of the paper lays out some basic facts about trade in recent years and provides a useful analytical framework for assessing the impact of trade flows on employment. The primary conclusion of this part of the paper is that trade was not the principal cause of the employment drop in manufacturing from 2000 to 2003. The second part of the paper analyzes the effects of outsourcing and offshoring in recent years, with a focus on jobs lost to India. This section concludes that these developments have had relatively modest effects to date on U.S. employment.

I largely agree with the paper's conclusions about the relatively small role of trade in the recent manufacturing job loss and the relatively limited effect of outsourcing and offshoring on employment. The empirical work is well done, and the evidence on the role of trade is credible.

In the first part of the paper, however, I believe the authors are a bit too quick to attribute the job loss to weak domestic demand. The endogeneity problem here is acute, and my sense is that rapid domestic productivity growth played a larger role than the authors suggest.[1] Recall that

---

1. Schultze (2004) also argues that rapid productivity growth was an important part of the job-loss story during this period.

Baily and Lawrence use data from the input-output tables to decompose employment change at the detailed industry level into a weighted average of the growth rate of value added less the growth rate of productivity for each component of interest: exports, imports, and domestic demand (equation 5 in the paper).[2] This industry-level decomposition is then aggregated to track the effects of trade on employment growth. Using this decomposition, the authors find that, of the 950,000 net manufacturing jobs lost per year between 2000 and 2003, only about 105,000 can be attributed to trade, with the remainder, about 845,000, attributable to weak domestic demand.

In this decomposition, productivity growth is taken as given and the domestic demand term is calculated as a residual. Thus, although this decomposition tells us something about the role of trade, it does not cut the knot of endogeneity and fully disentangle what else is going on. In particular, because productivity growth is taken as given, *the decomposition can assign no role to productivity growth as a source of job loss.* Baily and Lawrence clearly understand the endogeneity problem and point it out several times in the paper. Nevertheless, the reader is still left wondering what shock kicked off the large manufacturing decline. The phrase "weak domestic demand" has the flavor of a business cycle shock, but the recession of 2001 was quite mild by historical standards. Of course, the recession in manufacturing was quite severe, but noting that fact just begs the question of why it was so severe—was the underlying cause the implosion of the technology sector, the overhang of capital goods from the late 1990s, other sources of weak domestic demand, or rapid productivity growth?

One could argue that the main point of this part of the paper—that trade did not account for much of the employment decline in manufacturing—does not depend on identifying what other factors did cause the decline. However, I would argue that identifying those factors—whether it was weak domestic demand, rapid productivity growth, or some combination of the two—would make more credible the authors' argument that trade

---

2. The decomposition linking employment and trade is built up at a detailed level using the 1997 input-output tables. Implicitly, using these tables to assess trade flows from 2000 to 2003 assumes that intersectoral relationships have not changed since 1997. The fact that the 1997 table is the most recent available at a sufficiently disaggregated level highlights the need for the statistical agencies to produce input-output tables more quickly.

was not the main factor.[3] That is, accepting the conclusion that the manufacturing employment decline was not caused by trade might be easier if the primary explanation were not a factor calculated as a residual. Hence I will explore the productivity issue a bit further.

For the economy as a whole, rapid productivity growth is seen by many analysts as closely linked to the jobless recovery.[4] This observation is suggestive, and an alternative decomposition of the employment loss in manufacturing would assign a larger role to productivity growth. Of course, such a decomposition also would be subject to endogeneity issues, but it highlights that different conditioning assumptions could lead to different conclusions. Here are some pieces that could go into an alternative decomposition.

Consider the pickup in manufacturing productivity growth after 2001. Productivity growth in manufacturing averaged 3¾ percent a year from 1995 to 2001 but then picked up to an average annual pace of 6 percent from 2001 to 2003. Consider the counterfactual in which manufacturing productivity increased 3¾ percent a year from 2001 to 2003 rather than 6 percent. Then, taking output growth as given, manufacturing employment would have declined by about 340,000 less per year. Of course, in this counterfactual the workweek might have increased, and so the employment effect might have been less than 340,000, but since this analysis is only meant to be illustrative, I will stick with a figure of 340,000 jobs a year to keep things simple.

Over and above the job losses stemming from this burst of productivity, manufacturing employment has been experiencing longer-term decline. Between the peaks in manufacturing employment in 1989 and 1998, manufacturing employment declined by an average of about 50,000 a year. If this trend rate of decline has continued in recent years, manufacturing employment would have been declining by 50,000 a year during 2000–03, all else equal.

Consider as well the decline in technology sector employment related to the collapse of that sector and an overhang of high-technology capital

---

3. It is also possible that the shock was neither weak domestic demand nor productivity, but a third factor that caused both the productivity and employment outcomes. For example, greater-than-usual business caution could have led to sluggish employment growth and rapid productivity gains as firms pushed current employees harder.

4. For example, see Gordon (2003) and the discussions of that paper by Martin Baily and myself.

goods. As reported in table 1 of the paper, employment in computer and electronic products declined by about 175,000 a year during 2000–03.

Putting these pieces together (using the authors' estimate of the trade effect and of the employment decline in the high-technology sector), this illustrative alternative decomposition would parse the employment decline of 950,000 a year as shown in the first column below:

	Alternative decomposition	*Baily and Lawrence*
Total job loss during 2000–03 (annual average)	950,000	950,000
Due to:		
Trade	105,000	105,000
Faster manufacturing productivity growth	340,000	
Trend decline in manufacturing employment	50,000	
Collapse of the technology sector	175,000	
Other (including decline in domestic demand)	280,000	846,000

In this alternative decomposition, productivity-related factors (the third and fourth lines) together account for 390,000 of the yearly decline in manufacturing jobs, and the technology sector collapse for another 175,000. Taking account of these pieces leaves just 280,000 for the "other" category, compared with a residual of 846,000 (with rounding) in the Baily-Lawrence decomposition. The point of this exercise is not to say that the alternative decomposition is correct, but rather that alternative assumptions about what should be taken as given can lead to different conclusions about the source of the employment decline.

In considering whether productivity growth is a plausible explanation for the employment decline, it is important to distinguish between short-run and long-run effects of changes in aggregate productivity growth. The authors point out in their conclusion that the slowdown in productivity growth in the mid-1970s was associated with weak employment growth, whereas the productivity pickup of the second half of the 1990s was associated with strong employment growth. These patterns—which are related to long-lived changes in the underlying trend of productivity—suggest that changes in aggregate trend productivity growth are, if anything, positively associated with employment change.[5] However, there are plenty of exam-

5. To assess the effect of productivity growth on employment within manufacturing, as opposed to that in the economy as a whole, it is also necessary to delve into the relative rates of productivity growth across sectors and the elasticities of demand in different sectors. See *Economic Report of the President, 2004,* pp. 60–71, for a discussion.

ples of more cyclical or transitory movements in productivity in which strong aggregate productivity growth appears to be associated with weak employment growth. Indeed, in the early 1990s, a time of another jobless recovery, just such a thing happened. Decades earlier, in the early 1950s and again in the early 1960s, productivity growth was relatively rapid while employment growth was relatively sluggish.[6]

The analysis of outsourcing and offshoring in the second part of the paper is particularly valuable, because it debunks a lot of hype around these issues in the press. The data for this analysis are relatively sparse, and the concepts are less well defined than in the first part of the paper, inevitably making the analysis a little softer and squishier. Nevertheless, the authors present credible evidence that outsourcing and offshoring have not, to date, been major factors behind employment loss in the U.S. economy. I quite liked the simulations done with the Macroeconomic Advisers model. Although such simulations are not often included in academic papers, and despite possible arguments related to the Lucas critique, I believe these simulations provide useful insights into how (and how much) outsourcing and offshoring might plausibly affect employment going forward.

In addition, I commend the authors for their discussion of the quality (or productivity) of outsourced or offshored services relative to that of domestic employees. Many analysts seem to skip very lightly over this issue (implicitly assuming that the two groups of workers are of identical quality), even though it is an important link in sorting through the implications of outsourcing and offshoring.

Finally, although the authors focus primarily on *net* job loss, I suspect that, for the public at large, *gross* job loss is a more salient metric. I also suspect that any wage loss associated with trade or outsourcing or offshoring is a matter of great concern to many in the labor force, as is any trade-linked uncertainty about employment or wage prospects. The authors are careful to mention that losses to individuals can be large, even if the net employment effect for the economy as a whole is small. Nevertheless, given the current economic and policy environment, I suspect that the public and the political world will largely continue to focus on issues that go well beyond net job loss.

---

6. These observations are based on three-year moving averages of productivity and employment growth.

General discussion: Some Panel participants elaborated on the weakness in U.S. exports and how to interpret it. Edmund Phelps observed that U.S. firms moving operations offshore is an important part of the story, and that much of the offshoring of production to China is aimed at the Chinese rather than the U.S. consumer. Together with the strengthening dollar over much of the period in question, this offshoring worsens the U.S. terms of trade and the competitiveness of U.S. exports produced by U.S. labor and other U.S. inputs. This contrasts with the worrisome increase in supplies of imports, which improve our terms of trade. Susan Collins reported that BEA data on the overseas activities of U.S.-owned multinational corporations abroad showed that 75 percent of their output is sold in the host market, with an additional 12 percent sold in third markets, and only about 12 percent exported to the United States. This suggests that most of the increased activity abroad is reflected in lower exports rather than higher imports. She noted that the paper's macroeconomic model simulations treat shocks as a fall in import prices, with positive effects for the United States through improvement in the terms of trade. She reasoned that it would be more accurate to model the shocks as a reduction in the prices at which the United States can export, which would indicate a deterioration in the terms of trade as Phelps suggested. Collins added that it would be useful to distinguish clearly between outsourcing and offshoring. *Outsourcing* refers to jobs that are moved organizationally, from one ownership structure to a different one. *Offshoring* refers to moving jobs or activities from the home country to another country, within the same organizational structure. Austan Goolsbee added that the employment figures for manufacturing are likely to be distorted by the growing practice of outsourcing. The Census Bureau has not been able to identify when firms in manufacturing and elsewhere have terminated employees and rehired them or similar workers to do the same jobs under temporary contracts or through employment services.

William Nordhaus questioned the authors' treatment of productivity in the manufacturing sector, which implies that higher productivity will lead to proportionally lower employment. With manufacturing so open to foreign competition, the demand elasticity is likely to be high enough that increased productivity would lead to more jobs rather than less. He also questioned the assumption of a one-for-one job transfer from the United States to India, which the authors conceded provides only an upper limit for actual job loss. He noted that applying the job-for-job methodology to Chinese exports to the United States might show that tens of millions of

U.S. jobs were lost because of imports of Chinese manufactured goods. He suggested that the job-for-job calculation be compared with a dollar-for-dollar calculation converted to U.S. employment, which could provide a lower limit for U.S. job loss. Nordhaus also criticized the paper's use of the Forrester data as a baseline for longer-term projections, on the grounds that doing so gives them much greater credibility than they deserve.

Richard Cooper remarked that the public debate to which this paper contributes has been going on since 1820, yet little has been resolved, because economists use a general equilibrium framework whereas the public thinks in partial equilibrium or anecdotal terms. In addressing the public concerns in the first part of the paper, the authors use a partial equilibrium framework, taking macroeconomic developments such as exchange rate changes as givens. Yet the dollar was strong in part because of very extensive foreign investment in the United States, some of which was employment-creating. Thus the employment consequences of openness are quite different if one focuses broadly on U.S. engagement with the world economy rather than only on U.S. trade in manufactured goods.

Cooper also regarded the baseline simulation, under which the U.S. current account deficit falls to $100 billion in 2015 with substantial dollar depreciation, as unrealistic. He reasoned that the shock to the world economy, in particular the Japanese and European economies, from such a change in current account balances and exchange rates would be too large to tolerate. A baseline with a U.S. current account deficit in 2015 of $400 billion rather than $100 billion would be more realistic.

John Leahy observed that the paper's focus on job losses missed what might be the even greater public concern over incomes, particularly toward the lower end of the wage distribution. Over the longer run, unemployment is trendless, and little joblessness is permanent, whether initiated by trade or other developments. However, the effects of trade competition on prices and wages, which the authors do not address, are a different matter. He argued that what workers fear is competing against low-wage foreign workers and ultimately having to accept low wages themselves. Thus what trade will do to the wage distribution, particularly at the low end, is the relevant issue in the debate. Adam Posen added that the standard remedy, compensating those workers who lose their jobs to trade, does not fully address the political economy pressures raised by trade. Workers feel that their bargaining power and status are threatened, and income transfers do not overcome their risk aversion and sense of entitlement.

References

Atkinson, Robert. 2004. "Meeting the Offshoring Challenge." Policy Report. Washington: Progressive Policy Institute (July).

Autor, David H., Frank Levy, and Richard J. Murnane. 2003. "The Skill Content of Recent Technological Change: An Empirical Exploration." *Quarterly Journal of Economics* 118, no. 4: 1279–1333.

Bailliu, Jeannine, and Hafedh Bouakez. 2004. "Exchange Rate Pass-Through in Industrialized Countries." *Bank of Canada Review* (Spring), pp. 19–28.

Baily, Martin Neil, and Diana Farrell. 2004. "Exploding the Myths about Offshoring." San Francisco: McKinsey Global Institute (April).

Bardhan, Ashok Deo, and Cynthia Kroll. 2003. "The New Wave of Outsourcing." Fisher Center Research Reports 1103. Fisher Center for Real Estate and Urban Economics, University of California, Berkeley (repositories.cdlib.org/iber/fcreue/reports/1103).

Bhagwati, Jagdish, Arvind Panagariya, and T. N. Srinivasan. Forthcoming. "The Muddles over Outsourcing." *Journal of Economic Perspectives.*

Brainard, Lael, and Robert E. Litan. 2004. " 'Offshoring' Service Jobs: Bane or Boon—And What to Do?" Policy Brief 132. Brookings (April).

Burtless, Gary, ed. 1990. *A Future of Lousy Jobs? The Changing Structure of U.S. Wages.* Brookings.

Cline, William R. 2004. *Trade Policy and Global Poverty.* Washington: Institute for International Economics.

Ellwood, David T. 2001. "The Sputtering Labor Force of the 21st Century: Can Social Policy Help?" Working Paper 8321. Cambridge, Mass.: National Bureau of Economic Research (June).

Goldstein, Morris, and Mohsin S. Khan. 1985. "Income and Price Effects in Foreign Trade." In *Handbook of International Economics,* vol. II, edited by R. W. Jones and P. B. Kenen, chapter 20. Amsterdam: Elsevier Science Publishers.

Gordon, Robert J. 2003. "Exploding Productivity Growth: Context, Causes and Implications." *BPEA,* no. 2: 207–79.

Hooper, Peter, Karen Johnson, and Jaime Marquez. 1998. "Trade Elasticities for G-7 Countries." International Finance Discussion Paper 609. Washington: Board of Governors of the Federal Reserve System.

Houthakker, H. S., and Stephen P. Magee. 1969. "Income and Price Elasticities in World Trade." *Review of Economics and Statistics* 51, no. 2: 111–25.

Kirkegaard, Jacob F. 2004. "Outsourcing: Stains on the White Collar?" Washington: Institute for International Economics (www.iie.com/publications/papers/kirkegaard0204.pdf [September]).

Kletzer, Lori G. 2001. *Job Loss from Imports: Measuring the Costs.* Washington: Institute for International Economics.

Leamer, Edward E., and Robert M. Stern. 1970. *Quantitative International Economics.* Boston: Allyn and Bacon.

Mahdavi, Saeid. 2000. "Do German, Japanese, and U.S. Export Prices Asymmetrically Respond to Exchange Rate Changes? Evidence from Aggregate Data." *Contemporary Economic Policy* 18, no. 1: 70–81.

Mann, Catherine L. 2003. "Globalization of IT Services and White Collar Jobs: The Next Wave of Productivity Growth." Policy Brief PB03-11. Washington: Institute for International Economics (December).

_____. 1999. *Is the U.S. Trade Deficit Sustainable?* Washington: Institute for International Economics.

Marquez, Jaime R. 2002. *Estimating Trade Elasticities.* Advanced Studies in Theoretical and Applied Econometrics, Vol. 39. Boston: Kluwer Academic Publishers.

McCarthy, John C., and others. 2004. "Near-Term Growth of Offshoring Accelerating. Resizing U.S. Service Jobs Going Offshore." *Trends.* Cambridge, Mass.: Forrester Research Inc. (May).

McKinsey Global Institute. 2003. *Offshoring: Is it a Win-Win Game?* San Francisco: McKinsey and Company.

Richardson, J. David. 1970. "Constant-Market-Shares Analysis of Export Growth." Research Seminar in International Economics Discussion Paper 16. University of Michigan.

_____. 1971a. 'Constant-Market-Shares' Analysis of Export Growth." *Journal of International Economics* 1: 227–39.

_____. 1971b. "Some Sensitivity Tests for a 'Constant-Market-Shares' Analysis of Export Growth." *Review of Economics and Statistics* 53: 300–04.

Samuelson, Paul A. 2004. "Where Ricardo and Mills Rebut and Confirm Arguments of Mainstream Economists Supporting Globalization." *Journal of Economic Perspectives* 18 (Summer): 135–46.

Schultze, Charles L. 2004. "Offshoring, Import Competition and the Jobless Recovery." Brookings (www.brookings.edu/comm/policybriefs/pb136.pdf [September]).

Senhadji, Abdelhak S., and Claudio E. Montenegro. 1999. "Time Series Analysis of Export Demand Equations: A Cross-Country Analysis." International Monetary Fund *Staff Papers* 46, no. 3: 259–73.

Stone, Joe A. 1979. "Price Elasticities of Demand for Imports and Exports: Industry Estimates for the U.S., the E.E.C. and Japan." *Review of Economics and Statistics* 61, no. 2: 306–12.

Yang, Jiawen. 1998. "Pricing-to-Market in U.S. Imports and Exports: A Time Series and Cross-Sectional Study." *Quarterly Review of Economics and Finance* 38, no. 4: 843–61.

MIHIR A. DESAI
Harvard University

AUSTAN D. GOOLSBEE
University of Chicago

Investment, Overhang, and Tax Policy

THE PAST DECADE HAS seen an unusual pattern of investment. The boom of the 1990s generated unusually high investment rates, particularly in equipment, and the bust of the 2000s witnessed an unusually large decline in investment. A drop in equipment investment normally accounts for about 10 to 20 percent of the decline in GDP during a recession; in the 2001 recession, however, it accounted for 120 percent.[1]

In the public mind, the recent boom and bust in investment are directly linked due to "capital overhang." Although the term is not very precisely defined, this view generally holds that excess investment in the 1990s, fueled by an asset price bubble, left corporations with excess capital stocks, and therefore no demand for investment, during the 2000s. The popular view also holds that these conditions will continue until normal economic growth eliminates the overhang and, consequently, that there is little policymakers can do to remedy the situation, by subsidizing investment with tax policy, for example. Variants on this view have been espoused by private sector analysts and economists,[2] and the notion of a

We thank Mark Veblen and James Zeitler for their invaluable research assistance, as well as Alan Auerbach, Kevin Hassett, John Leahy, Joel Slemrod, and participants at the Brookings Panel conference for their comments. Dale Jorgenson was kind enough to provide estimates of the tax term by asset. Mihir Desai thanks the Division of Research at Harvard Business School for financial support. Austan Goolsbee thanks the American Bar Foundation and the National Science Foundation for financial support.

1. McCarthy (2003) documents the decline in equipment investment as a share of GDP for all business cycles since 1953 and shows the 2001 recession to be an outlier.

2. See, for example, Berner (2001); Graeme Leach, "The Worries of the World," *GCIEye* no. 1, 2002, accessed August 2004 (www.gcieurope.com/eye/GCIEye_Issue01. pdf), and Stephen Roach, "The Costs of Bursting Bubbles," *New York Times,* September 22, 2002, section 4, p. 13.

capital overhang has certainly been on the minds of leading Federal Reserve officials and researchers.[3]

Whether or not a capital overhang is the true explanation of the investment bust, it is clear that the drop in investment has motivated policymakers to try to stimulate investment through ambitious fiscal policy changes.[4] Under President George W. Bush, depreciation allowances for equipment investment have been increased twice, in 2002 and 2003, and in 2003 the tax rate on dividend income was cut sharply and that on capital gains income more modestly. These measures were mainly intended to increase after-tax returns and stimulate investment. The typical analysis of the investment collapse and policy response is summarized by the Republican chairman of the Joint Economic Committee:

> Excessive and bad business investments made during the stock market bubble have taken years to liquidate. In nine of the 10 quarters beginning with the fourth quarter of 2000, real business investment has declined. Fortunately, recent tax legislation signed into law in 2003 should promote business investment by increasing the after-tax returns from investing in capital assets and alleviating financing constraints among small and medium-size firms.[5]

Yet, after several years of tax cuts, investment has still not risen impressively compared with previous recoveries. This contrast has reignited claims that tax policy is ineffective at stimulating investment, although some make the more specific charge that tax policy is impotent when it follows a period of excessive investment.

This paper examines the evidence on the two related issues of capital overhang and taxes using data at the industry, the asset, and especially the firm level. Specifically, we address two questions: first, did "over"-investment in the 1990s *cause* the low investment of the 2000s, and, second, did investment in the 2000s become less sensitive to prices, and does this explain why tax policies, specifically the equipment expensing and the dividend tax cuts of 2002 and 2003, seem to have been ineffective in restoring investment to normal levels?

3. See, for example, Greenspan (2002), Ferguson (2001), Bernanke (2003), French, Klier, and Oppedahl (2002), Pelgrin, Schich, and de Serres (2002), Kliesen (2003), Doms (2004), and McCarthy (2004).
4. Unlike the behavior of investment, the behavior of tax policy in the 2000s is completely consistent with earlier time periods. Cummins, Hassett, and Hubbard (1994) have documented that a primary determinant of investment tax subsidies is a drop in investment.
5. Saxton (2003).

We begin by examining the degree to which growth in investment during the boom was correlated with a decline in investment during the bust across different assets and industries. There are, of course, many possible definitions of overhang or excess investment. We will *not* try to show that there was no overoptimism in product or capital markets. Clearly equity prices rose substantially and then fell, as did investment rates. Instead we investigate whether investment grew the most in those assets and industries in which it subsequently declined the most. We want to know if any aftereffects of the investment boom of the 1990s persisted into the 2000s—whether firms behaved differently because too much capital remained from the investment decisions of the 1990s.

The evidence across assets, industries, and firms suggests that, contrary to the popular view, there is little correlation between the investment boom of the 1990s and the investment bust of the 2000s. We also present some more specific evidence, using firm-level data, that investment behavior has remained just as responsive to the fundamentals (as measured by Tobin's q) regardless of how much a firm's investment grew or how much its market value rose in the 1990s. Essentially, we find that the explanatory power of the standard empirical model of investment has not deteriorated in the 2000s, despite the common perception that it has.

We then use that standard model to consider the impact of tax cuts. To estimate the impact of the dividend tax reduction, we revisit an enduring debate in public finance between the "new" view of dividend taxation, which says that dividend tax cuts do not reduce the cost of capital for marginal investments, and the "traditional" view, which says that such cuts do reduce the marginal cost of capital and thus stimulate investment. The evidence at the firm level strongly supports the new view and suggests that the dividend tax reductions enacted in 2003 had little or no effect on investment.

Finally, to estimate the impact of the changes in depreciation allowances, we estimate a tax-adjusted q model similar to that of Lawrence Summers,[6] but with greater emphasis on the importance of error in the measurement of q, as emphasized by Jason Cummins, Kevin Hassett, and

6. Summers (1981).

Glenn Hubbard.[7] The method introduced for handling these measurement error issues yields results that suggest that both tax policy and q are likely to have much larger effects on investment than found in the traditional literature, where coefficients are very small and imply implausibly large costs of adjustment. Even with the more reasonable adjustment costs, however, we show that the depreciation allowance changes of 2002 and 2003 changed the tax term by a relatively small amount: the estimated overall impact in these two years was an increase in investment of only 1 to 2 percent, far too small to offset the double-digit declines of the early 2000s.

Capital Overhang and Investment

Real investment was considerably higher than normal during the late 1990s. When recession years are excluded, investment from 1947:1 to 1995:2 averaged about 12 percent of GDP; the highest quarterly level was 15 percent in 1984:3. From 1996:1 to 2000:4, in contrast, this ratio *averaged* more than 16 percent, and it reached 18 percent at its peak. The distinctiveness of these investment rates holds even relative to the business cycle. Figure 1 shows that investment in the quarters leading up to the 2001 peak was higher than it had been during comparable periods in previous cycles. The popular view holds that this extra investment resulted from the excesses of the 1990s bubble.[8]

With this view in mind, figure 2 provides a counterpart to figure 1, showing the path of investment in the period after the trough quarter for the recovery that began in late 2001 and for the average of previous recoveries. The increase in investment in the current recovery, at least through the beginning of 2004, is notably smaller than in the average recovery. Taken together, these trends make it plausible to many observers that investment after the most recent trough was lower than in previous cycles precisely because investment in previous years had been higher.

Of course, these aggregate patterns do not establish any underlying connection between the rise and the fall. To test for a causal relationship, we believe, it is critical to disaggregate the investment data. Most aca-

7. Cummins, Hassett, and Hubbard (1994).

8. Tevlin and Whelan (2003) argue that much of the increase in gross investment can be explained empirically by falling prices of computers and their higher depreciation rates.

Figure 1. Real Investment Relative to Business Cycle Peak, Postwar Average and 1996–2000ᵃ

Index = 1.0 at peak

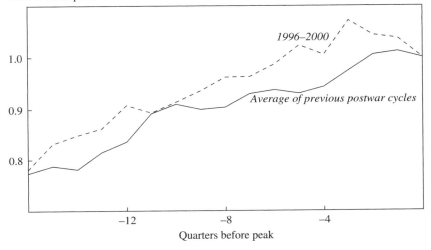

Quarters before peak

Source: Authors' calculations using National Income and Product Accounts data.
a. Investment is measured as a fraction of GDP.

demic work looking at the capital overhang has not done so, or has done so at a very broad level, emphasizing that the reversal in investment has been concentrated in information technology investment.[9] It is clear that the exuberance of the 1990s was not shared equally in all sectors. Industries such as telecommunications experienced huge increases in the 1990s in a way that railroads or mining, say, did not. We believe that any overhang, in the sense of excess capital remaining at the end of the boom, is inherently an industry- or firm-level phenomenon, which requires that we look at data at that level.

An additional reason to look at the industry- and firm-level data is that investment theory typically begins with the premise that there is a perfectly functioning secondary market for capital goods and a flat supply curve for capital. In such a world, firms with an overhang of unused capital equipment can simply sell it without incurring any loss. For the

9. Two papers by McCarthy (2001, 2004) are exceptions.

Figure 2. Real Investment Relative to Business Cycle Trough, Postwar Average and 2001–04ᵃ

Index = 1.0 at trough

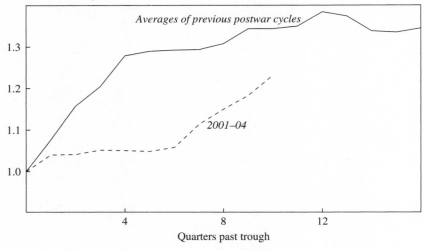

Quarters past trough

Source: Authors' calculations using National Income and Product Accounts data.
a. Investment is measured as a fraction of GDP.

popular view to make sense, then, either investment must be in some way irreversible (which leads to a rather different model),[10] or there must be some other type of adjustment cost associated with disinvestment.[11] Matthew Shapiro and Valerie Ramey have documented that, in some industries, a sizable wedge can develop between the purchase price of capital goods and the sale price.[12] These types of irreversibilities are likely to be firm or asset specific rather than applying to all types of investment in all sectors homogeneously. Fortunately, data on investment are available at the industry, asset type, and firm level, and, as we will show, the evidence at all three levels of disaggregation is generally the same.

10. As in, for example, Abel and Eberly (2002).
11. The adjustment costs could be at the firm level, or they might be external in the sense that the supply of capital goods in a particular industry is upward sloping as in Goolsbee (1998, 2001).
12. Ramey and Shapiro (2001). Evidence presented by Goolsbee and Gross (2000) is also consistent with that view.

Evidence at the Industry Level

We begin with the evidence on changes in investment at the industry level. Rather than rely on the more aggregated fixed asset data available from the Bureau of Economic Analysis (BEA), we turn to the Annual Capital Expenditure Survey (ACES) of the U.S. Census Bureau, which provides a finer industry disaggregation than is available elsewhere. The survey samples approximately 46,000 companies in more than 100 industries, categorized according to the 1997 North American Industry Classification System (NAICS). We narrow this categorization down to eighty-one nonoverlapping industries at approximately the three-digit NAICS level.[13]

The ACES provides measures of gross investment only and does not estimate industries' capital stock. Consequently, we cannot scale investment by lagged capital as is done in traditional empirical work on investment. Instead we simply investigate the change in total investment both for equipment alone and for equipment and structures combined. Empirical models of investment have struggled to explain the behavior of investment in structures, and it is not known whether this problem is due to mismeasurement in the tax term, unobservable factors in structures markets (such as liquidity and financing issues relating to the supply side of the market), or some other factor.[14] Since we cannot readily isolate equipment investment from structures investment in the firm-level data employed below, we have to assume that equipment investment and overall investment behave in the same way. Given that, by the 2000s, equipment accounted for something like 80 percent of nonresidential investment, this may not be too heroic an assumption, but the results in these areas will allow us to check the results in a circumstance where we have both sets of data.

Our goal with these data is to look for general evidence supporting the view that a capital overhang from the 1990s is a key factor determining investment in the 2000s. If overhang is quantitatively important, one might expect to find that those industries in which investment has fallen in the 2000s are the same as those in which investment grew substantially in

---

13. Before 1997, Standard Industrial Classification (SIC) codes were employed.

14. See, for example, Auerbach and Hassett (1992), who discuss the problems with estimating structures investment.

Brookings Papers on Economic Activity, 2:2004

the 1990s. To test this relationship formally, we performed a cross-sectional regression of the change in log investment by industry from 2000 to 2002 (the period widely viewed as the "collapse") on the change in log investment from 1994 to 1999 in the same industry, estimating the following equation:

$$(1) \qquad \ln(I_{i,\ 2002}) - \ln(I_{i,\ 2000}) = \alpha + \beta[\ln(I_{i,\ 1999}) - \ln(I_{i,\ 1994})] + \epsilon_i.$$

This test would show no evidence of reversion, of course, if all industries boomed and then busted together equally, since any such effect would simply appear in the constant term. Given that the investment growth of the 1990s was not likely to have been identical across industries, this equation provides a useful estimation strategy.

Table 1 presents, in the top panel, the results of estimating equation 1 by ordinary least squares (OLS) and, in the bottom panel, results for the same specifications employing median regressions, to ensure that the

Table 1. Regressions of Changes in Investment during 2000–02 on Changes in Investment during the 1990s, Equipment Only, Using Data by Industry[a]

Sample period	All industries 1-1	Manufacturing only 1-2	All industries 1-3	Manufacturing only 1-4
Ordinary least squares regressions				
1994–99	−0.084	−0.5315		
	(0.0693)	(0.1894)		
1997–99			−0.0582	−0.4204
			(0.0853)	(0.2047)
1994–97			−0.1435	−0.7878
			(0.1331)	(0.2704)
No. of observations	81	23	81	23
Adjusted R^2	.018	.273	.022	.330
Median regressions				
1994–99	−0.0205	−0.5836		
	(0.0994)	(0.2210)		
1997–99			0.0239	−0.5712
			(0.1392)	(0.2753)
1994–97			−0.1164	−0.8117
			(0.2206)	(0.4492)
No. of observations	81	23	81	23

Source: Authors' regressions using data from the Annual Capital Expenditure Survey of the U.S. Census Bureau.
a. The dependent variable in all regressions is the change in log capital expenditure on equipment from 2000 to 2002; the independent variable is the same change in log values in the same industry for the indicated sample period. Numbers in parentheses are standard errors.

results in the top panel do not purely reflect the role of large outliers. Column 1-1 reports the results from the basic overhang specification. The OLS and median regressions produce coefficients that are negative but very small and not significantly different from zero. To give a sense of the magnitude of this effect, a 1-standard-deviation change in the investment rate from 1994 to 1999 (0.53, or from the median of 0.38 to about the 85th percentile) is associated with only a 2.9 percent lower level of investment (less than one-twelfth of a standard deviation) from 2000 to 2002. This is modest evidence of an overhang, at best.

Given the serious decline of manufacturing in the most recent recession, and given that old-line manufacturing was not typically involved in the Internet boom, we further investigate the manufacturing sector separately. In column 1-2, which restricts the sample to the twenty-three manufacturing industries, the evidence for an overhang seems more pronounced. In both the OLS and the median regressions, there is a large and significant negative coefficient on the change in investment from 1994 to 1999. In the median regression, a 1-standard-deviation increase in the investment rate among manufacturing industries (a log value of 0.32) in 1994–99 corresponds to an almost 22 percent lower investment rate in 2000–02, which is equal to about two-thirds of the standard deviation of those changes. If one takes this larger effect as evidence of overhang (as opposed to a cyclical phenomenon), however, it should be noted that manufacturing industries accounted for only about 22 percent of total equipment investment and 18 percent of total investment in 2002, according to the ACES.[15] Consequently, on the present evidence, mean reversion for manufacturing can explain only a limited part of the aggregate collapse of investment.

The common explanation for capital overhang is that an abundance of funds raised in the capital market during the bubble encouraged the excess investment, particularly during the 1997–99 period. Indeed, the broadly disaggregated, cost of capital–type analysis done by Jonathan McCarthy suggests that there was no capital overhang at all until 1998, even in the high-technology investment goods sector (computers and communications equipment).[16] In columns 1-3 and 1-4, therefore, we con-

15. This is also consistent with the evidence cited by Bernanke (2003).
16. McCarthy (2003).

sider separately the periods from 1994 to 1997 and from 1997 to 1999 in order to isolate the effects of the bubble period and to take account of underlying growth trends in different industries that might mask investment reversion. Again there is little evidence of reversion across all industries, and there are larger negative coefficients in manufacturing. The later period, in which the overhang is alleged to have occurred, has a smaller coefficient than the earlier period, although the standard errors are not small enough to reject the hypothesis that they are equal. Rather than supporting the intuition of a bubble-induced capital overhang, this consideration of the two subperiods suggests some underlying, more secular mechanism associated with the continuing decline in U.S. manufacturing.

Table 2 considers the behavior of both equipment and structures investment. The results are qualitatively similar to those in table 1 in that they show little evidence of reversion, either generally or in manufacturing, featuring the dynamics discussed earlier.

Table 2. Regressions of Changes in Investment during 2000–02 on Changes in Investment during the 1990s, Equipment and Structures, Using Data by Industry[a]

Sample period	All industries 2-1	Manufacturing only 2-2	All industries 2-3	Manufacturing only 2-4
Ordinary least squares regressions				
1994–99	−0.0516	−0.5426		
	(0.0645)	(0.169)		
1997–99			−0.0677	−0.4786
			(−0.0871)	(0.1916)
1994–97			−0.0304	−0.6663
			(0.1001)	(0.2395)
No. of observations	81	23	81	23
Adjusted R^2	0.008	0.329	0.009	0.247
Median regressions				
1994–99	0.0533	−0.6793		
	(0.1066)	(0.2030)		
1997–99			0.0285	−0.5450
			(0.1182)	(0.3532)
1994–97			−0.1186	−0.6564
			(0.1184)	(0.3665)
No. of observations	81	23	81	23

Source: Authors' regressions using data from the Annual Capital Expenditure Survey of the U.S. Census Bureau.

a. The dependent variable in all regressions is the change in log capital expenditure on equipment and structures from 2000 to 2002; the independent variable is the change in log values in the same industry for the indicated sample period. Numbers in parentheses are standard errors.

Table 3. Regressions of Changes in Investment during 2000–02 on Changes in Investment during the 1990s, Using Data by Asset Type[a]

Sample period	3-1	3-2
Ordinary least squares regressions		
1994–99	−0.0945	
	(0.0970)	
1997–99		0.0388
		(0.1576)
1994–97		−0.2326
		(0.1611)
No. of observations[b]	34	34
Adjusted R^2	.029	.063
Median regressions		
1994–99	−0.1490	
	(0.1105)	
1997–99		0.0545
		(0.1270)
1994–97		−0.2407
		(0.1113)
No. of observations[b]	34	34

Source: Authors' regressions using National Income and Product Accounts data from the Bureau of Economic Analysis.

a. The dependent variable in all regressions is the change in log capital expenditure from 2000 to 2002; the independent variable is the same change in log values for the same asset type for the indicated sample period. Numbers in parentheses are standard errors.

b. Sample includes twenty-five categories of capital equipment and nine categories of structures.

Evidence at the Asset Level

Next we consider the general evidence on investment by type of investment good rather than by industry. We did this by testing our basic regression model (equation 1) using data by asset category instead of by industry. Using only the BEA data available for the whole period 1994–2002, we have twenty-five different categories of equipment and an additional nine categories of structures.[17] As in tables 1 and 2, the two panels of table 3 report both OLS and median regressions. (Weighting by the initial capital stock in these regressions provides very similar results, which we do not report here.) Those asset types that had the largest increases in investment from 1994 to 1999 are not systematically those that had the largest drop in investment from 2000 to 2002: the regressions

---

17. The categories of structures employed by the BEA change slightly over the period.

show a small and insignificant negative coefficient. This is equally true in the OLS and the median regression, and the coefficients have similar magnitudes. In the top panel, the estimate in column 3-1 indicates that an asset type whose log investment grew by 1 standard deviation (a log value of 0.36) more than the median asset from 1994 to 1999 would be expected to have a drop in log investment from 2000 to 2002 about one-sixth of a standard deviation larger than that of the median firm.

Column 3-2 repeats this analysis but splits the data into the early and late periods of the boom, 1994–97 and 1997–99, respectively. Here, although the coefficient estimates are imprecise, they are not consistent with the typical overhang story. If anything, the coefficients are again larger in absolute value in the earlier period than in the later period. Indeed, both of the point estimates in the later period are greater than zero, suggesting that those assets whose real investment grew most in the 1990s saw even greater investment growth in the 2000s. The irrational exuberance hypothesis would say just the opposite. Of course, in both cases the regressions do not control for anything but merely indicate the absence of a strong negative correlation. Using the firm-level data, we can further investigate these phenomena at the firm level, with better controls for observables related to investment opportunities.

Evidence at the Firm Level

Our firm-level sample includes all companies that appear in the Compustat research file from 1962 to 2003. Figure 3 plots the average investment rate (defined as capital expenditure divided by the beginning-of-period net capital stock) for manufacturing firms, for nonmanufacturing firms, and for firms involved in information businesses. Information businesses are defined as those in NAICS categories 334 (computer manufacturing) and 51 (information); this grouping is one we return to later, because the irrational exuberance of the late 1990s is commonly viewed as having been most extreme there. These data reveal the same pattern as the aggregate data: investment rates rose dramatically in the 1990s and then fell dramatically in the 2000s. We cannot say how representative the universe of publicly traded firms is of the rest of the economy, but in some ways the sheer magnitude of the firm-level sample makes it an overwhelmingly important component of aggregate investment on its own. Our calculations suggest that aggregate capital expendi-

Figure 3. Firm-Level Investment Rates by Sector, 1962–2003

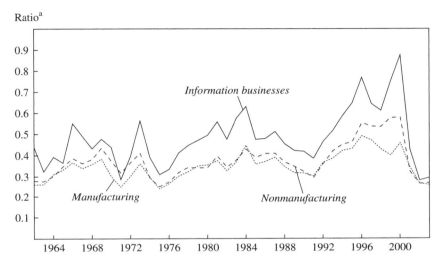

Source: Authors' calculations using Compustat data.
a. Ratio of current capital expenditure to the capital stock in the previous period, calculated as described in appendix A.

ture in the firms in the Compustat data constituted 85 to 90 percent of private, nonresidential investment in the United States for most of the last twenty-five years.[18] Our sample in 2003 does not include all firms, since some share of firms had yet to have their reports coded by Compustat at the time of our analysis. Nonetheless, the sample is large (more than 80 percent of the 2002 sample) and provides a perspective not afforded by the industry-or asset-level data, given their earlier cutoffs.

We begin with the general evidence that parallels the previous results in examining the changes in investment rates during the bust and the subsequent boom, but with the advantage that, in the firm-level data, we can compute the change in the investment rate because we have capital stock data for each firm. Our modified regression equation, then, is

18. One important shortcoming of the Compustat data (and common to virtually all empirical work that uses these data to study investment) is the inability to isolate domestic from international expenditure or the degree to which q measures worldwide rather than domestic investment opportunities.

Table 4. Regressions of Changes in Investment Rates during 2000–02 on Changes in Investment Rates during the 1990s, Using Data by Firm[a]

Independent variable	4-1	4-2	4-3
Ordinary least squares regressions			
Investment rate change, 1994–99	−0.0325		−0.0237
	(0.0234)		(0.0216)
Investment rate change, 1997–99		−0.0739	
		(0.0376)	
Investment rate change, 1994–97		−0.0174	
		(0.0252)	
Change in sales, 2000–02[b]			0.0364
			(0.0304)
No. of observations	3,249	3,225	3,172
Adjusted R^2	.002	.005	.004
Median regressions			
Investment rate change, 1994–99	−0.0170		−0.0120
	(0.0051)		(0.0051)
Investment rate change, 1997–99		−0.0351	
		(0.0063)	
Investment rate change, 1994–97		−0.0071	
		(0.0051)	
Change in sales, 2000–02[b]			0.0545
			(0.0040)
No. of observations	3,249	3,225	1,798

Source: Authors' regressions using data from Compustat.
a. The dependent variable in all regressions is the change in the firm's investment rate, as defined in the text, from 2000 to 2002. Numbers in parentheses are standard errors.
b. In percent.

$$(2) \qquad \left(\frac{I}{K}\right)^i_{2002} - \left(\frac{I}{K}\right)^i_{2000} = \alpha + \beta\left[\left(\frac{I}{K}\right)^i_{1999} - \left(\frac{I}{K}\right)^i_{1994}\right] + e,$$

where *I* is capital expenditure at the firm level and is scaled by the lagged capital stock K.[19]

As before, the top panel of table 4 presents the OLS results and the bottom panel the median regression results. Column 4-1 reports results for a specification that emphasizes the relationship between the change in investment rates over the 1994–99 boom and that over the 2000–02 bust. Given that a firm must have existed in 1994, 1999, 2000, and 2002 to appear in the sample for this regression, the sample size is somewhat

19. Appendix A describes how we compute the capital stock for each firm, following Salinger and Summers (1984) and Cummins, Hassett, and Hubbard (1994).

smaller than the full universe of firms. These results again show a very small and insignificant negative correlation in the changes in investment rates. The median percentage change in the capital stock from 2000 to 2002 was −0.3 percent. The estimated coefficients are indeed tiny compared with the median firm. The coefficient on the lagged investment change variable indicates that a firm whose increase in investment rate during the boom was 1 standard deviation (about 0.65) above that of the median firm would have seen its investment fall by about 0.02, or only about one-thirty-fifth of a standard deviation, during the bust. The bottom panel of table 4 repeats this specification but controls for outliers by using a median regression (particularly important when firm data are used), and here the coefficient is even smaller but statistically significant. A firm whose investment grew by 1 standard deviation more than the median during the boom would have seen its investment fall during the bust by only about one-seventieth of a standard deviation more than the median firm.

The regressions reported in column 4-2 of both panels in table 4 split the 1994–99 period into two parts as an additional control, to account for firms whose size is trending upward. Inclusion of this split, however, produced little change in the general result of a very small negative impact relative to trend. Finally, the regressions in column 4-3 include the percentage change in the firm's real sales as an additional control, to further take into account the fact that firms might be growing or shrinking over the period in a way that drives the investment results. (Recall the large coefficients on manufacturing investment in the industry-level data.) In this regression, sales growth is positively correlated with growth in investment, but the evidence on reversion is even a bit more modest than in the first two columns.

The evidence thus far, then, provides very limited support for the view that firms, asset types, and industries that had major increases in their investment in the 1990s experienced major drops in investment in the 2000s. This seems to suggest that overhang was not the dominant factor influencing investment in the later period. A more precise test is available, however, by relating overhang to the sensitivity of investment to fundamentals at the firm level.

Evidence on Overhang and the Sensitivity of Investment

The firm-level data allow us to further examine whether firms have been less responsive to changes in tax-adjusted q in the 2000s if they had significant valuation increases in the 1990s. If, in fact, firms experiencing large changes in market value exhibit a different response than other firms to tax-adjusted q in the 2000s, this could help explain why taxes have not seemed to have a major impact on investment. The next section and appendix B discuss in more detail our tax-adjusted measure of q and the model underlying it. There we provide a fuller discussion of the measurement issues and the predictions of that model, but we include this analysis here in order to fully address the overhang phenomenon. Our basic estimating equation will add an interaction term to the standard equation relating investment to q.

We investigate the relevance of two different measures of overhang in the 1990s: one based on equity values and one based on capital expansion. Table 5 reports results of regressions using the lagged change in q as a measure of the degree to which overhang is operative.[20] We create the variable $\Delta_{t-3}^{t-7} q_{it}^{2000+}$, which is the change in q observed in the period three to seven years before the current year and only for the time period 2000–03.[21] So, in 2002 for example, this variable would be the change in the firm's q from 1995 to 1999. Before the 2000s this variable is always zero. One view of the overhang hypothesis is that investment for firms with large capital overhangs from the 1990s should be less sensitive to fundamentals or tax rates.[22]

This yields the following investment equation:

$$(3) \qquad (I/K)_{it} = \alpha_i + \gamma_t + \beta_1 Q_{it} + \delta Q_{it}(\Delta_{t-3}^{t-7} q_{it}^{2000+}) + \beta_2(\text{cash}/K)_{it} + \epsilon_{it}.$$

Here α_i and γ_t are firm and year dummies, respectively, and Q is tax-adjusted q, as defined below. Column 5-1 of table 5 presents the results

20. We considered using the lagged change in the price-earnings ratio as the measure of firms with overhang, but this had the obvious problem that many firms had negative earnings.

21. Other lags, such as the change in q from five years ago to two years ago, yield similar results.

22. In a previous draft we also examined whether having had a large increase in K or in q during the 1990s led the *level* of investment at the firm to be lower, controlling for current q (as opposed to the increase changing the slope of the investment-q relationship). We found virtually no evidence that it did.

Table 5. Regressions Testing Sensitivity of the Firm-Level Investment-Q Relationship to Past Changes in q^a

Independent variable	All industries 5-1	All industries 5-2	Information businesses only 5-3	Manufacturing only 5-4	All industries 5-5
Q	0.0124	0.0221	0.0143	0.0137	0.0123
	(0.0014)	(0.0013)	(0.0032)	(0.0018)	(0.0014)
$Q \times \%\Delta q(t-3$ to $t-7)$, 2000 or after[b]	0.0006	0.0002	−0.0005	0.0010	0.0006
	(0.0004)	(0.0005)	(0.0011)	(0.0007)	(0.0004)
$Q \times \%\Delta q(t-3$ to $t-7)$, 1999 or before[c]					0.0003
					(0.0003)
Ratio of cash flow to capital stock	0.0198	0.0157	0.0069	0.0236	0.0198
	(0.0031)	(0.0024)	(0.0057)	(0.0042)	(0.0031)
Year dummies included	Yes	Yes	Yes	Yes	Yes
Firm dummies included	Yes	No	Yes	Yes	Yes
No. of observations	69,540	69,540	11,758	36,313	69,540
Adjusted R^2	.403	.039	.399	.377	.403

Source: Authors' regressions using data from Compustat.

a. The dependent variable in all regressions is the firm's investment rate in a given year, as defined in the text. Q is tax-adjusted q, defined as $[q/(1-\tau)] - [(1-\Gamma)/(1-\tau)]$, where Γ is the standard measure of the tax treatment of investment and τ is the corporate tax rate. Numbers in parentheses are standard errors clustered at the firm level.

b. Q times the change in q observed over the period three to seven years before the current year, where the current year is 2000, 2001, 2002, or 2003.

c. As above, where the current year is 1999 or before.

from estimating this equation over all firms. It shows that there is no significant difference in the investment-q relationship in the 2000s for firms that had larger run-ups in their stock prices in the 1990s. Indeed, the point estimate is actually positive, although small. Column 5-2 excludes the firm dummies, so that we are explicitly comparing results across firms rather than within a given firm. The result on the interaction term is very similar to that in column 5-1: positive and not significant.

Column 5-3 returns to the specification with firm dummies but restricts the sample to firms in information businesses; these are the firms most closely associated with the technology bubble. There is again no evidence that large increases in equity values in the 1990s have reduced the sensitivity of investment to the fundamentals in the 2000s. The point estimate on the interaction term is insignificant, although this time slightly less than zero. Column 5-4 repeats the analysis, this time for manufacturing firms only, and again there is nothing notable. Finally, column 5-5 investigates whether the relationship changed any differently in the 2000s than it did in earlier periods that followed asset price increases. The evidence suggests that it did not.

Table 6 repeats the exercise reported in table 5 but uses the lagged percentage change in capital for the firm during the 1990s as the measure of overhang. The advantage of the lagged change in q as the overhang measure in table 5 is that it picks up more directly the influence of asset price bubbles, which typically underlie the popular explanation of overhang. The lagged percentage change in the capital stock as used in table 6, in contrast, is a more direct measure of capital accumulation.

Table 6 reports estimates of the following equation:

$$(4) \quad (I/K)_{it} = \alpha_i + \gamma_t + \beta_1 Q_{it} + \delta Q_{it}(\%\Delta_{t-3}^{t-7} K_{it}^{2000+}) + \beta_2(cash/K)_{it} + \epsilon_{it},$$

where $\%\Delta_{t-3}^{t-7} K_{it}^{2000+}$ is the percentage change in the net capital stock of the firm between time $t-3$ and time $t-7$ for 2000–03 (in other words, the change in the capital stock during the mid-1990s).

Estimating this equation for the entire sample of firms, as reported in column 6-1, does show a significant negative coefficient on the interacted Q term, indicating that firms that had larger accumulations of capital in the 1990s did, indeed, show less sensitivity to the fundamentals in their investment behavior in the 2000s. Although the direction is consistent with the overhang view, the magnitude is extremely small. To see this, consider that the highest mean value of lagged capital growth was 1.37 in

Table 6. Regressions Testing Sensitivity of the Firm-Level Investment-Q Relationship to Past Changes in Investment[a]

Independent variable	All industries 6-1	All industries 6-2	Information businesses only 6-3	Manufacturing only 6-4	All industries 6-5
q	0.0124	0.0214	0.0155	0.0117	0.0137
	(0.0014)	(0.0012)	(0.0011)	(0.0017)	(-0.0015)
$Q \times \%\Delta K(t-3$ to $t-7)$, 2000 or after[b]	-0.0027	0.0008	-0.0021	-0.0023	-0.0030
	(0.0007)	(0.0004)	(0.0011)	(0.0009)	(0.0007)
$Q \times \%\Delta K(t-3$ to $t-7)$, 1999 or before[c]					-0.0013
					(0.0004)
Ratio of cash flow to capital stock	0.0168	0.0114	0.0058	0.0143	0.0168
	(0.0024)	(0.0017)	(0.0045)	(0.0033)	(0.0024)
Year dummies included	Yes	Yes	Yes	Yes	Yes
Firm dummies included	Yes	No	Yes	Yes	Yes
No. of observations	83,147	83,147	14,735	44,326	83,147
Adjusted R^2	.371	.035	.357	.337	.371

Source: Authors' regressions using data from Compustat.

a. The dependent variable in all regressions is the firm's investment rate, as defined in the text, in a given year. Q is tax-adjusted q as defined in table 5; K is the capital stock. Numbers in parentheses are standard errors clustered at the firm level.

b. Q times the change in the capital stock observed over the period three to seven years before the current year, where the current year is 2000, 2001, 2002, or 2003.

c. As above, where the current year is 1999 or before.

2002 (with a median value of past growth of 0.41). This value predicts that the coefficient on Q would fall by only 0.0037 (and only 0.0011 for the median). When we explicitly compare across firms by dropping the firm dummies (column 6-2), the point estimate becomes positive. Column 6-3 restricts the sample to information businesses as before; the coefficient on lagged capital growth, although slightly negative, is similarly modest. Column 6-4 repeats the analysis for manufacturing firms only and again finds similar results. Column 6-5 demonstrates that, with this measure of overhang, there is normally a small negative impact of lagged capital growth on current investment rates, even in the period before the 2000s. The difference in the coefficient between the 2000s and the pre-2000s period is only about 0.0017.

Taken together, the results in this section provide little evidence that capital overhang has played a key role in investment behavior in the 2000s. Low investment during the bust is not correlated strongly with excessive investment in the boom. Similarly, the sensitivity of investment in the 2000s to the fundamentals is not markedly different for firms overall or for those firms usually at the heart of the overhang view. In other words, the standard firm-level model using tax-adjusted q has not become noticeably worse at explaining investment. Accordingly, in the following section we use this model to analyze the impact of taxes.

q Theory, Investment Incentives, and Dividend Taxes: Theory and Empirics

As a prelude to using the tax-adjusted q model to study the impact of the Bush tax cuts, it is useful to consider the aggregate movements in q over the whole of the period that our firm sample covers, 1962–2003, in thinking about the root determinants of the behavior of aggregate investment in the 1990s and 2000s. Figure 4 plots average q for the corporate sector as a whole, measured as the total market value of all publicly traded firms as computed by CRSP (Center for Research in Security Prices) divided by the total stock of corporate capital as computed by the BEA in its fixed reproducible tangible wealth series. The series shows a historic rise in q in the mid-1990s and an unprecedentedly steep fall in the

Figure 4. Aggregate *q*, 1962–2002

Ratio[a]

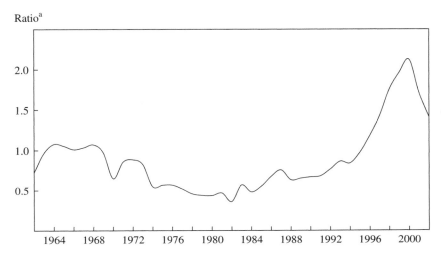

Source: Authors' calculations using BEA and Compustat data.
a. Ratio of the aggregate market value of all firms in the Compustat sample to the stock of corporate capital as computed by the BEA in its Fixed Reproducible Tangible Wealth series.

2000s.[23] Previous studies have found only very small coefficients on tax-adjusted *q,* and so this rise and fall in *q* might not imply much in the way of aggregate investment changes. We estimate the investment relationship, however, within a slightly different framework than is typical, to overcome possibly conflating measurement issues. It should be clear that, if the true coefficient on *q* for investment is not 0.02 but closer to 1, as argued below, the investment collapse is eminently comprehensible within the conventional framework. Clearly, within a standard *q* model of investment, an equity price bubble can still drive investment up and then down through movements in *q.* Such an account of the investment experience of the 1990s and 2000s is distinct from the intuition of a lingering overhang from the 1990s.

Of course, as critics have frequently pointed out, the fundamental question is why the coefficients on *q* in investment regressions are typically so low, implying extremely large adjustment costs. One of the key

23. A plot using the average of firm *q*s in our sample (not shown) yields a similar picture.

potential problems discussed in the literature has been the importance of measurement error in q. Marginal q is the variable of interest, but the data can provide only average q. At least some of the existing literature has argued that measurement error is at the root of the relatively weak empirical performance of traditional investment models.[24] This issue of measurement error is particularly important for thinking about the impact of taxation, as we demonstrate below.

If, in fact, an empirical implementation of the q model provides more reasonable coefficients through an alternative strategy of dealing with these measurement issues, then these estimates can serve as the foundation for analyses of the true marginal costs of adjustment and the impact of the various tax policy changes enacted during the Bush administration (the changes in depreciation allowances as well as the changes in dividend and capital gains taxes). The rest of this section undertakes such an analysis.

Tax-Adjusted q Theory, Dividend Taxes, and the Marginal Source of Funds

To use the q model to analyze the impact of taxes, particularly dividend taxes, we revisit the techniques for incorporating taxes into such models developed by Summers and by James Poterba.[25] A crucial issue in determining the impact of dividend taxes in this framework is what the marginal source of funds for firms' investments is. Briefly, if the marginal source of funds is retained earnings, then dividend taxes will have no impact on marginal investment incentives. But if the marginal source of funds is new equity, then dividend taxes will influence investment. This distinction is the subject of an enduring debate in public finance between the "new" and the "traditional" view of dividend taxation.

Appendix B works through the implications of the two views in some detail and provides alternative estimating equations. The investment model typically estimated in the literature follows the traditional view. In this view dividend taxes influence investment by, essentially, double-taxing corporate income. Assuming quadratic adjustment costs, this view generates the following investment-q relationship:

---

24. See, for example, Cummins, Hassett, and Hubbard (1994), Bond and Cummins (2000), and Goolsbee (2001).
25. Summers (1981); Poterba and Summers (1983, 1985).

(5)
$$\frac{I_t}{K_{t-1}} = \mu + \left(\frac{1}{\varphi}\right)\left(\frac{q_t}{1-\tau} - \frac{1-\Gamma}{1-\tau}\right),$$

where I is investment, K is the firm's capital stock, φ is the adjustment cost parameter, and μ represents an average investment rate. Under this assumption, net new equity finances investment, so that investment is determined by the point at which shareholders are indifferent between holding a dollar inside or holding it outside the firm. In a world without other taxes, the firm stops investing once $q = 1$. Of course, if investment is heavily subsidized (that is, if $\Gamma > \tau$), firms may even continue investing with $q < 1$, but the general idea is the same. Changes in dividend taxes will influence equity values and investment incentives by influencing the relative preference of investors to hold their money inside rather than outside the firm.

If, however, retained earnings are the marginal source of finance, the traditional investment-q relationship of equation 5 will not hold. In this case (again assuming quadratic adjustment costs), the relationship will follow

(6)
$$\frac{I_t}{K_{t-1}} = \mu + \left(\frac{1}{\varphi}\right)\left\{\left[\frac{q_t\left(\frac{1-c}{1-\theta}\right)}{1-\tau}\right] - \left(\frac{1-\Gamma}{1-\tau}\right)\right\},$$

where θ is the tax rate on dividends is and c is the accrual-equivalent tax rate on capital gains.

Equation 6 corresponds to the "new" (or "trapped equity" or "tax capitalization") view of the role of dividend taxation. In this view dividend taxes do *not* influence the tax term for marginal investments.[26] Instead they are fully capitalized into existing share prices. In other words, changes in dividend taxes serve solely as a penalty or windfall on existing firm values. To see the intuition behind this, consider a firm that uses retained earnings at the margin to finance investment, with dividends determined as a residual. In this model dividends are the only means of distributing earnings to shareholders. In this setting, given that retained

---

26. This view originates in the work of King (1977), Auerbach (1979), and Bradford (1981).

earnings are the marginal source of financing, investment is determined by the point at which shareholders are indifferent between receiving a dollar today as a dividend, with value $1 - \theta$, and having the dollar reinvested, yielding $(1 - c)q$. Accordingly, the firm will stop investing at the point $q = \dfrac{1 - \theta}{1 - c} < 1$ in a world of no other taxes, rather than at $q = 1$ as in the traditional case.

What is counterintuitive about the new view, as expressed in equation 6, is that although it argues that dividend taxes do not influence investment, the dividend tax rate appears in the investment equation. In contrast, equation 5, which exemplifies the traditional view, does not include a dividend tax term but corresponds to the view that dividend taxes do influence investment. The intuition for this is simply that, when dividend taxes get capitalized into share values, they influence q. This effect needs to be removed from the investment equation under the new view, because this part of q has no impact on investment. Alternatively, under the traditional view embodied in equation 5, a permanent dividend tax cut raises the value of q above 1, and this encourages further investment, just as any other increase in q does.

There is an old and contentious debate within public finance over which of these views is the more accurate. Proponents of the traditional view cite evidence on the effects of dividend tax rates on corporate dividend payout policy.[27] Furthermore, dividends seem more stable than the new view implies, and other means of distributing profits to shareholders, such as share repurchases, have become increasingly important. Proponents of the new view note that new equity issuances are still quite rare for most companies and that firms pay dividends even though dividends are tax disadvantaged. The arguments in this debate are considerably more involved than we can describe here.[28] Fundamentally, however, which view is more accurate is primarily an empirical matter. Surprisingly, except for the work on aggregate investment in the United King-

---

27. See the work of Poterba and Summers (1985), Chetty and Saez (2004), and Poterba (2004) and the papers they cite. Auerbach (2002) points out, however, that interpretation of the empirical evidence on this point is complicated by the fact that temporary cuts in dividend taxes should encourage dividend payouts, even under the new view.

28. Fuller assessments of both views can be found in Auerbach and Hassett (2003), Carroll, Hassett, and Mackie (2003), and Poterba and Summers (1985).

dom by Poterba and Summers,[29] there have been no direct attempts to test between the two views using investment data.

Poterba and Summers use thirty years of annual data from the United Kingdom to test between equations 5 and 6; their results support the traditional view. Although Alan Auerbach and Hassett have been critical of these findings for, among other things, failing to account for other macroeconomic and tax changes occurring at the same time,[30] these estimates are still the only direct empirical tests of how dividend taxes affect investment. Oddly, no one has extended the methods of Poterba and Summers to firm-level data, where it is possible to control for many aggregate factors. Nor has anyone ever applied their method to the United States, perhaps because, until the 2003 tax cut, U.S. dividend taxes did not change in isolation from other changes, but rather varied only through changes in personal income tax rates. Instead the empirical work testing the new versus the traditional view has adopted the indirect method of examining the relationship between dividend taxes and dividend payments (or the valuation of dividend payments by investors).[31]

The recent large changes in dividend taxes, however, make such an analysis possible. Indeed, testing between these two views (and making the required detour into the public finance debate) is critical for evaluating the impact of the Bush tax cuts on investment. If the marginal source of funds turns out to be retained earnings, the dividend tax cut will have little or no impact on marginal incentives to invest. Before explicitly testing between the two views, however, we lay out the basic tax-adjusted q model and illustrate why we believe measurement error is a primary reason that such models have implied high adjustment costs and have performed so poorly in the past.

Empirical Implementation of the Q Model

In computing q empirically, we use the historical and current Compustat database, which provides data on a panel of firms from 1962 through

29. Poterba and Summers (1983, 1985).

30. Auerbach (2002); Auerbach and Hassett (2003).

31. See, for example, Bernheim and Wantz (1995), Poterba (2004), Chetty and Saez (2004), and Poterba and Summers (1985), as well as the opposing evidence in Bolster and Janjigian (1991), Blouin, Raedy, and Shackelford (2004), and Ikenberry and Julio (2004).

2003.[32] For some firms we also match this sample to the earnings estimates provided by I/B/E/S (Institutional Brokers' Estimate System). Estimates of the tax term at the asset level are derived from data provided
generously by Dale Jorgenson.[33] As described in more detail in appendix A,
we follow Cummins, Hassett, and Hubbard and Robert Chirinko, Steven
Fazzari, and Andrew Meyer in using the BEA's capital flows table for
1997 to calculate the share of investment in each industry for each asset
type.[34] With that weighting, we calculate the weighted-average tax term in
each year for each four-digit industry in the Compustat data. Average
marginal tax rates on dividend and capital gains income (on an accrual
basis) are taken from Poterba.[35] Further discussion of the variable construction and the sources of data is provided in appendix A.

The measurement of q and, in turn, Q, hinges on constructing a measure
of the ratio of a firm's market value to its book value. The corporate finance
literature and the public finance literature have diverged somewhat in their
measurement of this ratio, and we consider both alternatives in the results
that follow. The corporate finance literature, as exemplified in the 1997
paper by Steven Kaplan and Luigi Zingales,[36] employs data from Compu-
stat to derive a measure of q as $\dfrac{BV\ Assets + (MV\ Equity - BV\ Equity)}{BV\ Assets}$,
where BV stands for book value and MV for market value, and all values
are taken from public financial records.[37] In contrast, the public finance
literature has emphasized the derivation by Salinger and Summers,[38]
which constructs q as $\dfrac{MV\ Equity + MV\ Debt}{MV\ Assets}$, where debt and equity
values are taken from financial reports, but the market value of assets is
imputed using perpetual inventory methods and valuations of inventory as
discussed in the data appendix to Cummins, Hassett, and Hubbard.[39]

---

32. Because of reporting conventions, the 2003 sample is somewhat smaller than the
sample in earlier years.
33. The data are described in more detail in Jorgenson and Yun (2001). Importantly,
the Jorgenson calculations do not take any future expectations of tax changes into account.
They use only the statutory tax rules for the year in question.
34. Cummins, Hassett, and Hubbard (1994); Chirinko, Fazzari, and Meyer (1999).
35. Poterba (2004).
36. Kaplan and Zingales (1997).
37. This numerator is also sometimes adjusted for deferred taxes.
38. Salinger and Summers (1984); see also Cummins, Hassett, and Hubbard (1994).
39. Cummins, Hassett, and Hubbard (1994).

Implicitly, this formulation takes the market value of debt to be its book value.

As with any firm-level analysis employing Compustat data to study investment, rules for considering extreme observations must be employed. Following studies such as that by Simon Gilchrist and Charles Himmelberg, we truncate our measures of q (and of investment and cash flow as a share of the capital stock) at the 1st and the 99th percentile.[40] Investment rates and cash flow rates are taken as the ratio of capital expenditure and operating cash flow before depreciation, respectively, to the capital stock.

Table 7 reports the results of estimating q models in our firm sample, under both of the two alternative definitions of q, as well as Q, that is, q adjusted for taxes, $\left(\dfrac{q_t}{1-\tau} - \dfrac{1-\Gamma}{1-\tau}\right)$. We postpone discussion of the relevance of dividend taxes, and so our estimating equation is equation 5 above, with and without consideration of taxes. Columns 7-1 and 7-4 of table 7 contrast the performance of the corporate finance and public finance measures of q without consideration of tax factors. Both coefficients are significant and positive, but the coefficient on the corporate finance q is much larger. Inspection of the public finance qs indicates that extreme values make up a large fraction of the sample and may contribute to this pattern. Comparison of columns 7-2 and 7-5 provides a similar result, with significantly larger coefficients on the corporate finance–based measure of Q. Nonetheless, the coefficients reflect the common difficulty in this literature, which is that these small coefficients translate into extremely high adjustment cost parameters (the inverse of the measured coefficient). Inclusion of both q and Q, in the specifications reported in columns 7-3 and 7-6, results in a similar pattern, but does indicate that tax-adjusted q outperforms q in explaining investment. This finding parallels the finding by Summers of the relevance of tax adjustments in improving the estimation of the q model.[41]

Given the relative performance of q and Q in the results reported in table 7, it is useful to consider separately the terms that make up Q to better understand the sources of the relatively small coefficients on Q. As discussed above, $Q = \dfrac{q_t}{1-\tau} - \dfrac{1-\Gamma}{1-\tau}$, and so the specifications in table 7 can

40. Gilchrist and Himmelberg (1998).
41. Summers (1981).

Table 7. Regressions Testing Sensitivity of the Firm-Level Investment-Q Relationship to q and Tax-Adjusted q Using Alternative Definitions[a]

Independent variable	Regressions using corporate finance definition of q			Regressions using public finance definition of q		
	7-1	7-2	7-3	7-4	7-5	7-6
q	0.0379		-0.1111	0.0007		-0.0030
	(0.0019)		(0.0174)	(0.0002)		(0.0018)
Q		0.0231	0.0863		0.0005	0.0023
		(0.0011)	(0.0102)		(0.0001)	(0.0010)
Ratio of cash flow to capital stock	0.0020	0.0006	0.0015	0.0003	-0.0013	-0.0013
	(0.0015)	(0.0015)	(0.0016)	(0.0015)	(0.0015)	(0.0016)
No. of observations	160,051	142,043	142,043	161,416	142,882	142,882
Adjusted R^2	.377	.376	.377	.368	.367	.367

Source: Authors' regressions using data from Compustat.

a. The dependent variable in all regressions is the firm's investment rate, as defined in the text, in a given year. Q is tax-adjusted q as defined in table 5. All regressions include year and firm dummies. Numbers in parentheses are standard errors clustered at the firm level.

naturally be recast to consider the separate effects for these two terms. Splitting Q in this manner has the advantage of allowing us to consider the role of measurement error in biasing the estimates previously obtained. More specifically, Cummins, Hassett, and Hubbard argue that mismeasurement of q means that using the estimated coefficients from standard investment regressions can dramatically understate the impact of investment taxes.[42] They emphasize large tax reforms as being times when the tax part of Q is not mismeasured, and they use these periods as the basis for comparing actual with projected investment. The specifications provided in table 7 take a simpler approach but in the same spirit. If measurement error in q is a problem, splitting Q into two parts has the advantage that the coefficient (or, more accurately, its absolute value) on the $\frac{1-\Gamma}{1-\tau}$ term should provide a better estimate of the true coefficient on q.[43]

Table 8 presents the results from splitting Q into its component parts. Specifically, the specification in the first column replaces Q with q scaled by 1 minus the corporate tax rate and terms for the equipment tax term and the structures tax term. It is difficult to measure a firm's relative investment in equipment and structures, and so we simply include both tax terms as separate regressors. Given the traditional difficulties in understanding the dynamics of incentives for investment in structures,[44] and given that equipment accounts for approximately 80 percent of corporate investment, we expect the equipment tax term to be much more precisely estimated. Controls for internal cash flow are included as well.

The key result from this table is that, although the q term remains small, the coefficient on the equipment tax term is considerably larger than typically estimated when just using Q and is close to 1 in absolute value.[45] The second column includes q without a tax adjustment and indicates, as with the results in table 7, that a tax-adjusted q term performs

---

42. Cummins, Hassett, and Hubbard (1994).

43. This assumes that the measurement errors are not correlated in the two series. We tried the same regressions in the exercise below, but excluding the q term and including only the tax terms, and found the coefficient on the tax term to be even slightly larger in absolute value, and so we are not as concerned about this issue.

44. See Auerbach and Hassett (1992).

45. We also tried including lagged q and tax term terms, but this had no impact on the results.

Table 8. Regressions Testing Sensitivity of the Firm-Level Investment-Q Relationship to Components of Tax-Adjusted q^a

Independent variable	Baseline regression	Including ordinary q in regression	Include controls for past depreciation allowances[b]	Include controls for debt shares[c]	Instrumental variables regression[d]
q/(1 − t)	0.0231	0.0858	0.0166	0.0245	0.2120
	(0.0011)	(0.0102)	(0.0011)	(0.0011)	(0.0054)
q		−0.1103			
		(0.0174)			
Tax term, equipment	−0.8895	−0.7865	−0.7078	−0.8949	−2.5351
	(0.3173)	(0.3162)	(0.2870)	(0.3163)	(1.1011)
Tax term, structures	−0.0169	−0.0064	−0.0333	−0.0127	−0.7902
	(0.0452)	(0.0453)	(0.0408)	(0.0450)	(0.2716)
Ratio of cash flow to capital stock	0.0005	0.0004	0.0090	0.0002	0.0170
	(0.0015)	(0.0015)	(0.0018)	(0.0015)	(0.0022)
No. of observations	141,629	141,629	111,059	141,245	46,154
Adjusted R^2	0.376	.377	.381	.378	—

Source: Authors' regressions using data from Compustat.
a. The dependent variable in all regressions is the firm's investment rate, as defined in the text, in a given year. All regressions include year and firm dummies. Numbers in parentheses are standard errors clustered at the firm level.
b. Controls for the present value of tax depreciation allowances on previously purchased investment, as described in appendix B.
c. Controls for the share of debt in firm financing.
d. Financial analysts' reported estimates of the firm's earnings are used as an instrument for firm q.

better than ordinary q. In this specification the coefficient on the equipment tax term remains significant and large. The third and fourth columns report two alternative robustness checks for these results that are modifications to the basic tax-adjusted q model. First, the theory does imply that the present value of tax depreciation allowances on previously purchased investment should be included in the value of the firm. This is frequently left out of empirical work on Q, since it is difficult to compute. In the third column we approximate the size of these tax shields as described in appendix A, and we add the value of these shields to the value of the firm in Q. This does not change the estimated results dramatically. We found this to be true for all of the major results in the paper, and, since computing the allowances requires reducing the sample by more than 30,000, we exclude them from the results that follow. Similarly, the model presented above follows most of the literature in assuming away any issues regarding debt financing. In the fourth column we incorporate the share of the firm's financing that comes from debt,[46] and the results are again similar.

The large coefficients on the tax term terms are worth dwelling on. First, the model predicts that these coefficients should be of the same magnitude as those on tax-adjusted q, but of opposite sign. Here, instead, the coefficients on the equipment tax term are considerably larger. With measurement error in q, the coefficient on the tax term may provide a more realistic estimate of the true coefficient. Such a coefficient is considerably closer to 1 and, consequently, corresponds to more realistic estimates of adjustment costs. Restricting attention to years with major tax reforms yielded similar estimates.[47]

To obtain some further evidence on the role of q mismeasurement as the reason for the small coefficient on the q term, we also modify the empirical strategy of Stephen Bond and Cummins,[48] within the framework of table 8. Their intuition is that earnings estimates by equity analysts as provided in the I/B/E/S database are a part of q that is based only on fundamentals.[49] Rather than use these estimates to create an alternative

46. Following Summers (1981).
47. These results are similar to findings by Cummins, Hassett, and Hubbard (1994).
48. Bond and Cummins (2000).
49. Cummins, Hassett, and Oliner (forthcoming) also look at investment equations that include analysts' earnings estimates.

q measure, however, we use them as instruments for q.[50] Employing the earnings estimates comes at considerable cost, given the shorter time frame covered by the I/B/E/S database (1983–2003) and the severely restricted number of firms covered by I/B/E/S. Nonetheless, we report in the fifth column of table 8 the results of this estimation. Several points are worth noting. First, as indicated by the tenfold increase in the coefficient on tax-adjusted q, mismeasurement of q seems important. Second, the coefficient on the equipment tax term rises considerably as well. Given the considerably smaller panel for these instrumental variables results, we rely on the coefficients on the equipment tax term term in the first column of table 8 as the best estimate of the true coefficient from a tax-adjusted q model. This analysis suggests that the true adjustment costs for investment are of plausible size, and so we use the model to estimate the impact of the Bush tax cuts. Finally, it is useful to consider whether the relevance of the q model is different in manufacturing industries, since many previous studies have restricted their sample to manufacturing. We prefer not to do this, since manufacturing accounts for only a small fraction of total investment. Table 9 replicates the analysis from the first column of table 8 and divides the sample. Although the reduced sample sizes reduce the power of these tests, the coefficients on the relevant tax term terms are quite similar in the two subsamples, suggesting that the model performs similarly well in both settings.

The Impact of Tax Cuts in the 2000s

During the George W. Bush administration two major changes have been made to the tax code to reduce taxes on capital. First, in 2003 the top capital gains tax rate was reduced from 20 percent to 15 percent, and the tax rate on most dividends was reduced from the ordinary personal income tax rate (which then had a maximum of 38.6 percent) to the capital gains tax rate. The second change substantially accelerated depreciation. In 2002 depreciation allowances for virtually all types of equipment investment were increased, as firms gained the right to immediately expense 30 percent of their purchases. In 2003 depreciation allowances

50. To be precise, we use the earnings estimates divided by $(1 - \tau)$ as an instrument for $q/(1 - \tau)$.

Table 9. Regressions Testing Sensitivity of the Firm-Level Investment-Q Relationship to Components of Q in Manufacturing and Nonmanufacturing Industries[a]

Independent variable	All industries	Manufacturing industries only	Nonmanufacturing industries only
$q/(1-t)$	0.0231	0.0210	0.0169
	(0.0011)	(0.0015)	(0.0011)
Tax term, equipment	−0.8895	−1.1545	−0.7034
	(0.3173)	(0.6943)	(0.2853)
Tax term, structures	−0.0169	−0.0035	−0.0307
	(0.0452)	(0.1762)	(0.0405)
Ratio of cash flow to	0.0005	0.0001	0.0090
capital stock	(0.0015)	(0.0022)	(0.0018)
No. of observations	141,629	68,680	111,059
Adjusted R^2	.376	.336	.381

Source: Authors' regressions using data from Compustat.

a. The dependent variable in all regressions is the firm's investment rate, as defined in the text, in a given year. All regressions are as specified in the first column of table 8. Numbers in parentheses are standard errors clustered at the firm level.

were increased again, as the fraction that could be immediately expensed increased to 50 percent. Each of these tax changes needs to be treated differently under the Q model.

Dividend Taxes

Although implementation of the dividend tax reduction was somewhat complex, essentially the maximum rate on dividends for individuals was reduced from the top rate on ordinary income (38.6 percent) to the capital gains tax rate (maximum of 15 percent). Advocates argued that this tax cut would reduce the tax term and stimulate business investment.[51] The Joint Committee on Taxation estimated that the dividend tax cut would reduce revenue by more than $100 billion from 2003 to 2008.[52] Given this high cost, it is worth assessing the impact of the cut. If the "new" view is correct, changes in dividend taxes have little or no impact on the cost of capital.

Table 10 reports results of our testing between the two views. In the first column we consider the relevance of dividend taxes by contrasting the predictions of equations 5 and 6 in one specification. The difference is

51. See Hederman (2004) and Larry Kudlow, "A Capital Idea from Microsoft," National Review Online, posted on July 23, 2004 (www.nationalreview.com/kudlow/kudlow200407230854.asp).

52. Joint Committee on Taxation (2003a).

Table 10. Regressions Testing Sensitivity of the Firm-Level Investment-Q Relationship to Capital Gains and Dividend Tax Rates[a]

	Sample period		
Independent variable	1961–2003	1961–1996	1997–2003
$q/(1 - t)$	−0.0158	−0.0067	−0.0652
	(0.0130)	(0.0154)	(0.0345)
$(1 - tcg)/(1 - tdiv) \times q/(1 - t)$[b]	0.0312	0.0241	0.0673
	(0.0105)	(0.0122)	(0.0291)
Tax term, equipment	−0.7795	−0.6258	0.748
	(0.3154)	(0.3219)	(2.6180)
Tax term, structures	−0.0081	−0.0237	9.464
	(0.0454)	(0.0459)	(2.7730)
Ratio of cash flow to capital stock	0.0004	0.0134	−0.0184
	(0.0015)	(0.0025)	(0.0023)
No. of observations	141,643	100,525	41,118
Adjusted R^2	.376	.426	.486

Source: Authors' regressions using data from Compustat.
a. The dependent variable in all regressions is the firm's investment rate, as defined in the text, in a given year. All regressions include year and firm dummies. Numbers in parentheses are standard errors clustered at the firm level.
b. tcg is the accrual-equivalent tax rate on capital gains and $tdiv$ the tax rate on dividends.

simply whether the q term is adjusted by the dividend tax preference parameter or not. In the empirical specification of the first column, we use all years for which we have firm data. The measure of q that is interacted with the $\left(\dfrac{1-c}{1-\theta}\right)$ term has a positive coefficient and is highly significant. The measure that is *not* interacted with the $\left(\dfrac{1-c}{1-\theta}\right)$ term is insignificant and actually has a negative coefficient. The two coefficients are significantly different from one another as well. In other words, although the marginal source of funds for these firms cannot be observed directly, their investment behavior is consistent with their treating retained earnings as the marginal source, and this implies that the new view is the correct one.

One major criticism of most previous analyses of the impact of dividend tax rates on investment and other economic behavior has been that changes in the rates themselves do not occur in isolation, but instead accompany changes in the top marginal rate on ordinary income.[53] In the later part of our sample, however (1997–2003), the tax changes that

53. See, for example, Auerbach (2002).

occurred are fairly specific in isolating the impact of dividend and capital gains taxes. In 1997 capital gains rates fell without any change in the top marginal income tax rate, and in 2003 both the capital gains rate and the dividend tax rate did so. This period, then, should be particularly instructive. For this reason (and because firm financing decisions may have changed over time with the rise of new equity issuances), we break the sample into the period before and the period including and after 1997. Results for these two subsamples are reported in the second and third columns of table 10. Both regressions show that the new view outperforms the traditional view, but the evidence is particularly strong for the later period.[54] Again, the evidence in all cases supports the new view and implies a small or negligible impact of dividend taxes on investment.

At the other extreme, in keeping with the discussion in Auerbach and Hassett, among others,[55] who have argued that the new view may apply for some firms and the traditional view for others, we calculate approximately how the dividend tax change would change the cost of capital if our findings were wrong and the traditional view held.[56]

Under the traditional view, the required after-tax rate of return r^* will be $r/[1 - p\theta - (1 - p)c]$, where r is the before-tax rate of return, p is the dividend payout rate, and c and θ correspond to the capital gains and dividend tax rates, respectively. The full cost of capital, assuming no inflation in the price of investment goods and a permanent change in tax policy, will then be $COC = (r^* + \delta)\left(\dfrac{1-\Gamma}{1-t}\right)$.

With a real interest rate of 5 percent, annual depreciation of 15 percent, a payout rate of 50 percent, and an accrual tax rate on capital gains equal to one quarter the statutory rate (as is commonly assumed in the literature), reducing the dividend tax from 38.6 percent to the level of the capital gains rate in 2003 for a fully taxable investor would be the

---

54. We also tried using only the personal tax rates from Poterba (2004) to take out any potential bias that the trends in corporate and nontaxable investor shares of dividends received might have on average marginal tax rates. This made no difference to our results and consistently showed evidence in favor of the new view. Note that our results are not identified by the level of the dividend tax term (which gets absorbed in the year dummies) but instead by the interaction with q.

55. Auerbach and Hassett (2002).

56. Carroll, Hassett, and Mackie (2003) simulate the impact in more detail under various assumptions.

equivalent of dividing the cost of capital by 1.035. The equipment tax term in 2003 was about 1.031, so this would have an effect on investment of approximately the same magnitude as converting the tax code to complete and immediate expensing of all equipment investment in 2003 (since dividing the tax term by 1.035 would yield a value of approximately 1, the same as immediate expensing). We will show in the next subsection, however, that changes to the tax term of that magnitude may not increase investment by much in the short run during this sample period.

The Impact of Partial Expensing

Although we find no impact of the dividend tax cuts on investment, the other tax incentives enacted during the early 2000s, specifically the depreciation allowance and partial expensing changes, directly reduced the tax term under either view of the dividend tax and should have stimulated investment. Their apparent failure to do so has led some to argue that tax policy is not effective.

MAGNITUDE OF THE CUTS. In 2002 President Bush signed a change in the tax code to allow for partial expensing of equipment; this change was made retroactive to cover all investment in 2002. In essence this rule change broke an investment into two parts. Thirty percent of the investment is immediately expensed. The remaining 70 percent is depreciated according to the normal schedule (which allows the firm to write off some portion in the first year, some portion in the second, and so on, for the tax life of the asset). Given that a fairly large share of the investment not being expensed already gets depreciated in the first year, this new law heavily weighted the depreciation allowances toward the first year.[57] In 2003 the law was changed again (and again made retroactive to cover investments made at any time during the year) to allow for first-year expensing of 50 percent of the investment. Although this provision was scheduled to expire at the end of 2003, it was extended to 2004 and may be extended further in the future—as of this writing, many legislators and commentators are arguing that it should be made permanent.

---

57. Cohen, Hassett, and Hansen (2002) provide a comprehensive analysis of the 2002 change.

These incentives were costly to provide, of course. The Joint Committee on Taxation estimated the cost of the changes in 2002 at about $35 billion and the cost of the higher expensing in 2003 and 2004 at about $32 billion and $53 billion, respectively.[58] Extending it indefinitely would presumably entail similar annual costs.

To estimate the effect of the changed investment incentives, we compute the increase in investment implied by the changes to depreciation allowances. The last two columns of appendix table A-1 report the change in the tax term from 2001 to 2003, averaged across industries at the three-digit NAICS level. The first column considers the overall change in the tax cost, and the second the change in the tax term for equipment only. Not surprisingly, the amounts differ across industries depending on the nature of the investment goods they purchase. Airlines, for example, invest mostly in equipment and mostly in long-lived assets such as aircraft. Long-lived assets that qualify for bonus depreciation receive the largest boost from allowing 50 percent immediate expensing (since they were depreciated over a longer period before) and thus provide the largest changes in the tax term. Firms in industries such as real estate and hotels invest little in equipment, and what equipment they buy tends to consist of computers and other short-lived assets for which immediate expensing is not as large an improvement.

The table shows that even these rather dramatic changes to the depreciation and expensing rules did not have a very large impact on the tax term. The average change in the equipment tax term across all firms is about 0.03 (0.02 after incorporation of the equipment share). Such a change is modest compared with changes such as the investment tax credit of 1962, its restoration in the early 1970s, or the increases in the depreciation allowance in 1981, all of which changed the overall tax term by around 0.10. Figure 5 depicts the industry-average equipment tax term over roughly the last half century and shows that the most recent changes in investment incentives have been modest by historical standards.

This relatively small effect stems from several factors. First, the value of an acceleration in depreciation allowances is a function of the corporate tax rate: with corporate tax rates already lower than they were in previous decades, altering depreciation schedules has a more muted effect. Second, the well-documented shift of investment toward computers and other

---

58. Joint Committee on Taxation (2002, 2003a, 2003b).

Figure 5. Aggregate Tax Term for Equipment,ᵃ 1950–2003

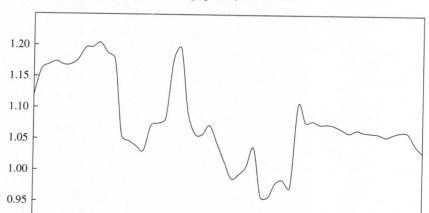

Source: Authors' calculations based on Jorgenson and Yun (2001).
a. Unweighted average of $q/(1-\tau) - (1-\Gamma)/(1-\tau)$ for 300 three-digit NAICS industries.

equipment with shorter lives has meant that accelerated depreciation provides less relief. The average net present value of depreciation allowances for equipment investment in 2001 was already approximately 90 percent of the investment value even before the tax cuts, suggesting that even complete expensing (raising the net present value to 1) would provide limited additional benefit. Given the smaller magnitude of the 2002 and 2003 cuts, it is unsurprising that such incentives could not overcome the dramatic drop in investment induced by the remarkable drop in q over the period. Our estimates suggest that these incentives do work as they are designed, but that their magnitude is simply too small to counteract the aggregate trend.

HOW MUCH DID THESE INCENTIVES INCREASE INVESTMENT? To estimate the precise impact of the tax changes on investment, we return to the tax-adjusted q model. To use that model to simulate the impact of the tax cuts in 2002 and 2003, we need to compute the transition path for investment in the standard q model.[59] Auerbach outlines a linearization that

---

59. See Abel (1981) and Summers (1981) for discussion.

makes this particularly easy,[60] and we adopt his notation to derive the predicted effects. Assuming a Cobb-Douglas production function with a capital share of $1 - a$, a real before-tax interest rate of r, quadratic adjustment costs of φ (the reciprocal of the true coefficient on Q in our regressions), and an adjustment cost-modified depreciation rate for capital in the firm of $\hat{\delta}$ (the specific formula for which is given below), Auerbach shows that, for an unanticipated permanent change in tax policy, the capital stock follows a simple partial adjustment model with $\dot{K}_t = \lambda_1(K^* - K_t)$, where K^* is the desired capital stock. The rate of adjustment $-\lambda_1$ follows the formula

(7)
$$\lambda_1 = \frac{r - \sqrt{r^2 + \dfrac{4a\left(r + \hat{\delta}\right)}{\varphi}}}{2}.$$

To compute this adjustment rate empirically, we assume a real interest rate of 5 percent. We compute a, the complement of the capital share, as 1 minus the gross output share of value added for each industry as reported in the disaggregated National Income and Product Accounts data for 1998. We take the true coefficient on Q to be 1, following the results above. We compute $\hat{\delta} = \delta[1 - (\varphi\,\delta)/2]$, using our value for φ and the industry-average depreciation rate on equipment or total investment, as computed from the weighted average by asset in the Jorgenson data using the industry weights in the capital flow table. This gives an annual adjustment rate for each firm. The average annual adjustment rate for all firms is about 33 percent, and the average value for each three-digit industry is given in appendix table A-1 (for structures and equipment as well as for equipment only). We then use the Cobb-Douglas production function to derive the optimal capital stock.[61]

---

60. Auerbach (1989).

61. Following the traditional literature, we make these calculations assuming that the elasticity of K^* with respect to the cost of capital is equal to -1, for a Cobb-Douglas production function for a given level of output. Such a figure is consistent with the empirical findings surveyed in Hassett and Hubbard (2002) but larger than the findings discussed in Chirinko (1993) or in Chirinko, Fazzari, and Meyer (1999). If labor were held fixed rather than output, our calculations would be scaled by $1/\alpha$, where α is the complement of the industry capital share (averaging about .66 to .70 in our data). To compute the total effect with varying output would require a full general equilibrium model for all sectors with industry-specific demand information. More details on the assumptions behind such calculations can be found in Coen (1969) and Hall and Jorgenson (1969).

To compute the effect of these policies over the past two years, we assume that the depreciation changes were unanticipated and thought to be permanent.[62] We first derive the optimal capital stock and amount of adjustment in the first year (2002). We then calculate the new optimal capital stock for 2003 (after the second tax cut) and the amount of adjustment based on the new gap between K^* and actual K (where actual K is higher than it was in 2001 because of the investment undertaken in 2002). Averaging for each three-digit industry and summing over the two years, we estimate the impact of the tax cuts on the capital stock for each industry (table 11). The average increase for the period is only about 1.0 to 1.5 percent, and so it is immediately clear why these tax cuts have seemed to have little success in stemming the investment declines: their short-run stimulus effect is too small. This is not a refutation of the view that taxes matter. The tax cuts were effective in changing incentives—they simply were not large enough to counteract the double-digit declines in investment rates observed in the 2000s. Changes to depreciation allowances simply do not have much impact when the system is already so close to full expensing and when aggregate declines in market value (and therefore in q) are so large. Since firms are moving asymptotically to the optimal capital stock, the effects of the policy change will be smaller in later years than in the first two years. After 2004 the average total increase will still be less than 2 percent.

Conclusion

This paper has addressed two major questions arising from the puzzling investment experience of the 2000s thus far: First, to what extent was the equity bubble of the 1990s correlated with the decline in investment in the 2000s? And second, why didn't the major tax cuts of 2002–03 do more to restore investment to normal levels?

---

62. That the changes were unanticipated is probably fairly accurate. An assumption of permanence seems reasonable, because although the changes were announced as temporary, from the moment they were passed many have been advocating that they be made permanent (and indeed the changes have already been extended to 2004). We assume permanence here because it considerably simplifies the computation of the investment path.

Table 11. Estimates of Change in Capital Stock Attributable to Tax Cuts of 2002 and 2003, by Industry

		Change in capital stock, 2002–03[a] *(percent)*	
NAICS code	*Industry*	*Using tax term for equipment and structures*	*Using tax term for equipment only*
481	Air Transp.	1.58	1.68
514	Information Servs. & Data Processing Servs.	1.47	1.79
492	Couriers & Messengers	1.44	1.52
561	Administrative & Support Servs.	1.43	1.63
213	Support Activities for Mining	1.42	1.61
487	Scenic & Sightseeing Transp.	1.42	1.63
488	Support Activities for Transp.	1.42	1.63
485	Transit & Ground Passenger Transp.	1.39	1.52
541	Professional, Scientific, & Technical Services	1.32	1.58
233	Building, Developing, & General Contracting	1.32	1.38
234	Heavy Construction	1.32	1.38
235	Special Trade Contractors	1.32	1.38
313	Textile Mills	1.31	1.58
314	Textile Product Mills	1.30	1.60
316	Leather & Allied Product Mfg.	1.30	1.54
323	Printing & Related Support Activities	1.30	1.57
322	Paper Mfg.	1.28	1.46
421	Wholesale Trade, Durable Goods	1.27	1.58
422	Wholesale Trade, Nondurable Goods	1.27	1.58
493	Warehousing & Storage	1.26	1.63
513	Broadcasting & Telecommunications	1.25	1.68
511	Publishing	1.25	1.55
114	Fishing, Hunting, & Trapping	1.25	1.68
621	Ambulatory Health Care Servs.	1.24	1.61
331	Primary Metal Mfg.	1.22	1.43
523	Securities, Commodity Contracts, & Other Fin.	1.20	1.59
334	Computer & Electronic Product Mfg.	1.19	1.58
321	Wood Product Mfg.	1.18	1.53
336	Transp. Equip. Mfg.	1.18	1.46
315	Apparel Mfg.	1.18	1.56
484	Truck Transp.	1.16	1.36
312	Beverage & Tobacco Product Mfg.	1.15	1.39
337	Furniture & Related Product Mfg.	1.14	1.50
332	Fabricated Metal Product Mfg.	1.12	1.35
524	Insurance Carriers & Related Activities	1.12	1.41
333	Machinery Mfg.	1.12	1.43
327	Nonmetallic Mineral Product Mfg.	1.11	1.35
339	Miscellaneous Mfg.	1.11	1.41
811	Repair & Maintenance	1.11	1.45
311	Food Mfg.	1.10	1.42
335	Electrical Equip., Appliance, & Component Mfg.	1.09	1.37

(*continued*)

Table 11. Estimates of Change in Capital Stock Attributable to Tax Cuts of 2002 and 2003, by Industry (*continued*)

		Change in capital stock, 2002–03[a] (percent)	
NAICS code	Industry	Using tax term for equipment and structures	Using tax term for equipment only
326	Plastics & Rubber Products Mfg.	1.07	1.29
622	Hospitals	1.03	1.82
324	Petroleum & Coal Products Mfg.	1.02	1.18
212	Mining (except Oil & Gas)	0.97	1.37
812	Personal & Laundry Servs.	0.95	1.43
113	Forestry & Logging	0.94	1.20
512	Motion Picture & Sound Recording	0.93	1.66
722	Food Servs. & Drinking Places	0.88	1.48
532	Rental & Leasing Servs.	0.86	1.00
325	Chemical Mfg.	0.86	1.28
522	Credit Intermediation & Related Activities	0.80	1.28
624	Social Assistance	0.77	1.59
482	Rail Transp.	0.73	1.39
562	Waste Management & Remediation Servs.	0.71	1.44
486	Pipeline Transp.	0.66	1.75
813	Religious, Grantmaking, Civic, Prof. & Similar	0.65	1.60
533	Lessors of Nonfin. Intangible Assets	0.63	1.10
111	Crop Production	0.61	0.70
444	Building Mtrl & Garden Equip. & Supplies	0.58	1.56
448	Clothing & Clothing Accessories Stores	0.58	1.56
443	Electronics & Appliance Stores	0.58	1.56
445	Food & Beverage Stores	0.58	1.56
442	Furniture & Home Furnishings Stores	0.58	1.56
447	Gasoline Stations	0.58	1.56
452	General Merchandise Stores	0.58	1.56
446	Health & Personal Care Stores	0.58	1.56
453	Miscellaneous Store Retailers	0.58	1.56
441	Motor Vehicle & Parts Dealers	0.58	1.56
454	Nonstore Retailers	0.58	1.56
451	Sporting Goods, Hobby, Book, & Music Stores	0.58	1.56
221	Utilities	0.56	1.36
623	Nursing & Residential Care Facilities	0.56	1.74
112	Animal Production	0.54	0.66
611	Educational Servs.	0.49	1.72
713	Amusement, Gambling, & Recreation	0.41	1.31
711	Performing Arts, Spectator Sports, & Related	0.38	1.54
211	Oil & Gas Extraction	0.26	1.48
525	Funds, Trusts, & Other Fin. Vehicles	0.18	1.46
721	Accommodation	0.18	1.46
531	Real Estate	0.03	0.72

Source: Authors' calculations using data from Compustat as described in appendix A.
a. Change in capital stock associated with changes in the expensing provisions by industry as described in the text.

The data at the firm, asset, and industry level do not support the popular explanation of how capital overhang affected the investment market in the 2000s. The general evidence shows that rapid growth of investment in the 1990s had very little correlation with the investment declines in the 2000s. The evidence further indicates that the firm-level relationship between investment and q has not changed noticeably in the recent period for firms that saw large increases in their market value or that invested heavily in the 1990s. Instead the rise and fall of equity prices, in the context of a conventional tax-adjusted q model that better accounts for measurement error in measuring marginal q, is the best explanation for the investment experience of the recent past.

This conventional tax-adjusted q model then serves as the basis for our analysis of the impact of the recent tax cuts and their seeming impotence. Our results show that the dividend tax cut, despite its high revenue cost, had minimal, if any, impact on marginal investment incentives. The results strongly favor the "new" view of dividend taxation, in which such taxes are capitalized into share prices and do not affect marginal incentives. Similarly, the partial expensing provisions passed in 2002 and 2003 were not large enough to provide much counterweight to the declines in aggregate investment. Our estimates suggest that tax policies contributed to an increase in the capital stock of only 1 to 2 percent.

APPENDIX A

Data Sources and Definitions

Firm-Level Financial Data

Annual data for all companies in the Compustat database, from 1950 on, are accessed through Wharton Research Data Services (WRDS).

Market Valuation of the Capital Stock

The Compustat series "Property, Plant, and Equipment—Total (Net)" is used as a measure of capital equipment; "Capital Expenditures (Statement of Cash Flows)" is used as a measure of capital expenditure. Each of these measures is converted to constant dollars by dividing by the current value of the producer price index (PPI) for capital goods, taken from the website of the Bureau of Labor Statistics.

Three factors enter into the current valuation of the capital stock. The first is changes in the prices of capital goods held over from previous years. Our conversion to constant dollars sidesteps this component. The second is additions to capital through investment expenditure. The third is depletion of capital on hand through depreciation.

The firm's current real capital stock can be thought of as the sum of the nondepreciated stocks of all previous years plus investment in the current year. Following Cummins, Hassett, and Hubbard (1994), and assuming a constant rate of depreciation δ, we calculate the current capital stock as

$$K_T = K_0(1 - \delta)^T + I_1(1 - \delta)^{T-1} + \ldots + I_{T-1}(1 - \delta) + I_T.$$

For example, the firm starts in period 0 with capital stock K_0, but only the nondepreciated part of this stock, $(1 - \delta)K_0$, remains to be carried over to the next period. Some of this carried-over capital is used up in producing output in the second period, leaving $(1 - \delta)^2 K_0$ to be carried over to the third period, and so forth. By period T, then, only $(1 - \delta)^T K_0$ is carried over from period 0. Similar reasoning explains the coefficients on the levels of investment carried over to period T from all previous years. I_T represents investment expenditure in period T.

Given the ending levels of the capital stock for all years, including the final year, and the final year's investment spending (all deflated by the PPI for capital goods), we can solve for the average rate of depreciation for each firm. This average rate of depreciation is then applied sequentially, from the first observed year for each firm to the last, to derive an estimated capital stock for each firm-year observation.

Conversion of Inventory from Book to Market Valuation

The Compustat series "Inventories—Total" is used as a measure of the current value of inventory holdings. As in Cummins, Hassett, and Hubbard (1994), we convert inventory levels from their book value to market value (on a last-in, first-out, or LIFO, basis) by adjusting the lagged book value of carried-over inventories for year-to-year changes in the prices of finished goods. How the adjustment mechanism is implemented depends on whether final inventories increase or decrease from one year to the next. If inventories increase, those goods carried over from the previous year are revalued at current prices, as is the net addition to total inventories:

$$\mathrm{Inv}_t^m = \mathrm{Inv}_{t-1}^m (P_t/P_{t-1}) + \Delta\mathrm{Inv}_t, \text{ if } \Delta\mathrm{Inv}_t \geq 0.$$

Essentially, under LIFO valuation rules, the ending levels of inventories include all goods that are carried over from the previous year plus unsold current production. All inventories carried into the current year remain at the end of the year and are revalued at current prices. The net addition to inventories is already measured at current prices and so needs no further adjustment.

On the other hand, if inventories decrease during the current year, it is assumed that all current production has been sold as well as some part of inventories carried over from the previous year. All goods remaining at the end of the year are then valued at current prices:

$$\mathrm{Inv}_t^m = (\mathrm{Inv}_{t-1}^m + \mathrm{Inv}_t - \mathrm{Inv}_{t-1})(P_t/P_{t-1})$$
$$= (\mathrm{Inv}_{t-1}^m + \Delta\mathrm{Inv}_t)(P_t/P_{t-1}), \text{ if } \Delta\mathrm{Inv}_t < 0.$$

Operating Income

The Compustat series "Operating Income before Depreciation" and "Operating Income after Depreciation" are used as measures of net income. Each was converted from nominal to real terms by dividing by the PPI for finished goods, taken from the website of the Bureau of Labor Statistics.

Analysts' Earnings Estimates

Consensus analysts' estimates of firms' earnings per share in future years were taken from the I/B/E/S summary statistics data maintained on WRDS. The variables in this file include the number of estimates and the mean, median, and standard deviation of estimates for a number of fiscal periods (quarters or years) into the future. We merged the Compustat firm-level financial data with the I/B/E/S firm-level analysts' estimates. We used the summary estimate made during the latest month before the end of the firm's fiscal year.

Asset-Level Tax Term

Data for the asset-level tax term come from Dale Jorgenson of Harvard University; his methodology is described in Jorgenson and Yun (2001). These data provide, for each asset type, an estimate of the net present value of depreciation allowances z, the investment tax credit rate, and the depreciation rate, as well as the capital stock and the average corporate tax rate. We compute Γ as ITC $+ tz$ and the full tax term as $(1 - \text{ITC} - tz)/(1 - t)$. The calculations are myopic in that they do not include the impact of expected future tax changes; current tax rates are assumed to be permanent. We modify the net present values of depreciation allowances in 2002 and 2003, to account for the changes in the partial expensing rules. We recomputed z, for 2002, using a 70-30 weighted average of the old z and 1; we do the same, but with 50-50 weights, for 2003.

Industry- and Firm-Level Tax Terms

To derive industry-level values of the tax term for equipment and structures as well as to derive industry-level depreciation rates, we use the 1997 capital flow tables of the BEA and compute the share of equipment and structures investment by asset type for each industry at approximately the three-digit NAICS level. We match these weights to the Jorgenson tax term figures by year for each asset type to compute a weighted-average tax term in each year for each industry. We then merge that series to each firm-year based on its first listed NAICS code in Compustat (table A-1).

Present Value of Depreciation Allowances on Past Investment

To estimate the value of A, the net present value (NPV) of depreciation allowances on past investments, we sort firms according to the weighted average of depreciation rates on the types of equipment in which firms in their industry invest. Using the inverse of this average depreciation rate as an estimate of the lifetime of the firm's capital, we assume that all firms in the industry have a discount rate of 10 percent and use double-declining-balance depreciation until straight-line depreciation exceeds it, and then switch to straight-line. We then multiply the NPV of the remaining depreciation allowances on investment from a given year in the asset's life by the investment-to-capital ratio lagged that many periods. For example, if the actual depreciation allowances for a three-year-lived good costing \$1 were one-third each year (pure straight-line depreciation), then the NPV of the allowances in the year of the investment would be $z_{age=0} = \left(.333 + \dfrac{.333}{1.1} + \dfrac{.333}{1.1^2} \right)$, the NPV of the allowances remaining one year later would be $z_{age=1} = \left(.333 + \dfrac{.333}{1.1} \right)$, and the NPV of allowances after two years would be $z_{age=2} = (.333)$. We would then compute the value of depreciation on previous investments as $A = t \left[z_{age=1} \left(\dfrac{I}{K} \right)_{t-1} + z_{age=2} \left(\dfrac{I}{K} \right)_{t-2} \right]$. Note that the NPV of depreciation allowances for current (time t) investment is not included in this measure (although it is in z); hence the computation of A for an industry whose asset life is three years has only two terms.

We compute the NPV assuming an asset life of three years for any firm for which the inverse of its average depreciation rate is between 3 and 4, four years for any firm for which the inverse is between 4 and 5, and so on, but with a cap at nine years (a few firms had average equipment lives of slightly over ten years).

Table A-1. Estimates of Adjustments to Tax Changes by Industry

NAICS code	Industry	Adjustment rate ($-\lambda_{1i}$)		Equipment share of total investment (percent)	Depreciation rate (δ)		Change in tax term, 2001–03	
		Equipment and structures	Equipment only		Equipment and structures	Equipment only	Equipment and structures	Equipment only
111	Crop Production	0.148	0.143	91	0.154	0.143	0.028	0.031
112	Animal Production	0.154	0.147	87	0.172	0.153	0.024	0.029
113	Forestry & Logging	0.318	0.304	85	0.164	0.145	0.022	0.027
114	Fishing, Hunting, & Trapping	0.272	0.262	81	0.106	0.094	0.033	0.043
211	Oil & Gas Extraction	0.315	0.252	21	0.172	0.091	0.007	0.033
212	Mining (except Oil & Gas)	0.300	0.286	82	0.135	0.118	0.023	0.030
213	Support for Mining	0.379	0.371	90	0.171	0.161	0.028	0.031
221	Utilities	0.240	0.207	58	0.140	0.092	0.019	0.038
233	Building, Developing, & Gen. Contracting	0.365	0.362	97	0.187	0.182	0.026	0.027
234	Heavy Construction	0.365	0.362	97	0.187	0.182	0.026	0.027
235	Special Trade Contractors	0.365	0.362	97	0.187	0.182	0.026	0.027
311	Food Mfg.	0.311	0.296	84	0.155	0.135	0.026	0.032
312	Beverage & Tobacco Product Mfg.	0.316	0.303	87	0.161	0.144	0.026	0.031
313	Textile Mills	0.335	0.324	88	0.128	0.117	0.029	0.034
314	Textile Product Mills	0.363	0.348	87	0.161	0.144	0.027	0.032
315	Apparel Mfg.	0.342	0.324	83	0.153	0.132	0.026	0.033
316	Leather & Allied Product Mfg.	0.344	0.332	89	0.156	0.142	0.028	0.032
321	Wood Product Mfg.	0.334	0.319	84	0.142	0.124	0.026	0.033
322	Paper Mfg.	0.307	0.301	93	0.135	0.128	0.030	0.033
323	Printing & Related Support	0.356	0.343	88	0.163	0.147	0.027	0.032
324	Petroleum & Coal Products Mfg.	0.243	0.237	91	0.155	0.144	0.030	0.033
325	Chemical Mfg.	0.286	0.268	80	0.180	0.150	0.022	0.030
326	Plastics & Rubber Products Mfg.	0.300	0.290	88	0.133	0.121	0.026	0.030
327	Nonmetallic Mineral Product Mfg.	0.302	0.291	88	0.154	0.139	0.027	0.031
331	Primary Metal Mfg.	0.345	0.332	88	0.156	0.141	0.026	0.030

Code	Industry							
332	Fabricated Metal Product Mfg.	0.339	0.328	89	0.162	0.147	0.024	0.029
333	Machinery Mfg.	0.371	0.353	85	0.196	0.171	0.023	0.029
334	Computer & Electronic Product Mfg.	0.395	0.377	86	0.212	0.186	0.024	0.030
335	Elect. Equip., Appliance, & Component Mfg.	0.327	0.312	86	0.166	0.147	0.025	0.030
336	Transp. Equip. Mfg.	0.366	0.353	88	0.171	0.155	0.024	0.029
337	Furniture & Related Product Mfg.	0.345	0.327	83	0.152	0.131	0.025	0.031
339	Miscellaneous Mfg.	0.334	0.320	86	0.162	0.144	0.024	0.029
421	Wholesale Trade, Durable Goods	0.402	0.383	86	0.208	0.183	0.024	0.029
422	Wholesale Trade, Nondurable Goods	0.402	0.383	86	0.208	0.183	0.024	0.029
441	Motor Vehicle & Parts Dealers	0.397	0.320	48	0.198	0.108	0.013	0.029
442	Furniture & Home Furnishings Stores	0.397	0.320	48	0.198	0.108	0.013	0.029
443	Electronics & Appliance Stores	0.397	0.320	48	0.198	0.108	0.013	0.029
444	Building Mtrl, Garden Supplies Dealers	0.397	0.320	48	0.198	0.108	0.013	0.029
445	Food & Beverage Stores	0.397	0.320	48	0.198	0.108	0.013	0.029
446	Health & Personal Care Stores	0.397	0.320	48	0.198	0.108	0.013	0.029
447	Gasoline Stations	0.397	0.320	48	0.198	0.108	0.013	0.029
448	Clothing & Clothing Accessories Stores	0.397	0.320	48	0.198	0.108	0.013	0.029
451	Sporting Goods, Book, & Music Stores	0.397	0.320	48	0.198	0.108	0.013	0.029
452	General Merchandise Stores	0.397	0.320	48	0.198	0.108	0.013	0.029
453	Miscellaneous Store Retailers	0.397	0.320	48	0.198	0.108	0.013	0.029
454	Nonstore Retailers	0.397	0.320	48	0.198	0.108	0.013	0.029
481	Air Transp.	0.313	0.309	96	0.124	0.121	0.036	0.038
482	Rail Transp.	0.288	0.253	59	0.097	0.064	0.020	0.034
484	Truck Transp.	0.350	0.339	90	0.184	0.169	0.025	0.028
485	Transit & Ground Passenger Transp.	0.367	0.360	94	0.192	0.182	0.028	0.030
486	Pipeline Transp.	0.336	0.273	48	0.177	0.098	0.017	0.037
487	Scenic & Sightseeing Transp.	0.391	0.377	90	0.193	0.176	0.027	0.031
488	Support for Transp.	0.391	0.377	90	0.193	0.176	0.027	0.031
492	Couriers & Messengers	0.402	0.397	96	0.209	0.202	0.027	0.028
493	Warehousing & Storage	0.383	0.364	84	0.180	0.156	0.025	0.031
511	Publishing Indus.	0.400	0.381	86	0.272	0.238	0.024	0.029
512	Motion Picture & Sound Recording	0.386	0.342	67	0.196	0.140	0.019	0.031

(continued)

Table A-1. Estimates of Adjustments to Tax Changes by Industry (continued)

NAICS code	Industry	Adjustment rate$(-\lambda_{ij})$ Equipment and structures	Equipment only	Equipment share of total investment (percent)	Depreciation rate (δ) Equipment and structures	Equipment only	Change in tax term, 2001–03 Equipment and structures	Equipment only
513	Broadcasting & Telecommunications	0.278	0.246	65	0.146	0.103	0.032	0.041
514	Info Servs. & Data Processing Servs.	0.448	0.428	87	0.258	0.228	0.026	0.030
522	Credit Intermediation & Related	0.347	0.311	72	0.276	0.206	0.018	0.026
523	Securities, Commodity Contracts, & Other	0.439	0.411	82	0.272	0.227	0.022	0.027
524	Insurance Carriers & Related	0.389	0.368	85	0.270	0.233	0.022	0.027
525	Funds, Trusts, & Other Financial Vehicles	0.419	0.260	19	0.296	0.077	0.005	0.026
531	Real Estate	0.182	0.097	5	0.193	0.026	0.002	0.027
532	Rental & Leasing Servs.	0.227	0.218	88	0.194	0.173	0.026	0.030
533	Lessors of Nonfinancial Intangible Assets	0.250	0.220	68	0.249	0.178	0.020	0.030
541	Professional, Scientific, & Technical Servs.	0.404	0.385	86	0.249	0.218	0.025	0.028
561	Administrative & Support Servs.	0.412	0.400	91	0.209	0.193	0.026	0.029
562	Waste Management & Remediation Servs.	0.352	0.307	61	0.190	0.131	0.016	0.029
611	Educational Servs.	0.447	0.340	41	0.214	0.099	0.010	0.029
621	Ambulatory Health Care Servs.	0.367	0.347	83	0.181	0.154	0.026	0.032
622	Hospitals	0.409	0.363	68	0.166	0.119	0.021	0.033
623	Nursing & Residential Care Facilities	0.414	0.328	44	0.172	0.087	0.012	0.031
624	Social Assistance	0.419	0.357	59	0.206	0.132	0.016	0.028
711	Performing Arts, Spectator Sports	0.365	0.273	36	0.192	0.084	0.010	0.031
713	Amusement, Gambling, & Recreation	0.346	0.277	43	0.165	0.087	0.010	0.027
721	Accommodation	0.334	0.232	20	0.160	0.052	0.005	0.031
722	Food Servs. & Drinking Places	0.382	0.343	69	0.171	0.126	0.018	0.028
811	Repair & Maintenance	0.368	0.342	78	0.175	0.142	0.023	0.028
812	Personal & Laundry Servs.	0.386	0.353	75	0.199	0.155	0.019	0.027
813	Religious, Grantmaking, Civic, Profess.	0.402	0.329	52	0.222	0.128	0.014	0.029

Source: Authors' calculations using data from Compustat.

Note that our measure is an approximation because it assumes that tax law remains unchanged over the whole sample period. In other words, the NPV of depreciation allowances on current investment, z, that we get from Jorgenson varies over time, but we do not have the entire depreciation schedules on which each z is based, and so we cannot let the calculation vary for A. We tried many different ways of computing A, for example adopting different assumptions about depreciation methods, different discount rates, and so on, and found they had negligible impact on the regression results.

APPENDIX B

Tax-Adjusted q with Dividend Taxes

WE BEGIN BY establishing the equilibrium condition that shareholders receive their required return, r, from holding equity that provides taxable dividends and capital gains, so that

(B1) $$rV_t = (1 - \theta)D_t + (1 - c)\{E_t[V_{t+1}] - V_t - V_t^N\},$$

where θ is the tax rate on dividends and c is the accrual-equivalent tax rate on capital gains. D_t denotes dividends paid to shareholders in period t, V is equity value, and V_t^N denotes equity contributions made in period t. Given that dividends and capital gains are alternative forms of returns to shareholders, it is useful to summarize the relative tax penalty on dividends and capital gains with the dividend tax preference parameter γ:

(B2) $$\gamma = (1 - \theta)/(1 - c).$$

Given that capital gains taxes are paid only when the gain is realized, γ is considered to be less than 1.[63] Solving equation B1 forward, and imposing the transversality condition that firm value cannot be infinite in a finite period, provides a value equation for the firm that implies

(B3) $$V_0 = \sum_{t=0}^{\infty} \beta_t E_0(\gamma D_t - V_t^N),$$

---

63. Even with similar rates on dividends and realized capital gains, $\gamma < 1$ is thought to hold. Typically, the accrual-equivalent c is usually taken as one-quarter of the statutory rate applicable to capital gains.

where β is the appropriate after-tax discount factor. Equation B3 corresponds to the straightforward intuition that firm value at time 0 is the present-discounted, tax-adjusted value of all future dividends, taking into account any equity contributions required to maintain a proportional shareholding in the firm.

Firm value maximization is subject to several constraints. Dividends and equity issuance are constrained to be nonnegative.[64] The firm's capital stock K evolves according to

$$(\text{B4}) \qquad\qquad K_t = K_{t-1}(1 - \delta) + I_t,$$

where δ is a constant proportional rate of decay and I is investment. The underlying cash flow identity for the firm is given by

$$(\text{B5}) \qquad\qquad (1 - \tau)[F(K_t, L_t) - w_t L_t - C(I_t, K_{t-1})p_t] \\ + V_t^N + \tau A_t = D_t + I_t p_t(1 - \Gamma_t),$$

where τ is the statutory corporate tax rate, $F(K, L)$ is firm output, L is labor, w is the wage rate, $C(I_t, K_{t-1})$ is an adjustment cost function for investment, and τA captures the tax value of depreciation allowances on previous investments. Variable p is the price of capital goods relative to output, and Γ is a summary measure of tax provisions that directly influence investment, such as the tax value of depreciation allowances and investment tax credits. The source and measurement of Γ are described in appendix A. In short, equation B5 states that a firm's after-tax cash flow and its new equity issuances are sources of funds, which are used for investment and for paying dividends, and the ps ensure that all terms are properly price adjusted.[65]

Given the expression for firm value in equation B3 and the constraints discussed above, firm value maximization employs the following Hamiltonian equation:

$$(\text{B6}) \qquad H_t = \gamma D_t - V_t^N - \lambda_t^1[K_t - K_{t-1}(1 - \delta) - I_t] - \lambda_t^2 D_t - \lambda_t^3 V_t^N.$$

---

64. As Poterba and Summers (1985) note, repurchases can be allowed without loss of generality. However, negative new equity issuances must be bounded by some maximum amount, an assumption justified by the IRS's ability to characterize large, regularized repurchases as dividends.

65. We abstract from debt and the presence of tax-deductible interest without loss of generality.

In this setting, λ_t^1, λ_t^2, and λ_t^3 correspond to the shadow values of capital goods, dividends, and negative equity issuances, respectively. Substituting the value of dividends from the cash flow identity in equation B5, we can rewrite equation B6 as

(B7)
$$H_t = (\gamma - \lambda_t^2)\{(1 - \tau)[F(K, L) - wL - C(I_t, K_{t-1})p_t] \\ + V_t^N + I_t p_t(1 - \Gamma) + \tau A_t\} - V_t^N - \lambda_t^1[K_t - K_{t-1} \\ (1 - d) - I_t] - \lambda_t^3 V_t^N.$$

Differentiating this Hamiltonian provides the relevant first-order conditions. The first-order condition for investment is provided by

(B8)
$$-(\gamma - \lambda_t^2)(1 - \tau)C_I p_t - p_t(1 - \Gamma) + \lambda_t^1 = 0,$$

and the conditions for dividends and net equity issuance are provided by

(B9)
$$D_t \geq 0; \, \lambda_t^2 \geq 0; \text{ and } D_t \lambda_t^2 = 0$$

and

(B10)
$$V_t^N \geq 0; \, (\gamma - \lambda_t^2 - 1 - \lambda_t^3) \geq 0; \text{ and } V_t^N(\gamma - \lambda_t^2 - 1 - \lambda_t^3) \\ = 0, \text{ respectively.}$$

Rearranging the investment first-order condition provided in equation B8 provides an expression for q that corresponds to the shadow price for capital:

(B11)
$$(\lambda_t^1/p_t) = q_t = (\gamma - \lambda_t^2)[(1 - \tau) C_I + (1 - \Gamma)],$$

where C_I is the marginal adjustment cost of new investment. In order to put this in more familiar terms, we specify a conventional, quadratic adjustment cost function:

(B12)
$$C(I_t, K_{t-1}) = (\varphi/2)[(I_t/K_{t-1}) - \mu]^2 K_{t-1},$$

where φ is the adjustment cost parameter and μ represents an average investment rate. This quadratic adjustment cost function allows us to represent equation B11 in more familiar terms. Differentiating the cost function with respect to I and substituting it into equation B11 yields

(B13)
$$\frac{I_t}{K_{t-1}} = \mu + \left(\frac{1}{\varphi}\right)\left(\frac{\dfrac{q_t}{\gamma - \lambda_t^2} - (1 - \Gamma)}{1 - \tau}\right).$$

Equation B13 is the basic estimating equation commonly used in the q-theory literature, with the slight peculiarity that q_t is divided by $(\gamma - \lambda_t^2)$. In the existing literature and our discussion below, $\left[\dfrac{q_t - (1 - \Gamma)}{1 - \tau} \right]$ is also referred to as Q rather than q. It will be important in our discussion of measurement error to note that Q is actually composed of two parts, associated with investment opportunities and taxes.

In order to consider under what conditions the additional, peculiar term disappears, it is critical to specify the marginal source of financing. To do so we return to the conditions B9 and B10 and consider the alternative cases where the marginal source of financing is either retained earnings or new equity issuance.

First, consider the case where the marginal source of finance is new equity issuances. In this case, $\lambda_t^3 = 0$ and, consequently, $\lambda_t^2 = \gamma - 1$, as indicated by equation B10. In this case equation B13 becomes its more familiar variant:

$$(B14) \qquad \frac{I_t}{K_{t-1}} = \mu + \left(\frac{1}{\varphi} \right)\left(\frac{q_t}{1 - \tau} - \frac{1 - \Gamma}{1 - \tau} \right).$$

Now consider the alternative case where the marginal source of finance is retained earnings rather than new equity issuance. This implies that dividends are positive and that $\lambda_t^2 = 0$. In turn, this implies that equation B13 can be rewritten as

$$(B15) \qquad \frac{I_t}{K_{t-1}} = \mu + \left(\frac{1}{\varphi} \right)\left\{ \left[\frac{q_t\left(\frac{1 - c}{1 - \theta} \right)}{1 - \tau} \right] - \left(\frac{1 - \Gamma}{1 - \tau} \right) \right\}.$$

Equations B14 and B15 provide alternative q-theory specifications for investment that incorporate different assumptions about the marginal source of finance and, consequently, about the role of dividend taxation in influencing investment.

Comments and
Discussion

Kevin A. Hassett: This paper by Mihir Desai and Austan Goolsbee examines the impact of recent corporate tax changes on investment behavior and investigates the impact of a possible capital overhang on investment. Since my fellow discussant will focus on the overhang issue, I will concentrate my remarks on the tax and investment side of the paper.

To summarize my conclusions: The paper is a good, state-of-the-art econometric effort that confirms many of the findings of the recent investment literature. The regression results are competently arrived at and believable. However, the authors' policy discussion and their discussion of the impact of recent tax reforms offer conclusions that do not follow from their results. In relating their results to the impact of current policies, the authors have favored some extreme assumptions that are not supported by their empirical work, all aligned in a manner to make the tax cuts seem ineffective. A more balanced assessment of the recent impact of the tax reforms would certainly be more favorable.

A LOOK AT THE LITERATURE. The first of the recent corporate tax changes reduced the user cost of capital by allowing firms to expense a fraction of their capital purchases. This expensing has been "temporary" from the outset, although there has been significant uncertainty about whether the expensing provisions would be allowed to expire. There is little dispute that this tax change will lower the user cost of capital. In a recent paper in the *National Tax Journal,* my coauthors and I found that this reduction would vary by asset class, averaging about 2 to 3 percent, if the change were viewed as permanent and if the expensing fraction were the original, lower number.[1] If instead the provision were expected

---

1. Cohen, Hansen, and Hassett (2002).

339

to expire, firms would have an incentive to shift investment forward. We found that this effect would reduce the current user cost by much more.

The second change was to lower the tax rate on dividends and capital gains. The effect of this change on the user cost depends on the marginal source of finance. In another recent paper, my coauthor and I found that approximately half of all firms behave as if they use new share issues as their marginal source of finance,[2] and approximately half behave as if they use retained earnings. Accordingly, relying on a third recent paper, in which my coauthors and I modeled the impact of dividend tax law changes,[3] I find that the reduction attributable to the recent changes would be quite large under the "old view" of dividend taxation and much smaller under the "new view." However, these conclusions depend crucially on unobservables. The most important of these are the marginal tax rates on dividends and on capital gains, which in turn depend on the nature of financial equilibrium. If, for example, a "Miller equilibrium" describes the world, the relevant rates are those at which the marginal investor is just indifferent between debt and equity, not the average observed rate. Across a range of assumptions, however, the dividend change reduces the cost of capital by about 7 percent on average, assuming that firms themselves are split 50-50 between the old and the new views.

More recent evidence consistent with the idea that there exist both old and new view firms includes work by James Poterba,[4] who has found that dividend payout responds significantly to tax changes, and by Raj Chetty and Emmanuel Saez,[5] who found that dividend payouts increased sharply after the recent change in the law. In a work in progress, Alan Auerbach and I are exploring share price responses to the dividend change and finding results that confirm the conclusions in our earlier paper. There thus appears to be a great deal of heterogeneity in the data, with some firms behaving according to the old view and some according to the new view.

Whether these changes would result in a stimulus to investment depends on the elasticity of investment with respect to the user cost. Glenn Hubbard and I, in our chapter in the *Handbook of Public Economics,* concluded that the literature is now leaning toward a relatively large elasticity.

2. Auerbach and Hassett (2002).
3. Carroll, Hassett, and Mackie (2003).
4. Poterba (2004).
5. Chetty and Saez (2004).

A number of recent papers have strengthened support for the conclusion that neoclassical fundamentals are important, by overturning past findings that cash flow is a much more important determinant of investment than the user cost or *Q*. For example, in a forthcoming paper, my coauthors and I find that cash flow does not matter in investment equations once one controls for measurement error in *Q*.[6] Thus liquidity constraints should not, the literature suggests, mute the possible effects of tax cuts.

THIS PAPER IN RELATION TO THE LITERATURE. This paper provides a very clear view of where the empirical investment literature is at the moment. The authors find that, once one controls for measurement problems, fundamentals such as taxes are hugely important in investment equations. Indeed, in most of their specifications, the estimated coefficient for the tax term is close to or exceeds 1 in absolute value. Confirming the findings of Jason Cummins, Stephen Oliner, and myself,[7] they also find that cash flow does not influence investment over and above the fundamentals.

The paper breaks from the literature in only one way. Using the same data as much of the previous literature, the authors follow an empirical strategy much like that of Poterba and Lawrence Summers in their seminal paper on the old and new views.[8] They reverse the Poterba and Summers result and find that the new view cost of capital explains investment. This departs significantly from the recent literature that has used dividend rather than investment behavior to assess the relative importance of the two views.

Their result favoring the new view is not very convincing, however. For one thing, they favor the new view on the basis of parameter estimates that are interacted with the *Q* variable, which the authors themselves concede is mismeasured. The new view *Q* estimate is slightly less absurd than the old view *Q* estimate, but both are an order of magnitude smaller than the coefficients on the separate tax terms. If the coefficients were the same as those on the tax terms, one might have more confidence in the results.

In addition, there is serious doubt that Desai and Goolsbee's approach has any power to distinguish between the two views. What mainly distinguishes the two models is a *marginal* tax wedge variable that is unobservable but approximated by an *average* taken from tax returns. That should

6. Cummins, Hassett, and Oliner (forthcoming).
7. Cummins, Hassett, and Oliner (forthcoming).
8. Poterba and Summers (1983).

Figure 1. Investor Tax Preference for Dividends versus Capital Gains, 1929–2003

Aggregate dividend tax preference parameter $(\theta)^a$

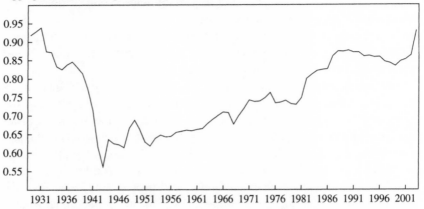

Source: Poterba (2004).

a. $\theta_t = \Sigma w_{h,t} * [(1-\tau_{div,h,t})/(1-\tau_{cg,h,t})]$, where $w_{h,t}$ is the share of corporate stock owned at time t by investor h, and τ_{div} and τ_{cg} are the marginal tax rates on dividends and long-term capital gains, respectively. Calculations assume that the effective capital gains tax rate is only one-quarter the statutory rate.

give one pause. Second, the tax wedge variable does not vary across firms. This means that the authors have *no* within variation to identify the two models, and they have very few real degrees of freedom. The correlation between the two relevant variables must be enormous—within a given year it is unity. Add year effects, and it is something of a miracle that their computer did not crash. It did not *only* because of the interaction with the noisy Q variable. That the two variables enter with opposite-signed co-efficients suggests that the design matrix may be ill conditioned, and this raises red flags. This is exactly why other recent empirical attempts to evaluate the relative importance of the two views have not attempted to do so with investment data.

Moreover, the tax wedge variable mostly follows a steady upward trend during this period (figure 1). Indeed, over the period observed in the paper, in only two years (1982 and 2003) did the variable deviate more than 5 percent, positively or negatively, from its value in the previous year. The explanation of the results may simply be a spurious trend relationship.

Or maybe not. It is quite uncertain whether this average wedge is the appropriate measure. It might be just as reasonable to use statutory tax rates for dividends. Indeed, one of the more interesting aspects of the recent tax changes is that the marginal dividend tax rate is no longer one of any number of tax rates but instead is a known parameter. We do not know what it is until the last observation. The accrual-equivalent capital gains tax rate is also a guesstimate. Do the results change if other, equally valid measures are used? The authors are too confident that they have the correct measure of the crucial variable.

Thus, where the paper agrees with the literature, it is on firm ground. Its disagreements with the literature may just be the result of poor design.

DID THE RECENT TAX CHANGES STIMULATE INVESTMENT? Given the authors' finding that tax variables affect investment, one might expect that they would conclude that the recent tax changes had a major impact on investment. They conclude otherwise for two reasons. First, they offer a misguided view of the recent data. Second, they greatly understate the user cost effects of the recent tax changes, and hence find a small impact on investment. I will respond to each of these in turn.

The authors argue that investment has not increased after these tax changes, but the chart they present in making this case is rather misleading. Equipment investment surged after the dividend tax cut (figure 2). We do not know yet whether this happened because of the cut, but surge it did. The authors conclude that it did *not* respond to tax policy only by cyclically adjusting the chart. But the current recovery may have been slower than past recoveries for a number of reasons unrelated to investment policy. The key question is, Did investment policy stimulate investment, ceteris paribus? The regressions that the authors run are not cyclically adjusted, nor should the prima facie evidence be. The authors appear to presume that a pro-investment policy can be judged successful only if it immediately returns investment to a point beyond its previous cyclically adjusted peak. I can think of no coherent rationale for such a view.

The authors understate the user cost reductions for two main reasons. First, they accept their own estimates and assume that all firms adhere to the new view. In doing so they neutralize most of the user cost effect of the recent dividend and capital gains tax cuts. Second, they assume that investors ignore the scheduled 2004 expiration of the partial expensing provision and instead assume that it will remain in effect. Recall that, if the provision does not expire, the user cost effects of the combined policies sum to about 9 to 10 percent. Given the authors' estimates, such a decline is an impressive stimulus.

Figure 2. Gross Private Domestic Investment in Software and Equipment, 1994–2004

Billions of chained 2000 dollars

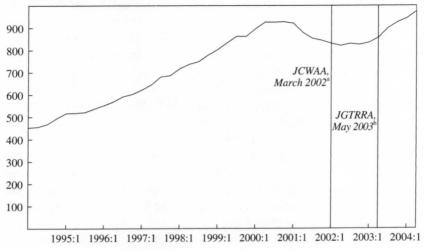

Source: National Income and Product Accounts.
a. Job Creation and Worker Assistance Act, which established a 30 percent depreciation bonus.
b. Jobs and Growth Tax Relief Reconciliation Act, which raised the depreciation bonus to 50 percent and cut dividend tax rates.

For partial expensing, the expiration is a big deal. For example, for seven-year-lived equipment, the percentage reduction in the Jorgensonian user cost in an expiration year (with only 30 percent partial expensing) is about 14 percent.[9] By assuming that the measure does not expire, the authors load the case in favor of their conclusion that, despite the high investment elasticity, the recent tax cuts had no effect. Using their coefficients and the more reasonable assumption that the expensing provision is expected to expire, one could just as easily generate, from their own model, a predicted 20 percent increase in equipment investment this year. And investment has been increasing sharply, supporting, casually at least, the view that policy has had the effect that the empirical evidence would predict. Their conclusions about the efficacy of current tax policy are likely the reverse of the truth.

9. Cohen, Hansen, and Hassett (2002, table 2).

CONCLUSION. The empirical evidence that the paper presents with regard to investment and the user cost supports the earlier literature in numerous ways and will likely be cited often as a competent and up-to-date estimation effort. The conclusions with regard to the new view versus old view debate differ from those of the earlier literature, but questions about the authors' specification suggest that the optimal Bayesian weight on these results is fairly low. In discussing policy, the authors' assumptions lead to an understatement of the user cost effects. Contrary to their claims, the evidence supports the view that the recent tax cuts likely had a significant impact on investment.

John V. Leahy: Mihir Desai and Austan Goolsbee have written a very interesting and provocative paper on the recent downturn in investment spending in the United States. In fact, they have written two papers. The first deals with one commonly attributed cause of the downturn, namely, "capital overhang." The second investigates the success of one of the intended solutions to this problem, namely, the Bush tax cuts. Sticking to my comparative advantage, I will address my comments to the paper on capital overhang.

Briefly stated, Desai and Goolsbee make two claims. First, they claim that there is little evidence of capital overhang in the cross section. To back this claim, they show that high investment in the 1990s is not associated with low investment in the 2000s regardless of whether one sorts the data by industry, by firm, or by type of capital. Second, they claim that there is little need for the capital overhang story, because a fundamentals story based on Tobin's q performs adequately. Variables associated with capital overhang provide no additional explanatory power in a standard q-theoretic model of investment.

My main quibble with the paper is that Desai and Goolsbee never write down an explicit model of capital overhang, without which the concept is not clearly defined. We have no way of knowing how capital overhang will manifest itself in their cross-sectional data, and we have no way of knowing whether or not their tests are efficient. Is high past investment a good measure of capital overhang at the firm level? Does the capital overhang story imply that high past investment is negatively correlated with current investment? A few examples will illustrate how different theories could lead one to different conclusions regarding these points.

In their introduction Desai and Goolsbee define capital overhang as the "view . . . that excess investment in the 1990s, fueled by an asset price bubble, left corporations with excess capital stocks, and therefore no demand for investment, during the 2000s." In this view an overhang is something that is irrational and unjustified.

But there is another, more benign view of capital overhang: that there was simply too much capital, not because of excessive investment or a stock market bubble, but rather because of a change in firms' view of the profitability of investment. Much happened between 1999 and 2001 that could have induced such a change: disillusion with the information technology revolution, the decline in stock prices, corporate scandals, Y2K, 9/11. In this view rationally optimistic firms accumulated capital during the 1990s, received new information around 2000, and found themselves with more capital than they desired. There is nothing here that is hard to reconcile with standard investment theory, and no reason that a standard q-theoretic model would have any greater difficulty dealing with this episode than it would with other cycles.

There are several ways to build such a change in perspective into a standard model of investment. One way would be to consider a neoclassical model of the business cycle and endow firms with a capital stock that is above the long-run equilibrium level because of past optimism regarding the profitability of investment. Such a model would be broadly consistent with the experience over the past five years. The real interest rate, investment, and employment would all fall below their steady-state levels, and consumption would rise above its steady-state level.

How would the Desai-Goolsbee tests look in this neoclassical model? Since firms do not differ in their response to aggregate news, the cross section would be uninformative. Moreover, since the model is completely standard, marginal q would be sufficient to explain investment. Terms associated with overhang would not provide any additional information.

This neoclassical model is a bit of a straw man, however. One would not expect that a shock would hit all firms equally, or that the degree of capital overhang would be the same across firms. One might therefore expect to see some evidence of capital overhang in the cross section. What form might this evidence take?

One way to model firm-level differences in the desire to invest would be to introduce "*Ss* dynamics" in the spirit of Giuseppe Bertola, Ricardo

Caballero, and Eduardo Engel.[1] In such a model, idiosyncratic shocks would lead to cross-sectional differences in firms' desire to invest, and frictions would prevent firms from adjusting immediately to their optimal capital stock. There would then be a gap between the marginal productivity of capital that triggers investment and that which triggers disinvestment: To induce investment, capital would need to be productive enough to cover both the cost of capital and the cost of adjustment. Similarly, for disinvestment to occur, the gains achieved by disinvesting would need to cover the adjustment costs. Capital overhang might be interpreted as a situation in which adjustment costs lead a firm to hold onto more capital than it would in the absence of these frictions.

What would be the correlation between past investment and current investment in such a model? It depends on the form of the adjustment costs and the common trend in the shocks. If fixed costs dominate, investment will tend to be lumpy. These lumpy investment episodes will tend to reduce the marginal productivity of capital and make subsequent investment less desirable. In such cases one might indeed expect to see a negative correlation between investment in the past and investment in the present. Russel Cooper, John Haltiwanger, and Laura Power have shown, however, that it may be very difficult to tease this correlation out of the data.[2] Unobserved heterogeneity in the adjustment costs and differences in trend growth in productivity both tend to bias the correlation in the opposite direction.

If instead the investment friction takes the form of irreversibility or a wedge between the purchase and the sale price of capital, the situation is entirely different. In this case past investment is a signal that a firm had a high marginal productivity of capital in the past. If the idiosyncratic shocks are uncorrelated with marginal productivity, such a firm is more likely to have a high marginal productivity of capital today as well. Absent other differences across firms, past investment would then be positively, not negatively, correlated with current investment.

How does capital overhang manifest itself in the irreversible investment model? Past investment in that case is not necessarily a good measure of capital overhang. Firms that invest are generally those with too little capital. It is therefore the other firms that are more naturally susceptible to overhang. A better measure might be an indicator of the irre-

1. Bertola and Caballero (1990); Caballero and Engel (1999).
2. Cooper, Haltiwanger, and Powell (1999).

versibility of investment, although even here the correlation between over-hang and investment might not accord with intuition. During a downturn, the firms that face the greatest irreversibilities and therefore suffer from the greatest threat of overhang may be precisely the firms that cut invest-ment the least. The irreversibility prevents them from disinvesting. The Desai-Goolsbee tests are not well targeted to this theory.

A common feature of most investment models is that investment is cor-related with the marginal product of capital, or, more precisely, the present value of the marginal product of capital. For the Desai-Goolsbee version of the capital overhang story to hold, one needs a model in which the high- and low-marginal-productivity firms switch places in or about 2000. Firms that had high marginal productivity in the 1990s need to have low marginal productivity in the 2000s. This switch would generate the nega-tive correlation between past investment and present investment that their data reject. Given that present values are dominated by expectations about the future, this switch can only happen as a result of a shock that drasti-cally alters firms' views of the future.

The lumpy *Ss* model generates this switch through a leapfrogging effect, in which firms with too little capital accumulate capital and surpass firms that start out with greater capital stocks. The following model might also fit these requirements: In the 1990s firms differed in their expected rate of productivity growth. Firms with high expected productivity growth invested more heavily than others, hoping to cash in on the expected future growth. For some reason, however, these expectations were not fulfilled, and by 2000 those firms that had expected high productivity growth found themselves with more capital than they desired, and they cut their invest-ment spending by a greater amount than did other firms. Note that in this model one does not need to take a stand on whether or not investment was excessive. The mistaken expectations could be the result either of irra-tional exuberance or of rational ignorance. One interpretation of the Desai-Goolsbee regressions is that this last story does fully not explain the data, although it may be part of the story if it is combined with some other story that generates a positive correlation in investment rates.

I enjoyed reading this paper. The questions it raises are interesting and important, and the authors' answers are provocative. The evidence pre-sented will prove an important contribution to our understanding of invest-ment behavior. Whether or not overhang is a good term to describe recent events remains an open question.

General discussion: Several panelists raised questions about the authors' definition and measure of the capital overhang. Olivier Blanchard and Daniel Sichel noted that the regressions using q as an explanatory variable cannot distinguish between two important hypotheses: first, that firms and markets are perfectly rational, and investment moves in step with promising fundamentals (that is, rational forecasts of the expected present value of marginal profits), and, second, that firms make investments on the basis of stock market valuations that include a bubble component. In both cases, ex post, the firms have accumulated too much capital and are now restraining investment: in the first case because their rational forecast was in error, and in the second because they responded to an irrational market. Since the authors do not explore whether the surge in investment or the rise in q in the late 1990s was justified by plausible forecasts of the fundamentals, they cannot analyze the reasons for the overinvestment.

William Nordhaus noted further that the authors' equations show only whether investment is surprisingly high or low relative to market valuations. Insofar as investment in the 1990s, for example in fiber optics, turned out to have a lower rate of return than was expected, both the market value and the need for investment will now be low. Since both the decrease in q and the decrease in investment are due to the same outside factor, the residuals from regressions of investment on q are not informative about whether earlier investment was excessive. Robert Gordon remarked that the experience of the late 1990s and early 2000s should remind us of the difficulty of attributing causation to q. It seems likely that both firms, in their investment decisions, and the market were overoptimistic about the profitability of the new economy. Ben Bernanke reminded the Panel that the empirical literature has found very small responses to changes in q, which implies that firms would have smoothed their investment through the bubble. He wondered whether there were significant positive residuals to q in investment equations in the late 1990s. Benjamin Friedman added that during the bubble period, for the first time since World War II, there was a significant net inflow of funds to the corporate sector from equity issuance. Kevin Hassett noted further that this was a period when there were many initial public share offerings, often by new, small firms accessing the stock market for the first time.

Nordhaus suggested that changes in the dispersion of investment across firms might provide some clues about the importance of any capital overhang from the 1990s. The firms the authors consider belong to very different industries, ranging from shopping centers to aircraft engine manufacturers. Many types of capital are nontransferable across sectors, implying upper and lower bounds on investment; the upper bounds due to capacity limits in the investment-producing sectors, and the lower bounds given by zero gross investment. Given industry-specific shocks, one would expect wide dispersion in investment rates across different industries even in normal times. If overhang were specific to particular industries in 2000, then one should observe greater dispersion of investment than usual. Nordhaus reported that the dispersion in the early 2000s does not appear to be significantly greater than during other cycles of the post–World War II period. Christopher House observed that, if overhang were firm specific, reflecting dispersion of optimism across firms, then even if that dispersion in the degree increased, there would be no reason to expect aggregate investment to have been excessive in the late 1990s. The fact that it was supported John Leahy's view that one should look for an explanation at the aggregate rather than at the firm level.

Turning to the discussion of the effects of dividend taxes on investment, House noted that the authors' analysis of tax incentives assumes that the recent tax cuts are permanent; the response would be quite different if agents expected the cuts to expire as the law mandates. Standard neoclassical analysis suggests that a temporary dividend tax cut should affect the timing of dividends, with little effect on investment. House also suggested that the Congressional Budget Office's projection of $130 billion in lost revenue from the changes to partial expensing is an overestimate. Extending the CBO's projection beyond 2005 reveals that increased revenue later on makes up for much of the short-run cost; the decline in the present discounted value of revenue would be much smaller than reported.

Peter Orszag pointed out that changes in the user cost of capital due to tax cuts depend on how the tax cut is financed. He suggested that, with reasonable values for the effects of deficit-financed tax cuts on interest rates, the user cost of capital might actually rise. In the same spirit, William Brainard remarked that, although the supply of saving may be elastic in the short run when resources are underutilized, in the long run what happens depends on the elasticity of saving with respect to after-tax rates of return. It is quite possible that increasing the after-tax rate of return actually decreases private saving, since defined-benefit pension plans are target savers, and most defined-contribution plans are designed to achieve a target replacement ratio. For such plans the income effect of rate changes dominates the substitution effect. The same is true for life-cycle savers whose intertemporal elasticity of consumption is less than 1, which is what most studies suggest. He also observed that, in an open economy, the marginal source of funds may be the saving of foreigners who are not affected by the U.S. tax rate on dividends.

References

Abel, Andrew B. 1981. "A Dynamic Model of Investment and Capacity Utilization." *Quarterly Journal of Economics* 96: 379–403.

Abel, Andrew B., and Janice C. Eberly. 2002. "Q for the Long Run." Working paper. University of Pennsylvania and Northwestern University (July).

Auerbach, Alan. 1979. "Wealth Maximization and the Cost of Capital." *Quarterly Journal of Economics* 93, no. 3: 433–46.

_____. 1989. "Tax Reform and Adjustment Costs: The Impact on Investment and Market Value." *International Economic Review* 30, no. 4, 939–62.

_____. 2002. "Taxation and Corporate Financial Policy." In *Handbook of Public Economics,* vol. 3, edited by Alan Auerbach and Martin Feldstein. Amsterdam: North-Holland.

Auerbach, Alan J., and Kevin A. Hassett. 1992. "Tax Policy and Business Fixed Investment in the United States." *Journal of Public Economics* 47, no. 2: 141–70.

_____. 2002. "Optimal Long-Run Fiscal Policy: Constraints, Preferences and the Resolution of Uncertainty." Working Paper W9132. Cambridge, Mass.: National Bureau of Economic Research (August).

_____. 2003. "On the Marginal Source of Investment Funds." *Journal of Public Economics* 87, no. 1: 205–32.

Bernanke, Ben. 2003. "Will Business Investment Bounce Back?" Remarks before the Forecasters Club, New York, April 24.

Berner, Richard. 2001. "Purging Excess—The Capacity Overhang." Presented at the Global Economic Forum, November 9, 2001 (www.morganstanley.com/GEFdata/digests/20011109-fri.html#anchor1 [accessed August 2004]).

Bernheim, B. Douglas, and Adam Wantz. 1995. "A Tax-Based Test of the Dividend Signaling Hypothesis." *American Economic Review* 85, no. 3: 532–51.

Bertola, Giuseppe, and Ricardo Caballero. 1990. "Kinked Adjustment Costs and Aggregate Demand." In *NBER Macroeconomics Annual 1990,* edited by Olivier J. Blanchard and Stanley Fischer. MIT Press.

Blouin, Jennifer L., Jana S. Raedy, and Douglas A. Shackelford. 2004. "Did Dividends Increase Immediately after the 2003 Reduction in Tax Rates?" Working Paper 10301. Cambridge, Mass.: National Bureau of Economic Research (February).

Bolster, Paul J., and Vahan Janjigian. 1991. "Dividend Policy and Valuation Effects of the Tax Reform Act of 1986." *National Tax Journal* 44, no. 4: 511–18.

Bond, Stephen R., and Jason G. Cummins. 2000. "The Stock Market and Investment in the New Economy: Some Tangible Facts and Intangible Fictions." *BPEA,* no. 1: 61–108.

Bradford, David. 1981. "The Incidence and Allocation Effects of a Tax on Corporate Distributions." *Journal of Public Economics* 15, no. 1: 1–22.

Caballero, Ricardo J., and Eduardo M. R. A. Engel. 1999. "Explaining Investment Dynamics in U.S. Manufacturing: A Generalized (S, s) Approach." *Econometrica* 67, no. 4: 783–826.

Carroll, Robert, Kevin A. Hassett, and James B. Mackie III. 2003. "The Effect of Dividend Tax Relief on Investment Incentives." *National Tax Journal* 56: 629–51.

Chetty, Raj, and Emmanuel Saez. 2004. "Do Dividend Payments Respond to Taxes? Preliminary Evidence from the 2003 Dividend Tax Cut." Working Paper 10572. Cambridge, Mass.: National Bureau of Economic Research (June).

Chirinko, Robert S. 1993. "Business Fixed Investment Spending: Modeling Strategies, Empirical Results, and Policy Implications." *Journal of Economic Literature* 31, no. 4: 1875–1911.

Chirinko, Robert S., Steven M. Fazzari, and Andrew P. Meyer. 1999. "How Responsive Is Business Capital Formation to Its User Cost? An Exploration with Micro Data." *Journal of Public Economics* 74, no. 1: 53–80.

Coen, Robert M. 1969. "Tax Policy and Investment Behavior." *American Economic Review* 59, no. 3: 370–79.

Cohen, Darryl S., Kevin A. Hassett, and Dorthe-Pernille Hansen. 2002. "The Effects of Temporary Partial Expensing on Investment Incentives in the United States." *National Tax Journal* 55, no. 3, 457–66.

Cooper, Russel, John Haltiwanger, and Laura Power. 1999. "Machine Replacement and the Business Cycle: Lumps and Bumps." *American Economic Review* 89, no. 4: 921–46.

Cummins, Jason G., Kevin A. Hassett, and R. Glenn Hubbard. 1994. "A Reconsideration of Investment Behavior Using Tax Reforms as Natural Experiments." *BPEA*, no. 2: 1–59.

Cummins, Jason G., Kevin A. Hassett, and Stephen D. Oliner. Forthcoming. "Investment Behavior, Observable Expectations, and Internal Funds." *American Economic Review.*

Doms, Mark C. 2004. "The Boom and Bust in Information Technology Investment." Federal Reserve Bank of San Francisco *Economic Review 2004,* pp. 19–34.

Ferguson, Roger. 2001. "Reflections on the Capital Good Overhang." Remarks to the Charlotte Economics Club, Charlotte, N.C., July 18.

French, Eric, Thomas Klier, and David Oppedahl. 2002. "Is There Still an Investment Overhang, and If So, Should We Worry about It?" Federal Reserve Bank of Chicago, *Chicago Fed Letter,* Special Issue 177a (May).

Gilchrist, Simon, and Charles Himmelberg. 1998. "Investment: Fundamentals and Finance." In *NBER Macroeconomics Annual 1998,* edited by Ben S. Bernanke and Julio J. Rotemberg. MIT Press.

Goolsbee, Austan. 1998. "Investment Tax Incentives, Prices, and the Supply of Capital Goods." *Quarterly Journal of Economics* 113, no. 1: 121–48.

_____. 2001. "The Importance of Measurement Error in the Cost of Capital." *National Tax Journal* 53, no. 2: 215–28.

_____. 2004. "Taxes and the Quality of Capital." *Journal of Public Economics* 88, no. 3–4: 519–43.

Goolsbee, Austan, and David B. Gross. 2000. "Estimating Adjustment Costs with Data on Heterogeneous Capital Goods." Graduate School of Business, University of Chicago.

Greenspan, Alan. 2002. "Economic Volatility." Remarks at the Federal Reserve Bank of Kansas City Symposium, Jackson Hole, Wyo., August 30 (www.federalreserve.gov/boarddocs/speeches/2002/20020830/default.htm).

Hall, Robert E., and Dale W. Jorgenson. 1969. "Tax Policy and Investment Behavior: Reply and Further Results." American Economic Revies 59, no: 388–401.

Hassett, Kevin A., and R. Glenn Hubbard. 2002. "Tax Policy and Business Investment." In *Handbook of Public Economics,* vol. 3, edited by Alan Auerbach and Martin Feldstein. Amsterdam: North-Holland.

Hederman, Rea S., Jr. 2004. "Tax Cuts Boost Business Investment." Heritage Foundation Web Memo (www.heritage.org/Research/Taxes/wm412.cfm [accessed August 2004]).

Ikenberry, David L., and Brandon R. Julio. 2004. "Reappearing Dividends." University of Illinois College of Business Working Paper (July).

Joint Committee on Taxation. 2002. "Estimated Revenue Effects of the 'Job Creation and Worker Assistance Act of 2002.' " Document JCX-13-02. Washington: U.S. Government Printing Office (March 6).

_____. 2003a. "Estimated Budgetary Effects of the Conference Agreement for H.R. 2 and the 'Jobs and Growth Tax Relief Reconciliation Act of 2003.' " Document JCX-55-03. Washington: U.S. Government Printing Office (May 22).

_____. 2003b. "Estimates of Federal Tax Expenditures for Fiscal Years, 2004–2008." Document JCS-8-03. Washington: U.S. Government Printing Office (December 22).

Jorgenson, Dale, and Kun-Young Yun. 2001. *Investment,* Vol. 3: *Lifting the Burden: Tax Reform, the Cost of Capital, and U.S. Economic Growth.* MIT Press.

Kaplan, Steven N., and Luigi Zingales. 1997. "Do Investment-Cash Flow Sensitivities Provide Useful Measures of Financing Constraints?" *Quarterly Journal of Economics* 112, no. 1: 169–215.

King, Mervyn A. 1977. *Public Policy and the Corporation.* London: Chapman and Hall.

Kliesen, Kevin L. 2003. "Was Y2K behind the Business Investment Boom and Bust?" Federal Reserve Bank of St. Louis *Review* 85, no. 1: 31–42.

Kudlow, Larry. 2004. "A Capital Idea from Microsoft." *National Review Online* (www.nationalreview.com/kudlow/kudlow200407230854.asp [accessed December 2004]).

McCarthy, Jonathan. 2001. "Equipment Expenditures since 1995: The Boom and the Bust." Federal Reserve Bank of New York *Current Issues in Economics and Finance* 7, no. 9: 1–6.

———. 2003. "Capital Overhangs: Has Equipment Investment Spending Suffered from a Hangover?" *Business Economics,* October, pp. 20–27.

———. 2004. "What Investment Patterns across Equipment and Industries Tell Us about the Recent Investment Boom and Bust." Federal Reserve Bank of New York *Current Issues in Economics and Finance* 10, no. 6: 1–7.

Pelgrin, Florian, Sebastian Schich, and Alain de Serres. 2002. "Increases in Business Investment Rates in OECD Countries in the 1990s: How Much Can Be Explained by Fundamentals?" OECD Economics Department Working Paper 327. Paris: OECD (April 15).

Poterba, James. 2004. "Taxation and Corporate Payout Policy." *American Economic Review* 94, no. 2: 171–75.

Poterba, James M., and Lawrence H. Summers. 1983. "Dividend Taxes, Corporate Investment, and 'Q.' " *Journal of Public Economics* 22: 135–67.

———. 1985. "The Economic Effects of Dividend Taxation." In *Recent Advances in Corporate Finance,* edited by Edward Altman and Marti Subrahmanyam. Homewood, Ill.: Richard D. Irwin Publishers.

Ramey, Valerie A., and Matthew D. Shapiro. 2001. "Displaced Capital: A Study of Aerospace Plant Closings." *Journal of Political Economy* 109, no. 5: 958–92.

Salinger, Michael A., and Lawrence H. Summers. 1984. "Tax Reform and Corporate Investment: A Microeconometric Simulation Study." Working Paper 0757. Cambridge, Mass.: National Bureau of Economic Research.

Saxton, Jim. 2003. "Economic Repercussions of the Stock Market Bubble: A Joint Economic Committee Study" (www.house.gov/jec/growth/07-14-03.pdf [accessed August 2004]).

Summers, Lawrence H. 1981. "Taxation and Corporate Investment: A q-Theory Approach." *BPEA,* no. 1: 67–127.

Tevlin, Stacey, and Karl Whelan. 2003. "Explaining the Investment Boom of the 1990s." *Journal of Money, Credit, and Banking* 35, no. 1: 1–22.